Lecture  notes...

Cavendish
Publishing
Limited

ENVIRONMENTAL LAW

TITLES IN THE SERIES

Lecture **CP** *notes...*

Cavendish
Publishing
Limited

ENVIRONMENTAL LAW

Susan Wolf, BA (Econ) Hons, LLB (Hons)
Senior Lecturer in Law
University of Northumbria

Anna White, LLB (Hons)
Lecturer in Law
University of Northumbria

First published in Great Britain 1995 by Cavendish Publishing Limited, The Glass House, Wharton Street, London WC1X 9PX

Telephone: 0171-278 8000 Facsimile: 0171-278 8080

British Library Cataloguing in Publication Data

Wolf, Susan
Environmental Law - (Lecture Notes Series)
I Title II Series, White Anna
344.10446

ISBN 1 85941 160 6

Cover photograph by Jerome Yeats
Printed and bound in Great Britain

Contents

Table of Cases

Table of Statutes

Table of Statutory Instruments

Table of PPGs

Table of European Legislation

Chapter 1

Elements of Environmental Law

A prerequisite of almost all legal textbooks is that they begin with a definition of key terms. This is clearly necessary where terms such as 'tort'and 'equity' are not used in general and are being introduced for the first time. 'The environment' on the other hand is a term which is used so frequently that any reader approaching the subject of environmental law will already have a preconceived notion of what the environment means. In its most general sense 'the environment' refers to our surroundings and is often understood to include not only the land, air and water but also our built environment and the condition of our local amenity and neighbourhood. The environment can, for others, mean something more specific and refer to the conservation of natural habitats and ecology. What is clear is that there has been a growing awareness of environmental issues and the need to protect the environment both at the very local level and also the global level – reflecting the maxim 'think global, act local'.

Although there are many interpretations of what is meant by 'the environment' it is still necessary to establish a central working definition as the basis upon which Environmental law operates and which defines the scope of this book. The Environmental Protection Act (EPA) 1990 provides a useful starting point. Under s 1(2):

> 'The "Environment" consists of all, or any of the following media, namely, the air, water and land; and the medium of air includes the air within buildings and the air within other natural or man-made structures above or below ground.'

This is clearly a very wide definition which encompasses environmental challenges ranging from ecological problems, such as damage to natural habitat and the conservation of flora and fauna, the 'working environment' with problems such as 'sick building syndrome' and more obvious problems such as noxious emissions into the atmosphere.

With such a wide ranging definition covering such diverse issues it would be impossible both within an Act of Parliament such as the EPA 1990 and within a textbook on environmental law to address all of these areas. This book, like the UK legislative framework, concentrates largely on the protection of land, air and water rather than the law relating

1.1   **The environment and pollution**

1.1.1   Defining the environment

to conservation and ecology. The central feature is the control of pollution of the environment specifically from industrial and commercial operations and it becomes necessary to define pollution.

1.1.2   The definition of pollution

There is not a single definition of 'pollution'. The Royal Commission on Environmental Pollution believes that it is neither practicable nor helpful to seek a comprehensive simple definition of pollution. In its Third Report, the Commission favours the following definition:

'The introduction by man into the environment of substances or energy liable to cause hazards to human health, harm to living resources and ecological systems, damage to structure or amenity or interference with legitimate uses of the environment.'

On the basis of this pollution is defined by reference to the potential effect of the introduction of substances or energy into the environment, rather than by the fact of the introduction itself. This emphasis on effect is echoed in the EPA 1990 which provides the following definition of pollution in s 1(3)

'The release (into any Environmental medium) from any process of substances which are capable of causing harm to man or any other living organisms supported by the Environment.'

Pollution occurs when there is the potential for harm. Harm to man is not confined to physical injury but encompasses 'offence caused to any of his senses or harm to his property', therefore smells and noise which may not cause injury can constitute pollution. Harm to living organisms can include harm to their health or interference with the ecological systems of which they form a part.

1.1.3   The nature of environmental problems

Images of environmental disasters are now common place in the media. On an international scale we have seen the poison gas incident at Bhopal, India (1983); the problems caused by contaminated land at Love Canal, USA (1978); the disaster at Chernobyl (1986), the effects of which are still with us today. These are but a few examples. Environmental problems are not only happening on an international level, there have been major polluting incidents in the UK, such as the Braer oil tanker disaster in 1993. Because of the often tragic consequences of these disasters they attract full scale international media attention. Less well publicised are the thousands of polluting incidents that receive little or no mention but which occur every day and may have irreversible Environmental consequences, such as the pollution of water courses or groundwater, land contamination or air pollution.

There has, however, been growing awareness of the long term consequences of environmental pollution with problems such as acid rain and global warming attracting public concern and demanding international responses from both government and industry. These problems have prompted international inter-governmental action, along with the growing popularity and influence of environmental pressure groups at the international, national and local level and the growing tide of 'green consumerism'. It is apparent that the protection of the environment rests not only with national governments but is an issue of common concern and common action. What is also clear is that the protection of the environment cannot be achieved simply through a legal framework. Environmental law can seek to regulate and control pollution and penalise polluters but it must also be supported by changing attitudes and behaviour towards the environment in order to be fully effective.

A further and very real problem concerning the environment is that we are faced with a legacy of pollution from our industrial past. The question of who pays for the remediation of historic pollution remains unresolved. The current legal framework offers no easy solution to this difficult problem, particularly in relation to contamined land, instead the existing legislation seeks to control current levels of pollution, prevent or reduce future pollution. This issue will undoubtedly feature in the future debates on environmental policy.

Although environmental protection has become a modern day issue and there is a tendency to date it back to the 1970s measures have existed to protect the environment well before this time. However, early legal controls were initiated not out of a desire to protect the environment per se but out of the recognition of dangers to health associated with pollution. The first 'environmental' statutes were undoubtedly intended to safeguard public health rather than the environment and it is still the case today that the two objectives remain closely linked.	**1.2** **The development of environmental law**

References to problems of air pollution date back to the 13th century, when in 1273 Edward I issued a decree prohibiting the burning of sea coal. Records show that a 'polluter' was executed in the 16th century for breaking air pollution laws. However the main starting point is undoubtedly the industrial revolution which had an enormous adverse impact on the environment of the UK and resulted in the adoption of measures to safeguard human health, and indirectly to protect the environment. Because of its lead in the industrial revolution, Britain is often referred to as the world's first industrial nation and as such has the oldest system of environmental regulation. Examples of early legislative attempts to deal with the problems of industrial pollution include the Public Health Act 1848 and the Alkali Act 1863, which established the Alkali Inspectorate, the world's first pollution control agency.

The late 19th century saw the enactment of a vast amount of 'environmental' legislation, much of which remained in place for a considerable period of time, some being replaced and overhauled as recently as 1990, with the enactment of the Environmental Protection Act.

The Public Health Act 1936 contained statutory nuisance provisions that had the joint objectives of safeguarding public health and, to a lesser extent, protecting the environment. The statutory nuisance provisions are now contained in the Environmental Protection Act 1990, and are of a considerable importance to both local authorities and the public, in the field of environmental protection.

The post-war period saw renewed concern for matters concerning the environment. In 1947 a new Town and Country Planning regime was created to control development and rebuilding. Although not strictly environmental legislation the Town and Country Planning Acts play a significant role in preserving the urban and rural environment and enable environmental objectives to be secured through the development control system. The relationship between the town and country planning regime and statutory pollution control mechanisms is an issue that has generated much attention and it has not always been clear where the boundaries between the two systems lie.

The environmental law framework as we know it today began to develop in the 1970s, with the enactment of the Control of Pollution Act 1974 (COPA). Although COPA was intended to provide a comprehensive framework for pollution control and provided a model for European Community waste legislation, it was enacted in a piecemeal fashion with some provisions never coming into force. The provisions of COPA have now largely been superseded by the Environmental Protection Act 1990 (EPA), which was hailed as an important piece of legislation that would provide the 'basic framework for pollution control until well into the next century'. The EPA 1990 has since been supplemented by the Noise and Statutory Nuisance Act 1993, and now the Environment Bill is due to update and replace certain provisions of the EPA.

In relation to water pollution, the Water Act 1989 provided the framework for the current operation and control of the water industry, water resources and the water environment. Water legislation has since been consolidated in 1991 by five new statutes including the Water Resources Act and the Water Industry Act.

Along with the burgeoning development of environmental legislation has been the development of environmental law as an academic and professional discipline. The subject of environmental law has grown in popularity not only on mainstream law courses but as an integral part of other courses such as environmental management and science. A number of law firms offer environmental legal advice and several promote themselves as environmental law specialists. The growth of this area of law has created a need for those who have a detailed knowledge of environmental law and its application. The 1980s saw increasing numbers of environmental lawyers, consultants and engineers whose role is to ensure that environmental obligations can be met.

1.2.1   Environmental law as a discipline

However despite its development as a branch of law it does not comprise one distinct set of legal rules, rather it is made up of law drawn from a variety of sources:

- environmental legislation;

- the torts of nuisance, negligence, trespass and the rule in *Rylands v Fletcher*;

- the town and country planning legislation;

- land law;

- consumer protection;

- public health legislation; and

- health and safety at work legislation.

The increasing amount of legislation in the field of environmental protection is a clear indication of the rate of change associated with environmental law. Although primary legislation such as the EPA provides the main framework of environmental law it is supplemented by an enormous quantity of secondary legislation. The EPA, for example, provides the Secretary of State for the Environment with powers to introduce, by means of regulation, detailed and technical provisions relating to large areas of the Act. It is essential that any student or practitioner of environmental law becomes familiar with the various sources of environmental law. These include:

1.2.2   Current sources of environmental law

- international treaties, conventions and protocols;
- European Community legislation;
- UK primary legislation;
- UK Statutory Instruments;
- case law;
- government departmental notes such as Planning Policy Guidance Notes;
- government circulars;
- Codes of Practice;
- Enforcement Authority Guidance Notes.

The environmental lawyer will also benefit from an awareness of environmental issues, and the technological aspects of environmental control which reflects the multi-disciplinary aspect of this area of law.

1.3 The international dimension of environmental law

The problems of acid rain and global warming testify to the fact that pollution does not respect national boundaries. The polluting activities of industrial nations such as the United Kingdom have contributed to environmental problems such as deforestation in Scandinavian countries. Global warming, caused by the emission of greenhouse gases such as carbon dioxide, methane, chlorofluorocarbons (CFCs) and nitrous oxide, is a major environmental concern and cannot be tackled on a fragmented national basis. It demands an international response. There are many other environmental problems that need to be tackled by international action, such as marine pollution and transfrontier shipments of waste.

The development of international law regarding environmental protection really began in 1972 with the United Nations Conference on the Human Environment. This conference was held in response to the ground swell of public awareness about environmental pollution, particularly in North America. The Conference, amongst other things, led to the introduction and development of the European Community's First Environmental Action Plan.

International law of the environment has contributed significantly to the development of EC law, and subsequently domestic law. This is well recognised in the UK government's environmental policy. In *This Common Inheritance* which sets out the framework for UK policy, it is stated that the threat of pollution 'can only be overcome if all nations work together ... One country's pollution can be every country's predicament'.

While the practical effects of international agreements may not be immediately apparent, it is clear that they focus attention onto environmental problems and provide the basis for co-operation in international environmental protection. The Earth Summit held at Rio de Janeiro in 1992 attracted worldwide attention and although it was criticised in some quarters, at the very least it brought together over 150 countries and numerous international pressure groups in a process that is still ongoing. Achievements at Rio included:

- The Framework Convention on Climate Change signed by 153 countries;

- Convention on Biological Diversity again signed by 153 countries;

- The Rio Declaration – A statement of 27 principles on Environment and development;

- Agenda 21.

Agenda 21 constitutes an Action Plan of the International Community in respect of the environment and development for the 21st century. It aims to integrate environmental concerns over activities such as water resources, energy and agriculture.

Chapter 3 traces the development of the European Community's environmental programme from the stage when the EC was primarily an economic community to today when environmental considerations are required to be taken into account in all of the Community's policy areas. European Community policy on environmental protection was not an objective of the Treaty of Rome 1957. Its incorporation into EC policy did not come until the 1970s when the First Environmental Action Programme was adopted in 1973. Since that time the EC has brought forward five multi-annual Action Programmes for the Environment. It has enacted over 300 pieces of legislation aimed at combating pollution and protecting the environment. Without doubt the EC plays an important role in developing environmental policy throughout the community on an integrated basis, controlling and preventing pollution in all Member States. Much of current UK environmental law stems from the implementation of Community law obligations.

The Community is now part way through its Fifth Action Programme which is based upon the principle of sustainable development and represents a major advancement on the earlier reactive approaches. The Action Programmes provide

1.4 The European Community dimension

the political framework for future environmental legislation. However the Community has been quick to recognise that environmental protection can not simply be achieved through traditional legal mechanisms and has introduced initiatives to support its legislative control of the environment. ENVIREG, MEDSPA, NORDSPA, ACE and LIFE are examples of Community financial support mechanisms aimed at promoting, for example, cleaner technologies.

European Community legislation has had a considerable impact across the EC in relation to air, water, waste. There are, however several key areas which have yet to be covered by environmental legislation, for example there is as yet no community wide guidance on contaminated land.

The objectives of EC environmental policy are:

- preserving, protecting and improving the quality of the environment;

- protecting human health;

- prudent and rational utilisation of national resources;

- promoting measures at international level to deal with regional or worldwide environmental problems.

The European Environment Agency, established in 1994, has the duty to provide the EC and Member States with 'objective, reliable and comparative information' which will allow environmental protection measures to be taken. The work of the agency is also open to other countries, and in particular the agency has extended it functions to monitoring pollution in eastern Europe.

1.5   UK environmental policy

The publication of *This Common Inheritance* (1990), the White Paper on the environment, was the first comprehensive statement of environmental policy in the UK. It contains reference to all of the main areas of environmental concern, namely the greenhouse effect, conservation and land use and pollution control in the environmental media of air, land and water. The cornerstone of this policy is the concept of 'stewardship' which means that everyone has a responsibility to act as stewards of the environment to preserve it for future generations. The White Paper asserts that the objective of sustainable development underpins the policy. Sustainable development is defined in the White Paper as 'not sacrificing tomorrow's prospects for a large illusory gain today'. However a more satisfactory definition is found in the Bruntland Report (see Chapter 3).

Both the UK Government and the EC emphasise in their policy documents the need for public participation in the protection of the environment. Referred to as the concept of stewardship in UK policy and shared responsibility by the EC there is a common recognition that environmental protection cannot be secured by government alone. The means by which this environmental stewardship is to be achieved is through a combination of regulation and market forces. Chapter 6 considers the role that pressure groups and individuals can play in protecting the environment.

1.5.1   The principle of stewardship

Environmental law can be said to have three main functions:

- prevention;
- setting environmental quality standards;
- clean-up/remediation.

1.6   The functions of environmental law

Prevention of pollution and environmental damage must surely be the optimum objective of environmental regulation. However, the extent to which this aim is achieved by UK environmental regulation is limited as it can only apply to new processes. Prevention of pollution has no bearing on the large legacy of historic pollution which exists in this country, all that can hopefully be achieved in this latter respect is clean-up or remediation. The regime established under Part I of the EPA has as its main objective the prevention of damage to the environment. By controlling emissions to all three environmental media, air, land and water, the Integrated Pollution Control is attempting to prevent serious environmental damage. The Water Resources Act also includes provisions aimed at preventing water pollution, for instance through the designation of Water Protection Zones and Nitrate Sensitive Areas.

1.6.1   Prevention of pollution

Falling between the objectives of prevention and cure lies the environmental legislation that establishes acceptable levels of pollution, or environmental quality standards. This is probably the most acceptable type of pollution control for industry, as it recognises the need to allow the operation to continue, whilst monitoring and controlling its harmful emissions. In many cases it is neither appropriate, nor possible, to eradicate pollution altogether as other factors must be taken into consideration. Polluting activities create goods and services, employment, wealth and amenity. Modern society could not function without the industrial processes which pollute the environment and they must therefore be allowed to continue in a controlled manner.

1.6.2   Setting environmental quality standards

1.6.3 Remediation	Clean-up of environmental damage is also an objective of environmental legislation. It is necessary to safeguard against the failure of the previous objectives, where pollution has caused environmental damage. There are several clean-up provisions in current environmental legislation, examples include s 161 of the Water Resources Act 1991 under which Acts the NRA can clean-up actual or threatened pollution and s 59 EPA 1990 in relation to waste.

1.7 Environmental crimes

The principal means of enforcing environmental legislation is through the creation of numerous criminal offences. The offences are discussed in detail throughout the various chapters of this book, however they share some common features that are discussed below. Broadly speaking the offences fall into the following categories:

- causing pollution;
- permitting pollution;
- breach of licence conditions;
- breach of statutory duty;
- failure to comply with notices.

1.7.1 Causing pollution

Causing pollution is an offence under various provisions of environmental law, for example it is an offence to knowingly cause controlled waste to be deposited under s 33(1)(a) EPA 1990 and also causing poisonous, noxious or polluting matter to enter controlled waters is an offence under s 85(1) WRA 1991. The courts have considered the meaning of 'causing' in many cases and have established that it lays down an offence of strict liability. To cause pollution requires some positive act, but not necessarily an intention to pollute or to be negligent. It is sufficient that there is a direct relationship between the activities of the defendant and the offence complained of. Any break in the chain of causation may be enough to avoid liability.

In the leading case of *Alphacell v Woodward* (1972), the House of Lords held there was no need to prove negligence or fault in relation to a causing offence. Thus, Alphacell were guilty of 'causing' a discharge into the River Irwell above the consented biochemical oxygen demand. Lord Wilberforce stated that causing 'must involve some active operation or chain of operations involving as the result the pollution of the stream'. This test has been reiterated in later cases.

The effect of the strict liability nature of the 'causing' offence was clearly demonstrated in *Wrothwell Ltd v Yorkshire*

Water Authority (1984). In this case a company director poured herbicide down a drain which he thought led to a public sewer. However the drain led to a nearby stream. He was found guilty of causing pollution despite his lack of intention. The intervening actions of a third party may provide a defence, as in *Impress (Worcester) Ltd v Rees* (1974), and *Welsh Water Authority v Williams Motors (Cwmdu) Ltd* (1988).

Invariably statutes provide a separate offence of 'permitting' pollution. For example s 85(1) of the Water Resources Act 1991 creates the offence of knowingly permitting poisonous, noxious or polluting matter to enter controlled waters. Whilst 'causing' requires a positive act on the part of the defendant, 'permitting' an event' may apply to passive situations. See *Price v Cromack* (1975) and *Wychavon DC v National Rivers Authority* (1993).

1.7.2   Permitting pollution

Pollution control in this country is largely exercised through the system of licensing. It will not be an offence to pollute the air land or water in most circumstances providing the polluting activity has been authorised by the relevant regulatory authority. It will be an offence not to comply with the conditions imposed in such an authorisation. For example, under s 33(6) it is an offence to contravene the conditions of a Waste Management Licence and it is also an offence not to comply with the conditions attached to a discharge consent issued by the National Rivers Authority under the Water Resources Act.

1.7.3   Breach of licence conditions

The principal offence falling under this heading is breach of the statutory duty of care created under s 34 of the EPA in relation to the handling of waste. All waste holders are subject to the duty of care irrespective of whether they require a Waste Management Licence. For a further discussion of the duty of care in relation to waste see Chapter 11.

1.7.4   Breach of statutory duty

The Regulatory Authorities have the power to serve a variety of notices in order to either prevent a nuisance occurring, to prohibit a polluting activity or to require remedial work to take place. Examples of such notices include the Statutory Nuisance Abatement Notice under s 80 EPA and a Prohibition Notice under s 23 EPA. Failure to comply with the terms of a notice within the prescribed time constitutes a criminal offence. It is however usually possible to lodge an appeal against such notices.

1.7.5   Failure to comply with a notice or other requirement

1.7.6	Defences to criminal proceedings	Although the offences described above are strict liability offences the statutes which create them usually provide some form of defence, in particular that the best practicable means were employed to prevent or counteract the effect of a nuisance. The main statutory defences include:

- best practicable means;

- that all reasonable precautions were taken;

- that the defendant acted under instruction from his employer and neither knew or had reason to suppose his actions were in contravention of the law;

- acts done in an emergency;

- reasonable excuse;

- the offences were committed due to the act or default of some other party.

1.7.7	Environmental prosecutions	The prosecution policies of both HMIP and the National Rivers Authority are discussed in Chapter 5. However one of the dilemmas faced by the pollution control authorities is that they are not under a duty to prosecute and they have to exercise their discretion as to whether a prosecution is the best means of securing compliance with the statutory controls. It is in part because of the criminal nature of environmental law that this problem arises. There are those who argue that environmental offences are not criminal in any real sense and that environmental law should be 'de-criminalised'. The purpose of criminal law is usually to punish the wrong doer or to protect the public, whereas the purpose of environmental law is largely to prevent or control pollution.

1.7.8	Penalties	Since environmental offences are criminal in nature they are dealt at first instance either by the magistrates' court or the Crown Court. The courts have the power to impose a range of penalties although they largely rely on the use of fines. The levels of fines are limited in the magistrates' court but the Crown Court can impose unlimited fines. In deciding upon the level of fines the courts should be aware that in some instances commercial gain has featured as one of the motives for the pollution; in other words the cost of compliance with the pollution controls has been considered against the likely level of fine. In addition to fining the courts can impose a custodial sentence. For instance the Crown Court can imprison a person for up to two years for offences in relation to Integrated Pollution Control and waste offences. In addition the courts have certain other enforcement powers which they can use, these include:

- enforcement by injunction;

- compensation orders;

- confiscation of proceeds of offence;

- statutory powers to order the effect of the offence to be remedied;

- power to deprive offender of property.

Often the adverse publicity associated with a conviction will be more harmful to the defendant than a fine particularly where the person or company in question wishes to promote an environment-friendly image or where the results of the pollution incident are hazardous to human health. In addition an order for costs will normally be made against the defendant.

Section 157 EPA provides that where an offence is committed by a company and it can be shown that a director, manager or similar person in the company either consented, connived or was negligent, then criminal liability can attach individually as well as on a corporate basis. A manager is only someone who is part of the 'controlling mind' of the company. See *R v Boal* (1992). Similar provisions exist under s 217 of the Water Resources Act 1991.

1.7.9   Individual liability for environmental crimes

The environmental protection mechanisms discussed throughout this book are largely concerned with the legal framework for preventing and combating pollution or environmental nuisances. However, environmental protection cannot be secured simply through the command and control system of regulation. As society has become increasingly aware of environmental problems it has begun to exert pressure for greater environmental responsibility on the part of polluters. Individuals concerned about the environment have been able to exert power by using consumer purchasing power to send strong signals to manufacturers about the levels of environmental friendliness which is to be expected.

1.8   Pressure for environmental responsibility

This has manifested itself in the upsurge in demand for 'green' products which have been either produced in an environmentally friendly manner, or which are themselves less damaging to the environment. Supermarkets provide a good example of this with growing ranges of products such as recycled toilet rolls, chlorine free bleach and CFC free aerosol products. Manufacturers have been quick to respond to these demands and to meet the needs of the new 'green consumer'. It is clear that market forces have played a large part in 'persuading' manufacturers of the need to 'clean up their act'.

Growing numbers of companies are promoting their environmental credentials. The Co-op Bank promotes its policy of non investment in environmentally damaging products, the Body Shop produces a range of environmentally friendly products and promotes environmental issues. Even companies such as Rover, the car manufacturer, and B&Q, the DIY retailer, have introduced environmental management systems.

Industry is beginning to take up the challenge of environmental protection through various environmental management schemes. The British Standards Institution has published BS 7750, the first standard on environmental management systems. It is a voluntary certification system, the objective being to protect the environment through a quality management approach. It has now been adopted by more than 15,000 companies. Many companies are also instituting environmental management systems such as waste minimisation schemes, which in addition to protecting the environment are also generally more cost effective.

1.8.1   Environmental politics

The 1980s saw a increasing popularity in the 'green' movement and green politics. Although the Green Party has never won a seat in the Westminster Parliament, the European Parliament currently has over 20 MEPs from European Green Parties. The main political parties in this country were quick to recognise the electoral advantages of green issues and they all have environmental policies firmly on their agendas. In the UK, the environment is generally seen as a non-party political issue; all measures taken to help the environment receive cross party support. This can be seen in the debates during the passage of environmental legislation.

1.8.2   Green pressure groups

The rise in the awareness of green issues has also resulted in an explosion in the membership of environmental pressure groups on an international level, such as Greenpeace and Friends of the Earth. Friends of the Earth International operates in over 50 countries and Greenpeace boasts some 4.5 million supporters in over 158 countries. In the UK, there are some 300,000 paid-up supporters of Greenpeace, and Friends of the Earth has over 300 local groups. In addition there are many more pressure groups either concerned with specific problems such as the protection of wildlife, or with local environmental problems. For example, groups of people have joined together to protest against the marine disposal of the Brent Spa oil platform and the government's road building programme through Twyford Down. Pressure groups play an important role in raising awareness of environmental problems, assisting in the development of law and policy and in the enforcement of legal controls. The ways in which pressure groups can participate in the functioning of environmental law are discussed more fully in Chapter 6.

A number of principles underpin the framework of environmental law. These principles are enshrined in the EC Treaty (Art 130) and form the basis for the large volume of EC legislation which takes effect in this country. The principles are discussed below.

1.9   Principles of environmental law

The polluter pays principle is one which is aimed at ensuring that the costs of environmental damage caused by polluting activities are borne in full by the person responsible for such pollution; the polluter. The principle means:

1.9.1   The polluter pays principle

- the polluter should pay for the administration of the pollution control system; and

- the polluter should pay for the consequences of the pollution – for example, compensation and clean-up.

In the UK environmental framework it can be seen that the polluter pays principle applies to both these factors. On the one hand, the polluter pays for the administrative framework via the scheme of fees and charges levied by the regulatory authorities. The costs associated with pollution prevention, such as the installation of abatement technologies, should also be borne in full by the polluter. However, the question remains to what extent the polluter actually pays. Often the polluter will be an industrial operator and will deflect any increase in costs associated with pollution control on to the consumer.

The polluter should also bear the financial consequences of the pollution. A variety of legislative provisions seek to ensure this for example s 161 of the Water Resources Act 1991. In practice, particularly in relation to historic pollution, it is not always possible to identify the polluter or attach liability and the costs of remediation fall onto other parties. It is sometimes hard to see the application of this principle in practice.

Early UK and EC environmental legislation was largely concerned with so-called 'end of pipe' solutions, dealing with existing problems of pollution. The preventive principle first gained ground in the context of EC law and was included in the 1986 Single European Act. The preventive principle requires more forward thinking actions on the basis that 'prevention is better than cure' and steps should be taken to

1.9.2   Preventive principle

prevent or minimise the effects of pollution before the polluting process begins. There is however, very little EC legislation which has applied the preventive principle as an objective, one example is the Environmental Assessment Directive, 85/337. An example of such preventive legislation in the UK is the Integrated Pollution Control regime, but only so far as it relates to new operations. The preventive principle cannot be said to apply to existing operations because there has already been the opportunity for pollution, the legislation is merely limiting its effects.

1.9.3   The precautionary principle

The precautionary principle was introduced by the Treaty on European Union, which states that it is the basis for environmental protection in the EC and also in the UK. The essence of the principle is that in the absence of firm scientific evidence as to the effect of a particular substance or activity the protection of the environment should be the first concern. There is no need to wait for conclusive scientific proof before preventive action is taken. In other words the environment will be given the benefit of the doubt.

1.10   Environmental terms

One of the features of Environmental law is the frequent use of jargon. The legislation abounds with acronyms which are central to the regulatory framework. Terms such as BATNEEC and BPEO are integral to the system of Integrated Pollution Control (IPC) and therefore demand explanation.

1.10.1   BPM – Best Practicable Means

BPM stands for Best Practicable Means. Although the requirement that Best Practicable Means are employed in various aspects of environmental legislation. there is in fact no statutory definition. The meaning of BPM is explained in several sources, for instance HMIP Guidance Notes, and has also been considered by the courts in relation to the defence of BPM.

The central feature of BPM is that it is a flexible standard, allowing for individual circumstances. The concept of BPM is not new, it dates back to 1842 when it was applied to smoke control in Leeds. It was also mentioned in the Public Health Act 1936, The Alkali Acts (1863, 1874 and 1906) and the Control of Pollution Act (COPA) 1974. However BPM as an environmental standard has now largely been superseded by the concept of BATNEEC (see below). Best Practicable Means appears a defence in relation to some Statutory Nuisance proceedings and also in relation to noise offences under COPA 1974. To rely on the defence it is necessary for the defendant to prove that the best practicable means were used to prevent or counteract the effects of the nuisance. Best

Practicable Means are defined in s 79(9) EPA the details of which are considered in Chapter 14.

The concept of BPEO was first introduced under s 7(7) of the EPA 1990 as part of the system of Integrated Pollution Control (IPC). The concept of BPEO was promoted by the Royal Commission on Environmental Pollution. There is no definition of BPEO in the EPA, although the Royal Commission on Environmental Pollution considered the concept in its 11th Report 'Best Practicable Environmental Option':

> 'A BPEO is the outcome of a systematic consultative and decision making procedure which emphasises the protection and conservation of the environment across land, air, and water. The BPEO procedure establishes, for a given set of objectives, the option that provides the most benefit or the least damage to the environment as a whole, at acceptable cost, in the long term as well as in the short term.'

The essential feature of BPEO is that regard is had by the regulatory authority (HMIP) to the overall effect of a polluting process on all environmental media It therefore necessitates a degree of compromise in which an increase in the discharges of waste to water may be more than offset by a reduction in the emissions to air. HMIP will seek to ensure when authorising a process that the overall levels of discharges secure the best practicable environmental option. BPEO is achieved by applying BATNEEC.

The concept of BATNEEC is found in the Environmental Protection Act and is the cornerstone of the system of Integrated Pollution Control and Local Authority Air Pollution Control. BATNEEC means Best Available Techniques Not Entailing Excessive Cost. The EPA requires that BATNEEC is used by all prescribed processes in order to:

1   prevent the release of substances prescribed for any environmental medium into that medium or, where that is not practicable by such means for reducing the release of such substances to a minimum and for rendering harmless any such substances which are so released; and

2   for rendering harmless any other substances which might cause harm if released into any other environmental medium.

Processes subject to IPC will be required to use the best available techniques not entailing excessive cost in order to achieve the Best Practicable Environmental Option. For a discussion of how BATNEEC and BPEO operate see Chapter 9.

1.10.2   BPEO – Best Practicable Environmental Option

1.10.3   BATNEEC – Best Available Techniques Not Entailing Excessive Cost

Guidance Notes produced by the Department of Environment define BATNEEC as follows:

- Best – the most effective techniques for minimising, preventing or rendering harmless noxious emissions. There may be more than one 'best' technique.

- Available – the techniques must be available to the operator. They need not be in general use, but they must be available generally, or specifically to the operator. It must be proven to work in the context the operator works in.

- Technique – The use of the word 'technique' has a wide meaning as it refers both to technology and to the method of operation. It allows for the consideration of issues such as the design of the process, the components, training of staff involved, supervision and management of the site.

- Not Entailing Excessive Cost – This is a reflection that in environmental law the protection of the environment must be balanced alongside other factors, especially economic concerns. When applying the BATNEEC standard it must not be excessive in relation to the environmental benefit it achieves, and must therefore be subject to some cost/benefit analysis for the process in question. The NEEC requirement does not relate to whether or not the operator finds the costs excessive.

1.11 The Environment Bill 1994

Environmental law is a rapidly expanding area of law. This is clear when one considers that the first comprehensive attempt at pollution control in 1974 has now largely been superseded by the Environmental Protection Act and that there are over three hundred pieces of EC environmental legislation. At the time of writing the Environment Bill before Parliament will introduce further changes into the framework of environmental control.

The Environment Bill was finally introduced by the government on 1 December 1994 some two years after it was first proposed. The principal aim of the Bill is the creation of a new Environment Agency for England and Wales. Over 50% of the Bill is concerned with the establishment of the Environment Agency and its administrative function. The remaining parts of the Bill cover a range of environmental issues including:

- pollution from abandoned mines;

- the creation of independent authorities for National Parks;

- producer responsibility for waste streams;

- hedgerow protection;

- grants for conservation and enhancement of the countryside;

- the extension of the framework for statutory nuisance including contaminated land.

The Environment Agency provisions are due to come into force immediately the Bill receives Royal Assent, and it is anticipated that the majority of the remaining provisions will come into force on 1 April 1996.

The details of the functions and duties of the new Environment Agency are discussed in Chapter 5. Briefly the Agency will be responsible for the following functions:

1.11.1   The Environment Agency

- functions currently exercised by the National Rivers Authority, which will be abolished;

- waste management functions exercised by the Waste Regulation Authorities;

- HMIP's responsibilities under Pt I of the EPA 1990;

- functions relating to radioactive substances;

- certain enforcement functions under the Health and Safety at Work Act 1974.

The contaminated land provisions in the Environment Bill are of considerable interest for all those who followed the progress of the ill-fated s 143 of the EPA 1990. The Environment Bill will create a further 18 sections to be included within the statutory nuisance provisions of the EPA 1990, ss 78A–78R. The Bill introduces a new definition of contaminated land which is dependent on the potential for harm to the health of living organisms, ecosystems and property. Excluded from the definition are offence to man's senses and harm to amenity.

1.11.2   Contaminated land

Under the Environment Bill control of contaminated land is divided between the Environment Agency and local authorities. The local authorities will be under a duty to inspect their areas for contaminated land and closed landfill sites. Once such sites are identified a plan for remediation must be formulated. The local authority will also be required to identify land other than closed landfill sites which are classed as 'special sites' which will fall under the control of the Environment Agency. Remediation notices are to be prepared by the relevant authority and served on an appropriate person, namely an owner or occupier.

The local authorities are also under a duty to keep registers of information relating to contaminated land in their area, although unlike those proposed under s 143 EPA these may be in any form.

1.11.3   Water pollution from abandoned mines

The Environment Bill will insert a new chapter into the Water Resources Act 1991 which deals specifically with water pollution from abandoned mines. One of the criticisms of the Water Resources Act was that it excluded abandoned mines from the control of the NRA. It is proposed that mine operators should give the Agency six months notice of any proposed abandonment. Failure to give notice will constitute a criminal offence.

Elements of Environmental Law

The term 'environment' can be defined very widely. However the Environmental Protection Act 1990 defines it in the following way:

> 'The "environment" consists of all, or any of the following media, namely, the air, water and land; and the medium of air includes the air within buildings and the air within other natural or man-made structures above or below ground.'

Pollution is defined by reference to the potential effect of the introduction of substances or energy into the environment rather than the fact of the introduction itself. This emphasis on effect is echoed in the EPA 1990.

The environment and pollution

Environmental law is now considered to be a branch of law in its own right. However, it does not comprise one distinct set of legal rules, rather it is made up of law drawn from a variety of sources:

Environmental law

- environmental legislation;
- the torts of nuisance, negligence, trespass and the rule in *Rylands v Fletcher*;
- the town and country planning legislation;
- land law;
- consumer protection;
- public health legislation; and
- health and safety at work legislation.

The main sources of environmental law are:

Sources of environmental law

- international treaties, conventions and protocols;
- European Community legislation;
- UK primary legislation;
- UK Statutory Instruments;
- case law;
- government departmental notes such as Planning Policy Guidance Notes;
- government circulars;

- Codes of Practice;
- Enforcement Authority Guidance Notes.

The international dimension

International agreements play an important role in shaping both EC and UK environmental law and policy. The EC has introduced over 300 pieces of legislation concerned with the environment.

The functions of environmental law

Environmental law can be said to have three main functions:

- prevention;
- setting environmental quality standards;
- clean-up/remediation

Environmental crimes

Environmental law creates numerous criminal offences which carry the possibility of unlimited fines or even imprisonment. In the main the criminal offences can be categorised into the following broad headings.

- causing pollution;
- permitting pollution;
- breach of licence conditions;
- breach of statutory duty;
- failure to comply with Notices.

Principles of environmental law

Environmental law is based upon a number of principles which underpin policy and legislation. These are:

- the polluter pays principle;
- the preventive principle;
- the precautionary principle.

In addition legislation has introduced various standards of activity. These are:

- BPM: Best Practicable Means;
- BPEO: Best Practicable Environmental Option;
- BATNEEC: Best Available Techniques Not Entailing Excessive Cost.

Chapter 2

European Community Environmental Law

No study of UK environmental law would be complete without a detailed consideration of EC environmental law. It is clear that EC environmental measures have played a key role in shaping UK law. The European Community has adopted over three hundred measures which have an impact upon the environment or relate to environmental protection. These measures have had to be implemented into UK law and any, even cursory, inspection of the range of UK environmental laws will give evidence to that fact alone. However the EC has also played an important role in shaping UK environment policy and policy objectives. Many of the UK Governments stated aims reflect EC policy ambitions.

It is therefore self evident that any student (or indeed practitioner) of environmental law must not only have a knowledge of the specific environmental provisions of EC legislation, they must also have a clear understanding of the nature of EC law; how it can be enforced; how it may be challenged and in particular how it operates within the domestic legal system.

This chapter examines the institutional arrangements within the European Community with reference, where appropriate, to the environment; it covers the legislative procedures, enforcement of community law and concludes with a discussion of the effect of community law in the domestic legal system. These issues are clearly of significant importance, however, it is not appropriate in a textbook on environmental law for lengthy discussion on all of the issues involved and therefore readers are recommended to consult an EC law textbook for further detailed analysis.

The next chapter (Chapter 3) is also concerned with EC environmental law and deals with the following issues:

- The development of the European Community's environmental policy and law. In particular it considers how the Community has become a key actor in the environment field, albeit in its early years it had no legal basis on which to do so. Consideration is also given in this chapter to the relationship between the ECs environmental programme and other areas of Community law, in particular the aim to achieve a common market in which goods and services can move freely. The issue of whether

Member States can introduce more stringent environmental laws than those laid down by the EC is also dealt with.

- The substantive nature of EC environmental policy and some of the principle features of the current Environmental Action Plan. The chapter highlights some of the key environmental Directives which are considered elsewhere in this book.

The full text of Treaty Arts 130(r–t) is reproduced at Appendix 1.

2.2 The development of the European Union

The European Economic Community was established by the Treaty of Rome in 1957. Since that time the Community has grown from an initial membership of six (Belgium, France, Germany, The Netherlands, Luxembourg and Italy) to 15 following the accession of the United Kingdom, Denmark and Ireland in 1973, Greece in 1979, Spain and Portugal in 1986 and Austria, Finland and Sweden in January 1995. Following German reunification in 1989, East Germany was absorbed into the Community, subject to certain special transitional arrangements. It was anticipated that Norway would join at the same time as Austria, Finland and Sweden but following a 'no vote' in the Norwegian Referendum, the Norwegian Government was not able to proceed to membership. In addition Cyprus, Malta and Turkey have applied to join.

2.2.1 From EEC to EC

Not only has the Community grown in size it has also considerably increased its spheres of influence by becoming very much more than an association of states pursuing economic goals. The Community can now legitimately take action in a range of areas, including environmental protection, which were never envisaged as Community interests in its formative years. The Treaty of Rome has been amended by the Single European Act 1986, itself a Treaty despite its rather modest title, and the Treaty on European Union signed at Maastricht on 7 February 1992, and which took effect in November 1993. The Single European Act (SEA) 1986 introduced a number of significant changes to the Rome Treaty designed to, *inter alia*, speed up the decision making process in Europe so that a programme of over 280 measures could be enacted in order to create the Single European Market by the self imposed deadline of 31 December 1992. The SEA also established for the first time that the Community could legitimately take action in the field of environmental protection.

The Treaty on European Union (TEU) was an altogether more complex Treaty. On the one hand, it created the European Union (EU) which essentially is an institutional framework for political co-operation between the Member States. However, the TEU also amended the EEC Treaty itself. Article G of the TEU introduced significant amendments to the EEC Treaty in relation to Community interests, and also procedural changes (the main one being the creation of a new legislative procedure which strengthened the power of the Parliament). A further significant change brought about by the Treaty on European Union was the change in the name of the European Economic Community to the European Community (EC). This change of name is more than symbolic and reflects the fact that the Community has developed to such an extent that it can no longer be regarded simply as an economic community pursuing economic goals.

Article 2 of the EC Treaty, which lays down the aims of the Community and as such is pivotal in determining the legal competences of the community institutions, has been amended by the SEA and the TEU. In 1957 the Treaty of Rome stated that the task of the Community was to establish a common market, progressively approximating the economic policies of the Member States to promote throughout the Community a 'harmonious development of economic activities, a continuous and balanced expansion, an increase in stability, an accelerated raising of the standard of living and closer relations between the States belonging to it'. Following the amendments to the Treaty by the SEA and the TEU the aims are more widely stated :

2.3   The aims of the European Community

> 'The Community shall have as its task, by establishing a common market and an economic and monetary union and by implementing the common policies of activities referred to in Arts 3 and 3(a) to promote throughout the Community a harmonious, and balanced development of economic activities, sustainable development and non-inflationary growth, respecting the environment, a high degree of convergence of economic performance, a high level of employment and of social protection, the raising of the standard of living and quality of life, and economic and social cohesion and solidarity among Member States.'

This expansion of Community interests has been one of the key concerns for those who fear the moves towards a federal Europe. The Treaty on European Union stimulated enormous debate and, as a consequence, it did not come into effect until November 1993, following the difficulties of ratification in some Member States. In 1996 an Inter-governmental conference will begin the process of reviewing the Treaty again.

2.4   Community competencies

The institutions of the European Community are entrusted with the power to enact secondary legislation in order to further the aims of the Community. It is Art 3 of the Treaty which sets out which actions can be taken in pursuit of those aims. In other words Art 3 defines what actions can be taken, or to use the jargon, it defines the Community's competences. If the Community institutions take action in an area which the community is not legally competent, then any such action may be annulled by the European Court of Justice exercising its powers of judicial review under Art 173. Again, Art 3 has also been subject to positive amendment and now runs to a very wide-ranging list of legitimate actions. Article 3 now states:

'For the purposes set out in Art 2, the activities of the Community shall include, as provided by this Treaty and in accordance with the timetable set out therein:

(a) the elimination, as between Member States, of customs duties and quantitative restrictions on the import and export of goods, and of all other measures having equivalent effect;

(b) a common commercial policy;

(c) an internal market characterised by the abolition, as between Member States, of obstacles to the free movement of goods, persons, services and capital;

(d) measures concerning the entry and movement of persons in the internal market as provided for in Art 100C;

(e) a common policy in the sphere of agriculture and fisheries;

(f) a common policy in the sphere of transport;

(g) a system ensuring that competition in the internal market is not distorted;

(h) the approximation of the laws of the Member States to the extent required for the functioning of the common market;

(i) a policy in the social sphere comprising a European Social Fund;

(j) the strengthening of economic and social cohesion;

(k) a policy in the sphere of the environment;

(l) the strengthening of the competitiveness of Community industry;

(m) the promotion of research and technological development;

(n) encouragement for the establishment and development of trans-European networks;

(o) a contribution to the attainment of a high level of health protection;

(p) a contribution to the education and training of quality and to the flowering of the cultures of the Member States;

(q) a policy in the sphere of development co-operation;

(r) the association of the overseas countries and territories in order to increase trade and promote jointly economic and social development;

(s) a contribution to the strengthening of consumer protection;

(t) measures in the spheres of energy, civil protection and tourism.'

It is clear from this list that the activities of the Community are wide-ranging, but on closer inspection they are not all necessarily compatible. Whilst activities aimed at protecting the environment, consumer protection and a high level of health protection may be complementary, others are not. There is a tension between the aims of securing the strengthening of the competitiveness of Community industry and environmental protection. The need to promote economic growth usually comes at an environmental cost. The creation of new businesses may make the EC more competitive in the global market and may indeed create much needed jobs and opportunities, but there will be environmental consequences and these need to be taken into account. The Community has recognised that the goal of economic growth cannot be pursued without consideration for the environment and that in promoting growth today account needs to be taken of the consequences for future generations. This view is reflected in the current desire to pursue sustainable and non-inflationary growth respecting the environment. The principle of sustainable development is considered more fully in Chapter 3.

2.5 Sources of EC law

The EC Treaty is the primary source of European Community law since it is from the Treaty that the Community institutions derive their power to enact secondary legislation. The Treaty is often described as *Traité Cadre*, which means that it is a framework treaty which sets out broad general principles and aims, but leaves the institutions to 'flesh-out' and implement these aims by means of secondary legislation. The institutions of the Community are entrusted under Art 4 of the Treaty to carry out their respective functions, which includes the capacity to enact secondary legislation. However the institutions must only act within the powers conferred upon them by the Treaty and, as stated above, if they bring forward legislation in areas which the community is not legally competent then such measures may be annulled on the ground of lack of competence (the equivalent of the *ultra vires* doctrine in English law). This is important because it prevents the Community taking action in those areas which are legitimately the domain of Member States and it prevents a transfer of power beyond that which the Member States agreed in the signing of the Treaty.

Therefore it is clear that all EC Secondary legislation must derive from the Treaty and must have a legal basis. This is a particular point which has been of importance in the area of environmental law and will be considered more fully in Chapter 3.

2.5.1	EC secondary legislation	Article 189 of the Treaty defines the legislative powers of the institutions and the types of legal instruments available. Because these Acts derive from the Treaty, they are regarded as secondary legislation and are hierarchically inferior to the Treaty which is the primary source of EC law. It is important to be familiar with the distinctions between the types of secondary legislation. However, a note of caution: the classification laid down below is not always straightforward. An Act is not always what it says it is, consequently the Court of Justice will look at the substance rather than the form, and has held that where a regulation fails to lay down general rules it may be a disguised decision.

The cases of the *Confédération Nationale des Producteurs de Fruits et Legumes v Council* (1962), are of particular relevance in the context of judicial review proceedings.

2.5.2	Regulations	Regulations have general application, are binding in their entirety and directly applicable in all Member States. Regulations apply equally to all 15 Member States and can therefore be used to ensure that the law is exactly the same throughout the Community. For this reason Regulations take effect within Member States either on the date specified in the Official Journal of the European Communities (all Regulations and, indeed, Directives must be published in the Official Journal – see Art 191 EC Treaty) or, in the absence of a specified date, the Regulation takes effect 20 days after publication. Since Regulations are binding in their entirety and directly applicable, there is no need for Member States to

implement the Regulation in order for it to take effect. In fact, national implementation of Regulations has been held in *Leonesio v Ministero dell'Agricoltura e delle Foreste* (1971) to be incompatible with the aims of the Regulations.

Directives differ from Regulations in a number of respects. Article 189 states that :

> 'A Directive shall be binding as to the results to be achieved, upon each Member State to which it is addressed, but shall leave to the national authorities the choice and form of methods.'

2.5.3   Directives

Although Directives are generally addressed to all Member States, it is possible for Directives to be directed to only one or a few Member States, and it is equally possible for Directives to be addressed to all Member States but with different conditions (such as deadlines for implementation). Directives state the 'aim to be achieved', which is binding upon the Member State, but leave the choice and means of implementation to the discretion of the Member State. Therefore Directives provide that implementation should be within a certain timetable or by a certain deadline. Member States are obliged to ensure that there is effective implementation of the Directive within the specified time period. Implementation by means of a government circular will not be sufficient. Member States usually submit a copy of the implementing legislation to the Commission so that the Commission can review whether or not there has been compliance. In the UK, implementation is usually done by means of Statutory Instrument. The European Communities Act 1972 provides powers for Ministers to introduce delegated legislation giving effect to Community obligations in Directives.

The majority of EC environmental 'acts' take the form of Directives rather than Regulations. This means that Member States play a large part in the implementation of EC environmental law and that they exercise some discretion in terms of how to achieve the aims laid down by the Community. This use of Directives rather than Regulations has a number of consequences however. At the practical level, it means that students and practitioners of environmental law should become familiar with the skills involved in 'tracking' Directives and their subsequent implementation. Since this will invariably be by means of Statutory Instrument it will necessarily involve finding out whether a Statutory Instrument has been introduced or not.

However, Directives are problematic in another respect insofar as there is clearly the scope for Member States to fail to implement them, either on time or indeed at all. Alternatively there are cases where implementation takes place in form, but there may not be effective implementation in terms of adequate enforcement or remedies available. It is interesting to note that the Fourth Environmental Action Programme (1987–1992) stated that one of the principal aims was to ensure that Member States apply Directives fully both in terms of legal implementation and practical implementation. Given that Directives are prone to such problems, it is reasonable to wonder why they are the principal means of enacting Community environmental legislation. By leaving the choice and form of implementation to the Member States, there will automatically be divergences of approach. On the other hand, Directives provide a flexible means of ensuring harmonised standards whilst taking account of the differing legal and administrative systems within the Member States and, to some extent, reflect the principle of subsidiarity which is so central to the Treaty.

Directives have generated considerable case law, both within the national legal systems of the Member States and also by the ECJ. The direct effect, or otherwise, of Directives is considered more fully below.

2.5.4	Decisions

A Decision is an individual Act 'binding in its entirety upon those to whom it is addressed'. Decisions can be addressed to Member States but can equally be addressed to individuals and companies. Because it is a binding Act, a Decision has the force of law and does not require any implementation. Decisions are frequently used by the Commission in the field of competition law but are rarely used in environmental law.

2.5.5	Recommendations and Opinions

In addition to Regulations, Directives and Decisions, the Treaty also makes provision for recommendations and opinions, which are not legally binding. However, the Court of Justice held in *Grimaldi v Fonds des Maladies Professionnelles* (1988) that recommendations and opinions should be of persuasive influence to national courts.

2.5.6	Case law of the European Court of Justice

Clearly where the court gives a ruling in an individual case, that ruling is binding on the parties to the proceedings. However, that decision is also binding in all subsequent cases. National courts are bound to follow rulings of the Court of Justice by virtue of Art 5, which provides that Member States (which includes the national courts) are bound to ensure fulfilment of the obligations arising out of the Treaty, or resulting from actions taken by the institutions of the

Community (which includes the ECJ's decisions). Moreover s 3(2) of the European Communities Act requires national courts to take judicial notice of any decision of the European Court of Justice. The case law of the ECJ has provided a rich source of Community law. It is the Court of Justice which is responsible for developing the principles of supremacy and direct effect and, as such, has been successful in securing the integration of Community law into the domestic legal systems. In its most active phases, the court has been criticised for judicial law making.

To understand how environmental policy and legislation is developed in the Community, it is necessary to be aware of the way in which legislation is enacted and the role of the respective Community institutions. This is particularly important when one considers the amount of environmental legislation that the Community has thus far enacted and the way in which influences can be brought to bear to affect its content (or, indeed, existence). It is also important to understand the role of the respective institutions in the enforcement of EC environmental law and the actions that they can take in the event of a breach of the community laws. The issue of enforcement is of particular importance in the light of what has already been said about the use of Directives in the field of environmental law. Since the implementation of most EC environmental law rests with the Member States themselves, the Community must have the means available to ensure that such implementation is both effective and uniformly applied.

2.6   The institutional framework

Within the Community, no one institution is solely responsible for passing legislation, instead the law-making process involves the Council, the Commission, the Parliament and, in some instances, the Economic and Social Affairs Committee and the newly-created Committee of the Regions. Neither is there one single law-making procedure. Instead there are several, each of which involves the institutions in a number of different relationships. The Parliament can not be regarded as the legislative body in the same way in which the UK Parliament is. Instead, the European Parliament participates, in varying degrees, in the overall process of enacting legislation, although in some instances it may play no role at all. The institution with the greatest influence is the Council of Ministers.

2.6.1   The institutions

The Council of the European Union (formerly called the Council of Ministers prior to the TEU) is made up of 15 representatives from the Member States. The representatives

2.6.2   The Council of the European Union

must be Ministers of State who are authorised to commit their respective governments. When Ministers attend Council meetings, they represent their governments and generally pursue national interests. The composition of the Council alters, depending on the subject under discussion; general council meetings are usually attended by Foreign Affairs Ministers, environment meetings are attended by Environment Ministers and so on. Where high level policy meetings are the subject of discussion, then the Council may consist of Heads of State. However, the Heads of State are also required by the Treaty to meet at least twice a year and, when they act in this special capacity, they meet as the European Council. Each Member State takes over the presidency of the Council for a period of six months.

2.6.3	The functions of the Council of Ministers

The duty of the Council is to 'ensure that the objectives set out in the Treaty are attained' and to ensure the overall co-ordination of the general economic policies of the Member States. The Council, by virtue of Art 145, has the power to take decisions which places it in the most powerful position in terms of enacting legislation (although, as is shown below, it interacts with the other institutions in a variety of ways, depending on the specific legislative procedure that is used).

Because the Council has this power of decision-making, the way in which it votes and takes decision on legislative proposals is of utmost significance. Clearly if decisions were always take by a simple majority (ie eight out of 15) there would be scope for legislation to be regularly enacted despite the disagreement of seven Member States. Therefore, although the Treaty specifies that decisions will usually be taken by simple majority unless otherwise provided for, the Treaty does go on to provide otherwise in most instances and, in fact, simple majority voting is rare. The provisions of the Treaty require some decisions to be taken by 'qualified majority'.

2.6.4	Qualified majority voting

In these instances each Member State has a weighted vote, the weight depending on the size of population. Therefore the larger member States (France, Germany, Italy and the United Kingdom) each have 10 votes, Spain has eight, Belgium, Greece, the Netherlands and Portugal carry five votes, Austria and Sweden have four votes, Denmark, Ireland and Finland each have three and Luxembourg, the smallest Member State, has two votes.

Where a qualified majority is required in favour of a proposal, then 62 out of the total of 87 votes must be cast in favour of the proposal. In other words at least 25 votes are required to block a proposal. The system is complicated by a compromise agreement whereby, if the Member States achieve a total of between 23 and 25 votes against a qualified decision, then the Council is obliged, within certain limits, to try and reach a compromise solution. This system of weighting was introduced by the Single European Act essentially to speed up decision-making in order to achieve the self-imposed deadline of achieving the Single Market programme by 1992. It also provides a means of decision-making/voting which prevents the larger Member States effectively out-voting the smaller Member States.

Qualified majority voting is used now in relation to the majority of legislation required to complete the Single Market. Thus, most harmonising measures introduced under Art 100a will require a qualified majority vote by the Council. Qualified majority voting is also used for environmental protection measures enacted under Art 130s.

In certain circumstances, the Treaty still requires that decisions are agreed unanimously. Fiscal measures, measures relating to the free movement of people or professional training are some of the areas that still require a unanimous vote. As far as environmental measures are concerned, where the proposed measures concern Town and Country Planning, land use (with the exception of waste management and management of water resources), and energy supply, the Council are required to act unanimously. Where a unanimous vote is required, there is a much greater likelihood that the proposals will be delayed for lengthy periods until a compromise can be reached which satisfies all the Member States. It is not unknown for some proposals to have taken as long as 16 years to be agreed. The Environmental Assessment Directive is a case in point.	2.6.5 Unanimous voting
The European Commission is made up of twenty Commissioners. Commissioners are appointed by common accord of the governments of the Member States. Once appointed as a Commissioner, an individual must act in the interests of the Community, not taking instructions from any national government. Their independence must be beyond doubt. Each Member State appoints at least one, whilst the larger Member States and Spain put forward two. The Commissioners are now appointed for five years and these terms may be renewed. The Commission is headed by a President. Commissioners are each given a specific portfolio for which they are responsible.	2.6.6 The European Commission

2.6.7	The Commission Services	The Commission Services (the civil service of the Community, based largely in Brussels) is divided into a series of departments which are known as Directorate Generals. Headed up by an administrative and permanent Director General, each DG reports to a specific Commissioner. The Directorate Generals are classified by number, with DG XI taking responsibility for the Environment, Nuclear Safety and Civil Protection.

2.6.8	The functions of the Commission	The functions of the European Commission are laid down in Art 155 of the EC Treaty. The Commission acts in the capacity of executive and also plays a key role in the formation of legislation. In addition, the Commission exercises considerable powers in relation to the enforcement of Community law, having the right to bring Member States before the Court of Justice. In this respect the Commission is regarded as the 'watchdog' of the Community or is sometimes referred to as the 'Guardian of the Treaties'. The Commission's role in the enforcement of Community law is dealt with more fully at para 2.8.

The Commission is responsible for proposing and initiating legislation. Prior to the Treaty on European Union only the Commission had this power, albeit that it was not explicitly stated in the Treaty but was implied. The Council can of course suggest proposals to the Commission, but it has no legal power to insist that legislation is brought forward, although it clearly exercises considerable political power. However, since the Treaty on European Union, the Parliament now enjoys the right to require the Commission to propose any legislation that it suggests. The Council can only take legislative action on proposals that have been initiated by the Commission.

2.6.9	The European Parliament	The Parliament was originally called the European Assembly and was made up of representatives from national parliaments. However, in 1979 direct elections to the Parliament were held for the first time and the Assembly changed its name to European Parliament as required by the Single European Act. The Parliament is now made up of 626 directly elected representatives, known as Members of the European Parliament or MEPs. At present, the electoral systems in the different Member States vary, with most States electing by means of proportional representation. The Treaty requires, however, that a uniform electoral system is eventually adopted.

2.6.10	The functions of the European Parliament	The Parliament's functions and powers have grown significantly since 1957. Prior to the Single European Act 1986,

the Parliament acted largely in an advisory and supervisory capacity. Its involvement in the legislative procedure was limited to giving an opinion on proposed legislation, but only in relation to those areas of legislation where the Treaty specifically provided that the Parliament should be consulted. In some areas of legislation, the Council could take decisions without the need for any consultation with the Parliament (this non-consultation procedure still exists today).

However, the Parliament, as befitting the only directly elected community institution, pressed for greater powers and in particular a greater involvement in the legislative process. Its powers were increased by the Single European Act, which gave it the right in certain circumstances to be consulted twice in relation to certain proposals and, even more significantly, by the Treaty on European Union, which introduced the so-called co-decision procedure, giving the Parliament effectively a right to veto certain legislative proposals. The way in which the Parliament votes in relation to proposals before it are specified in the Treaty. Unless otherwise provided by the Treaty, the normal voting arrangement would be by a simple majority of votes cast. However, the Treaty specifies, particularly in relation to the procedures known as 189b and 189c (see below), that in some instances an absolute majority is required.

The Parliament currently exercises a range of functions. Its role in the legislative process is described more fully below. It also acts in a supervisory capacity in relation to the Commission and, to a lesser extent, the Council. The Parliament has the power to dismiss the whole of the Commission with a vote of censure, provided that it can achieve a two-thirds majority in favour of such action. Although the Parliament has threatened such action on two occasions, it has never done so. The Parliament also conducts its own version of question time when it requires Commissioners to answer Parliamentary questions, either verbally to the Parliament or in writing. It is in this way that the Parliament exercises a degree of control over the Commission, and this reflects the checks and balances that are built into the institutional framework. The Council of Ministers also reports to the Parliament. At the end of each presidency period, the outgoing President of the Council reports to the Parliament on the achievements during the presidency period.

Since the Treaty on European Union, the Parliament has been given the power to set up a Committee of Inquiry to investigate alleged contraventions or maladministration in the implementation of Community law and has also been required to appoint an Ombudsman for Maladministration.

2.6.11   The Parliament and the environment

The political composition of the Parliament is wide-ranging, with large representations from both the left and right of the political spectrum. However, in the current Parliament there are 23 representatives from Green Parties. The Parliament also has its own select Committee on Environment, Public Health and Consumer Protection which has about 50 members. The Parliament receives a number of petitions from environmental pressure groups and these are usually passed on to the Commission to deal with under the Art 169 proceedings (see below). The value of petitioning Parliament is that it can lend a political impetus to the process which may be persuasive when the Commission decides upon enforcement proceedings.

2.6.12   The European Court of Justice

Article 164 of the Treaty provides that the role of the European Court of Justice (ECJ) is to 'ensure that in the interpretation and application of this Treaty the law is observed'. Various other Treaty Articles deal with its jurisdiction in relation to cases brought by Member States, against Member States, against the institutions themselves and also its relationship with the national courts of the Member States. These will be discussed more fully below in relation to the enforcement of Community law. The Court itself is made up of 15 judges chosen from people whose independence is beyond doubt. The Court is assisted by nine Advocate Generals who help the Court by presenting an analysis of the cases before the Court and also, importantly, their recommendations in the form of an opinion. The Court reaches its decisions in private and presents a single judgment known as a collegiate judgment. This means, in fact, that there is no record of any dissenting judgment. It is often very useful when reading judgments of the Court to also read the opinion of the Advocate General. Whilst the judges are not bound to follow the Advocate Generals' recommendations, where they do the opinion provides a very useful indication of the Court's reasoning.

In addition to the Court of Justice, there is also the European Court of First Instance, which was created in 1988 to alleviate some of the workload of the ECJ. The Court of First Instance, however, has limited jurisdiction and cannot give preliminary rulings under Art 177, or deal with cases brought by or against the Member States. The Court can act as a Court of First Instance in EC competition law cases and judicial review cases brought by 'natural and legal persons'.

The following diagram provides a detailed breakdown of the number of MEPs' votes in Council and Commissioners for each of the 15 Member States.

Member State	MEPs	Votes at Council	Commissioners
Austria	21	4	1
Belgium	25	5	1
Denmark	16	3	1
Finland	16	3	1
France	87	10	2
Germany	99	10	2
Greece	25	5	1
Ireland	15	3	1
Italy	87	10	2
Luxembourg	6	2	1
Netherlands	31	5	1
Portugal	25	5	1
Spain	64	8	2
Sweeden	22	4	1
United Kingdom	87	10	2
TOTAL	626	87	20

The process of enacting Community secondary legislation is complex; however, there are two underlying fundamental principles which govern it. The first is that, in order to enact EC secondary legislation, the Treaty must provide a legal basis for such action. In other words, there must be a legal basis for secondary legislation. The Community institutions have no power to enact legislation that does not serve the aims of the Community. To do so would mean that they were acting *ultra vires*. However, it should be noted that Art 235 of the Treaty provides a residual power to enable the institutions to take action to achieve community objectives, notwithstanding an explicit legal basis. Article 235 is dealt with more fully in chapter 3.

2.7 The legislative procedure

The second point of importance is that the Treaty defines how the relevant legislation will be enacted. The legislative procedure that will be employed to enact the secondary legislation depends entirely upon the Treaty Article under which the legislation is based. This point is of particular importance in the field of environmental law, where it is possible to enact environmental legislation either under Art 100a or under Art 130. Article 100a and Art 130 both prescribe the procedure to be used, which, in the case in hand, are in fact different procedures. Article 100a requires measures to be adopted under the co-decision procedure, whereas Art 130 requires the co-operation procedure.

Legislative proposals are initiated by the Commission. In practice, the Commission consults with a variety of groups as to the content of the legislation and it is in this way that environmental pressure groups can influence the content of environmental legislation. Once the proposal has been drafted and agreed by the Commission, it is sent to the Council of Ministers.

There are a number of ways in which the proposal will be dealt with from this point, however the main procedures are as follows:

- Council legislation without consultation of the European Parliament: where the Council takes a final decision on the Commission proposal without the involvement of the Parliament;

- The Consultation Procedure: in this procedure the Parliament must be consulted before the Council reaches its final decision. The Council must take account of the Parliament's opinion, although the opinion is not binding on the Council;

- The Co-operation Procedure: introduced by the Single European Act 1986. This procedure is strictly called the Art 189(c) procedure. The procedure enables the Parliament to have two opportunities to consider the proposal (rather like adding a second reading to the process). The Parliament can suggest amendments to the draft proposal. If the Council does not accept the Parliamentary amendments, then it is forced to act unanimously in order to enact the legislative proposal. It is in this way that the Parliament exerts some influence on the content of legislation;

- The Co-decision Procedure or Art 189(b) procedure: this is a new procedure introduced by the Treaty on European Union. The procedure is complicated but greatly enhances the role of the Parliament. The effect of the co-decision procedure is to provide for the possibility of a third reading. The procedure follows that of the co-operation procedure until the final stage. Where the Council does not approve Parliamentary amendments, a conciliation committee of equal numbers of the Council and the Parliament attempt to agree a joint text. If the joint text cannot be agreed, then the proposed measure fails.

In addition to these main procedures, there are others – such as the Assent procedure, and the Conciliation procedure.

Since there are clearly differences between the procedures, in terms of the powers of the Parliament and the voting in the Council of Ministers, the question of which Treaty Article should be used has significant implications, and is dealt with more fully in Chapter 3 in relation to environmental legislation.

Member States are obliged to fulfil their Community law obligations and not to do anything which would jeopardise the attainment of the Treaty.

2.8   Enforcement of Community law

Member States are required by Art 5 to fulfil their obligations as members of the Community. They are specifically required to take all appropriate measures, whether general or particular, to ensure fulfilment of the obligations arising out of the Treaty, or resulting from action take by the institutions. Such action embraces both policy, secondary legislation and decisions of the Court of Justice and Court of First Instance. In addition, Member States must not take any measures which could jeopardise the attainment of the Treaty objectives.

2.8.1   Member States' obligation to comply with EC law: Art 5

Failure to fulfil obligations can take many forms:

* introducing legislation in contravention to the Treaty: This happened in relation to the Merchant Shipping Act 1988 which contravened the basic principle of non-discrimination on the grounds of nationality and resulted in the *Factortame* litigation and the case *Commission v United Kingdom* (1989);

* failure to implement Directives either at all, or on time: The Commission has brought numerous actions against Member States on these grounds. For example, the case of *Commission v United Kingdom* (1993);

* partial or incorrect implementation of a Directive;

* inadequate enforcement of a Directive.

The main direct sanction against Member States is provided for by Art 169 of the Treaty, which enables the European Commission to commence legal proceedings against Member States before the European Court of Justice. Article 169 provides for two pre-litigation stages before court proceedings are taken. If the Commission believes that a Member State is in breach of its community obligations, it can inform the Member State in question by means of a letter of formal notice, known as an 'Article 169' letter, which sets out the nature of the infringement and the course of action to be taken. This only usually happens after informal negotiations have been exhausted. The letter must state all the grounds for complaint. Member States must then be given an adequate time period to make their observations on the alleged breach. If the Commission is still not satisfied that the Member State is

2.8.2   Direct actions against Member States

complying with its obligations, then it can take the next step of issuing a 'reasoned opinion'. This formally records the infringement and requires the Member State to take the necessary action to bring the infringement to an end. Normally the Member State will be given a deadline by which it must take appropriate action.

Following these two pre-litigation steps, the Commission can, if it chooses, commence legal proceedings against the Member State before the Court of Justice (such cases appear as the *Commission v United Kingdom* or *Commission v Italy* and so on). The number of cases brought before the ECJ under Art 169 are increasing each year. A number of points need to be made in relation to Art 169 proceedings:

- The Commission often acts on the basis of complaints made by aggrieved citizens or pressure groups. The number of complaints received in 1993 was 1,040. In addition, the Commission also receives numerous petitions (23 in 1993) from pressure groups, trades unions and so on. It is in this respect that individuals and pressure groups can exert pressure on the Commission to deal with breaches of environmental law. Complainants do not have to satisfy any legal or sufficient interest in the matter complained of. Therefore Art 169 provides an inexpensive means by which interested parties can seek to enforce Community law ;

- The Commission is not bound to investigate or follow through all complaints nor is it bound to commence Art 169 proceedings. In fact the Commission exercises discretion at all stages. This was confirmed by the Court of Justice in *Star Fruit Company v Commission* (1989) ;

- Member States have raised various mitigating factors and defences but these have rarely succeeded. In *Commission v Ireland* (1981), concerning Ireland's failure to implement Directive 77/91, the Court held that a Member State may not plead provisions, practices or circumstances existing in its internal legal system in order to justify a failure to comply with obligations resulting from Community Directives.

The following tables indicate the number of Article 169 letters, reasoned opinions and legal actions commenced in 1993 and 1994.

	Art 169	Reasoned opinions	To ECJ
1993	1206	352	44
1994	974	546	89

In 1993 of the 1,206 letters of formal notice 90 were concerned with environmental law matters, resulting in 26 reasoned opinions and seven cases before the European Court of Justice.

Actions against Member States in 1994

Belgium	10
Denmark	0
France	8
Germany	5
Greece	17
Ireland	12
Italy	12
Luxembourg	6
Netherlands	4
Portugal	5
Spain	9
UK	1

In addition to Art 169, Art 170 provides for a similar procedure enabling one Member State to bring an action against another Member State. It is very rare for Member States to resort to Art 170. Member States are, in fact, required to ask the Commission to commence proceedings, and only when the Commission has failed to issue a reasoned opinion does this option become available. However, it is more likely that Member States will resolve their differences at the political level through the Council of Ministers rather than resorting to legal action before the ECJ.

Where a Member State is found to be in breach of its Community obligations, the Court of Justice will issue a declaration to that effect. Failure to comply with the declaration and remedy the situation will result in the Member State being in breach of both Art 171 and Art 5. Prior to the TEU, the Court's powers were limited to issuing a declaration. However, its powers have been enhanced by the TEU and the Court now has the power to impose a fine where a Member State continues to breach its obligations after a Court declaration. The fine is not automatic; the Commission is required to recommence proceedings against the defaulting Member State before a fine can be imposed.

2.8.3   Fines

The Treaty also gives the Court of Justice the jurisdiction to review the acts of the Community institutions and to annul them on specific grounds. The power of the Court in this respect is important, because it acts as check on the other

2.8.4   Judicial review of Community law

Community institutions which have been given significant powers under the Treaty. Article 173 specifies which 'acts' are reviewable, who may bring judicial review proceedings, the grounds on which review proceedings may be brought and the time limits for bringing such actions.

Judicial review in Community law is complex particularly in relation to actions brought by aggrieved individuals.

2.8.5	Reviewable acts

The Court can review the legality of acts adopted jointly by the European Parliament and the Council, of acts of the Council, of the Commission and of the European Central Bank other than recommendations and opinions and of acts of the European Parliament intended to have legal effect *vis-à-vis* third parties. 'Acts' are not defined other than in the negative sense, in that they do not include recommendations or opinions, which, of course, are not legally binding. It is clear therefore that Regulations, Directives and Decisions are 'acts' in this sense and therefore 'reviewable acts'. However the Court of Justice has not confined the interpretation of 'acts' to secondary legislation and, in various cases, has held that they include all measures taken by the institutions which are designed to have legal effect irrespective of their nature or form.

2.8.6	Who can bring an action?

Article 173 draws a distinction between the Member States and the institutions on the one hand, and natural and legal persons on the other. The Member States and the Council and the Commission are so-called privileged applicants. They can commence judicial review proceedings in relation to any reviewable act, they do not have to demonstrate or prove a legal interest. In other words, they automatically have standing. The Parliament does not have the same general right, but can bring an action to protect its prerogative powers. The position with regard to individuals or 'natural or legal persons', a classification which encompasses environmental pressure groups, is unfortunately much more complex and restrictive.

Article 173 states that any natural or legal person may institute proceedings against 'a decision addressed to that person, or a decision which, although in the form of a regulation or a decision addressed to another person, is of direct and individual concern to himself'.

In essence there are three situations where a non-privileged person can bring actions for judicial review:

(a) where the applicant is directly addressed;

(b) where a Regulation is really a disguised decision;

(c) where the decision is addressed to another person, which can include a Member State (*Plaumann & Co v Commission* (1963)).

In the cases of (b) and (c) the applicant also has to prove that the reviewable act is also of direct and individual concern. The tests laid down by the Court of Justice in relation to direct and individual concern have been very restrictive, making it extremely difficult for individuals to overcome this hurdle of standing. There is as yet no automatic right for pressure groups to bring judicial review actions.

Once an applicant has established that he/she has standing then they must then go on to establish the grounds for review. These are laid down in Art 173(2) and can often overlap in individual cases. These are:

- lack of competence;

- infringement of an essential procedural requirement;

- infringement of the Treaty or of any rule of law relating to the application of the Treaty; and

- misuse of power.

2.8.7   Grounds for review and time limits

Given that Art 169 proceedings can only be brought by the Commission and that individuals have in practice so little access to the Court of Justice under Art 173, it is vital to understand how Community law can be enforced within the national legal system by domestic courts. The European Court of Justice has established through its rulings, that individuals can raise issues of Community law in the context of legal proceedings in order to secure rights under Community law. So, for example, it is possible to use EC law to establish legal rights (*Marshall v Southampton Area Health Authority* (1986)), or as a defence in criminal prosecutions (*Ratti*).

2.9   Indirect enforcement through the national courts

In order to ensure that Community law is applied by national courts in a uniform manner, Art 177 provides that the domestic courts can refer matters of interpretation and validity of EC law provisions to the Court of Justice in order to obtain a ruling. This is known as the preliminary rulings procedure.

The Court of Justice has jurisdiction to give preliminary rulings concerning the interpretation of the Treaty, the validity and interpretation of acts of the institutions of the Community and the interpretation of the statutes of bodies established by an act of the Council. It is worth emphasising

2.9.1   The preliminary rulings procedure

that the Court can only interpret the Treaty; it cannot, as is the case with secondary legislation, question its validity.

If a question arises in the context of national court proceedings about an issue of EC law then that court or tribunal may, if it considers that decision is necessary to enable it to give judgment, request the Court of Justice to give a ruling. This is known as the Art 177 procedure. It enables national courts to refer questions on interpretation of EC law to the Court of Justice. Once the Court of Justice gives its preliminary ruling, the national court is bound by it and must apply it to the facts of the case. The Court of Justice is not deciding on the facts or the outcome of the national court case, neither is it acting as an appeal court. Instead it is essentially co-operating with the national court in order that the Community law provisions may be interpreted correctly. The Court of Justice is well placed to give this authoritative interpretation of Community law given its 'panoramic view' of the community and of its institutions (*per* Lord Bingham in *Customs and Excise Commissioners v Aps Samex* (1983)). When the national court seeks a preliminary ruling from the Court of Justice, the court proceedings are suspended until the Court has given its ruling. This has been known to take as long as two years although the period has now fallen to about 15 months.

The Court of Justice cannot pass judgment on the compatibility of domestic law with EC law. In circumstances where the Court has been asked to do this (since it is usually in cases involving a conflict between domestic and EC law that questions of interpretation are raised) the Court of Justice frequently rephrases the question from the national court in order to provide the interpretation of the relevant community law provision.

| 2.9.2 | When should a national court refer a question to the Court of Justice? |

The Treaty draws a distinction between courts which may refer a question and courts which shall. Art 177(3) states that courts from which there is no judicial remedy (no right of appeal) shall refer, whereas other (lower) courts exercise a discretion. Despite this distinction a court need only refer if it considers that a decision from the Court of Justice is necessary in order to enable it to give judgment. Therefore all courts exercise a discretion in determining whether a referral is necessary. In *Customs and Excise v Aps Samex* (1983) Lord Bingham gave the following guidance:

> '... if the facts have been found and the Community law issue is critical to the court's final decision, the appropriate course is ordinarily to refer the issue to the European Court of Justice unless the national court can

with complete confidence resolve the issue itself.

In considering whether it can with complete confidence resolve the issue itself, the national court must be mindful of the difference between national and Community legislation; of the pitfalls which face a national court when venturing into an unfamiliar field; of the need for uniform interpretation throughout the Community and of the great advantages enjoyed by the Court of Justice in construing Community instruments.'

The exercise of discretion is qualified in relation to questions concerning the validity of Community law raised in the context of national litigation. In *Firma Foto-Frost v Hauptzollamt Lubeck Ost* (1988), the Court of Justice explicitly stated that national courts do not have the power to declare acts of the Community institutions invalid. Therefore, where a question about the validity of Community law is raised, then the national court must seek a preliminary ruling from the Court of Justice.

2.9.3   A court must refer on questions of validity

The Art 177 procedure has provided the main vehicle for the Court of Justice to develop the principles of direct effect and supremacy dealt with in the following section. Many individuals have benefited from the Art 177 procedure as a result of the ECJ interpreting various EC provisions in such a way as to deem them directly effective and thus enforceable in national courts. There have been relatively few Art 177 rulings concerning environmental law. In the UK the first reference on an environmental law matter was made at the time of writing by the House of Lords in the case of *R v Secretary of State for the Environment, ex parte Royal Society for the Protection of Birds*, (1995).

2.9.4   Importance of Art 177 procedure

Commentators have described Community law as 'unique' in international law terms, largely because of the extent to which Community law penetrates the domestic legal systems of the Member States and confers enforceable legal rights upon individuals. The Court of Justice has itself stated that the Community:

2.10   The Community as a new legal order

'constitutes a new legal order of international law for the benefit of which the states have limited their sovereign rights, albeit within limited fields and the subjects of which comprise not only Member States but also their nationals.'

This statement was made by the European Court of Justice in the leading case of *Van Gend en Loos v Nederlandse Administratie der Belastingen* (1962). At the time when the court made this statement, the role of the Community was limited.

However, since that time the Community has extended its competences and the transfer of sovereign rights referred to in the judgment extends to less limited fields. The issue of the transfer of power away from Member States has caused major problems for a number of the Member States, particularly when those states sought to ratify and incorporate the new Treaty on European Union into their domestic legal systems. An expression of this concern came with the Danish 'no' vote in the referendum held on whether the Danish government should ratify the new Treaty. Therefore, a principal amendment to the Treaty on European Union was the introduction in Art 3B of the principle of subsidiarity.

| 2.10.1 | Subsidiarity |

This provides that in areas which do not fall within the Community's exclusive competence, the Community shall only take action if and so far as the objectives of the proposed action cannot be sufficiently achieved by the Member States and can therefore, by reason of the scale or effects of the proposed action, be better achieved by the Community. Furthermore, any action by the Community shall not go beyond what is necessary to achieve the objectives of the Treaty, recognition of another fundamental principle of Community law – the principle of proportionality.

| 2.10.2 | The relationship between Community law and UK law |

The relationship between EC law and national law is one which has dominated many Articles and text books and which is usually covered within the context of most Constitutional or Public law courses. Therefore, it is not the intention of this section to cover this subject in great detail. However, in view of the volume of Community environmental law that has been introduced, it is necessary to reflect on the way in which Community law is incorporated into the English legal system and, in particular, on the issues arising when there has not been adequate implementation of Directives. European Community law is incorporated into English law by the European Communities Act 1972 (as amended).

2.11 Supremacy of Community law

The EC Treaty does not specifically make reference to the issue of supremacy or the relationship between Community law and national law. However, this relationship is of the utmost importance. The Court of Justice has in a number of famous decisions made it clear that priority is to be accorded to EC law and that EC law should prevail over conflicting national provisions. To allow otherwise would undermine the very being of the Community and its principal aim of establishing a common market.

As early as 1962, in the case of *Van Gend en Loos*, it was established by the European Court of Justice that the Member States had limited their sovereign rights and that the Community constituted a new legal order. The Court went further in *Costa v ENEL* (1964) when it stated that :

'the transfer by the States ... to the Community legal system of the rights and obligations arising under the Treaty carries with it a permanent limitation of their sovereign rights against which a subsequent unilateral act incompatible with the concept of the Community cannot prevail.'

National courts are required to apply provisions of Community law and to give full effect to those provisions and, if necessary, to set aside any conflicting provisions of national legislation, even if adopted after the relevant community law provision (*Amministrazione delle Finanze dello Stato v Simmenthal* (1978)).

In addition to the principle of supremacy, the Court of Justice has also addressed the problem of the effect of Community law throughout the Member States. The aim of the Community is to achieve a common market where goods, people, services and capital can move freely. It is therefore necessary to achieve uniformity throughout the Community of standards and provisions established at Community level. This need to secure uniformity of Community law is evidenced by the nature of regulations and also by the presence of the Art 177 procedure. However, a large amount of Community law, particularly environmental law, takes the form of Directives, and Directives do not guarantee immediate uniformity in the same way that Regulations do. The failure by a Member State to implement a Directive can distort the standards laid down at community level and can potentially leave people in one Member State with fewer rights than those in another where there has been full implementation. However, the Court has asserted that Member States should not be able to rely on their failure to implement a Directive and has developed a number of principles which enable community law to take effect even where there has not been formal implementation by the state. These are:

2.12   Effect of Community law

1. *Direct effect*. The concept of direct effect allows litigants in national courts to rely directly on the terms of EC measures, notwithstanding that those terms have not been implemented into the domestic legal system. However,

certain conditions must be satisfied before a measure can be directly effective;

2. *Indirect effect or the duty of interpretation.* The concept of indirect effect stems from the obligations placed on national courts to interpret national law in a accordance with community law;

3. *Damages against the State.* In certain circumstances damages may be awarded in favour of individuals who have suffered loss as a result of the failure of a Member State to implement Community law properly.

2.12.1	Direct effect of Community law

The concept or principle of direct effect has been developed by the Court of Justice in a number of cases dealing with Treaty Articles, Regulations, Directives and Decisions. It was first established in the *Van Gend en Loos* case in relation to Art 12 of the Treaty. In the course of an Art 177 reference the Court of Justice ruled that Art 12 was capable of direct effect and could be relied upon by individuals before national court and tribunals. The ECJ stated that:

'The objective of the EEC Treaty, which is to establish a common market, the functioning of which is of direct concern to interested parties in the Community, implies that this Treaty is more than an agreement which merely creates mutual obligations between the contracting states.'

As a consequence, Van Gend en Loos was able to rely on the Treaty Article to secure enforceable rights in the Dutch courts.

2.12.2	Conditions for direct effect

The ECJ laid down three conditions which must be satisfied in order for a provision to be directly effective:

(a) the content of the relevant provision must be both clear and precise;

(b) the relevant provision must be unconditional; and

(c) the provision must leave no room for the exercise of discretion by the Member State.

Following the *Van Gend en Loos* case, the Court has held a large number of Treaty Articles to be directly effective. The criteria laid down have been applied generously and, as a result, even measures which are not particularly clear or precise have been deemed to be capable of direct effect. In addition to Treaty Articles, the Court has established that EC secondary legislation is also capable of direct effect. Regulations which are described in Art 189 as 'directly applicable' may also be directly effective if they can satisfy the test laid down by the Court.

It was thought that Directives, by their nature, could not be capable of direct effect because they could not satisfy the requirement that they leave no room for the exercise of discretion by the Member State. However, the existence of discretion concerning the means of implementation of Directives has not prevented them from being directly effective. The Court in *Van Duyn v Home Office* (1971) established conclusively that Directives were capable of direct effect and therefore could be enforceable at the suit of individuals in the national courts, providing they could satisfy the requirements laid down in *Van Gend en Loos*. (It should be noted that these tests are applied not to a Directive as a whole but to the relevant provision that is being considered, such as an Article of a Directive or a particular paragraph.) It follows that Directives are only capable of direct effect after the period for implementation by the Member State has expired (*Publico Ministero v Tullio Ratti* (1979). Until expiry of the implementation period, Member States are free to rely on existing national law, even if it conflicts with the requirements of a Directive which is not yet due for implementation.

2.12.3 Direct effect of Directives

It is clearly not possible to state that all EC environmental measures are capable of being directly effective, since many are couched in very vague and uncertain terms and others are dependent on certain criteria being satisfied and will not satisfy the requirement that the provisions are unconditional. However, Ludwig Kramer, the leading author on EC environmental laws, suggests that certain types of provision may be capable of direct effect, in particular Directives which lay down specific maximum values for permissible discharges, or provisions which prohibit the use or discharge of certain specified substances. He asserts that certain Directives such as the Drinking Water Directive, and also the Environmental Impact Assessment Directive, are capable of direct effect. The latter Directive is one which has caused considerable controversy and the question of its direct effect is dealt with in Chapter 13 on Planning and Pollution Control.

2.12.4 Direct effect of environmental measures?

Unfortunately, there have not been sufficient cases before the Court of Justice concerning the question of direct effect of environmental measures to reach any firm conclusions about the subject.

As far as Directives are concerned, it is well established that litigants in national proceedings can only benefit from the direct effect of a Directive in actions against the State or an emanation of the State (*Marshall v Southampton Area Health*

2.12.5 No horizontal direct effect of Directives

Authority (1986)). Therefore, one of the particular problems in relation to Directives is that they will not be directly enforceable against individuals (to use the jargon, they are said not to be horizontally directly effective). The Court of Justice has been consistent in the line that it has taken in relation to Directives, maintaining that they can only be directly enforceable against the State or an emanation of the State and that they are not capable of being directly effective against individuals. The consequence of this is that individuals and environmental pressure groups cannot rely on the direct effect of an unimplemented Directive against private companies. This 'anomaly' was illustrated in the case of *Dori–Recreb* (1992) where a number of Dutch environmental groups brought an action in the Dutch courts against a Belgian company. The environmental groups alleged that the company had discharged chemicals into the River Maas in breach of the provisions of Directive 76/464. The Belgian government had failed to implement the Directive and the environmental groups claimed that the company had abused the failure of the Belgian government. The Dutch court, however, dismissed the application on the ground that the Directive was addressed to the Member State and was not capable of being directly enforceable against an individual (the Belgian company).

2.12.6	An emanation of the State?

Because of this limitation in relation to the direct effect of Directives, it becomes necessary to define what is meant by the State or an emanation of the State. The Court of Justice has interpreted the phrase widely. In *Foster v British Gas* (1991), it was held that bodies responsible for the provision of public services and which have greater powers than are normally accorded to individuals or corporations are to be construed as emanations of the State. The issue has raised its head more recently in the case of *Unison v South West Water* (1994).

The case is of particular importance in environmental law because it involved the question of whether South West Water could be construed as an emanation of the State. The action was brought by the trades union, UNISON, concerning a Directive relating to employment issues. However, the decision of the court is of significance. Blackburn J held that South West Water was an emanation of the State because the company was 'a State authority'. He asserted that the relevant question was not whether the body in question is under the control of the State, but rather whether the public service in question is in control of the State. The fact that the overall control of water services is exercised by the State was the relevant factor, not the legal form of the body, nor the fact that the body was a commercial concern. Blackburn J went on to say:

> 'It is also irrelevant that the body does not carry out any of the traditional functions of the state. It is irrelevant too that the state does not possess day-to-day control over the activities of the body.'

The judgment is of particular significance since it paves the way for other Directives, in the field of environmental law in particular, to be directly effective against the water companies, as emanations of the State.

Whilst the direct effect doctrine may assist individuals to obtain enforceable legal rights in the national courts in actions against the State or emanations of the State, it will not assist individuals bringing actions against other individuals. This is a clear anomaly but has been justified by the Court of Justice on the grounds that because Directives are addressed to Member States they may not of themselves impose obligations on an individual. However, the Court of Justice has put forward other ways in which individuals can seek to rely on Directives, even where the Directives are not capable of direct effect (because they cannot satisfy the relevant conditions) or where the action is a horizontal one against another individual. The first of these approaches is sometimes called 'indirect effect', but a more appropriate way of describing it is the 'duty of interpretation'. The approach was first put forward in the case of *Von Colson v Land Nordrhein-Westfalen* (1983) and later extended in impact in the case of *Marleasing SA v La Commercial Internacional de Alimentacion SA* (1989).

In *Von Colson*, the Court held that national courts (as emanations of the State and therefore equally bound by Art 5 of the Treaty) are under a duty to interpret national law, as far as possible, in the light of the Directive which generated the national legislation. In other words, the national legislation should be construed to give effect to the purpose of the Directive.

The judgment in *Marleasing*, which affirmed the position in *Von Colson*, was really quite remarkable in that the Court of Justice came to the view that the duty of interpretation also extended to national provisions whether they were introduced before or after a Directive. The Court stated that in applying national law:

> '... whether the provisions in question [ie the national provisions] were adopted before or after the Directive, the national court called upon to interpret it is required to do

2.13   The duty of interpretation approach

so, as far as possible, in the light of the wording and the purpose of the Directive in order to achieve the result pursued by the latter ...'

The response of the English courts has been mixed. In *Webb v EMO Air Cargo (UK) Ltd* (1993), Lord Keith stated that the Court of Justice had, in the *Marleasing* decision, only required national courts to construe national legislation to give effect to a Directive only if it was possible to do so. He went on to say that it would only be possible to do so where a domestic law was 'open to an interpretation consistent with the Directive whether or not it is also open to an interpretation inconsistent with it'. However, in the case of *Wychavon District Council v Secretary of State and Others* (1994), the High Court showed itself to be very unwilling to apply this principle. The case concerned the Environmental Assessment Directive and is covered in detail in the chapter on Planning and Pollution Control.

2.14 Damages against the State

In *Francovich and Bonfaci v Italian State* (1991), the European Court of Justice extended yet further the impact of Directives. The case is important in that lays down the principle that Member States may be sued for damages as a result of their failure to implement a Directive. The Court in its previous judgments had been clear that Member States should not be able to benefit from their failure to implement Directives in actions brought against the State by individuals and that Member States could not plead their failure to implement by way of defence. The *Francovich* judgment was a further extension of this and may well prove to be important in the enforcement of environmental Directives.

The facts are as follows: Mr Francovich was owed six million lire by his insolvent employers. However, because he was unable to enforce a judgment against them, he brought an action against the Italian government for compensation. Under a Council Directive aimed at protecting employees in the event of the insolvency of their employers, Member States were required to ensure that a system was set up to meet outstanding pay arrears for employees in the event of their employers' insolvency. The Italian government had not implemented the Directive and had not set up any system to act as guarantor in these circumstances. Francovich however could not rely on the direct effect of the Directive since it was not sufficiently clear and precise. However, the Court of Justice held that, subject to three conditions, damages are available against the State for failure to implement the Directive.

The conditions for State liability are:

- the result prescribed by the Directive should be the grant of rights to individuals;

- it must be possible to identify those rights on the basis of the provisions of the Directive; and

- there must be a causal link between the breach of the State's obligation and the loss and damage suffered by the injured parties.

If these conditions are satisfied, there is a right on the part of individuals to obtain reparation from the State. The *Francovich* decision is extremely important. It opens the way for individuals who can prove explicit legal rights under Directives to sue the State for damages, providing they can prove the causal link referred to. As far as environmental law is concerned, it may prove difficult to identify the grant of rights to individuals arising from Directives. It will also be difficult (as is the case in much environmental litigation) to prove causation. However, it may be that the *Francovich* case will provide a further deterrent against the non-implementation of Directives by Members States. Combined with the possibility of fines under Art 171 of the Treaty, Member States run the risk of serious financial consequences for non-implementation of Directives.

2.14.1   The conditions for State liability

Summary of Chapter 2

European Community Environmental Law

The European Economic Community was established in 1957 by the Treaty of Rome. The EEC had an initial membership of six. Since that time the Treaty has been amended by the Single European Act 1986 and the Treaty on European Union 1992 which established the European Union. The EEC is now called the European Community (EC). The membership has grown from six to 15. The aims and competences of the Community have also expanded and the EC can no longer be regarded simply as a community pursuing economic goals.

The development of the European Union

The European Community Treaty is the primary source of EC law which lays down the overall aims of the EC (Art 2) and Community competences (Art 3). As a framework Treaty it requires fleshing out by means of 'secondary legislation' in the form of:

Sources of EC law

- Regulations;

- Directives;

- Decisions;

- Recommendations and Opinions (which have no binding legal force).

The institutions of the Community are entrusted to achieve the tasks laid down in the Treaty and to this end they have the power to enact the secondary legislation.

The institutional framework

Member States are obliged (Art 5) to fulfil their Community law obligations and not to do anything which would jeopardise the attainment of the Treaty. As such they must not introduce laws which conflict with EC law and they must take all the appropriate steps to implement Directives effectively and by the time specified in the Directive.

Enforcement of Community law

The Court of Justice is charged with ensuring that Community law is observed (Art 164). Its jurisdiction is laid down in further Treaty Articles:

- Articles 169–171 – the Court can make a declaration that a Member State has failed to fulfil its Community law obligations and it can also fine a Member State that fails to comply with such a declaration. Actions against Member States are brought by the Commission;

- Article 173 – the Court can judicially review the 'acts' of the community institutions on the grounds laid down in that Article. 'Acts' have been construed in the widest sense. Member States and the institutions are 'privileged applicants' whereas natural and legal persons have to satisfy the test of 'direct and individual concern';

- The preliminary rulings procedure (Art 177) – enables national courts to ask the Court of Justice to interpret relevant provisions of EC law. The interpretation given by the Court of Justice is binding on all Member States and must be followed by the national courts.

The Community as a new legal order

European Community law has been described as a 'new legal order'. It provides for legal rights which may be directly enforceable within the national courts. The Court has developed various ways in which individuals can benefit from Community law provisions, even where Member States have failed to implement those provisions:

- Direct effect – Treaty Articles, Regulations, Directives and Decisions may be directly effective providing they can satisfy the tests laid down in *Van Gend en Loos*;

- National Courts – are under a duty (by virtue of Art 5) to interpret national legislation in the relevant area in order to give effect to a Directive (*Marleasing*);

- Member States – may be liable in an action for damages if it can be established that there is a direct relationship between the losses suffered by a person as a consequence of the states failure to implement a Directive (*Francovich*).

Chapter 3

The Development of a Community Environmental Policy

When the European Economic Community, was formed in 1958 by the Treaty of Rome, the major concern of the founding members was the creation of a common market throughout the six Member States. The Treaty of Rome concentrated primarily on economic issues and there was no specific reference to the environment. It was not until the 1986 Single European Act that Title VII 'Environment ' was incorporated into the Treaty, giving the Community a legal competence in the field of environmental protection for the first time. However, despite the lack of an explicit legal basis the Community had in the intervening years taken numerous measures to protect the environment. It had also managed to develop its own interventionist environmental policy using other powers under the Treaty, namely Arts 100 and 235.

The position today is that the Community has a well-developed environmental policy, enjoys specific powers to enact legislation in the environmental field and has enacted about 300 measures largely in the form of Directives. In fact, it could be said that environmental policy has equal standing with economic and social policy. Environmental policy now enjoys a unique status in Community law by virtue of Art 130r that requires environmental protection requirements to be integrated into the definition and implementation of other Community policies.

As stated above, the Treaty of Rome made no reference to the environment. The authors of the Treaty and founding members were principally concerned to establish a common market for goods. Article 2/3 of the Treaty stated the aims of the Community as 'establishing a common market and progressively approximating the economic policies of Member States, to promote throughout the Community a harmonious development of economic activities, a continuous and balanced expansion, an increase instability, an accelerated raising of the standard of living and closer relations between the States belonging to it'.

Since the institutions of the Community can only legally act within the limits of the powers conferred upon them by the EC Treaty, legislation in the early days of the Community was largely concerned with economic issues and market regulation. However, despite the absence of any specific

3.1 Introduction

3.2 Environmental policy and law before the Single European Act, 1957–1986

powers, the Community did in fact introduce a large number of Directives which impacted either directly or indirectly upon the environment. As early as 1967, the Community had introduced a Directive on the classification, packaging and labelling of dangerous substances. The introduction of the legislation was aimed not specifically at protecting the environment, but rather at harmonising standards in relation to the packaging and labelling of dangerous substances, but it nevertheless had indirect implications for the environment. This early legislation was introduced either under Art 100 or Art 235.

3.2.1	Articles 100 and 235

Article 100 provided for measures to be introduced to secure the approximation of laws affecting the functioning of the common market. Environmental measures enacted on the basis of Art 100 were justified on the basis that different levels and standards of environmental protection in the different Member States would interfere with the creation of a common market by distorting competition. In other words, if the standards of environmental protection are low in one Member State compared to another with more rigorous standards, then industrialists in the former state spend less on meeting environmental protection standards than industrialists in the latter Member State. This disparity may give the industrialist in the Member State with the lower standards a competitive edge (in a sense they will be benefiting from a hidden subsidy) and this may distort the patterns of trade. An example of a Directive enacted under Art 100 is Directive 78/659 on the quality of freshwater needing protection or improvement in order to support fish life. Although it is clear that this is an environmental protection measure in its own right, the preamble to the Directive states that: 'differences between the provisions ... in the various Member States as regards the quality of waters capable of supporting the life of freshwater fish may create unequal conditions of competition and thus directly affect the functioning of the common market.'

Article 235, on the other hand, is a sort of residual power which enables action to be taken by the institutions even where the Treaty has not provided the necessary powers, but where it is 'necessary to attain, in the course of the operation of the common market, one of the objectives of the Community'. Measures such as Council Directive 79/409 on the Conservation of Wild Birds were adopted under Art 235 exclusively. The justification for the Wild Birds Directive in particular was that the conservation of wild birds was necessary to attain the Community's objective of improving living conditions throughout the common market. Therefore, the measure was justified rather tentatively by reference to Art 2 of the Treaty of Rome. In the same way Art 235 has been used to justify other policy areas such as regional policy which were not explicitly stated within the Treaty, but which were construed as being Community interests.

These early measures were not introduced as part of a coherent strategy on the environment which, at this stage, the Community did not have. However, the early 1970s saw a ground-swell in public opinion about the environment and also marked the beginning of the Community's environmental policy. In 1972 a United Nations conference was held in Stockholm to consider the human environment. The Conference was significant because it marked the beginnings of international co-operation in the field of the environment, and it is from this date that environmental law has become a legitimate and important area of international law. It is also important in Community law terms because it was followed by the Paris Summit in October 1972, when the Heads of State and governments of the Member States of the Community declared:

3.2.2 The Stockholm Conference and the emergence of a Community environmental policy

> 'Economic expansion is not an end in itself. Its firm aim should be to enable disparities in living conditions to be reduced. It must take place with the participation of all the social partners. It should result in an improvement in the quality of life as well as in standards of living. As befits the genius of Europe, particular attention will be given to intangible values and to protecting the environment, so that progress may really be put at the service of mankind.'

Following this recognition of the importance of protecting the environment, the Commission was requested to draw up an Action Programme on the environment. This first Action Programme for the period 1973–76 was adopted in 1973. Since that time the Community has produced four more Action Programmes:

3.2.3 Environmental Action Programmes

Action Programmes	Period	Citation
First	1973–1976	C112, 20.12.73
Second	1977–1981	C139, 13.6.77
Third	1982–1986	C46, 17.2.83
Fourth	1987–1992	C328, 7.12.87
Fifth	1993–2000	C138, 17.5.93

The Action Programmes are essentially political statements, which outline the Community's intentions for legislation and other activities in the years ahead. The First Action Programme started with a general statement of the objectives and principles of a Community environmental policy and then went on to list the actions that the Commission would bring forward. It also listed 11 principles which are still largely applicable today. These are dealt with in more detail at para 3.9 below.

Although the Community had begun to develop an environmental policy as early as 1973, it still faced the problem that there was no real constitutional basis for that policy. Legislation was still largely enacted on the basis that different standards of environmental protection throughout the community would distort competition, would hamper the establishment of a common market and had to be justified accordingly. However, the Single European Act provided for the first time a specific legal basis upon which the Community could legislate in the field of environmental protection.

3.3	**The Single European Act 1986**

The Single European Act (SEA) marked a key stage in the development of the European Community's environmental protection policy. The SEA resulted in the incorporation of a new Title specifically on the environment into the EEC Treaty and in doing so introduced Art 130 paras r–t into the Treaty. (These Articles have subsequently been amended by the Treaty on European Union and are included in full in Appendix 1.)

In addition, Art 100 was also amended by the SEA and a new Art 100a was introduced, which provided that qualified majority voting in the Council of Ministers would be the normal voting procedure in relation to the harmonising measures pursued under this Article. This change was introduced essentially to speed up the decision-making process in relation to harmonising measures needed to complete the Single Market by 1992. A further amendment in relation to the new Art 100a was the requirement that the Commission would, when making proposals which concern environmental protection, take as a base a high level of protection. This was significant because it was recognition in the Treaty itself that approximation measures enacted under Art 100a could legitimately be concerned with environmental protection and was also important in so far as it meant that environmental measures were not exclusively in the domain of Art 130.

The Treaty on European Union, signed in Maastricht in 1992, gave effect to a number of significant amendments relating to environmental law. These can be briefly stated as follows:

- The EEC became the European Community, or EC, in recognition that it is more than just an economic community;

- Article 2 refers to sustainable and non-inflationary growth respecting the environment;

- Article 3 established that there should be a policy in the sphere of the environment;

- Article 100a was amended so that the procedure used for harmonising legislation is the co-decision procedure (see Chapter 2), thus allowing the Parliament the right of veto in relation to such legislation;

- Article 130 was amended and, in particular, changed the legislative procedure so that, with certain exceptions, environmental legislation could now be enacted using the co-operation (or Art 189c) procedure, thus giving the Parliament a greater degree of control than it had previously. The amended Article also built in the requirement that Community environmental policy should aim at a high level of protection.

Even before the Single European Act was amended to incorporate a Community competence in the field of the environment, the European Court of Justice had recognised that the environment and environmental protection was an 'essential' component of Community policy, even to the extent that protection of the environment could hinder the free movement of goods within the Community, one of the fundamental principles of Community law.

In *Procureur de la République v ABDHU* (1983), the Court stated that there could be no doubt that the protection of the environment constitutes an objective of general interest which the Community could legitimately pursue. The case involved an action in the French courts to dissolve the Association de défense de bruleurs d'huiles usagées, an association established in 1980 to defend the interests of manufacturers, dealers and users of heating appliances designed to burn fuel oil and waste oils. In their defence, the Association contested the validity of Directive 75/439 which aims to protect the environment against the risks from waste oils. The Association contested that the Directive was contrary to the principles of freedom of trade, free movement of goods and freedom of competition. The French court sought a ruling from the Court of Justice on the interpretation and validity of the Directive, using the Art 177 preliminary rulings procedure. In reaching its decision that the Directive was valid, the Court held that:

'The Directive must be seen in the perspective of environmental protection, which is one of the Community's essential objectives.'

One of the significant features about the Court's judgment in this case is that it came to this conclusion at a time when the Treaty did not provide any specific explicit legal basis for environmental action. The case predated the introduction of Art 130r–t. The view that environmental protection could constitute one of the Community's essential objectives was reinforced and developed in *EC Commission v Denmark* (1988), known as the *Danish Bottles* case.

3.5.1   The *Danish Bottles* case

The *Danish Bottles* case is important because it raises two very important issues. First, it considered the question of whether Member States could introduce more stringent environmental laws than the rest of the Community; and, second, because it also concerned the related issue of the relationship between environmental protection and the free movement of goods as required by Art 30 of the Treaty. It therefore merits detailed attention.

The Danish Government, concerned about the environmental consequences of litter and waste from discarded metal cans, instituted a system requiring beer and soft drinks to be marketed only in containers that could be reused. The use of metal cans was forbidden. Containers needed to meet the requirements laid down and be approved by the Danish National Agency for the Protection of the Environment. Non-approved containers were permitted subject to very strict limits and also to a deposit and return system. Although the object of the system was to reduce the numbers of discarded metal tins, it had as an effect a potential restriction on competition. Manufacturers of beers and soft drinks outside Denmark could sell their products throughout the Community but not in Denmark unless they could comply with the Danish deposit and return system. Therefore the Danish manufacturers were in effect protected from external competition.

The European Commission commenced proceedings against the Danish government under Art 169 of the EEC Treaty, on the grounds that the approval system constituted a breach of Art 30 which secured the right for goods to move freely throughout the Community. The Court held that the approval system was incompatible with Art 30 but accepted that the deposit and return system was lawful. In reaching its conclusions, the Court clearly stated that 'the protection of the environment is a mandatory requirement which may limit the application of Art 30 of the Treaty' however, it came to the conclusion that the approval system was contrary to the principle of proportionality or, in other words, the aims of environmental protection could have been secured by less restrictive means.

It has been established thus far that both the Treaty and the Court of Justice in its case law have recognised the importance of Community environmental policy. One would be forgiven for thinking that, after the Single European Act and the provisions of Art 130r–t, the development of Community environmental law from that point in time was simply a matter of developing new environmental initiatives and laws under that Treaty Article. However, the introduction of Art 130r–t brought with it a number of particular problems. As stated above, prior to its introduction the Commission had to rely on Arts 100 and 235 to justify environmental measures, and sometimes measures were challenged by Member States. The introduction of this new explicit legal base, however, did not mean that from 1987 onwards all environmental legislation would be enacted under Art 130r–t. It is still clearly the case that some legislation is intended to protect the environment *per se*, whereas other legislative acts are intended to approximate standards. The question therefore became 'which was the correct legal basis for environmental action? – Art 100a (as it had become) or Art 130?'

3.6   Environmental legislation after the Single European Act

The issue of which is the correct legal basis is not simply one of academic importance. The choice of Treaty Article upon which EC secondary legislation is based has very real legal (and political) consequences. It is important for the following reasons:

3.6.1   The correct legal basis?

• The European Court of Justice has the jurisdiction to review and annul secondary legislation on the basis that the legislation is either *ultra vires* (ie there is no legal basis for the relevant legislation) or on the grounds that there has been an infringement of an essential procedural requirement, which would include cases of legislation being enacted using the 'incorrect' legal basis.

• The Treaty stipulates which of the legislative procedures is to be used in relation to specific types of legislation.

Therefore, legislation enacted under Art 100a is to be adopted using the co-decision procedure, whereas legislation enacted under Art 130r–t uses the co-operation procedure (with certain exceptions in Art 130s(2)). This in turn determines the voting arrangements in the Council of Ministers and the amount of control that can be exerted upon the legislation by the European Parliament. From the Parliament's perspective it exercises more control over Art 100a legislation than it does over legislation under 130r–t. The Council on the other hand exercises more control over legislation under Art 130r–t. Hence the question of which Treaty Article is used becomes one of political significance and may have a bearing on the final content of the legislation;

• The purpose of legislation enacted under Arts 100a and 130 is intrinsically different and has consequences in terms of whether Member States can introduce more stringent environmental controls. The purpose of Art 100a is to secure a uniform standard throughout the Community and Member States are not able to introduce different standards and thus distort the functioning of the common market (albeit there is a limited exception to this under Art 100a(4) which is dealt with later). Article 130r–t on the other hand is concerned with environmental protection in its own right and Art 130t specifically enables Member States to maintain or introduce more stringent protective measures, although such measures must be compatible with the Treaty and they must be notified to the Commission.

The use of the correct Treaty Article is, therefore, of real practical and legal importance and has been particularly so in relation to EC environmental law. The issue of whether the correct legal basis has been used, therefore, can give rise to legal challenge before the Court of Justice exercising its powers of judicial review (under Art 173) and has in fact caused problems in terms of the smooth implementation of environmental policy. In particular, the institutions themselves have disagreed over the proper legal basis for environmental action. The EC Council has favoured Art 130r–t, because of its desire to retain the greatest degree of control over such legislation, whereas the Commission and the Parliament have preferred the use of Art 100a. A number of occasions have arisen where there has been dispute over which is the correct Article to use and, in fact, the issue is still not fully resolved. The issue fell to be considered by the European Court of Justice in *EC Commission v EC Council* (1989), known as the *Titanium Dioxide* case.

In 1989, the European Commission brought an action against the Council of Ministers, arguing that it had incorrectly used Art 130s for the adoption of the Titanium Dioxide Directive. When the Commission had originally proposed the Directive, it had put it forward as an internal market harmonisation measure under Art 100a. However, the Council of Ministers subsequently decided (unanimously) to alter the legal basis and adopt the Directive under Art 130s.

The Court of Justice decided in favour of the Commission. The Court noted that the Titanium Dioxide Directive had two aims; the first was to protect the environment from titanium dioxide pollution and the second was to harmonise the conditions relating to the titanium dioxide industry in the Community. The Court held that, where there are two aims and, therefore, two possible legal bases, then normally both should be used. However, in this instance it was not possible to use both Arts 100a and 130 since the legislative procedures required under both were different. Therefore one single legal basis had to be used. The Court came to the conclusion that the correct basis was Art 100a. In reaching this decision the Court referred to the second paragraph of Art 130r which states that 'Environmental protection requirements shall be a component of the Community's other policies'. They took this to mean that Arts 130r–t were not the only provisions of the Treaty concerned with Environmental protection.

Environmental measures could therefore legitimately be enacted under other Treaty Articles. In relation to Art 100a, the Court noted that the Commission, when initiating proposals in the health, safety, consumer and environment spheres must take as a base a 'high level of environment protection'. According to the Court, this meant that the objective of protecting the environment contained in Art 130r could also be achieved through harmonisation measures based under Art 100a. The Court therefore effectively came to the decision that measures enacted under Art 130r–t were concerned solely with the protection of the environment, whereas Art 100a covered initiatives designed to protect the environment and promote the Single Market.

The judgment of the Court of Justice in the *Titanium Dioxide* case was welcomed by the Commission. Not only did it uphold the Commission's argument, it also effectively gave the go-ahead for environmental protection measures to be incorporated as part of the Single Market programme. However, the Court of Justice was asked to consider the issue once again in *Commission v Council (Waste Disposal)* (1991). Like the *Titanium Dioxide* case, this case involved a judicial

3.6.2   The *Titanium Dioxide* decision

3.6.3   The correct legal basis reviewed again

review action brought by the European Commission against the Council of Ministers for its use of Art 130s in the adoption of Directive 91/156 on waste disposal. The Commission contested that the Directive had been incorrectly adopted under Art 130s and that it should have been adopted as an Art 100a measure. However, the Court came to a different conclusion in this case.

The Court held that, whilst it was true that waste had to be regarded as a product which should be able to move freely around the community, mandatory environmental protection requirements justified exceptions to the free movement of waste. In these circumstances, the Directive could not be intended to promote the free movement of waste within the Community. There was not sufficient justification for recourse to Art 100a where harmonisation of conditions of the market was only an ancillary effect of the measure adopted. The judgment in this case may have an effect upon the Commission's programme of legislation in so far as that, unless the Commission can clearly justify measures as harmonisation measures, they must proceed under Art 130s.

3.7 Stricter environmental rules in Member States and the freedom of movement of goods

Another very important difference between the use of the two Treaty Articles is the extent to which Member States can introduce stricter environmental protection rules than the community-wide rules or standards. This is an issue of twofold importance.

On the one hand, it is a matter of concern to those Member States that place a particularly strong emphasis upon environmental protection and wish to secure the highest levels of protection. For some Member States, harmonisation suggests harmonising down rather than up, and this is unsatisfactory to them. This will be an important issue to Sweden and Austria, in particular, which have in place certain environmental protection measures which are stricter than prevailing community wide measures.

On the other hand, the second and inextricably related issue is the extent to which stricter environmental protection rules can be permitted where they hamper or restrict the freedom of movement of goods required by Art 30. This issue has already be referred to in the *Titanium Dioxide* case, above at para 3.6.2, but is considered more fully below.

3.7.1 The relationship between environmental protection and the free movement of goods

The free movement of goods throughout the Community is regarded as one of the fundamental cornerstones of EC law. Article 30 of the EC Treaty prohibits quantitative restrictions and measures of equivalent effect which restrict the free circulation of goods. Measures which are introduced by

Member States which have the effect of hindering the free circulation of goods across borders, therefore, are prohibited. Even where measures apply equally to domestic and imported goods (known as indistinctly applicable measures) the measures may still breach Art 30 where they affect inter-State trade. The types of measure which have been held to breach Art 30 range from more obvious measures such as bans and import quotas to 'buy national' campaigns which have the effect of discriminating against imports. Art 30 has been used widely in litigation and its scope has been widely defined by the Court of Justice (see *Procureur du Roi v Dassonville* (1974)).

Article 36 provides a list of six exceptions to Art 30 whereby Member States may attempt to justify any measures which breach Art 30. The list is exhaustive. Breaches of Art 30 may be justified on the grounds of public morality; public policy or public security; the protection of health and life of humans, animals or plants; the protection of national treasures possessing artistic, historic or archaeological value; or the protection of industrial or commercial property. However, Art 36 stipulates that measures can not be justified whatsoever if they constitute a means of arbitrary discrimination or a disguised restriction on trade between Member States. The terms of Art 36 have been subject to a narrow interpretation by the Court of Justice, which has been keen to preserve the fundamental freedom of goods, and the Court has not been willing to extend the list of exceptions provided by Art 36. In terms of environmental protection measures, it may be possible to justify them on the basis that they are necessary to protect the health and life of humans, animals or plants. However, the Court has been very reluctant to permit measures under this particular head. The burden of proof falls squarely on Member States to demonstrate that a measure is necessary to achieve the protection claimed and, importantly, that the measure is proportionate to the aims. In the main, the cases have been concerned with measures aimed at protecting the health of humans rather than plants or animals. Article 36, therefore, provides little support for national environmental protection measures which effect inter-State trade.

Measures which have the effect of discriminating against imported goods may, however, be permitted if they apply equally to domestic and imported goods and they satisfy the requirements laid down by the Court of Justice in the case known as *Cassis de Dijon (Rewe-Zentrale) v Bundesmonopolverwältung für Branntwein* (1979). The Court stated that in the absence of Community measures or standards Member States were free to regulate the production and marketing of goods and that:

> 'Obstacles to movement in the Community resulting from disparities between the national laws relating to the marketing of the products in question must be accepted in so far as those provisions may be recognised as being necessary in order to satisfy mandatory requirements relating in particular to the effectiveness of fiscal supervision, the protection of public health, the fairness of commercial transaction and the defence of the consumer.'

Therefore, in relation to indistinctly applicable measures (those which apply to all goods irrespective of whether they are produced nationally or imported) Member States can, in the absence of Community measures, introduce national measures which are necessary to satisfy certain mandatory requirements. Unlike the terms of Art 36 which is exhaustive, the list of matters which constitute 'mandatory requirements' has been extended to include environmental protection. The *Danish Bottles* case (*Commission v Denmark*), referred to above at para 3.5.1, resulted in environmental protection being added to the list of issues that could constitute a mandatory requirement. Thus, in the absence of relevant Community environmental protection measures, Member States may be able to introduce national rules which have the effect of restricting the free movement of goods, but are necessary to secure the necessary requirement of environmental protection. It should be noted that the rule in *Cassis de Dijon* only applies in the absence of Community standards. The programme of harmonisation pursued by the Commission will reduce the effectiveness of this ruling.

3.7.2   **Stricter environmental protection measures: Art 130t**

Article 130t provides that the protective measures adopted under Art 130s shall not prevent any Member State from maintaining or introducing more stringent protective measures providing that these measures are compatible with the Treaty. In other words, a Member State may introduce Environmental protection measures which go beyond those adopted by the Community under Art 130, but they must not infringe other Treaty provisions, particularly Art 30. Therefore, Art 130t provides a balance between the Member States right to adopt measures, against the right of the Community to legislate in this area.

3.7.3   **Stricter environmental protection measures: Art 100a(4)**

Measures introduced under Art 100a are introduced with the intention of approximating laws and, therefore, Member States ought not to apply national measures which differ from Community measures adopted under this Article. However, there is one specific exception provided for in Art 100a(4) whereby Member States may, in certain circumstances, apply stricter rules. The provision only operates when the Community harmonisation measure is adopted by the Council acting by a qualified majority. Where a Member State (which presumably has voted against the harmonising measure in question) wishes to apply different national measures relating to the protection of the Environment, they must obtain the consent of the Commission to do so. The Member State in question must notify the Commission of its intentions and the Commission must then confirm (or otherwise reject) the national provisions. In reaching its decision, the Commission must verify that the national measures in question are not a means of arbitrary discrimination or a disguised restriction of trade between the Member States. Further provision exists for the Commission or any Member State to bring the matter before the Court of Justice if they believe that a Member State is improperly using the powers provided for in Art 100a(4). Such a challenge was mounted by France in the so called *PCP* case.

France v The Commission of the European Communities (1993) concerned the use of Art 100a(4). Following the adoption of Directive 91/173 (which was amending Directive 76/769) Germany applied for a derogation under Art 100a(4). Directive 91/173 was adopted under Art 100a and concerned the marketing and use of substances and preparations containing pesticide and preservative pentachlorophenol (PCP). At the time of its adoption, Germany had in place much stricter standards, setting lower concentration limits on PCP. The Council of Ministers had reached a decision on the Directive by qualified majority vote, with Germany voting against the measure. Germany sought to maintain its own stricter standards and therefore asked the Commission for confirmation under Art 100a(4). The Commission granted Germany the derogation, despite strong opposition from France, Italy and Greece who were concerned about the impact of the German measure on imports of their leather goods into Germany. The case involved an action for judicial review under Art 173 of the Treaty brought by France against the Commission's decision. The Court, accepting that the Commission's decision was a reviewable act, held that Art 100a(4) should be interpreted restrictively and that it is up to the Member State seeking the derogation to prove that the measure is both necessary and proportionate, and that there are no other suitable means of achieving the aim pursued in a manner which is less restrictive of the free movement of

3.7.4   **The *PCP* case and Art 100a(4)**

goods. Once again, as in the *Danish Bottles* case, stricter environmental measures must be proportional.

3.8 **The Community's Environmental Action Programmes**	The European Community's First Action Programme for the Environment was adopted by the Council of Ministers on 22 December 1973. It set Community-wide objectives to resolve urgent pollution problems concerning water, air and soil. More importantly, it also established 11 principles upon which the Community's environmental policy is based (see para 3.9 below). The Second, Third and Fourth Action Programmes continued in much the same vein as the first, only providing refinements to the Community's objectives. They concentrated upon specific environmental media: air, water, waste. In particular, many of the policy aims, subsequently translated into Directives, were concerned with setting emission limits. They were seen largely as 'end of pipe' solutions or 'fire fighting' measures. However, they were not entirely reactive in nature and over the subsequent Programmes there was a growing emphasis on prevention rather than cure. The Fifth Action Programme represents a departure and change in thinking. On 26 June 1990, the Heads of State of the Member States called for the Fifth Action Programme to be drawn up on the principles of sustainable development, preventative and precautionary action and shared responsibility.
3.8.1 The Fifth Environmental Action Programme – 'Towards Sustainability'	The Fifth and current Environmental Action Programme covers the period 1993 to the year 2000 and, to that extent, differs from the previous Programmes in that it covers a seven year period rather than five (although there is provision for a review of this Programme in 1995). The programme also marks a more important departure from previous Programmes in its approach. Entitled *Towards Sustainability* the latest Programme does not concern itself with the protection of specific environmental media, such as air, water or land. Instead, the Programme concentrates on five key sectors of activity which have significant impacts on the state of the environment. The five sectors are: Industry, Energy, Transport, Agriculture and Tourism. In the field of transport, for example, the Commission has produced a Green Paper on transport entitled *Sustainable Mobility*. This recommends the transfer from private transport use to more public transport and considers using fiscal measures such as road pricing and higher fuel prices to reduce demand. Agriculture, as another key sector is responsible for a significant amount of environmental damage and there is recognition that the Common Agricultural Policy has been responsible for a negative impact on the environment. The aims of the Fifth

Action Programme are to reduce the impact of agriculture on the environment by encouraging farmers to see themselves as 'guardians of the countryside' and to reduce in particular the pollution from nitrates and phosphates.

The emphasis in the Fifth Action Programme is sustainable development. One of the best definitions of sustainable development is the one provided in the Bruntland Report *Our Common Future* which set the agenda for discussions about the relationship between economic growth and protection of the environment. The report states that sustainable development is:

> '… economic development which meets the needs of the present generation without compromising the ability of future generations to meet their own needs.'

The Treaty on European Union introduced the principle of Sustainability explicitly into the EC Treaty for the first time in Art 2.

3.8.2 Sustainability

Another feature of the Fifth Environmental Action Programme is the emphasis that is placed on 'shared responsibility'. Inherent in the Fifth Action Programme is the belief that everyone shares a responsibility towards the state of the environment and that there must be an 'optimum involvement of all sectors of society'. To this end, it will be necessary to change patterns of behaviour of producers, consumers, government and citizens, and there is a greater need for information campaigns to raise public awareness. Access to environmental information is seen as a key element in enabling citizens to assist with the monitoring of pollution throughout the community and also as a means of exercising consumer preferences for 'green' products and producers.

3.8.3 Shared responsibility

The Action Programmes provide the broad policy framework from which the Commission can initiate legislative proposals. However, the Fifth Action Programme recognises that environmental protection cannot be secured entirely by legal and regulatory measures. In a review of the measures available to improve the environment, the Commission states that future environmental policy will be based on four types of measure:

3.8.4 Types of environmental measures

- regulatory instruments;

- market-based measures;

- support measures such as education, information and research; and

- financial support mechanisms.

3.9   Objectives and principles of Community environmental policy

The environmental policy and programme of the Community is based upon a number of fundamental principles which underpin the legislative framework These principles, like the policy that stems from them, have evolved over time. The First Action Programme listed 11 key principles, which although they have developed since, still form the basis of Community policy. These 11 principles are:

1. Pollution should be prevented at source rather than dealt with after the event;

2. Environmental issues must be taken into account at the earliest possible stage in planning and other technical decision-making processes;

3. Abusive exploitation of natural resources should be avoided;

4. The standard of knowledge in the EU should be improved to promote effective action for environmental conservation and improvement;

5. The polluter should pay for preventing and eliminating 'nuisances', subject to limited exceptions and transitional arrangements;

6. Activities in one country should not degrade the environment of another;

7. The EU and the Member States must in their environmental policies have regard to the interests of developing countries and should aim to prevent, or minimise, any adverse effects on their economic development;

8. There should be a clearly defined long-term European environmental policy that includes participation in international organisations and co-operation at both regional and international levels;

9. Environmental protection is a matter for everyone in the EU at all levels; their co-operation, and the harnessing of social forces, is necessary for success. Education should ensure the whole Community accepts its responsibilities for future generations;

10. Appropriate action levels must be established – local, regional, national, Community and international – for each type of pollution area to be protected;

11. Major aspects of national environmental protection policies should be harmonised. Economic growth should not be view from purely quantitative aspects.

A number of these principles are of significant importance and have now been incorporated formally into the Treaty by Art 130 and are consequently enforceable by the European Court of Justice. The principles discussed below have also shaped UK evironmental policy and underpin the framework not only for EC legislation but also UK legislation. Art 130r sets out the basic principles of environmental policy.

Article 130 identifies the aims of Community Environmental policy and the fundamental principles upon which legislative action should be taken. The full text of Art 130 can be found at Appendix 1 but the key elements are considered below.

3.9.1 Current environmental policy and principles

The objectives of the Community's environmental policy are that it should contribute to:

- preserving, protecting and improving the quality of the environment;

- protecting human health;

- the prudent and rational utilisation of natural resources; and

- promoting measures at international level to deal with regional or worldwide environmental problems.

Community policy is based on the following principles:

- the precautionary principle;

- the preventative principle; and

- the polluter pays principle.

One of the most unique features about the Community's environmental policy is its status in relation to other policy areas. Article 130r(2) requires that environmental considerations are a mandatory component of decisions in all policy areas. 'Environmental protection requirements must be integrated into the definition and implementation of other Community policies.' This special status was confirmed by the Court of Justice in *Commission v Belgium* (1992).

3.9.2 Environmental policy and other Community interests

Community policy on the environment is required to contribute to promoting measures at the international level to deal with both regional and worldwide environmental problems. In the early days of its environmental policy, the EC was mainly concerned with controlling pollution within the Community. However, it was soon recognised that pollution has no frontiers and that there is a need to co-operate with non-EC countries. Article 130r(4) requires that both the Community and the Member States, within their

3.9.3 International involvement

respective spheres of competence, co-operate with third world countries and with the competent international organisations such as the United Nations.

3.10	**Environmental legislation**	The European Community has enacted over 300 legislative Acts which are either directly or indirectly concerned with environmental protection. It is clearly not possible within the scope of this book to cover all of this legislation, the majority of which has been incorporated into UK law and is rightly regarded now as domestic law. However, it is possible to identify certain types of legislation and it is clear that the Community has adopted various approaches aimed at combating pollution and protecting various environmental media. The approaches taken may be categorised as follows:
3.10.1	Quality standards approach	A number of Directives set quality objectives and limit values for different media. With regard to water, for example, five Directives have been adopted which establish water quality objectives for different uses of water. The most important is Directive 75/440 which establishes the quality required for surface water which is intended for drinking. Directive 80/778 sets standards for water intended for human consumption, 78/659 for fish and 79/923 for shellfish, and also Directive 76/160 which sets standards for water used for bathing purposes. Directives setting air quality objectives and limit values include 82/884 – lead and 85/203 – nitrogen dioxide.
3.10.2	Control of dangerous substances	Another approach that the EC has adopted is to control the use, discharge or emission of dangerous substances. Framework Directive 76/464 is particularly important in this regard since it is concerned with the control of certain dangerous substances into the aquatic environment. This Directive provides a list of dangerous substances which are either to be eliminated (List 1 substances) or to be progressively reduced (List 2 substances). Subsequent daughter Directives have since been adopted relating to specific discharges of dangerous substances from industrial discharges. These include Council Directives 82/176 and 84/156 – mercury, Directive 83/513 – cadmium and 84/491 – lindane. Additionally Directive 86/260 (as amended) deals with certain other dangerous substances.
3.10.3	Vehicle emission standards	Directive 70/220 was introduced to minimise air pollution from car exhaust fumes, and did this by prescribing limit values for certain gaseous emissions. This was followed by a similar Directive, 72/306, in relation to diesel engines. These have been amended by subsequent legislation, increasing the

stringency of the controls. Now all new petrol engine cars must be fitted with a three-way catalytic converter by virtue of Directive 91/441.

Certain Directives aim to restrict the level of polluting substances in products. For example, Directive 78/611 set the maximum content of lead in petrol.

3.10.4   Product quality standards

The 1993 Annual Report of the European Commission states that, in 1993, the Commission sent 90 Art 169 letters concerning breaches of EC Environmental law and issued 26 reasoned opinions. (See Chapter 2 for a discussion of the procedures involved in enforcement of Community law.) In 1993, there were seven cases before the ECJ involving environmental law. However, the report does more than simply provide statistics; it deals with certain problem areas. Certain Directives have caused more problems than others, notably the Environmental Assessment Directive, the Wild Birds Directive 79/409 and Directives relating to waste and discharges into the aquatic environment. There have also been complaints about the implementation of the Environmental Access to Information Directive in the UK. However the report states that 'the lion's share of infringements of Community environment Directives relate to Directive 85/337'. For a detailed discussion of the problems with this Directive, see Chapter 13 on Planning and Pollution Control.

3.11   Enforcement of environmental legislation

The report indicates that the incorrect application of environmental law is most commonly detected through complaints from community citizens and through questions put to Members of the European Parliament. It is certainly the case that Directorate General XI does not have the resources to police and monitor compliance with the legislation and is dependent upon receiving these complaints. The Community has been criticised for being quicker to make environmental laws rather than introducing procedures to ensure that they are implemented properly. Unlike Directorate General IV which is concerned with competition policy, DG XI does not benefit from specific powers of investigation. In the field of competition law, the Commission has the power under Council Regulation 17/62 to carry out investigations (including the so-called dawn raids of companies) and to conduct hearings to enforce Arts 85 and 86 of the Treaty.

3.12	**The European Environment Agency**	In May 1990 the Council of Ministers adopted a regulation (Council Regulation 1210/90) setting up the European Environmental Agency. After much debate about its location, the agency was eventually set up in Copenhagen. The agency is supported by an Environmental Information and Observation Network. The major criticism of the agency is that it has, as yet, no enforcement role.
3.12.1	Functions of the EEA	The functions of the EEA are discussed in Chapter 5. Within two years of the agency coming into operation, it is intended that a proposal is presented to the Council of Ministers setting out possible extensions to the Agency's functions. One possible extension to its role could be in the actual monitoring of the implementation of EC environmental legislation. Although the Commission is responsible for doing this, it is clear that it does not have the resources to carry out the function fully and it might be appropriate function for the Agency to assist in this task.

The Development of a Community Environmental Policy

Since the creation of the EEC, almost 40 years ago, the Community has greatly extended its spheres of influences (competences). Originally an Economic Community, the Treaty of Rome did not provide a legal basis for the Community to take any action in the field of eEnvironmental protection;

The Community's activities in relation to the environment can be dated back to the UN Conference on the Environment held in Stockholm in 1972 and which led to the Community's first Environmental Action Programme;

Before the Single European Act, the Community had no specific legal basis to adopt Environmental protection measures, but nevertheless adopted many measures under Arts 100 or 235;

The Court of Justice in *Procureur de la République v ABDHU* (1983) affirmed that environmental protection was an essential component of Community policy notwithstanding the absence of an explicit legal basis.

Environmental policy and law before the SEA

The SEA introduced Arts 130r–t which provided for the first time a legal basis on which the Community institutions could introduce measures aimed at protecting the environment in its own right, rather than having to justify them as harmonisation measures under Art 100a.

The Single European Act 1986

Despite the introduction of Art 130r–t, certain measures were still adopted under Art 100a. This led to challenges before the Court of Justice (*EC Commission v EC Council* (1989), known as the *Titanium Dioxide* case);

Environmental legislation after the SEA

Community environmental policy is based on fundamental principles which underpin the legislative measures:

- precautionary principle;
- preventative principle;
- polluter pays principle.

The Fifth Environmental Action Programme which sets the agenda for action until the year 2000 places an emphasis on sustainable development.

The Community's Environmental Action Programmes

Chapter 4

The Common Law and Civil Liability

The development of environmental law owes a great deal to the common law, in particular the torts of public and private nuisance, negligence, trespass and the rule in *Rylands v Fletcher*.

The application of these torts to the field of environmental protection developed significantly in the late 19th century, largely in response to the need of landowners and industrialists to protect their interests in land. The common law has provided the basis for the development of environmental legislation, which has, to a large extent, modified and supplemented the common law principles to establish a more rigid framework of control, better suited to both the protection of the environment and the needs of industry. The current legal framework for environmental protection is largely made up of statutory provisions; however, even today, the common law is recognised as having a valid place within this framework. Although reliance on the torts of nuisance, negligence, trespass and the rule in *Rylands v Fletcher* has diminished in recent years as more specific environmental legislation is being enacted, the common law is still recognised as having a legitimate role in protecting the environment.

This chapter will examine the application of the principal torts relating to environmental actions, namely nuisance, negligence, trespass and the rule in *Rylands v Fletcher*, giving examples of successful actions, and finally discussing the future of the common law as a means of environmental protection.

4.1   Introduction

The essential function of the common law is to protect interests in land; the fact that it has developed to prevent or rectify any damage of an environmental nature is really an indirect consequence of this primary objective. As a result of this, the use of the common law has diminished in recent years as more reliance is placed on legislative provisions, although it is still used in numerous cases – for example, in circumstances where there is no remedy available under statute or by individuals and pressure groups such as the Anglers' Association to gain relief from, or compensation for, environmental damage. The recent case of *Cambridge Water Company v Eastern Counties Leather plc* (1994) is an example of

4.1.1   The purpose of the common law

this. It was brought under the heads of nuisance and the rule in *Rylands v Fletcher* because the pollution pre-dated the Water Resources Act 1991. The impact of the House of Lords' decision in this case will be discussed later in para 4.13.

Despite the decline in importance attached to the common law, it is still seen as the area which gives rise to the most potential liability by banks, lending institutions, landowners and developers. Such institutions are taking their lead from the United States, where litigation on environmental issues is extremely common. The major problem for business in relation to the common law is the uncertainty of the outcome of the case, as often there are no precedents, for the extent of the damages which can be awarded against the polluter is unknown.

4.2   Remedies

The common law offers various remedies which will be sought by the plaintiff depending upon the particular circumstances of each case. Each remedy is discussed below.

4.2.1   Damages

The object of damages in the law of tort is to put the plaintiff into the position he would have been in had the harm or damage not happened. This is particularly difficult to calculate in relation to environmental damage, because it is often the case that the cost of environmental damage can never be calculated for many years, as clean-up may take several years or the damage can never be fully rectified.

The most common form of damages to be awarded by the courts are compensatory damages, where the plaintiff is compensated for any loss that has been suffered.

There are several other forms of damages which may be awarded and these are not uncommon in actions concerning environmental issues, for example:

- *Aggravated damages* – are awarded where the court wishes to express disapproval of the defendant's conduct and compensate the plaintiff who has suffered more than would normally be expected;

- *Punitive/exemplary damages* – are awarded where it is the court's intention to punish the tortfeasor by adding an additional award onto the compensatory damages awarded, which may also have the effect of deterring others from acting in a similar fashion. The award of exemplary damages is largely governed by the rules established in *Rookes v Barnard* (1964), in which it was stated that damages of this type could only be awarded in three strict classes of cases:

(a) where servants of the government act in an oppressive, arbitrary or unconstitutional way. In *Gibbons v South West Water Services* (1992), a claim in private nuisance, it was held that this could not apply to private individuals or corporations;

(b) where the defendant's conduct was calculated to profit from the tort. This is particularly appropriate in environmental cases, because often industrial operators feel that it would be more profitable to continue with the polluting activity and to face the consequences when paying damages, rather than to cease production or to operate with less polluting techniques;

(c) where the statute expressly permits the payment of exemplary damages.

In addition, or as an alternative to damages, the plaintiff may seek an injunction. An injunction allows the court to require the defendant to discontinue the operation which is causing the damage.

4.2.2   Injunction

Injunctions can be:

* *mandatory* – in which case the court will order the defendant to 'undo' the wrongful act;

* *prohibitory* – thereby ordering the defendant not to commit a wrongful act, for example operating a process which is resulting in damage to the plaintiff's land.

The plaintiff may apply for an interim or interlocutory injunction which would prevent the offending action being continued pending the arrangement of a full hearing.

The effects of an injunction can be especially damaging for those upon whom it is imposed, for example, in an Irish case, *Bellew v Cement Ltd* (1948), an injunction closed a cement factory for three months. The effects of such an injunction are obviously detrimental to business and may deter further polluting operations by the same firm or by others fearing similar results. To this extent an injunction can act as a much greater deterrent than a prosecution under statute, where the fines may have considerably less impact than the financial and commercial damage caused by the closure or restriction of the operation.

The courts have the discretion to award damages and to order an injunction should it be felt to be necessary, for example, where an industrial operation has caused environmental damage, and will continue to do so unless action is taken to prevent or modify the operation.

4.2.3 Abatement

The remedy of abatement dates back many years, although it is rarely used today as its use is not encouraged by the courts. However, it has developed under statute and is the main remedy for statutory nuisance. Under the common law, abatement is known as the 'self help' remedy, because an occupier of land affected may take action to abate the damage.

The definition of abatement was given in *Blackstone's Commentaries on the Laws of England Book III*:

> 'And the reason why the law allows this private and summary method of doing one's self justice, is because injuries of this kind, which obstruct or annoy or such things as are of daily convenience and use, require an immediate remedy; and cannot wait for the slow progress of the ordinary forms of law.'

This point was discussed in *Burton v Winters* (1993) in which it was stated that the abatement was a summary remedy which was only justified in clear and simple cases where the nuisance or trespass would not justify the expense of legal proceedings, or in an emergency where an urgent remedy is required.

A common example of abatement was given in *Smith v Giddy* (1904) in which it was held that the plaintiff was entitled to cut back the overhanging branches of his neighbour's ash and elm trees which were damaging the growth of his fruit trees.

4.3 General defences to intentional torts

An action in the law of tort may fail if the defendant can prove reliance on one of the general defences discussed below. There are also defences which are specific to particular torts, which will be discussed in each section.

4.3.1 Statutory authority

If the tort has been authorised by a statute, then this will provide a complete defence, and will not allow the injured party to recover damages. The exact application of the defence of statutory authority will depend on the statute in question.

The defendant must prove that the conduct complained of has arisen as an inevitable result of the activity authorised by the statute, and that the defendant has exercised reasonable care in carrying out that activity.

The authority to carry out the activity must be expressly or impliedly authorised by the statute.

An example of implied authority was given in *Allen v Gulf Oil Refining Ltd* (1979). The Gulf Oil Refining Act 1965 authorised the compulsory purchase of land, by the defendants, for the construction of a refinery. It did not explicitly authorise the operation of the refinery. The plaintiff claimed that the operation of the refinery caused a nuisance. The House of Lords held that the defence must apply because the operation of the refinery was implied by the statute and was therefore authorised.

However, this defence may not succeed where the Act specifically envisages that an action in nuisance may be brought. The case of *Lloyds Bank v Guardian Assurance, Trollope and Colls Ltd* (1986) is an example of this.

In the case of *Budden v BP Oil Ltd and Shell Oil Ltd* (1980), the Court of Appeal accepted an argument put forward by the defence that they had complied with the relevant statutory provision, s 75(1) of the Control of Pollution Act 1974, and accepted that the statutory standard establishes the common law standard. However, the question of whether an authorisation or consent from a regulatory authority such as the National Rivers Authority constitutes statutory authority remains unclear.

Meaning literally no injury is done to a person who consents, the defence of *volenti non fit injuria* can be pleaded by the defendant. In order for this defence to succeed, the plaintiff must voluntarily assume the risk. In order to do this, the plaintiff must be in position to make a choice as to whether or not to assume the risk, and he must also know of the nature and extent of the risk.	4.3.2 *Volenti non fit injuria*

The defence of necessity is used where the defendant must choose between causing damage to the plaintiff's property and preventing some greater damage to the public or to a third party. This defence is effective in limited circumstances. Where the defence is raised, it can only succeed if the necessity did not arise from the defendant's negligence. It must also be proved that the defendant has acted in the public benefit, or for the protection of his own property. When determining the applicability of the defence, it is necessary for the courts to judge which of the possible outcomes would be preferred. The limitation attached to the defence of necessity is that the defendant must have acted as a reasonable man in order to avoid a greater danger.

4.3.3   Necessity

Section 1 of the Law Reform (Contributory Negligence) Act 1945 provides:

4.3.4   Contributory negligence

'Where any person suffers damage as the result partly of his own fault and partly of the fault of any other person or persons, a claim in respect of that damage shall not be defeated by reason of the fault of the person suffering the damage, but the damages recoverable in respect thereof shall be reduced to such extent as the court thinks just and equitable having regard to the claimant's share in the responsibility for the damage.'

The burden of proof is placed on the defendant to establish that the plaintiff contributed to the damage resulting in his injuries.

This allows the amount of damages to be reduced in line with the plaintiff's contribution to his own loss or injury. Damages are often reduced by anything from 10% to 75%, and even a 100% reduction is not unknown.

4.4	**The common law actions**	The following sections will examine the general principles of each tort which are necessary to establish liability. Each section will contain a general introduction, a definition, the parties involved in an action, defences, remedies and an example of its application for environmental protection purposes.
4.5	**Nuisance**	Actions in nuisance may be categorised into private nuisance, public nuisance and also statutory nuisance as contained in ss 79–82 of the Environmental Protection Act 1990, and supplemented by the Noise and Statutory Nuisance Act 1993. Statutory nuisance is dealt with in Chapter 14. A distinction must be made between the three types of nuisance because they are each significantly different from the others. The tort of private nuisance attempts to reconcile the competing interests of landowners; public nuisance is a crime which protects public rights, although an individual may bring an action where he has suffered damage over and above that suffered by the public generally; a statutory nuisance is one which is largely controlled by local authorities exercising their statutory powers.

Today the tort of nuisance is recognised as the area of common law which has contributed most significantly to environmental protection. It is the area of tort which is most commonly relied upon in cases concerning damage to the environment and there are many recorded examples of the tort of nuisance being used in such a way. In *St Helens Smelting Co v Tipping* (1865), a nuisance action was brought in respect of noxious vapours from the defendant's copper smelting work which damaged the plaintiff's trees and crops. In *Sturges v Bridgman* (1879), the action was brought as a result of noise and vibration caused by a confectioner's pestle and mortar.

The basic principle of private nuisance is the balance between competing rights of neighbours to use their property as they wish. It must be stressed that not every interference with another's use or enjoyment of land can constitute a private nuisance. In order to be actionable, the conduct complained of must constitute an unreasonable interference with an occupier's interest in the beneficial use of his land.

4.6   Private nuisance

Private nuisance was defined in *Read v Lyons & Co Ltd* (1947) as 'unlawful interference with a person's use or enjoyment of land or some right over, or in connection with it'.

4.6.1   Definition

The key issue in an action based on nuisance is that the court must judge whether the defendant is using his property reasonably. In *Saunders-Clark v Grosvenor Mansions and D'Allesandri* (1900), Buckley J stated the importance of this requirement of the tort of nuisance:

4.6.2   Reasonableness

> '... the court must consider whether the defendant is using his property reasonably or not. If he is using it reasonably, there is nothing which at law can be considered a nuisance: but if he is not using it reasonably ... then the plaintiff is entitled to relief.'

However, this statement must be qualified by the fact that in coming to a decision as to the reasonableness of the defendant's conduct, the following factors will be taken into account:

- locality;
- duration;
- sensitivity of the plaintiff;
- intention of the plaintiff;
- the utility of the defendant's conduct.

Each of these is discussed below.

Where the injury consists of interference with the use and enjoyment of the land, the locality principle is used as a means of determining whether there is an actionable nuisance.

4.6.3   Locality

The question of locality was raised in *Sturges v Bridgman* (1879), in which Thesiger, LJ stated:

> 'What would be a nuisance in Belgrave Square would not necessarily be so in Bermondsey.'

The issue of locality was tackled recently in the case of *Gillingham BC v CV Medway (Chatham) Dock* (1992), which questioned the effects of a grant of planning permission on the nature of the locality. The area in question was the Chatham

Royal Naval Dockyard, owned by the Medway Dock Company, who applied for planning permission to re-open the dock as a commercial port. This necessitated the passage of a large number of heavy goods vehicles from the surrounding residential area into the port.

Planning permission was granted. When the port became operational, many residents complained that the increased traffic through the area was a nuisance. The local authority subsequently brought an action against CV Medway (Chatham) Dock in public nuisance. In the judgment it was suggested that the grant of planning permission could change the character of a neighbourhood:

'Where planning consent is given for a development or a change of use, the question of nuisance will thereafter fall to be decided by reference to a neighbourhood with that development or use and not as it was previously.'

The judgment in this case was, however, by no means conclusive as questions were raised, but not entirely answered, in particular: to what extent could conditions be introduced to regulate antisocial activities?

This issue has been addressed more recently in *Wheeler and Another v J J Saunders Ltd and Others* (1995). In this case, planning permission had been granted for two pig-rearing houses. The plaintiffs brought a successful action in private nuisance which was a result of the smells from the pig houses. The question raised in the action was whether the planning permission provided a defence against the nuisance claim. The Court of Appeal accepted that a grant of planning permission might change the character of a neighbourhood, but Staughton LJ rejected the proposition that a planning permission automatically authorised any nuisance that would arise as a result of it.

The judgments delivered in the *Gillingham* and *Wheeler* cases have the effect of warning developers that they must still take action to ensure that their operations comply with the relevant statutory authority, and also that they do not constitute an unreasonable interference with the rights of private citizens.

4.6.4   Duration of the nuisance

There is a general rule that if the plaintiff is seeking an injunction this will not be granted if the nuisance can be classed as temporary or occasional. There are exceptions where the application of this rule could be deemed unreasonable. An example of such unreasonableness was given in *De Keyser's Royal Hotel Ltd v Spicer Bros Ltd* (1914). The case was brought on the grounds that the defendants' building operations were so loud that guests at the hotel were unable to sleep, and after dinner speakers were unable to make themselves heard. It was held that the defendants were not carrying out the operations in a reasonable and proper manner.

Where the plaintiff is deemed to be abnormally sensitive, there can be no actionable nuisance. This was explained in *Robinson v Kilvert* (1889), in which the plaintiff claimed that heat from the defendant's property which was situated in the basement, was having an adverse effect on the brown paper stored at his premises. It was held that there was no actionable nuisance because:

> 'a man who carries on an exceptionally delicate trade cannot complain because it is injured by his neighbour doing something lawful on his property, if it is something which would not injure anything but an exceptionally delicate trade.'

4.6.5 Sensitivity of the plaintiff

The rationale behind this principle is consistent with the law of nuisance, namely that each owner of property should have a right to reasonably use and enjoy his land.

An example of abnormal sensitivity was given in the case of *Heath v The Brighton Corporation* (1908). In this case the vicar of a church sought an injunction to restrain the noise from the defendant's power station. The vicar failed because the noise was neither interrupting services nor had it affected attendance at church, it merely irritated the vicar.

The defendant's motives may be some indication of the reasonableness of his conduct. In *Christie v Davey* (1893) and *Hollywood Silver Fox Farms v Emmett* (1936), the defendants' actions, which were motivated by malice, were found to be unreasonable.

4.6.6 Intention of the defendant

If the defendant is carrying out operations which provide a general benefit to the whole community, then the nuisance will be more reasonable or justifiable than if his motive is purely selfish or malicious.

4.6.7 Utility of the defendant's conduct

It is a long-established principle that, in order to sue in nuisance, the plaintiff must have an interest in the land affected. This will include the occupier of the land, a tenant in possession, and it can extend to those with a variety of legal interests in land.

4.6.8 Who can bring an action in private nuisance?

The recent Court of Appeal decision in *Khorasandjan v Bush* (1993), a case concerning harassing telephone calls to the daughter of the householders, may have overturned the property requirement in allowing an action brought by someone without the legal interest in land to succeed. However, this decision has yet to be considered more fully by the judiciary for this assertion to be made.

4.6.9	Against whom can a nuisance action be brought?

A nuisance action can be brought against the following:

1   The creator of the nuisance: the party who creates the nuisance may always be sued. This is the case whether or not the creator of the nuisance is the occupier of the land at the time, as decided in *Thompson v Gibson* (1841) ;

2   The occupier of the premises: the occupier will be liable in two situations:

- if he himself creates the nuisance; or
- if the nuisance is caused by his servant or agent.

In *Leakey v National Trust* (1980), it was stated that where the nuisance is not being created by the occupier, he is only expected to do what is reasonable in his individual circumstances to prevent or minimise a known risk to his neighbour;

3   The landlord: there is a generally recognised rule that a landlord will generally not be liable because he is not in occupation of the property, unless he has authorised the nuisance, as in *Tetley v Chitty* (1986). In this case, the local authority, as landlord, was held liable for the noise caused by go-karting activities because the authority knew, or should have known, of the nuisance before the property was let.

4.6.10	Examples of actions in private nuisance

In *Manchester Corporation v Farnworth* (1930), an action succeeded in respect of crops damaged by toxic emissions from a generating station. It was held that the defendants had not done sufficient to prevent the nuisance.

In *Kennaway v Thompson* (1981), a successful nuisance action was brought following a nuisance created by the noise from motor-boat racing on a lake near the plaintiff's house. On appeal an injunction was granted restricting the activities on the lake.

4.7	**Public nuisance**

The tort of public nuisance shares many of the elements of private nuisance, although there are several distinguishing factors, namely, who may bring an action in public nuisance. It is also possible for the nuisance to be actionable as both a public and private nuisance.

Public nuisance was defined in the case of *Attorney-General v PYA Quarries* (1957) :

> 'A public nuisance is one which materially affects the reasonable comfort and convenience of a life of a class of Her Majesty's subjects who come within the sphere or neighbourhood of its operation; the question whether the number of persons affected is sufficient to constitute a class is one of fact in every case and it is sufficient to show that a representative cross-section of that class has been so affected for an injunction to issue.'

4.7.1   Definition

Public nuisance is classed as a criminal offence and the case is brought by the Attorney-General, who may seek an injunction to prevent a public nuisance.

For a private claimant to seek damages in a case of public nuisance, he must prove that he has suffered some special damage over and above that suffered by the general public. It is not necessary for the plaintiff to have an interest in land. Damages may be available to compensate for personal injury and for economic loss from the responsible party.

4.7.2   Who can bring an action in public nuisance?

As in private nuisance, an action may be brought against the following:

- the creator of the nuisance;
- the occupier of the premises;
- the landlord.

4.7.3   Against whom can the action in public nuisance be brought?

The case of *R v South West Water Authority* (1991) was brought following the water pollution incident at Camelford, which attracted a considerable amount of press coverage at the time.

In July 1988, 20 tonnes of aluminium sulphate was put into the wrong tank at a water treatment works. Although the alarm was raised almost immediately, remedial action was not taken for several hours, during which time there were reports that the water smelt and tasted foul, that it was black, it burnt mouths and hair and stuck fingers together. It was later reported that the water had caused considerable personal injury in the form of hair loss, nail deformities, rheumatism, diarrhoea and memory loss.

The action was brought as criminal proceedings against South West Water Authority. The Authority was found guilty of committing a public nuisance for supplying water contaminated with aluminium sulphate which endangered the health or comfort of the public. The Authority was fined £10,000 and was held to be responsible for costs of £25,000.

4.7.4   Examples of actions in public nuisance

4.8   Defences in public nuisance and private nuisance actions

The following are defences in public and private nuisance actions:

- Statutory authority;

- Contributory negligence;

- Prescription (only available in private nuisance). The law will not allow an action in nuisance to succeed if the state of affairs which constitutes the actionable nuisance has continued for more than 20 years. For this defence to succeed, the plaintiff must know that the actionable nuisance has run from the beginning of this 20 year period, as was decided in *Sturges v Bridgman* (1879);

- Consent of the plaintiff. In circumstances in which the plaintiff has consented, either expressly or impliedly, to the nuisance, the defendant cannot be liable, unless there is some negligence on his part. An example of this defence was given in *Kiddle v City Business Properties Ltd* (1942);

- Ignorance. Ignorance of the nuisance can only be classed as a defence if it is not a result of the defendant's failure to act with reasonable skill and care in order to discover the nuisance;

- Other defences. Many other defences have been raised, although few have been successful; for example, it would be no defence for the defendant to argue that the plaintiff had 'come to the nuisance', nor could the defendant argue that the activity is of some use to the public in general, although it may be an issue which is considered in determining whether the defendant's use of the land is reasonable.

4.9   Remedies in nuisance actions

Remedies in nuisance actions are:

- abatement;

- injunction;

- damages.

Damages are certainly available for physical damage to the plaintiff's property, although it is not clear if damages can be awarded for personal injury. Some commentators feel that an action under negligence may be the only way to claim damages for personal injury. It is also possible that damages for economic loss may be available although there is no clear judicial guidance on this point.

The tort of negligence is rarely used in actions relating to environmental protection despite its wide application across numerous areas of legal dispute. The disadvantages associated with an action in negligence are, however, sufficiently great as to limit the availability of actions in negligence in cases of environmental protection:

4.10   Negligence

- the courts have shown great reluctance in awarding compensation for pure economic loss, therefore it is essential that the case is based on damage or personal injury; and

- as with other areas of common law, the evidential burden is great. There are many difficulties associated with proving a causal link between the defendant's actions and the damage suffered by the plaintiff, and further proving that a duty of care was owed by the defendant, that this was breached, and that there was resultant damage.

There are, however certain advantages associated with an action in negligence;

- there is no need to prove an interest in the land which is affected, as there is in a action based on private nuisance;

- there is no requirement to demonstrate loss by other members of the public, which is necessary in cases brought on the grounds of public nuisance.

A definition of negligence was given by Lord Wright in *Lochgelly Iron and Coal Co v McMullen* (1954):

4.10.1   Definition

> 'Negligence means more than heedless or careless conduct ... it properly connotes the complex concepts of duty, breach and damage thereby suffered by the person to whom the duty was owing.'

In order to establish negligence, the plaintiff must prove the following:

- that a duty of care is owed to the plaintiff by the defendant;

- that there is a breach of this duty;

- there is damage resulting from this breach of duty; and

- that the damage was foreseeable.

The general duty of care in negligence was established in *Donoghue v Stevenson* (1932). The general principle behind the duty of care is the 'neighbour principle' – meaning that 'you must take reasonable care to avoid acts or omissions which you can reasonably foresee would be likely to injure your

4.10.2   Duty of care

neighbour'. The neighbour is defined as 'persons who are so closely and directly affected by my act that I ought reasonably to have them in contemplation as being so affected when I am directing my mind to the acts or omissions which are being called into question'.

This principle has developed over the years and it would now appear that the requirements for establishing a duty of care are:

- foreseeability of damage;

- a proximate relationship between the parties;

- that it is just and reasonable to impose such a duty.

The standard of the duty of care varies considerably, although the basis of this duty is taken as that which would be exercised by the reasonable man in the same situation, *London Graving Dock Co v Horton* (1951). Where the duty of care relates to a specialised area, then the duty of care expected is one which would be expected from someone with those skills in the same profession, as was decided in *Bolam v Friern Hospital Management Committee* (1957). Where industrial practices are concerned, one must look to standards which are deemed reasonable by the industry concerned.

In the case of *Dominion Natural Gas Co v Collins & Perkins* (1909), it would appear that where hazardous substances are involved in the industrial practice then the standards will be judged highly:

'What that duty is will depend on the subject matter of the things involved. It has, however, again and again been held that in the case of articles dangerous in themselves, such as loaded firearms, poisons, explosives and other things ejusdem generis, there is a particular duty to take precaution imposed upon those who send forth or install such articles when it is necessarily the case that other parties will come within their proximity.'

4.10.3   Breach of duty of care

Once the duty of care has been established, it is necessary to go on to establish that the defendant was in breach of this duty of care and, further, that this breach resulted in damage. In order to determine whether there has been a breach of the duty of care, it is necessary to look at the conduct of the defendant and ask whether he has achieved the standard of care that is necessary if he is not to be liable. The standard used is that of the 'reasonable man'. This is an objective standard and as such no concessions are made for individual weaknesses. The courts will look at the following factors to determine whether the defendant has acted as a reasonable man:

- the likelihood of harm;
- the seriousness of the risk;
- the end to be achieved;
- the cost and practicability of avoiding the risk.

An action in negligence can only be brought where the negligence has caused, or contributed to, personal injury or damage to property. The courts usually use the 'but for' test to determine whether the defendant's breach of duty was the cause of the damage

Damage must also be reasonably foreseeable, as the defendant will not be liable for the unforeseen consequences of his negligent act. (See further *Overseas Tankship (UK) Ltd v Morts Dock & Engineering Co Ltd (The Wagon Mound)* (1961).)

4.10.4   Foreseeable damage arising from the breach of the duty of care

There is no need to prove an interest in the land which is affected, as there is in an action based on private nuisance. It is not necessary to demonstrate loss by other members of the public, which is necessary in cases brought on the grounds of public nuisance.

4.10.5   Who can bring an action in negligence?

An action can be brought against any party where it can be proved that he owns a duty of care to the plaintiff, that there was a breach of this duty and that this resulted in foreseeable damage or injury. There are, however, policy factors which will limit actions against certain defendants, for example, judges, solicitors and barristers.

4.10.6   Against whom can an action in negligence be brought?

It may be possible to raise the defence of statutory authority, if an operation is complying with relevant authorisations (see para 4.3.1).

4.10.7   Defences

Damages: it is a general principle of the tort of negligence that it is possible to claim damages for physical damage, to the person or to property, and for loss consequential to this damage. It is not possible to claim for pure economic loss. (See further *Murphy v Brentwood District Council* (1990).) Following this, it would be possible to claim damages for injuries caused by a chemical spillage which causes damage to people and property; it would be possible to claim for the clean-up costs; but it would not be possible to claim money for lost profits for the time the site was shut.

Injunction: in *Miller v Jackson* (1977), it was held that an injunction is not an available remedy in an action based in negligence.

4.10.8   Remedies

4.10.9	Examples of actions in negligence	*Edgson v Vickers plc* (1994) presents a common example of the tort of negligence for environmental purposes. In this case, the widow of a man who contracted mesothelioma – an industrial disease associated with contact with asbestos – in the course of his employment, sought damages for the negligence of his employers, Vickers. It was held that there was a breach of the relevant regulations, therefore Vickers were in breach of their duty of care.

A current example of a claim in negligence may be found in the forthcoming case of *Andrews v Southern Water Services* (1994), in which the plaintiff alleges that water in which he was surfing was polluted with sewage, and from which he contracted Hepatitis A. The claim is also proceeding under the head of public nuisance.

In *Scott-Whitehead v National Coal Board* (1987) the defendant, a regional water authority, was found to be negligent for failing to advise a farmer that the water he was abstracting from a stream to irrigate his crops contained a strong chlorinated solution.

This area of negligence has potential to be developed in respect of environment agencies which fail to advise of pollution, providing that the requirements of duty of care, breach of this duty and resultant damage can be proved.

4.11   Trespass

The tort of trespass on land has many functions. Its application for environmental purposes is a more recent development, although its use for such purposes appears to be limited as there are few reported cases.

There is some overlap between trespass to land and private nuisance, although it may be easier to bring an action on the basis of trespass because there is no requirement to prove actual damage as there is with nuisance. This is an obvious advantage and it may make an action in trespass in respect of fly-tipped waste, for example, more likely to succeed than an action in private nuisance.

4.11.1   Definition

Trespass to land is the unjustifiable physical interference with land, arising from intentional or negligent entry onto the land. A continuing trespass may be caused by continuing entry onto the land or by allowing physical matter to remain on the land.

The key issues which must be present in order for an action for trespass to land to be brought are:

1   that the trespass was direct;

2   that the act was intentional or negligent;

3   a causal link must be proved between the directness of the act and the inevitability of its consequences.

This was discussed in the case of *Gregory v Piper* (1829). In which it was stated that in order to be direct, the injury must result from an act of the defendant. An example of this may be found in *Jones v Llanrwst Urban District Council* (1911), in which it was held that sewage, which had been released into a river which had passed downstream and settled on the plaintiff's land, was direct and amounted to trespass.

4.11.2   Direct

If the trespass is indirect, then any action should be brought through the law of nuisance.

In order for a trespass to be actionable, it is necessary to prove the defendant's intention or negligence. The intent requirement essentially means that the defendant, or something under his control, must voluntarily enter the plaintiff's land, not that he intended to trespass. Involuntary entry onto, or into, the plaintiff's land is not sufficient to constitute trespass.

4.11.3   Intentional or negligent

It is also imperative to establish a causal link between the directness of the act and the inevitability of its consequences. If the effects of the act are indirect, there can be no trespass; however, there may be a remedy for nuisance or negligence.

4.11.4   Causal link between the directness of the act and its effects

Any person who is in exclusive possession of the land can bring an action in trespass. Exclusive possession refers to the occupation or physical control of the land.

4.11.5   Who can bring an action in trespass?

As trespass is actionable *per se*, the party bringing the action does not have to prove that the trespass has caused actual damage.

The action can be brought against the wrongdoer who has interfered with the possession of the land. An example of this would be where someone has exceeded permission to remain on the land.

4.11.6   Against whom can a trespass action be brought?

Defences are:

4.11.7   Defences

•   necessity;

•   licence: a licence gives the express or implied authority which will prevent the trespass from being actionable.

Remedies are:

4.11.8   Remedies

•   Damages. The amount of damages awarded in actions of trespass will usually depend upon the act complained of, particularly as trespass is actionable without any evidence of damage being caused. If the trespass is deemed to be trivial, then the damages awarded will usually be nominal. Substantial damage will, however, result in an appropriate award of compensation. However, where the trespass has physically damaged the land the level of damages awarded will reflect the reduction in the value of the land rather than the costs of remediation, as in *Lodge Holes Colliery Co Ltd v Wednesbury Corporation* (1908), which does not necessarily provide a satisfactory environmental solution.

- Injunction. It will generally be easier to obtain an injunction in an action for trespass than under any other Tort because there is no need to prove any damage.

The plaintiff may require an injunction to prevent a continuing trespass, for example to prevent the recurrence of tipping.

| 4.11.9 | Examples of actions in trespass |

The dumping of rubbish on land is a common form of trespass, even if it causes very little damage, as in *Gregory v Piper* (1820) in which the defendant disposed of his rubbish in such a way as to block a right of way. Some of the rubbish rolled against the plaintiff's wall and it was held that the defendant was liable in trespass.

Blocking the highway is also classed as trespass, as was determined in the case of *Randall v Tarrant* (1955). This may apply to incidents of, for example, where rubbish is fly-tipped or where there has been a chemical spillage from a lorry.

The early authority of *Harrison v Duke of Rutland* (1893) also establishes that it is a trespass to unlawfully interfere with the rights of the owner of the subsoil beneath the highway. This principle could be relied upon in cases of contamination of land or groundwater.

4.12 The rule in *Rylands v Fletcher*

It is generally thought that the rule in *Rylands v Fletcher* (1868) originates from the development of the tort of nuisance. This view was supported by the decision in *Cambridge Water Company v Eastern Counties Leather plc*, discussed in para 4.13 below.

4.12.1 Definition

The principles of the rule were established in the judgment delivered by Blackburn J in the case of *Rylands v Fletcher*:

> 'We think that the true rule of law is, that the person who for his own purposes brings on his lands and collects and keeps there anything likely to do mischief if it escapes, must keep it in at his peril, and, if he does not do so, is

prima facie answerable for all the damage which is the natural consequence of its escape.'

The rule basically imposes strict liability on anybody who brings onto and keeps on their property anything which is likely to do mischief if it escapes.

In *Read v Lyons* (1947), the necessary factors for establishing liability under the rule in *Rylands v Fletcher* were clarified. They are:

| 4.12.2 | Which factors must be established for the rule to apply? |

- dangerous thing likely to do mischief;

- brought on to land;

- escape;

- non-natural user of the land.

The first essential factor in the application of the rule in *Rylands v Fletcher* is that it applies to 'anything likely to do mischief if it escapes'. There are numerous examples of 'dangerous things', including oil (*Smith v GW Ry* (1926)); noxious fumes (*West v Bristol Tramways Co* (1908)); and explosions (*Miles v Forest Rock and Granite Co (Leicestershire) Ltd* (1918)).

| 4.12.3 | Dangerous thing likely to do mischief |

In determining the 'dangerous thing' the courts will use a factual test 'whether the thing is likely to do mischief if it escapes'. Following the decision in *Cambridge Water v Eastern Counties Leather plc* (1994), it would appear that there is a requirement that the damage is foreseen as a result of the escape, and possibly that the escape itself is foreseeable (see para 4.13.5 below).

It is not enough for the dangerous thing to be naturally present on the land, it must have been brought onto the land. In *Giles v Walker* (1890) there was no liability for self-sown thistle-down which blew from the defendant's land onto the plaintiff's land. There may be liability in nuisance in such circumstances (see para 4.6).

| 4.12.4 | Brought on to land |

There must also be an escape of the 'dangerous thing' from land before there can be any liability under the rule in *Rylands v Fletcher*. It is not sufficient that there was merely the potential for escape. This was defined in the case of *Read v Lyons*, in which it was stated that escape meant an 'escape from a place when the defendant has occupation, from the place where the occupant has occupation or control over land, to a place which is outside his occupation or control'.

| 4.12.5 | Escape |

4.12.6   Non-natural user of the land

It is a fundamental principle of the rule that the defendant should have brought onto his land something which was not naturally there. The term 'natural' was interpreted in *Rylands v Fletcher* to mean 'that which exists in or by nature and is not artificial', although more recent cases have centred around the wider definition which covers the concept that a non-natural use is one that brings with it 'increased danger to others and must not merely be the ordinary use of land or such a use as is proper for the general benefit of the community', as was defined in *Rickards v Lothian* (1913). This was followed in *Read v Lyons* by what was essentially a policy decision, that uses which provide some public benefit would be classed as 'natural'. This point was illustrated in *British Celanese Ltd v AH Hunt (Capacitors) Ltd* (1969):

> 'The manufacturing of electrical and electronic components ... cannot be adjudged to be a special use ... The metal foil was there for use in the manufacture of goods of a common type which at all material times were needed for the general benefit of the community.'

The *Cambridge Water Company v Eastern Counties Leather plc* (1994) decision may alter the 'non-natural user' requirement. In determining what was a non-natural user, the House of Lords took a fairly broad approach, in line with the original concept of non-natural use, which was that there should be a distinction between something naturally occurring, for example a flood, and an artificial creation such as a reservoir.

A possible reason for this view is that there is less need to restrict possible claims on the natural user ground because of the House of Lords' assertion that foreseeability would be an essential requirement which would limit unfounded claims.

4.12.7   Remoteness

The House of Lords, in *Cambridge Water Company v Eastern Counties Leather plc*, stressed the connection between nuisance and the rule in *Rylands v Fletcher* and suggested that the latter was merely an extension of the former:

> '... it would moreover lead to a more coherent body of common law principles if the rule was to be regarded as essentially an extension of the law of nuisance to isolated escapes from land.'

As a result of making this connection, it was stated *inter alia* the escape must be foreseeable:

> 'The historical connection with the law of nuisance must now be regarded as pointing towards the conclusion that foreseeability of damage is a prerequisite of the recovery of damages under the rule.'

It is not clear whether it is necessary to have an interest in land to bring an action under the rule in *Rylands v Fletcher*, as there are several cases where the plaintiff has not had an interest, although it was suggested in *Read v Lyons* that some interest in land will be necessary.

The House of Lords' decision in *Cambridge Water Co v Easter Counties Leather plc* suggests that the rule in *Rylands v Fletcher* is merely an extension of the law of nuisance and if this is so, the ordinary principles of nuisance will apply, namely that the plaintiff must have an interest in land. However, this position may have been altered following the judgment in *Khorasandjian v Bush* (1993) (see para 4.6.8).

It would appear that the defendant does not need to have any proprietary interest in the land, it is enough that he merely controls the 'dangerous thing', as was stated in *Rainham Chemical Works v Belvedere Fish Guano* (1921). This suggestion is consistent with the law of nuisance and reflects the close link between nuisance and *Rylands v Fletcher*.

Although it is widely acknowledged that the rule in *Rylands v Fletcher* created a regime strict liability, the liability is not absolute and the courts have developed a number of defences:

- statutory authority;

- necessity;

- Act of God.

  The Act of God defence is very limited, as it can only apply to 'forces of nature which no human foresight can provide against, and of which human prudence is not bound to recognise the possibility', as defined in *Tennent v Earl of Glasgow* (1864);

- common benefit.

  Where the 'dangerous thing' is for the benefit of both the defendant and the plaintiff, the defendant will not be liable for its escape. This defence is very close to the defence of consent;

- independent act of a third party.

  The unforeseeable act of an independent third party is a defence where the defendant has no control over his actions. The burden of proving this defence lies with the defendant.

  Where the third party's act could have been foreseen or action could have been taken to prevent the consequences

4.12.8 Who can bring an action under *Rylands v Fletcher*?

4.12.9 Against whom can an action in *Rylands v Fletcher* be brought?

4.12.10 Defences

then the defendant will still be liable. An example of this was given in *Northwestern Utilities v London Guarantee and Accident Co Ltd* (1936);

• Default on the part of the plaintiff.

Where the plaintiff suffers as a result of his own act or default the defendant cannot be liable. Where there is contributory negligence on the part of the plaintiff, the provisions of the Law Reform (Contributory Negligence) Act 1945 applies.

| 4.12.11 | Remedies |

Because the rule in *Rylands v Fletcher* has its origins in nuisance, the remedies available appear to be the same as those for public nuisance, namely:

• damages – although in *Read v Lyons* it was decided that damages would not be available for personal injury;

• injunction – although there is little judicial guidance on this point.

| 4.12.12 | Examples of actions on the rule in *Rylands v Fletcher* |

In *West v Bristol Tramways Co* (1908), the defendants were found liable under the rule in *Rylands v Fletcher* for damage to plants at the plaintiff's market garden which was caused by fumes given off by the defendant's creosote.

4.13   The case of *Cambridge Water Company v Eastern Counties Leather plc*

The House of Lords decision in the case of *Cambridge Water Company v Eastern Counties Leather plc* (1994) has made a considerable impact on the interpretation and application of the common law to environmental problems and may have important implications for the development of civil liability for environmental harm.

4.13.1   The facts of the case

In September 1976, the Cambridge Water Company bought a piece of land which was formerly used as a paper mill at Sawston, Cambridgeshire, attached to which was a licence to abstract water from a borehole on the site. Cambridge Water Company began to abstract the water for public consumption in June 1979. Unknown to the water company was the fact that the water was contaminated by a solvent which had leached into the aquifer from a nearby tannery operated by Easter Counties Leather. The spillages of the solvent occurred regularly between 1950 and 1976, after which the tannery began to operate more efficiently. This contamination was not considered an issue until, in 1976, the EC issued Directive 80/778 relating to the standards of drinking water for human consumption and contained figures relating to the maximum levels of perchloroethylene which could be present in the water. The water abstracted from the borehole from Eastern

Counties Leather was found to exceed these limits and use of the borehole was discontinued.

It was originally thought that the action would be brought under the Water Resources Act 1991; however this proved to be impossible as the pollution pre-dated its enactment. Cambridge Water Company began proceedings against Eastern Counties Leather on the grounds of nuisance, negligence and the rule in *Rylands v Fletcher*.

The action was dismissed in nuisance and negligence because it was decided that the defendants, Eastern Counties Leather, could not have foreseen the damage caused to the aquifer arising from their tannery operations.

4.13.2   The High Court's decision

Kennedy J also considered the application of the rule in *Rylands v Fletcher* and decided that the solvent used by Eastern Counties Leather was a 'natural use' of the land.

The High Court decision was reversed by the Court of Appeal and Cambridge Water Company were awarded £1,000,000 in damages, plus costs.

4.13.3   The Court of Appeal's decision

The decision of the Court of Appeal was based on the tort of nuisance and the case of *Ballard v Tomlinson* (1885). The Court of Appeal decided that the pollution of the aquifer by Eastern Counties Leather plc constituted an interference with Cambridge Water Company's 'natural rights' to abstract naturally occurring water which comes beneath his land by percolation through undefined underground channels. It was decided that interference with this natural right to abstract uncontaminated groundwater constituted an actionable nuisance.

The Court of Appeal did not comment of the rule in *Rylands v Fletcher* because it was thought to be 'inapposite in the present case'.

The Court of Appeal's reversal of the High Court's decision was alarming for those who were responsible for causing pollution and provided hope for those in the same position as Cambridge Water Company who were seeking redress for Environmental damage.

Appeal to the House of Lords was inevitable.

The decision of the House of Lords was awaited with a great deal of interest as it was widely anticipated that the outcome would considerably affect the future application and development of the common law, and that it would clarify the principles of the common law relating to environmental damage.

4.13.4   The House of Lords' decision

The judgment contained pronouncements on the relationship between nuisance and its effects on the rule in *Rylands v Fletcher* and the element of foreseeability. These elements are discussed below.

4.13.5   Foreseeability

The House of Lords considered the issue of foreseeability in great detail. The following passage indicates the tone of the judgment:

> '... it by no means follows that the defendant should be held liable for damage of a type which he could not reasonably foresee; and the development of the law of negligence in the past 60 years points strongly towards a requirement that such foreseeability should be a prerequisite of liability in damages for nuisance, as it is of liability in negligence.'

Lord Goff went on to state that foreseeability of harm 'is a prerequisite of recovery of damages in private nuisance, as in the case of public nuisance'. Therefore there can only be liability where the interference is of a type which can be reasonably foreseen by a person in the defendant's position. In *Cambridge Water Company v Eastern Counties Leather plc* it was decided that the damage caused to the aquifer by the method of delivering the solvents was not reasonably foreseeable at the time the pollution occurred.

The element of foreseeability is an ever changing factor in light of developments in awareness of environmental problems, and it could now be argued what was not foreseeable in 1976, would be foreseeable today. Certainly, in the light of more scientific evidence about the effects of pollutants and stringent EC controls, it will be increasingly difficult to sustain the argument that pollution is not foreseeable.

4.13.6   Nuisance and the rule in *Rylands v Fletcher*

The House of Lords considered the relationship between nuisance and the rule in *Rylands v Fletcher*, accepting the view that the rule is 'to be regarded as essentially an extension of the law of nuisance to isolated escapes from land.' In looking at the 'non-natural user' element, the House of Lords indicated that the decisions in previous cases such as *Read v Lyons*, in which a munitions works was classed as a natural user, could not stand today.

> '... the storage of substantial quantities of chemicals on industrial premises should be regarded as an almost classic case of non-natural use.'

The judgment further states that the non-natural use distinction as a means of limiting the application of the rule may be unnecessary because of the introduction of the foreseeability requirement.

Also contained in the judgment was a statement referring to the development of the common law as a means of environmental protection. It was implied that it was the function of parliament, rather than the courts, to create a statutory regime of liability for environmental damage:

> 'But it does not follow from these developments that a common law principle, such as the rule in *Rylands v Fletcher*, should be developed or rendered more strict to provide for liability in respect of such pollution. On the contrary, given that so much well informed and carefully structured legislation is now being put in place for this purpose, there is less need for the courts to develop a common law principle to achieve the same end, and indeed it may well be undesirable that they should do so.'

The judgment has been viewed by many environmentalists as being restrictive because of the affirmation of requirement of foreseeability in nuisance and the rule in *Rylands v Fletcher*. Critics of the judgment say that only very rarely will it impose liability for pollution cases such as this one. However, many commentators feel that the judgment was the only reasonable and practicable step to be taken in the circumstances, because it is unfair to penalise anyone for operations which were considered perfectly normal and effective at the time. Neither is the judgment as restrictive as some originally interpreted, as it can provide the basis for liability where the polluter knowingly pollutes; this would cover the example of the wilful and careless polluter, or the environmental 'vandal'.

It is clear that the common law does have a valid role to play in the protection of the environment. Below is a discussion of both the advantages and disadvantages of the common law in relation to actions arising out of damage to the environment.

The first fundamental problem associated with the use of the common law to secure environmental protection is that it cannot prevent damage to the environment; its purpose instead is to compensate the owner of the land affected. The remedies can provide such compensation which may finance the remediation. This, however, is contingent upon some environmental damage being done, which is contrary to the aims of current environmental policies which are seeking to prevent the generation of pollution. The availability of compensation to remediate the environmental damage may not necessarily clean up the environmental damage satisfactorily.

4.13.7   The courts and environmental protection

4.13.8   The implications of the judgment

4.14   An evaluation of the common law as a means of environmental protection

4.15   Disadvantages

Because the development of the common law control has taken place over a number of years and at a time when the environment was not highly regarded, it does not meet the specific needs of environmental protection for a number of reasons:

- it operates on the basis of 'cure' rather than prevention;

- the common law creates an uncertain level of liability;

- it permits individuals to be guardians of the environment only on an *ad hoc* basis, given the uncertainty of establishing that the behaviour complained of was unreasonable and the evidential difficulties associated with this.

Modern environmental laws which have been developed in response to specific environmental problems are better placed to address the needs of environmental protection because they contain express standards and provisions which relate directly to many industrial operations.

Current environmental regulation is also better suited to the needs of industry as it provides standards of acceptable environmental behaviour, namely through the Integrated Pollution Control regime as discussed in Chapter 9. Through this legislative framework industry can also seek advice and guidance as to acceptable levels and types of pollution from the environmental agencies, namely HMIP and the NRA. Their functions are detailed throughout this book, especially in Chapter 5.

In the late-19th century it was established that the courts could not assume the place of the legislature in such cases. This was affirmed in *Cambridge Water Company v Eastern Counties Leather plc*, in which it was stated that it would not be appropriate for the courts to develop the common law principles further (see para 4.13.7 above).

In a recent consultation paper issued by the Department of the Environment entitled *Framework for Contaminated Land*, the government asserts that the common law should continue to exist in its present form, and that it would be inappropriate to extend the common law through statutory provisions in order to include further defences such as a state of the art defence, or one based on environmental due diligence.

4.15.1   Evidence

It may be very difficult to establish the source of the pollution, and further to establish a causal link between the pollution and the damage caused. This is largely because pollution can occur in many ways, it may be an isolated incident, it may result from incidents occuring over a period of years.

Anyone wishing to use such evidence may need to employ specialist consultants to determine the source and the effects of the pollution, which often causes considerable delay and expense when bringing an action under the common law.

The cost of financing a common law action is often extremely prohibitive, especially as the availability of legal aid in such cases is very restricted. A current example of a legally-aided action is the Docklands litigation (*Hunter v Canary Wharf* (1994)).

4.15.2   Costs

Where legal aid is not available, it is usually only the wealthy who can take action, an example of this being the rock star Roger Daltry, who brought an action in respect of agricultural pollution which damaged his fish farm in *Beju-Bop Ltd v Home Farm (Iwerne Minster) Ltd* (1990).

The financial problems are exacerbated by the fact that an unsuccessful plaintiff may have to bear the defendant's legal costs as well as his own.

An action in the law of tort brought following environmental damage is often one that is hard fought by the defendant, who may be a large multinational company. They wish to avoid defeat because this may damage the image of the company, with the potential seriously to affect trade adversely. In order to avoid defeat, the defendants will spend a considerable amount of money on legal advice, representation and presentation of alternative scientific evidence, often far more than the plaintiff can afford.

An example of such a case is that of *Hanrahan v Merck, Sharp and Dohme* (1988), an Irish case, which had it not been for the sheer determination of the plaintiff, and the hardship suffered by him and his family to raise the finances necessary to appeal, would not have reached the Supreme Court, where the earlier decision in favour of *Merck, Sharp and Dohme* was reversed.

The introduction of contingency fees by the Law Society may have a considerable impact on environmental litigation.

4.15.3   Remoteness

The House of Lords decision in *Cambridge Water Company v Eastern Counties Leather plc* introduced the element of foreseeabilty as a prerequisite for recovery in nuisance, and probably into the rule in *Rylands v Fletcher*. See, further, para 4.13.5 above.

The introduction of the foreseeability element will have the effect of limiting the claims of historic pollution. However, as foreseeability is to be determined from the state of knowledge at the time the pollution takes place, it is unlikely that a great deal of the pollution which is currently taking place will be unforeseeable.

| 4.15.4 | The Limitation Act 1980 |

A further limitation as to the effectiveness of the common law in the protection of the environment is that the Limitation Act 1980 applies. Section 2 of the Act provides:

- 'An action founded on tort shall not be brought after the expiration of six years from the date on which the cause of action actually accrued';

- Where the action is brought in respect of personal injury the basic limitation period is reduced to three years under s 11(4) of the Act, although the court has discretion to override this limitation period if it would be equitable to do so;

- The limitation period is calculated 'from the date on which the cause of action occurred'. The reason for the existence of the limitation period is that it would be unfair on the defendant if an action could be brought against him for an indefinite period of time.

4.16 Advantages

The strengthening of the statutory framework for the control of environmental pollution and environmental damage may have diminished reliance on the common law. However, it still remains an important weapon in several circumstances:

- for environmental pressure groups, a prolific source of litigation are Anglers' Associations which have been very successful in recent years (see Chapter 6);

- for individuals who are affected by environmental damage and for whom there is no relief under statutory provisions. There are many examples of this type of action;

- for enforcement agencies, such as NRA of HMIP where a prosecution under a statutory provision cannot stand.

An action under the common law may also supplement the statutory provisions. For example, in the case of *NRA and Anglers Co-operative Association v Clarke* (1994), the NRA attempted to prosecute a pig-farmer, Mr Clarke, who was responsible for the release of 3,000,000 gallons of slurry which entered the river Sapiston in Suffolk, affected 75 kilometres of the river Sapiston, the Little Ouse, and destroyed a fishery. The action against Mr Clarke was brought under s 31(1)(a) and s 32(1)(a) of COPA 1974, and under s 4(1) of the Salmon and Freshwater Fisheries Act 1975. The Court of Appeal decided that the pig farmer could not be liable because his knowledge of the discharge could not be proven. Had the NRA based the action on 'causing' pollution, they may have succeeded.

Following the failure of the action under the statute, the NRA, along with the Anglers Co-operative Association who were representing the interests of the local angling club, then proceeded with a civil action against Mr Clarke. This time the action succeeded and the NRA were awarded £90,000 to cover their legal costs, to investigate the extent of the damage to the fishery and pay for restocking.

The Anglers Co-operative Association were awarded £8,400 for legal expenses, and the local angling club were awarded £8,450 in damages.

• where the pollution has taken place before the relevant legislation has come into force. This was the case in *Cambridge Water Company v Eastern Counties Leather plc* where the pollution pre-dated the Water Resources Act 1991.

The remedies available in successful common law case actions against environmental damage are often appropriate to compensate individuals who suffer from such damage, although they may not be the most effective in remedying or deterring continuing pollution. A significant advantage of an action under common law over statutory provisions is that, under the principal torts, the plaintiff may recover damage for loss or personal injury. This is only rarely possible under statute. one example, however, is s 73(6) of the EPA 1990 which is discussed in para 4.17 below.

The remedies available in cases based on the common law are not specifically intended to meet modern environmental challenges; rather, their aim is to address affected property rights. However, they do seek to provide some sort of redress for the damage caused to the environment by virtue of the remedies of damages and an injunction. The remedy of abatement is of limited application and is discussed above at para 4.2.3.

The availability of damages is of considerable importance. Often the award of damages to the aggrieved party can provide the finances for the remediation of environmental damage. This remedy is particularly useful in cases of contaminated land because it is usually possible to clean up this contamination, albeit at great cost. However, there are many areas of environmental damage which cannot be rectified, all the damages would do in a case such as this would be to compensate the owner of the land whose interests were affected.

Injunctions can be granted in a variety of situations. They may be prohibitive, in which case they will simply require that the defendant should cease operations to prevent further damage from occurring; they may be mandatory, in which case the defendant will be required to take some positive action, such as the clean-up of a contaminated site. Both types of injunction may be granted on a *quia timet* basis, which would prevent damage being done where there was a threat of it occurring.

A major advantage associated with an action based on the law of tort is that the action need not be brought on one ground alone, it is not uncommon for the torts of nuisance, negligence, trespass and the rule in *Rylands v Fletcher* to be tested in one case. For example, in *Cambridge Water Company v Eastern Counties Leather plc* a judgment was originally sought on the application of nuisance, negligence and the rule in *Rylands v Fletcher*, although the House of Lords' judgment only contained reference to *Rylands v Fletcher* and nuisance.

4.17	Civil actions under statute

The general policy behind current environmental legislation is that it provides some sort of public accountability for damage to the environment. This is followed through in the Environmental Protection Act 1990, and also the Water Resources Act 1991.

The possibility of a common law action as a means of environmental protection has already been discussed above. However, legislation can also provide a means by which individuals can pursue civil claims against others for the breach of environmental law in order to obtain compensation, and to this extent has supplemented the common law.

Civil liability actions arising from statutes are available as follows:

- express statutory rights to be compensated for certain types of damage;

- breach of statutory duty;

- certain statutory provisions which extend, or sometimes restrict, rights under the common law.

Each of these will be considered in turn.

It may also be possible for an individual to privately prosecute a polluter for an offence under the statute, providing such action is not prohibited by the statute. An example under environmental legislation is s 23(1) EPA 1990.

An example of such an express provision is s 73(6), which states that where any damage is caused by waste which has been deposited in or on land, any person who deposited, or knowingly caused or knowingly permitted it to be deposited so as to commit an offence under s 33(1) or s 63(2) is liable for the damage caused.

Section 73(6) also provides that where the damage was wholly the fault of the person who suffered it, or the person who suffered voluntarily accepted the risk of the damage, the defences of contributory negligence and *volenti non fit injuria* will be allowed.

It is not necessary for a prosecution to be brought, it is enough that the offence has been committed.

A further example is s 60 of the Water Resources Act 1991 which provides for damages where the NRA under s 39 of the Act has granted water abstraction rights which impair the existing rights of third parties.

4.18   Express statutory rights to damages

The general rule defining breach of statutory duty was established in *Bishop of Rochester v Bridges* (1831).

> '... where an Act creates an obligation and enforces performance in a specified manner ... that performance cannot be enforced in any other manner.'

A breach of statutory duty is only actionable where it can be shown by the court that Parliament intends that the statute should grant a civil remedy, or, if the duty is owed to individuals rather than to the State as a whole, then a civil remedy will exist for the plaintiff to claim damages in private nuisance. Many environmental statutes which prohibit an activity or make it a criminal offence also provide for some degree of civil liability.

The question of civil liability for breach of statutory duty is addressed in both the Environmental Protection Act 1990 and the Water Resources Act 1991.

In order to bring an action for breach of statutory duty, plaintiff must prove the following:

1   that the statute creates an obligation;

2   that the statute intends to allow a civil action;

3   that the harm suffered by the plaintiff is within the general class of risks at which the statute is directed;

4   that the plaintiff is a member of the class of persons protected by the statute;

5   that the defendant has breached the statute; and

6   that this breach has caused the damage complained of.

4.19   Breach of statutory duty

4.19.1	Defences	There are two defences available for breach of statutory duty.

- *Volenti non fit injuria.* The defence of *volenti non fit injuria* applies to cases of breach of statutory duty.

   This was decided in *ICI v Shatwell* (1965), in which the House of Lords held that it applied in cases of breach of statutory duty except where there is a statutory provision to the contrary. This defence is not available where a worker sues his employer for breach of employer's statutory duty.

- Contributory negligence.

4.19.2 Example of actions in breach of statutory duty

Gibbons & Others v South West Water Services (1992) was a class action brought on behalf of 80 plaintiffs in respect of damage suffered by them when their drinking water supplies were contaminated with aluminium sulphate. The plaintiffs claimed for damages on the grounds of breach of statutory duty, public nuisance and breach of contract. The defendants, South West Water Services, admitted liability for breach of statutory duty and the plaintiffs were awarded compensatory damages. The plaintiffs appealed because they also claimed exemplary and/or aggravated damages; however, the original decision was upheld.

4.20 Statutory provisions which alter rights under common law

Statutory nuisance provisions in the EPA which have extended the tort of nuisance still allow an individual to bring action in a magistrates' court against a person who has created the nuisance, s 82. This section is used where the local authority has not acted to prevent or abate the statutory nuisance.

An individual aggrieved by statutory nuisance may bring an action under s 82 of the EPA 1990 (which re-enacts s 99 of the Public Health Act 1936). These proceedings will be brought against the person responsible for the nuisance. If the responsible party cannot be found, the owner of the premises may be liable, or where more than one person is responsible for the nuisance, each party may be liable under s 82 'whether or not what any of them is responsible for would by itself amount to a nuisance'.

This action can only be brought through the magistrates' court; there is no power for an individual to serve an abatement notice. Notice of the individual's intention to bring proceedings must be given to the responsible parties. In the case of a noise nuisance three days' notice must be given, and in all other cases 21 days' notice must be given.

Work is currently in progress within the European Commission on the preparation of a Draft Directive on Civil Liability for Damage to the Environment Caused by Waste. The purpose of the proposed Directive is to harmonise the systems of civil liability which are in place in Member States across the European Union. The concept of civil liability in relation to environmental damage is already established in some Member States: it already exists in Germany, Belgium, France and Italy, and has recently been introduced in the waste management sector in Spain.

The different systems in place in the Member States may lead to unequal conditions for competition among Member States, thereby creating artificial currents of investment and wastes from those countries where less stringent standards apply for the operators.

The proposed Directive has a preventative intention to encourage the polluter to take action to minimise the risks at the earliest possible stage. Its objectives are:

- to apply the polluter pays principle on terms conducive to completing the goal of the Single Market;

- to establish a uniform system of liability;

- to ensure that industry's waste related costs are reflected in the price of the product or service giving rise to the waste.

The Directive proposes to place primary liability on the producer of the waste; this could include any person who imports waste into the European Community, and persons responsible for waste installations. Where the producer of the waste cannot be found, then liability will be extended to the person who has control.

It is not yet clear whether this draft Directive in its current amended form will be adopted. The issue is currently being considered in a wider dialogue on environmental liability.

4.21   The EC and civil liability

The Common Law and Civil Liability

The statutory framework of environmental control is supported by the common law torts of public and private nuisance, negligence, trespass and the rule in *Rylands v Fletcher*. Although the main purpose for such torts is essentially to protect interests in land, they have developed considerably in the field of environmental protection.

The application of these torts for environmental purposes has recently been discussed in *Cambridge Water Company v Eastern Counties Leather plc*. In particular, the case examined the torts of nuisance and the rule in *Rylands v Fletcher*. The judgment contained pronouncements on the following elements:

- foreseeability;
- the relationship between nuisance and the rule in *Rylands v Fletcher*;
- the role of the courts and the common law in securing environmental protection;
- damages;
- injunction;
- abatement.

Remedies

There are several defences common to all intentional torts, and there are also those specific to individual torts.

Defences

The disadvantages associated with the common law are:

- not specific to the needs of environmental protection;
- not suited to the needs of the polluters;
- evidential difficulties;
- costs;
- the limitation period.

Disadvantages associated with the common law

Advantages associated with the common law

The advantages associated with the common law are:

- useful where there is no statutory provision;

- can be relied upon where the pollution pre-dates the statute;

- the common law is widely tested by individuals and pressure groups, who are often successful;

- actions may be based on more than one ground, thereby increasing chances of success.

Civil actions under statute

Individuals may also bring actions for civil liability under statute:

- where there is express statutory right to damages;

- where statutory provisions extend existing common law rights;

- in the tort of breach of statutory duty.

The EC is also developing a Directive on Civil Liability for Damage Caused by Waste. This will establish a community-wide regime of civil liability.

Chapter 5

The Role and Powers of the Regulatory Authorities

On 15 July 1992, the Secretary of State for the Environment announced to Parliament the Government's intention to create a new authority with overall responsibility for the protection of the environment. At the time of writing, the Environment Bill was before Parliament, its principal aim being the creation of the Environment Agency which is due to be set up in April 1996. The need for a 'one-stop' organisation with overall responsibility for environmental protection and pollution control is clear. At present, responsibility for the various aspects of environmental protection and pollution control is divided between a number of different authorities, whose functions sometimes overlap. The local authority sector in particular is responsible for a number of environmental protection functions, as well as controlling development through the Town and Country Planning regime. Local authorities exercise powers in relation to waste, air pollution, hazardous substances and statutory nuisances, albeit at different tiers of local government and in different departments. This fragmentation of environmental control reflects the way in which environmental legislation has developed in this country, largely in a piecemeal fashion and often in response to pollution incidents or problems.

At the time of writing, the creation of the new Environmental Agency was still being considered by Parliament. The proposals contained in the Environment Bill are considered below at para 5.9.

This chapter describes the composition, function and powers of the main statutory environmental protection authorities as they stand prior to the establishment of the new Environment Agency proposed in the Environment Bill. However, before considering each organisation in turn, it is possible to identify certain areas in common between them which illustrate the main mechanisms for pollution control in this country. Within the framework of legal regulation of the environment and pollution control the authorities in general fulfil the following main functions:

- Controlling pollution of the environment by giving prior 'permission' to pollute in a controlled manner. The principal tool of environmental protection is through

5.1 Introduction

5.2 The role of the regulatory authorities

regulation and control of polluting processes by a means of prior consent. Processes that pollute the various environmental media of air, water and land need to obtain permission from the relevant regulatory authority or authorities. Through the consent systems, the volume of substances discharged into the environment are controlled by means of conditions attached to the various consents. These prior permissions take various forms, such as a Waste Management Licence, a Water Discharge Consent or an Air Pollution Authorisation. The regulatory authorities which are responsible for administering the system use conditions to achieve certain environmental quality objectives and also meet obligations arising from Community law;

• Monitoring compliance with environmental controls. The various authorities described in this chapter and throughout the book are responsible for ensuring that the conditions laid down in 'authorisations' are being met. Compliance with conditions is enforced through a system of sanctions and criminal offences. The authorities are endowed with various powers of inspection and they employ specialist inspectors who enjoy a variety of powers, such as entry onto land and the ability to take samples which may later be used in evidence in court proceedings. Monitoring is also usually required as a condition of the permission or authorisation. Failure to monitor will usually be a breach of condition and therefore an offence, as is the falsifying of information on monitoring records. The results of monitoring exercises are available for public inspection in the public registers of information that the authorities are required to maintain;

• Enforcement of statutory controls. The various statutes described in this book, principally the Water Resources Act 1991 and the Environmental Protection Act 1990, create a number of criminal environmental offences. The various types of environmental offences have been discussed in Chapter 1 and are covered in detail in the various chapters on media-specific controls. Operating without the statutory 'permissions' usually amounts to a criminal offence, as does breaching the conditions imposed in any such permissions. To this extent the system of prior authorisation has been described as the 'cornerstone' of environmental law enforcement. The regulatory authorities are responsible for enforcing the regulatory controls and have the powers to prosecute offenders. Prosecution is usually seen as a last resort means of enforcement and the authorities have a variety of other enforcement tools, such as the power to revoke a licence or issue an Enforcement Notice which may be more effective as a means of control. Enforcement may also be secured more informally by means of a letter or the threat of prosecution. In addition, the regulatory authorities described below have various means at their disposal to require polluters to take steps or carry out works to abate environmental harm, or in certain circumstances to take remedial action.

In addition to these common functions, both the National Rivers Authority and Her Majesty's Inspectorate of Pollution conduct research into various aspects of pollution and pollution control and act in an advisory capacity to government and industry. HMIP, for example, are required to monitor developments in pollution abatement techniques and negotiate with industry to determine the availability of the best techniques not entailing excessive cost to be employed by processes falling under their regulatory control.

From the point of view of an industrialist operating a factory which discharges effluent into a stream, river or the sewers; emits gases and/or smoke into the atmosphere; and/or produces waste materials on site, it is not always clear which agencies are responsible for the control of such activities. Where a new industrial development is proposed, the developer will need to obtain a variety of authorisations from a number of different organisations, each exercising statutory powers aimed at protecting the environment. In order to avoid criminal liability, it is imperative that all the necessary authorisations are obtained before the development goes ahead. For this reason, good legal advice should be taken to ensure that all the necessary steps are taken to ensure compliance with all of the relevant procedures.

For any new development, it will be necessary to obtain planning permission from a local planning authority before the development can go ahead. However, the developer may also need to seek further authorisations from the local authority depending on the nature of the project. For example, it may be necessary for the developer to obtain a noise consent from the local authority for the noise generated during the construction period. The developer may need to obtain a Waste Management Licence or register with the Waste Regulation Authority, which will normally be the County Council. He may need to obtain Local Authority Air Pollution Control authorisation if the development is a prescribed process. There may be a need to obtain chimney height

5.2.1   The regulatory authority maze

approval from the local authority, or possibly even a hazardous substances consent.

In addition the developer may need to obtain a consent from the National Rivers Authority to discharge into water. Alternatively if the process is prescribed for central control it may require Integrated Pollution Control authorisation from Her Majesty's Inspectorate of Pollution. There may be a need to abstract water from a local river, in which case NRA approval will be required. There might be a need to discharge trade effluent into the drains, and in these circumstances the consent of the sewerage undertaker must also be obtained.

It becomes clear from looking at a hypothetical scenario such as this (the very stuff of seminars!) that the developer will need to understand the statutory controls that regulate the development and the bodies that are responsible for controlling the various matters. Failure to obtain the correct permissions may result in a criminal prosecution. Fines may be unlimited and the Crown Court has the power to impose a custodial sentence of up to two years. Recent cases suggest that the courts are becoming more willing to impose large fines and exercise the option of imprisonment. Additionally, both the Water Resources Act 1991 and the Environmental Protection Act 1990 provide that prosecutions may also be brought against company directors, managers, secretaries or other such officials in certain circumstances.

It is not only from the point of view of the industrialist that the picture is confusing. With so many organisations involved, it is difficult to establish an overview of what polluting activities are going on where. Although HMIP was established in 1987 with the aim of achieving a more coherent approach to pollution control through the system of IPC (see Chapter 9), there is clearly still the need for a more integrated approach to pollution control than the system that currently exists. Whilst the authorities themselves have been active to publicise their work and increase public awareness of their respective roles, the picture is still not entirely free of confusion. The government therefore sees the new Environment Agency as a means to develop a consistent and uniform approach to environmental protection which, hopefully, will also mean that the regulation and control of pollution becomes more transparent and understandable to those subject to such controls.

5.3   The existing Environmental Protection Authorities

This chapter will consider the overall structure and responsibilities of the main bodies currently involved in environmental protection and pollution control. The detailed description of their respective pollution control activities, functions and powers are dealt with in the chapters dealing with specific environmental legislation.

The main environmental protection authorities are:

- the Department of the Environment;

- Her Majesty's Inspectorate of Pollution;

- the National Rivers Authority;

- the local authorities.

In addition to these, a number of other organisations play a role in relation to environmental protection either in terms of promoting new legislation, acting in an advisory capacity or dealing with environmental regulation more indirectly. This chapter will consider the role of the following organisations that can be said to fall into these other categories:

- Royal Commission on Environmental Pollution;

- Sewerage Undertakers;

- Office of Water Services;

- Health and Safety Executive;

- English Nature and the Welsh Countryside Council;

- European Environment Agency.

5.3.1   The Department of the Environment

The Department of the Environment has principle responsibility for environmental legislation and policy and also for promoting new environmental legislation. It is responsible for issuing many of the Regulations which provide the detailed mechanisms for environmental control. The Department also issues various Guidance Notes and Circulars which are intended to assist either the regulatory authorities or applicants seeking consents from the various bodies. However, despite its name, the Department of the Environment is not solely or exclusively concerned with environmental protection. On the one hand, it is responsible for a number of other areas such as housing, energy, construction, local government and planning. On the other hand, because the environment is not something that can be considered in isolation, other government departments such as the Ministry of Agriculture and the Department of Transport play a role in terms of environmental protection.

Organisationally the Department of the Environment (DoE) has a number of specialist divisions dealing with the various aspects of environmental law. These are:

- The Directorate of Environmental Policy and Analysis – which is responsible for environmental policy and also provides the main link with the European Community;

- Directorate of Air, Climate and Toxic Substances – which is responsible for a wide range of activities, including air pollution (it supervises the activities of the local authorities in respect of their air pollution control activities) and chemical safety;

- The Water Directorate – which is responsible for overseeing all aspects of water supply and water quality;

- The Directorate of Pollution Control and Wastes – which deals with all aspects relating to waste policy and law. The Directorate is responsible, in particular, for overseeing the Waste Management Licensing system and provides guidance to the Waste Regulatory Authorities and the waste industry;

- Planning and Development Control Directorate – which is the directorate that controls the planning and development control system. It is responsible for developing planning policy and also for administering the role of the Secretary of State in the planning system;

- The Rural Affairs Directorate – which deals with wildlife and habitat conservation, National Parks, access to the countryside and sites of special scientific interest.

The Department's stated aims for environmental protection are to:

- promote sustainable development;

- ensure prudent use of natural resources and to minimise waste;

- prevent and minimise pollution of air, land and water in cost effective ways;

- increase informed public participation in environmental decision making and the involvement of all sectors, especially business;

- ensure environmental concerns are reflected in all the Government's work both at national and international level;

- reduce the burden of regulation, and make markets work for the environment;

- protect the rnvironment, and save money, by encouraging better management methods and by promoting the cost-effective use of energy.

A glance through most of the chapters of this book will indicate that the Secretary of State for the Environment plays a key role in regulating environmental protection. This involves, *inter alia*:

- dealing with appeals against decisions of the enforcement agencies, although in practice appeals are dealt with by the Planning Inspectorate;

- issuing directions, for example to HMIP concerning applications or to meet various EC law obligations;

- exercising various discretionary powers, for example in the designation of Special Protection Areas under the Habitats Directive ;

- reviewing waste-disposal plans and waste-recycling plans.

Although the Department of the Environment is the lead department for environmental policy, other government departments have a significant role to play. It is established government policy that all government departments are under a duty to ensure that environmental considerations are taken into account in the development of all policies and programmes. So, for example, the Department of Transport is required to consider the environment in respect of its road building programme and the problems that heavy traffic can cause as a result of congestion in towns and cities. The relationship between transport and the environment is already recognised as of importance by the European Community, which published a Green Paper on *Transport and the Environment* and is highlighted in the Planning Policy Guidance Note on Planning and Transport. In addition other areas of government, notably the Ministry of Agriculture, Fisheries and Food (MAFF) take action which impinges on the environment. MAFF is responsible for agricultural policy and has taken a number of steps to protect the environment as part of that policy. MAFF also has important responsibilities under the Water Resources Act 1991 and in particular provides the appeal mechanisms from decisions taken by the National Rivers Authority.

Prior to the formation of HMIP in 1987 control of pollution was the responsibility of a number of central government inspectorates: the Alkali Inspectorate (which was formed in 1863 and which was later called the Industrial Air Pollution Inspectorate); the Radiochemical Inspectorate; the Hazardous Waste Inspectorate and the Water Pollution Inspectorate. (The functions of the Water Pollution Inspectorate were transferred to the National Rivers Authority by the Water Act 1989.)

HMIP operates in England and Wales; separate organisations operate in Scotland and Ireland. It is currently part of the Department of the Environment (unlike the National Rivers Authority); however it operates on a regional basis with a central office at Romney House in London. HMIP is headed up by the Chief Inspector and Director and its regional responsibilities are discharged by inspectors in the regions. All of the regulatory work is handled by the regional offices; there are currently seven regions. HMIP currently has over 430 staff. In addition, HMIP has a Technical Guidance Branch and a Monitoring Branch.

5.4.2   Responsibilities of HMIP

HMIP's responsibilities were increased in 1990 by the Environmental Protection Act and it now regulates over 200 categories of industry, 5,000 major industrial plants and 8,000 premises storing radioactive material. It now has responsibility in England and Wales for the following areas of Environmental protection:

(a) regulation of the most seriously polluting processes through the system of Integrated Pollution Control introduced by Part 1 of the Environmental Protection Act;

(b) regulation of sites which use, store or dispose of radioactive material under the Radioactive Substances Act 1993;

(c) responsibilities under the Health and Safety at Work Act 1974 in relation to the air emissions of IPC processes;

(d) duties under the Water Industry Act 1991 to act on behalf of the Secretary of State with regard to special category effluents discharged into the sewers;

(e) research on pollution control and also on radioactive waste disposal;

(f) statutory consultee in environmental assessments;

(g) oversight of the work of local Waste Regulation Authorities;

(h) maintenance of public register on IPC authorised processes.

In carrying out these functions, HMIP is meant to serve the government, industry and also the citizen. In particular HMIP provides expert advice and support to government departments on a wide range of environmental issues. HMIP officials are involved in European Community working groups and other international bodies.

HMIP draws its powers from a number of statutory provisions including:

- Alkali etc, Works Act 1906;

- Health and Safety at Work Act 1974;

- Environmental Protection Act 1990;

- The Water Resources Act 1991;

- The Radioactive Substances Act 1993.

Once an industrial process has been authorised by HMIP, the Inspectorate has responsibility to ensure compliance with the conditions and standards laid down in the authorisations, through a system of monitoring. Usually the authorisation itself will require the holder to carry out routine monitoring and to report the results to HMIP on a regular basis. These monitoring results, plus any obtained directly by HMIP Inspectors are placed on the public register. In addition to this, HMIP inspectors can carry out their own site inspections, either on a regular or ad hoc basis or in response to any complaints received. In recognition of the significant role that monitoring plays, a new Monitoring branch of HMIP was established in August 1991.

5.4.3   Duties: responsibilities to monitor

The enforcement powers of HMIP were substantially increased by the Environmental Protection Act 1990. HMIP has the power to revoke authorisations granted and also to halt a process where there is imminent risk of serious pollution. In addition it has the power to bring prosecutions against offenders whic if upheld in the magistrates' court, can lead to a fine of up to £20,000. For other cases, taken in higher courts, penalties can lead to an unlimited fine and/or a period of up to two years' imprisonment. To assist HMIP in the process of enforcement, its inspectors have considerable powers of investigation, particularly under s 17 EPA, to enter premises and take samples.

5.4.4   Enforcement powers

HMIP has the power to prosecute where processes are operating in the absence of the appropriate authorisation or where conditions of authorisations are being breached. These powers to prosecute are dealt with in more detail in chapter 9 on Integrated Pollution Control. However HMIP has been criticised for its poor prosecution record and contrasted with the National Rivers Authority which has shown that it is much more willing to prosecute offenders. The following statistics illustrate the number of HMIP prosecutions since its formation in 1987:

5.4.5   Prosecutions record

HMIP prosecutions:

1987–88	3
1988–89	2
1989–90	4
1990–91	1
1991–92	11

In its publicity material (*Protecting Britain's Environment – The Work of Her Majesty's Inspectorate of Pollution*) it states that:

'Breaches of authorisations are normally dealt with quickly and effectively with the co-operation of the operator. But where this does not produce the necessary results, HMIP uses its powers of enforcement and prosecution.'

The emphasis in practice is on ensuring compliance with the co-operation of the operator and this will normally be secured informally be an Inspector's letter. As stated above, HMIP can also use its other tools of enforcement by issuing either an Enforcement or Prohibition Notice. Prosecution is usually a last resort means of enforcement.

5.4.6	Technical guidance

In order to assist both industrialists and the Chief Inspectors, HMIP publishes a considerable amount of guidance material. Following the introduction of Integrated Pollution Control, HMIP has started to issue a new series of guidance notes covering all IPC processes. These guidance notes give advice on matters such as the best available technology for the particular process, pollution abatement techniques, operating procedures and importantly the emission standards to be achieved.

5.4.7	Cost recovery

One of the government's stated ambitions for HMIP is that it should be self-financing, recovering its costs from charges made for authorisations, variations, etc of IPC processes. This reflects the notion that the polluter should pay, not just for remedying pollution but also for the costs of pollution control. A charging scheme was introduced in April 1990. HMIP is required, by the EPA, to set fees and charges so that income and relevant costs balance 'so far as practicable'. However, in 1992/1993 HMIP did not achieve this and there was a significant shortfall.

5.5	**The National Rivers Authority**

The National Rivers Authority (NRA) is the main regulatory body with responsibility for controlling pollution of water, although it shares responsibilities with Her Majesty's Inspectorate of Pollution in relation to those industrial processes that are governed by the Integrated Pollution

Control Regimes of the Environmental Protection Act. The NRA was set up by the Water Act 1989, at the same time as water privatisation, to provide integrated management of river basins and the water environment in England and Wales. It took over the functions previously exercised by the Water Authorities. Although the NRA was established by the Water Act 1989, its constitution, function and powers are now governed by the 1991 Water Resources Act, and all the following sections relate to the 1991 Act. The NRA exercises a range of functions beyond pollution control; for example it is responsible for flood protection. However, in the context of environmental protection, the NRA has shown itself to be a strong regulator.

The NRA was established as an independent public body and does not enjoy Crown Immunity. However, it is nevertheless accountable to the Secretary of State for the Environment. The Secretary of State can issue directions to the NRA, although he can only do so after consultation with the authority unless the direction is issued in an emergency situation. There is also a requirement that details of any directions issued by the Secretary of State are published in the authority's annual report. The NRA has been identified by the Department of the Environment as the 'competent body' to implement the requirements of numerous EC Directives concerning water quality.

Unlike Her Majesty's Inspectorate of Pollution, the National Rivers Authority is a non-departmental body. NRA has its national headquarters in Bristol but is structured on a regional basis with the wight regions corresponding to the catchment boundaries of the former regional Water Authorities. In 1993, NRA Northumbria and NRA Yorkshire were amalgamated, and NRA South West and NRA Wessex Regions were merged to form NRA South Western.	5.5.1 Organisational structure

The corporate membership of the NRA can vary between eight and 15 members. Two are appointed by the Minister of Agriculture, Fisheries and Food whilst the remaining members are appointed by the Secretary of State for the Environment. In appointing members the Secretary of State or the Minister must have regard to the desirability of appointing people who have experience of, or some capacity in, matters relevant to the functions of the authority.

The NRA is assisted by a number of regional advisory committees that act in a consultative role to the Authority, providing advice on those areas within their spheres of influence. These committees were established under s 7 of the	5.5.2 Advisory committees

WRA 1991. There are three main advisory committees that operate in each region:

- Regional Rivers Advisory Committees;
- Regional Flood Defence Committees;
- Regional Fisheries Advisory Committee.

In addition there is an Advisory Committee for Wales. The advisory committees give advice in relation to their specialist field. Therefore, for example, the Rivers Advisory Committee is consulted on any proposals relating generally to the manner in which the Authority carries out its functions in that area and the Fisheries Committee will be consulted on the way the NRA carries out responsibilities relating to fishing licences. These advisory committees have however no specific formal powers.

The members of the advisory committees are appointed by the NRA. The advisory committees are open to the press and to the public, unlike the meetings of the NRA.

5.5.3   Functions

When the NRA was established in 1989, it inherited the functions of the water authorities relating to pollution control, water resource management, flood defence, fisheries, navigation and conservation and recreation. Its functions are laid down in s 2 of the 1991 Act and cover the following areas:

- maintaining and improving water quality in controlled waters;
- regulating discharges into controlled waters;
- monitoring the extent of water pollution;
- managing and safeguarding water resources (abstraction);
- conserving amenity and promoting recreation;
- flood defence and land drainage;
- regulating fisheries (under the Salmon and Freshwater Fisheries Act 1974).

5.5.4   Powers

NRA Officers have a wide number of powers by virtue of ss 169–173 of the Water Resources Act. The so-called 'River Police' enjoy powers of entry, can take samples and collect evidence. These powers are considered more fully in chapter 8 on Water Pollution.

5.5.5   Duties

The Water Resources Act places the National Rivers Authority under a number of statutory duties. The consequence of this is that the NRA must have regard to these duties when exercising its various functions and it may also be amenable to judicial review if it fails to take into account the duties it is under.

The NRA is required by s 16 of the Water Resources Act to generally promote (to the extent that it considers desirable) the conservation and enhancement of the natural beauty and amenity of inland and coastal waters and of land associated with such waters; the conservation of flora and fauna which are dependent on the aquatic environment; and the use of such waters and land for recreational purposes.

The NRA also has a duty to consider water supply issues and by virtues of s 15 it must have regard, when exercising any of its powers, to have particular regard to the duties that are imposed on any water undertakers or sewage undertakers by Parts II–IV of the Water Industry Act 1991.

The policy of the National Rivers Authority is to provide strong effective regulation in order to secure real environmental improvements of controlled waters. However, it does not view regulation as the only means at its disposal. It places an emphasis on changing attitudes and, hopefully, resulting behaviour. As part of its pollution prevention campaign, the NRA has produced a short promotional video entitled 'Pollution doesn't pay'. The video has been made widely available to businesses promoting the benefits of compliance and good practice.

5.5.6   NRA policy

Since its creation in 1989, the NRA has shown itself to be more willing to prosecute offenders than HMIP. Although prosecution figures are not conclusive of a strong enforcement policy, the statistics are telling. Between 1989 and the end of 1994 the NRA had made over 2,200 successful prosecutions. These resulted in over £5,000,000 in fines.

5.5.7   Prosecutions policy

The system of Integrated Pollution Control (IPC) established by Part I EPA is concerned with controlling the emissions of waste to air, land and water. HMIP, the body responsible for regulating the most seriously polluting processes that are prescribed for IPC, are required, when determining whether and how to authorise a prescribed process, to have regard to achieving the best practicable environmental option. To this end, they are responsible for authorising discharges made into controlled waters, as well as emissions to air. Processes prescribed for Integrated Pollution Control must obtain authorisation from HMIP, failure to do so is a criminal offence. HMIP determine conditions concerning the discharges into controlled waters and therefore exercise the powers normally exercised by the NRA. However, HMIP is

5.5.8   Overlap with HMIP

required to consult the NRA before it sets conditions and, effectively, the NRA has the power to indirectly determine any conditions which should be attached.

5.6   The local authorities

The local authorities are perhaps the most difficult to describe in this brief overview. This is because they carry out a wide range of environmental functions and these functions are performed at different tiers of the local government structure. Some functions are carried out at county council level – such as waste regulation – whereas as others are the responsibility of the district council or the London Borough Council. Where local government is featured in the environmental regulation described in the following chapters, the appropriate level will be defined. In addition, the various functions are carried out within different local authority departments, with the planning and environmental health departments playing the leading roles. Many of the powers, for instance in relation to statutory nuisance, are delegated to officers who have to make on the spot determinations about statutory nuisance complaints.

This section intends only to provide a brief overview of the main environmental protection functions carried out by local authorities:

• Waste regulation is performed by the Waste Regulation Authorities, the Waste Disposal Authorities and the Waste Collection Authorities. This involves both the county and district councils. The functions of each of these are dealt with in Chapter 10 on Waste on Land;

• Responsibility for the planning control system which requires local planning authorities to take environmental considerations into account in the preparation of development plans and also in respect of planning applications. Planning authorities are also involved in Environmental Impact Assessments;

• District councils are responsible for investigating and abating statutory nuisances under the EPA;

• Local authorities are responsible under the Clean Air Act 1993 for controlling emissions of dark smoke and can control smoke emissions through the creation of Smoke Control Areas;

• Local authorities are responsible for authorising prescribed processes under Part 1 of the EPA for Local Authority Air Pollution Control. This function is carried out by the district councils;

- Hazardous Substances Authorities.These are normally the local planning authorities. See Chapter 10 at para 10.17.4.

Although HMIP and the NRA are the principal players in the pollution control field a number, other organisations make a significant contribution towards achieving environmental protection.

5.7 Other bodies concerned with environmental protection

5.7.1 The Royal Commission on Environmental Pollution

The Royal Commission on Environmental Pollution was established in February 1970 as a standing body to:

'advise on matters, both national and international, concerning the pollution of the environment; on the adequacy of research in this field; and the future possibilities of danger to the environment.'

It is a permanent body made up of experts in environmental matters who are appointed on the advice of the Prime Minister.

The Royal Commission has played an extremely important role in the development of current environmental legislation, not least because of its expert advice and also because it has had the opportunity to give objective advice on different choices to be made and actions to be taken. The Royal Commission has published a number of reports, which are referred to in this book. The reports provide a valuable insight into a variety of environmental problems and invariably set the agenda for debate and consultation. The reports are intended to give advice to government but in fact they have been very influential on UK environmental policy.

5.7.2 Sewerage undertakers

The sewerage network is operated by private companies known as sewerage undertakers. Notwithstanding the fact that they operate as private companies, the sewerage undertakers are responsible for licensing discharges into public sewers through the system of trade effluent consents.

5.7.3 Office of Water Services

The Office of Water Services (OFWAT) was established in 1989 following privatisation of the water supply industry. Its principal function is to regulate the water supply industry 'in the public interest'. Although OFWAT is not specifically an environmental agency, it is required to ensure that the water undertakers have regard to their general environmental duties as laid down in the Water Industry Act 1991.

5.7.4 The Health and Safety Executive

The Health and Safety Executive (HSE) is responsible for the administration of the Health and Safety at Work Act 1974. However, the boundaries between health and safety of workers and protection of the environment are not always clear and the HSE, in fact, fulfils a number of functions related to environmental protection. In particular, the HSE is involved in the regulation of certain activities which, if not carried out properly, could have serious environmental consequences. These include the regulation of asbestos installations handling hazardous substances. In addition, the HSE acts as a statutory consultee in relation to applications for Integrated Pollution Control authorisation.

| 5.7.5 | English Nature and the Countryside Council for Wales |

Part VII of the EPA 1990 created English Nature and the Countryside Council for Wales out of the former Nature Conservancy Council. English Nature operates in England and the Countryside Council operates in Wales. English Nature does not have any pollution control powers or means of enforcement. Instead it acts as the Government's statutory body on nature conservation and is responsible for promoting nature conservation generally. The powers of English Nature are contained in the Wildlife and Countryside Act 1981 as amended.

5.8 The European Environmental Agency

The European Environment Agency was set up in 1994, following the adoption by the Council of Ministers in May 1990 of Council Regulation 1210/90. After considerable debate as to where it should be located it was eventually decided that it should be based in Copenhagen. The functions of the agency are as follows:

- to provide the Member States with objective, reliable and comparable information about the environment;

- to ensure that the public is properly informed about the state of the environment.

The Management Board of the EEA is made up of one representative from each Member State, two representatives from the European Commission and a further two designated by the European Parliament.

The European Environment Agency is assisted by the European Environment Information and Observation Network.

The main criticism of the agency, as it currently exists, is that it has no role to play in the enforcement of environmental law.

5.9 The future and the new Environment Agency

In November 1994, the Environment Bill was introduced before Parliament, its principal purpose being the creation of a new Environment Agency for England and Wales. The government sees the new Environmental Agency as a means of developing a consistent and cohesive approach to environmental protection which, hopefully, will also mean that the regulation and control of pollution is more readily understandable to those who are subject to the controls.

The agency will bring together a number of functions currently exercised by HMIP, NRA and the Waste Regulatory Authorities (these are generally the County Councils except in Metropolitan County areas and London). In particular the agency will be responsible for the following functions:

- The agency will assume the functions currently exercised by the NRA. As a consequence of which the NRA will be abolished;

- The waste management functions exercised by the Waste Regulation Authorities;

- HMIPs responsibilities under Part I of the Environmental Protection Act (see Chapter 9 on Integrated Pollution Control);

- Functions relating to radioactive substances;

- Certain enforcement functions under the Health and Safety at Work Act 1974.

The agency will be placed under certain statutory duties which it must have regard to when exercising any of its functions:

5.9.1   Duties of the new agency

- in the same way that the NRA is currently under such a duty, the new agency will also be obliged, to the extent that the agency considers desirable, to promote the conservation of the natural beauty and amenity of inland and coastal waters and land surrounding them, the conservation of nature and the promotion of recreational use of such waters;

- it will be under a duty to consider the desirability of protecting the cultural heritage and of preserving freedom of access to woodland, mountains, moors, heathlands, downs, cliffs, the foreshore and other places of natural beauty.

The Environment Agency will be assisted by Regional Environment Protection Advisory Committees. These Regional Advisory Committees must be consulted when the Environment Agency decides how it is to carry out its functions in the respective regions. These regional committees are to be made up of people who have experience of, or capacity in, matters relating to environmental management.

5.9.2   Regional Environment Protection Advisory Committees

| 5.9.3 | An effective Agency ? | The reaction to the proposed Environment Agency has been mixed. Despite the fact that the creation of such an integrated agency has been long awaited (and long promised), there is already a feeling that the new agency is 'compromised even before it begins' (Council for Protection of Rural England). Environmental pressure groups such as Friends of the Earth have also reacted with similar comments. |

5.9.3   An effective Agency ?

The reaction to the proposed Environment Agency has been mixed. Despite the fact that the creation of such an integrated agency has been long awaited (and long promised), there is already a feeling that the new agency is 'compromised even before it begins' (Council for Protection of Rural England). Environmental pressure groups such as Friends of the Earth have also reacted with similar comments.

5.9.4   Lack of independence?

The proposal that the Agency is made up of members nominated by the Secretary of State for the Environment and the Minister for Agriculture has generated concerns about the independence of the Agency. Concern has been expressed about the degree of Ministerial control and the extent to which Ministers can give guidance to the agency with respect to its aims and objectives. This concern has not just come from environmentalists or environmental pressure groups, but has also been voiced by Lord Crickhowell, Chairman of the National Rivers Authority. In the second reading debate in the House of Lords (December 1994), Lord Crickhowell warned against the wide-ranging powers which the Government was taking to intervene in the Agency's work. In a telling criticism, the Chairman of the NRA has stated that: 'Almost everything that the Agency does, its regulatory arrangements, charging schemes, corporate plan and financial arrangements, has to be approved by Ministers.'

5.9.5   Constraints on the way in which the Agency can operate

Pressure groups have also indicated concern about the terms upon which Ministers have required the Agency should exercise its functions. In particular, an issue that has caused considerable disquiet is the requirement that the Agency, when it considers whether and in what manner it will exercise any of its powers, must take into account the costs which are likely to be incurred as a result of the exercise of that power. In taking into account these costs, the Agency will be required to weigh the costs against the benefits which are likely to accrue. In other words, there is a requirement that the Agency consider the cost and benefits of exercising any of its powers. This requirement has led, not surprisingly, to the view that environmental quality will be sacrificed to commercial interests. This desire to be cost-effective is also evident in the statements that were made by the Minister when the Bill was introduced into Parliament.

The Role and Powers of the Regulatory Authorities

Responsibility for pollution control and environmental protection currently rests with a number of regulatory authorities. However at the time of writing the Environment Bill is proceeding before Parliament, its principal aim being the creation of a new Environment Agency.

The role of the regulatory authorities

Overall responsibility for the environment is vested within the Department of Environment although other government departments such as the Ministry of Agriculture, Fisheries and Food and the Department of Transport also play a key role in environmental protection through the development of their policies.

The Secretary of State for the Environment plays a key role in regulating environmental protection. This involves, *inter alia*, in:

- dealing with appeals against decisions of the enforcement agencies, although in practice appeals are dealt with by the Planning Inspectorate;

- issuing directions, for example to HMIP concerning applications or to meet various EC law obligations;

- exercising various discretionary powers, for example in the designation of Special Protection Areas under the Habitats Directive;

- reviewing waste-disposal plans and waste-recycling plans.

The main environmental protection authorities discussed in this book are as follows:

The main environmental protection authorities

- Her Majesty's Inspectorate of Pollution;

- the National Rivers Authority; and

- the local authorities.

Her Majesty's Inspectorate of Pollution (HMIP) was created in 1987. Its responsibilities were increased in 1990 by the Environmental Protection Act and it now regulates over 200 categories of industry, 5,000 major industrial plants and 8,000 premises storing radioactive material.

In the context of this book its main responsibility is the regulation of the most seriously polluting processes through the system of Integrated Pollution Control introduced by Part I of the Environmental Protection Act.

The National Rivers Authority (NRA) is the main regulatory body with responsibility for controlling pollution of water, although it shares responsibilities with Her Majesty's Inspectorate of Pollution in relation to those industrial processes that are governed by the Integrated Pollution Control Regimes of the Environmental Protection Act.

The local authority sector plays an important part in controlling pollution and environmental protection. Its main functions can be summarised as follows:

- Waste regulation is performed by the Waste Regulation Authorities, the Waste Disposal Authorities and the Waste Collection Authorities. This involves both the county and district councils.

- Responsibility for the planning control system which requires local planning authorities to take environmental considerations into account in the preparation of development plans and also in respect of planning applications. Planning authorities are also involved in Environmental Assessments;

- District councils are responsible for investigating and abating statutory nuisances under the EPA;

- Local authorities are responsible under the Clean Air Act 1993 for controlling emissions of dark smoke and can control smoke emissions through the creation of Smoke Control Areas;

- Local authorities are responsible for authorising prescribed processes under Part I of the EPA for Local Authority Air Pollution Control. This function is carried out by the district councils;

- Hazardous Substances Authorities.

Other bodies concerned with environmental protection

A number of other agencies play an important role in the area of environmental protection. These include the:

- Royal Commission on Environmental Pollution;

- Office of Water Services;

- Sewerage Undertakers;

- English Nature and the Welsh Countryside Council;

- Health and Safety Executive;

- European Environment Agency.

Chapter 6

Pressure Groups, Individuals and the Environment and Access to Information

The principle of public participation in the area of environmental protection is one which seems to enjoy support from all levels of government. There appears to be general recognition that the protection of the environment cannot be left entirely to those public and regulatory agencies which have statutory responsibility for the environment or pollution control. On the one hand, these agencies are often not sufficiently resourced and would be hard pushed to monitor and regulate all discharges, emissions or pollution incidents. They rely and depend on members of the public to report incidents and draw their attention to unusual discharges or emissions. On the other hand, there is also a valid view that the pollution control authorities should not be left alone to fulfil their role but should in some way be accountable or at least responsible to the citizen.

The participation of citizens in the protection of the environment is recognised at international, European Community and national level. Inextricably linked with the desire to encourage and promote public participation is the recognition that access to information is vital. Individual citizens must be able to obtain information about the state of the eEnvironment; they must be able to find information on emissions and discharges from the regulatory bodies; and, importantly, this information must be easily accessible and freely available.

This chapter will specifically consider the issue of public participation in the enforcement of environmental law and the rights of environmental associations and pressure groups to take legal action, either to bring prosecutions after incidents have occurred, or to ensure compliance with environmental law in order to avoid any breaches. In particular, the following issues will be considered:

- the principle of stewardship and the importance of public participation;

- the importance of environmental pressure groups;

- the ways in which environmental pressure groups can use EC law to secure better protection of the environment;

6.1   Introduction

- the means by which pressure groups and individuals can seek to enforce environmental law themselves, principally by means of judicial review;

- the possibilities of bringing private criminal prosecutions under the main statutory provisions;

- environmental protest; and

- access to information about the environment.

6.2   Recognition of the need for public participation

6.2.1   International recognition

At the United Nations conference on environment and development held in Rio de Janeiro in 1992, over 150 States and the EC agreed to Principle 10 of the Rio Declaration that 'Environmental issues are best handled with participation of all concerned citizens, at the relevant level'.

6.2.2   European Community recognition

The EC's Fifth Environmental Action Programme also envisages an important role for the citizens of Europe in ensuring that environmental legislation is enforced:

'Individuals and public interest groups should have practicable access to the courts in order to ensure that their legitimate interests are protected and that prescribed environmental measures are effectively enforced and illegal practices stopped.'

Environmental pressure groups have been particularly active at the European level in two principal ways. First, by participating in the development of environmental law and policy and, second, by monitoring compliance with EC environmental law and complaining to the European Commission about cases where EC law has been breached or inadequately enforced. The Fourth Environmental Action Programme (1987–1992) stated that one of the aims of the EC's environmental policy was to ensure that Directives are not only legally implemented, but are also practically enforced. This monitoring of compliance does not rest entirely with the European Commission or the national regulatory authorities but is supported by individuals and pressure groups.

6.2.3   National recognition

The Department of the Environment has produced a publication called *Green Rights and Responsibilities: A Citizens Guide to the Environment*, which sets out the government's thinking on public participation in environmental protection.

In the Secretary of State's Foreword to the *Guide*, the following statement is made:

'Government provides the law and institutions within which we exercise our environmental rights and discharge our responsibilities. But unless each one of us plays our own part, no amount of law-making will make any difference to the quality of the environment.'

These environmental rights are described as:

- the right of access to environmental information which is held by public bodies;

- the right to participate in the decision-making process on environmental issues; and also,

- the right to seek appropriate remedies in the event of a breach of environmental laws or failure to provide environmental services.

There is a long history of environmental pressure groups in the UK and they are considerably expert in mobilising public opinion. There are now numerous environmental pressure groups (note, they are often referred to as non-governmental organisations or NGOs) some of which have very large memberships and are interested in global environmental and conservation issues. Greenpeace, Friends of the Earth and the World Wide Fund for Nature are the obvious ones. In addition, there are many groups which are formed around specific issues, such as the protection of birds or particular species of animal. The Royal Society for the Protection of Birds enjoys a particularly large membership, is well-resourced and has shown itself to be prepared to take legal action to protect specific bird habitats.

Today the large pressure groups such as Greenpeace and Friends of the Earth boast large membership numbers throughout the world, in countries as diverse as Guatemala, Russia and Tunisia. These groups have developed into large organisations with significant financial and technical resources and also highly trained staff (and often volunteers) ranging from scientists to lawyers. The larger pressure groups have become skilled in organising professionally run campaigns and mobilising public support.

Environmental pressure groups have been able to exert an influence on both the introduction and enforcement of EC environmental law and have been able to use EC environmental law rights to bring legal actions within the national courts of the Member States.

Given that so much of our current environmental legislation emanates from the Community and that the UK is obliged under Art 5 of the EC Treaty to implement and enforce such legislation, pressure groups have realised the importance of

6.3   Environmental pressure groups

6.3.1   Using EC environmental law to protect the environment

6.3.2   Lobbying at the European level

influencing the content of legislation at the European level. Indeed, the same can be said for almost all areas of Community law, and Brussels now is a major centre for professional lobbyists. Environmental pressure groups representing a wide range of general and specific interests have been particularly active in bringing pressure on the Community institutions to influence the content of legislation. This has involved lobbying the European Parliament and the Commission, suggesting amendments, providing technical advice and participating in the drafting of Directives. There are numerous examples of successful lobbying at the EC level.

6.3.3   **Environmental pressure groups and the enforcement of EC environmental law**

Although it is generally only the larger and well-resourced pressure groups that can exert influence on the law-making process and the content of environmental legislation, almost all environmental pressure groups can play a role in the enforcement of EC environmental law. However, this is subject to at least two limitations: first, not all groups will have the financial and technical resources to bring costly legal actions, particularly where they run the risk of having to bear the other side's costs. Second, not all pressure groups will be able to challenge decisions made by planning authorities, the regulatory authorities or the Secretary of State by means of judicial review actions because of the difficulties in proving that they have *locus standi*. However, most groups can play a role in terms of monitoring compliance with EC law and they all have the right to complain directly to the European Commission when they believe that EC law is being breached.

6.3.4   **Article 169 direct actions**

The European Commission receives thousands of complaints each year from pressure groups, their members and also aggrieved citizens concerning the breach of environmental law. The legal action brought by the Commission (under Art 169 of the Treaty) against the United Kingdom, *Commission v United Kingdom* (1993), concerning breaches of the Bathing Water Directive reputedly resulted from a complaint received by the Commission on a postcard from an aggrieved holidaymaker at Blackpool. However, the Commission is not under a duty to follow up every complaint and it exercises its discretion as to whether to take any action against the Member State involved (see Chapter 2 for further discussion). Therefore, although the Art 169 procedure offers aggrieved citizens and pressure groups an inexpensive means of attempting to secure compliance, it does not guarantee that the Commission will take any action.

In addition to the possibility of complaining to the Commission, environmental pressure groups may also, where relevant, seek judicial review of EC Acts under Arts 173 and 175 of the Treaty. Article 173 involves the review of Acts, whereas Art 175 is concerned with omissions or the failure of the institutions to act. According to the Treaty, natural and legal persons (as opposed to the institutions and the Member States) can only seek judicial review against a decision addressed to that person or against a decision which, although in the form of a Regulation or a Decision addressed to another person, is of direct and individual concern to the former. Unlike the Member States and the community institutions, individuals and pressure groups have limited access to the ECJ in judicial review actions. Not all 'acts' are reviewable, only decisions or regulations which are decisions in substance. The test for *locus standi* is that a person is directly and individually concerned. In a number of cases largely concerned with market regulations, the Court of Justice has placed a very restrictive interpretation on what is meant by the phrase 'direct and individual concern', effectively barring many applicants from bringing such actions. The test which was laid down in the leading case of *Plaumann* (1963) is that a person other than one to whom a decision is addressed will only be individually concerned:

> 'if that decision affects them by reason of certain attributes which are peculiar to them, or by reason of circumstances in which they are differentiated from all other persons, and by virtue of these factors distinguishes them individually just as in the case of the person addressed.'

In terms of environmental law, two problems become immediately apparent. First, most environmental measures are in the form of Directives and are therefore *prima facie* not reviewable in judicial review actions brought by individuals. It is rare for the Commission to take a formal decision concerned with environmental protection but, as the case below illustrates, they can take decisions which have a bearing on the enforcement of environmental laws, albeit indirectly. Second, the *locus standi* test itself is very difficult for environmental pressure groups to satisfy. Notwithstanding that, the Court of First Instance, which has first instance jurisdiction in judicial review actions brought by natural and legal persons, has, like the English courts, recently been forced to consider the position of environmental pressure groups in the following case.

6.3.5   Challenging Community environmental law before the Court of Justice

6.3.6   *Stichting Greenpeace*   This case illustrates the importance of judicial review as a
          Council and others v   means of ensuring that environmental policy and law are
          EC Commission (1993)   enforced and complied with, not only by the pollution control
authorities but also by the authors of the policy and law, in
this instance the European Commission. The Commission,
which is responsible for initiating legislation and ensuring
compliance was, in this case, challenged by a number of
applicants because of its decision to award financial assistance
through the structural funds (regional funds to support
infrastructure projects in certain regions throughout the
community) for a project which had not been made subject to
the Environmental Assessment Directive.

The project in question involved the construction of two
power plants in the Canary Islands. The applicants included
local farmers and residents, two Canary Island environmental
groups and Greenpeace. They sought annulment of the
Commission's decision to award a 12,000,000 ECU grant aid
towards the projects on the grounds that the grant was made
for a project for which an environmental assessment should
have been carried out and that the Commission had itself
violated EC environmental law. Somewhat ironically, the
Commission argued that the applicants were not individually
concerned by the structural funds decision.

6.4   Judicial review in English law

The regulation and control of polluting activities is exercised
by public regulatory authorities which have responsibility,
amongst other things, for exercising their discretion and
granting 'permission' to pollute in a controlled manner
through the various licensing systems described in this book.
This can be seen in the Environmental Protection Act where
authorisations are required for prescribed processes, either
from HMIP or a local authority; consents are required for
certain discharges into controlled water; and waste
management licences are required for final disposals by
deposit of waste on land. These 'permissions' are granted on
application from the pollution control authority, subject to
conditions. Alternatively they may be refused. Rights of
appeal in respect of applications lie not to the courts, but to
the Secretary of State. The Secretary of State's involvement is
not, however, confined to dealing with appeals concerning
applications. Rights of appeal to the Secretary of State exist in
a number of other circumstances, for instance in relation to
refusals to vary authorisations and revocations.

Decisions taken by the pollution control authorities, and
the Secretary of State using powers conferred under statute,
are public law decisions and as such are amenable to judicial
review. It is therefore critical that individuals and pressure

groups have access to the courts in circumstances where they wish to challenge the way in which the former have, or have nor, exercised their discretion properly.

The remedies of *mandamus, certiorari* and prohibition are only available in respect of the exercise of public power or public law matters. Therefore, where an applicant seeks to obtain one of these remedies they can only do so against decisions made by public bodies and not against bodies exercising private power. In most cases, it is clear which bodies are operating as public bodies in that they derive their powers from a statutory source, although in fact not all functions which arise from a statutory framework have the necessary public law element and equally bodies which derive their powers from other sources than statute (or the common law) may be involved in public law matters. This was demonstrated in *R v Panel on Take-Overs and Mergers, ex p Datafin plc* (1987). However, in most cases the public law element necessary for obtaining these remedies is to be found in the statute which establishes the body in question.

6.4.1	Judicial review remedies

The concept of a citizen's action is one which presumes that citizens generally should be able to bring judicial review actions in the public interest without having to show any individual harm over and above that of the general community. Although no such right of action exists in English public law, it has received some judicial support. In particular Lord Diplock in *R v Inland Revenue Commissioners, ex p National Federation of the Self-Employed and Small Businesses Ltd* (1982) asserted that :

6.4.2	The question of standing: do environmental pressure groups have *locus standi*?

> 'It would, in my view, be a grave lacuna in our system of public law if a pressure group, like the federation, or even a single public-spirited taxpayer, were prevented by outdated technical rules of *locus standi* from bringing the matter to the attention to the court to vindicate the rule of law and get the unlawful stopped.'

However, it remains the case in English law that, in order to challenge administrative decisions, it is necessary for the person or persons seeking judicial review to demonstrate the requisite *locus standi*. The rules developed by the courts in this area have, until more recently, been restrictive and have in a number of instances been to the detriment of environmental pressure groups.

The case of *R v Secretary of State for the Environment, ex p Rose Theatre Trust* (1990) illustrates the restrictive approach to judicial review actions brought by pressure groups on public interest and environmental protection matters. Developers

6.4.3	*Rose Theatre Trust*: the restrictive approach

had been granted planning permission to build an office block on the site of an Elizabethan theatre, the Rose Theatre, in London. A Trust company had been set up by numerous campaigners to preserve the ruins of the Theatre, which was of particular historical importance because it boasted two first performances of Shakespeare's plays. The Rose Theatre Trust sought to persuade the Secretary of State to designate the site as one of national importance and include it in the list of monuments under the Ancient Monuments and Archaeological Areas Act 1979. If the Secretary of State had done this, it would have meant that no work could begin on the site without his consent. The Secretary of State agreed that the site was of national importance but decided that it would not fall within the relevant legislation. The Theatre Trust brought the action for judicial review alleging the illegality of the Secretary of State's decision. The question was whether or not the Trust had:

> '... "sufficient interest" to bring such an action. Members of the Trust argued that since they had entered into correspondence with the Secretary of State they had the necessary interest. However, the Court found that the Trust did not have *locus standi*. In reaching this decision, the court held that a challenger must show that he has: "sufficient interest in the application to which the matter relates".'

Schiemann J stated that it was necessary to consider the Statute to determine whether it afforded standing to these individuals in this instance. On the facts of the case, the court held that no individual could point to anything in the Statute that would serve to give them a greater right or interest than any other that the decision would be taken lawfully. The case resulted in a great deal of criticism and was a blow to the notion of public interest litigation. Among other things, in the Rose Theatre case it appeared that the court was not concerned that no one could sue in such a situation, leaving the decision of the Secretary of State beyond rebuke.

The restrictive approach laid down in *Rose Theatre Trust* was, however, not followed in the judicial review action brought by the pressure group Greenpeace against HMIP in which the court was willing to grant *locus standi* to Greenpeace.

6.4.4   The *Greenpeace* case

This case (*R v Her Majesty's Inspector of Pollution, ex p Greenpeace (No 2) (1994)*) involved a challenge brought by Greenpeace against the decision by HMIP in relation to the THORP reprocessing plant at Sellafield. British Nuclear Fuels Ltd (BNFL) argued that Greenpeace had failed to establish a sufficient interest and that their application should be set aside. However, this argument was not accepted by the Court. Mr Justice Otton held Greenpeace was an eminently respectable and responsible organisation and that their genuine interest in the matter was sufficient for them to be granted *locus standi*. In reaching this welcome decision, the Court took into account the following of factors:

- the nature of Greenpeace as a campaigning group whose prime objective was the protection of the environment;

- the fact that Greenpeace had been accredited by the United Nations and several other international bodies.

Mr Justice Otton went on to say that a denial of standing would mean that the people represented by Greenpeace would not have 'an effective way to bring the issues before the court'. In saying this, Otton J declined to follow the decision in *Rose Theatre Trust* where the court was seemingly unconcerned about this particular issue. Otton J stated that a denial of standing to Greenpeace would have meant that an application for judicial review would have had to have been brought either by an individual employee of BNFL or a near neighbour. Neither would have had the resources or the expertise to bring such an action and this would have resulted in a less well-informed challenge which would have stretched the court's resources.

The decision in this case is greatly welcomed. With a less restrictive view on the sufficient interest requirement, environmental pressure groups such as Greenpeace, which represent people who are directly affected by the challenged decision or action, are more likely to succeed in achieving *locus standi*. However, a note of caution: in the judgment, the court referred to the advantages of an application from Greenpeace who, with its particular experience in environmental matters and its access to experts in the realms of science, technology and law, could bring a focused relevant and well-argued challenge. It seems, therefore, that the larger national or international groupings are more likely to satisfy the test than small *ad hoc* or localised groups without the benefit of a 'deep-pocket' and expert back-up.

The trend towards recognising the standing of pressure groups was given further support in the case *R v Secretary of State for Foreign Affairs, ex p World Development Movement Ltd* (1995). Rose LJ held that the World Development Fund had sufficient interest to challenge the government's aid for the Pergau dam scheme, on the basis that there were few other parties that could challenge the decision and also because of the prominence of the World Development Movement in the protection of aid to under developed countries.

| 6.4.5 | Law Commission recommendations on standing of pressure groups |

The case law on *locus standi* is complex and it is, *inter alia*, why the Law Commission in 1994 has recommended a streamlining of judicial review procedures to make them more accessible and effective. The Commission has in particular made a number of recommendations about *locus standi*. The rules on standing should make it clear that, in appropriate cases, applications for judicial review may be brought by interest groups as well as individuals adversely affected by a decisions and that un-incorporated associations should be permitted to seek judicial review in their own names through a member applying in a representative capacity.

One further problem which warrants consideration is the fact that the rules on standing vary considerably throughout the different Member States within the EC. In practice therefore, pressure groups may be able to bring judicial review proceedings to secure compliance with environmental law in one Member State but may not be able to do so in another. Some countries throughout the world have established that environmental pressure groups have a right of action without the need to show any material or legal interest.

6.5 Private prosecutions

The enforcement of environmental law is not the monopoly of the pollution control authorities. Their lack of resources to monitor and deal with all incidents has already been commented upon. Neither the NRA, HMIP or, indeed, the local authorities exercising their pollution control functions, have the financial or manpower resources to ensure full enforcement of the environmental controls laid down in statute or in the permissive authorisations granted. It is for these reasons that the individuals and pressure groups can play an extremely important role in the enforcement of environmental law by bringing private criminal prosecutions. The environmental legislation considered in this book contains a number of provisions which enable citizens to bring their own prosecutions against those who commit offences under the specific legislation. The Environmental Protection Act 1990, for example, provides considerable scope for citizens to bring private prosecutions (except in the case of Part IV of the Act, which deals with genetically modified organisms). However, it appears that these rights have not been widely recognised or taken up. There are several reasons why this might be the case and these will be returned to below.

At common law it is a well-established rule that a citizen has the right to bring a private prosecution under an Act of Parliament. This was stated in the case of *R v Stewart* (1896). The High Court allowed a private prosecution to be brought by the Royal Society for the Prevention of Cruelty to Animals under the Diseases of Animals Act 1894. The Court held that a citizen has a right to prosecute under any Statute unless an Act specifically precludes that right in clear words. Various Statutes do specifically provide provisions which explicitly give individuals the right to enforce the statutory provisions by means of private prosecutions and clearly these rights are of particular importance in the context of pressure groups and the environment. But even in the absence of a specific statutory provision, an individual or pressure group can still bring a private prosecution under an Act of Parliament, providing that the Act does not expressly and clearly preclude such a right.

In the context of environmental protection where most businesses have statutory authority to pollute to some extent (in accordance with the conditions imposed in authorisations etc), it is necessary to establish whether an offence has been committed. Access to information about polluting activities is essential, and the Public Registers described below should provide the information necessary in order to assist people in identifying the firms or businesses that are committing offences. From the information on the registers, it should be possible, for example, to ascertain who is responsible for a particular discharge into a river, what the discharge consent conditions are, whether there has been any monitoring, any notices served, or previous offences. Where a person or group of persons believes that an offence has been committed, is being committed or is likely to be committed, the easiest and cheapest course of action will be to complain to the regulatory authority and ask them to take enforcement action. It has already been stated that the pollution control authorities do not have the resources to monitor every discharge or emission all of the time and they therefore rely on reports and complaints brought by people in this respect. For instance, the Anglers' Associations will often be the first to draw the NRAs attention to pollution incidents and fish kills. In fact, the NRA has a 24-hour hot-line telephone number for people to report incidents to them.

However, the alternative course of action is for an individual or pressure group to bring a private prosecution (often using the information obtained from the public registers). An example of a statutory right to bring a private prosecution is s 79 EPA where the aggrieved citizen is given

6.5.1   The right to bring a
private prosecution

the right to prosecute statutory nuisances. This is one of the more well known 'rights' and is covered in Chapter 14 on Statutory Nuisance.

6.5.2	Problems for private prosecutors

Although private prosecutions are becoming more commonplace, there are a number of problems associated with starting such litigation which has resulted in a relatively limited number of cases. It may not always be necessary to commence a legal action; it is possible that the threat of litigation will produce the desired results. The financial cost of commencing a criminal prosecution must be taken into account. Very often, prosecutors will need to employ scientific evidence to 'prove beyond reasonable doubt' that the defendant was responsible for the offence. The legal costs will also be considerable.

Problems arise in relation to admissible evidence. Private prosecutors are not entitled, like the pollution control authorities, to enter premises and take samples, records etc. They therefore have to rely on other evidence, such as samples taken by the individuals themselves at points of discharge and information on the public registers.

6.6   Environmental protest

Most environmental protest is peaceful and involves people from a wide cross-section of society and across all age groups. Protest can take many forms, ranging from exercising purchasing power in favour of 'green' or 'ecological' products, such as recycled toilet rolls and organic vegetables, to demonstrating in the streets and preventing work being undertaken that is going to destroy the environment. The rise of green consumerism and the demand for environmentally-friendly products and, indeed, services is a powerful weapon. Companies are increasingly taking steps to improve their environmental record and image in order to capture the increasing market. Even financial institutions, such as the Co-operative Bank, promote themselves to consumers as the 'greenest', and many major retailers, such as IKEA and B&Q, promote their green credentials.

6.6.1	The right to protest?

In recent times, certain environmental protests have attracted considerable media attention, particularly in circumstances where protesters have 'occupied' land to prevent a development going ahead, or have blocked pipes in order to prevent the discharge of dangerous substances into the sea. The protest at Twyford Down is one particular example. Environmental protest has not generally been violent, unlike some of the protests and demonstrations, for example, against the Community Charge where, at times, considerable disorder resulted. Instead, environmental protest has been generally very peaceful. However, where protest involves some form of public disorder then the police will be able to resort to powers under the Public Order Act 1986 or other provisions such as the Highways Acts 1980 and 1986. Environmental protesters are not immune from the occasional examples of disorder and they will be subject to the same repercussions as any other protester committing a breach of the peace or an obstruction of the highway.

One of the most important, if not *the* most important, requisites for individuals and pressure groups to take action is that they are equipped with the necessary information. There is a view that public access to information on the environment lends itself to improved environmental protection. Since most environmental offences involve the carrying out of unauthorised activities, the public needs to have access to information to ascertain whether the activity is authorised or not and, if it *is* authorised, whether all of the conditions attached to the authorisation are being complied with. Environmental information may also be used for less litigious purposes, for instance by consumers to identify the environmental track record of certain companies. Businesses have traditionally favoured less disclosure of information and have perceived the registers as a threat. The various provisions do allow certain information to be excluded from the public, but these provisions do not offer the opportunity for firms to exclude information simply on the grounds that it would be detrimental to their image.

6.7   Access to information

The Royal Commission on Environmental Pollution can take much of the credit for ensuring the introduction of statutory provisions which established the creation of publicly accessible registers relating to pollution controls. The Royal Commission on Environmental Pollution, in its Second Report, suggested that the arguments in favour of retaining environmental information on a confidential basis were not well founded:

6.7.1   Royal Commission on Environmental Pollution

> 'We doubt some of the reasons for this confidentiality and our doubts are shared by many of the witnesses from industry with whom we have spoken. It is a practice which on occasion hinders the flow of information and it leads to risks of misunderstanding on the part of the public which may be harmful to industry and government alike.'

In its Tenth Report the Royal Commission recommended that the public should be entitled to the fullest possible information on all forms of environmental pollution and that the onus should be placed on the polluter to substantiate a claim for exceptional treatment. It accordingly recommended that a guiding principle behind all legislative and administrative controls relating to environmental pollution should be a presumption in favour of unrestricted access for the public to information which the pollution control authorities receive by virtue of their statutory powers, with protection for secrecy only in those circumstances where a genuine case can be substantiated. It was also suggested that cases where genuine secrets are involved are, in fact, comparatively rare.

The basic premise of the Royal Commission's arguments is that the public has a right to know, that there is a need to restore public confidence in the enforcement system and, importantly, that the public has a beneficial interest in the environment.

The Environmental Protection Act 1990 introduced important new provisions requiring that information held by the regulatory bodies empowered by the Act be available for inspection by the public. The stated aim was that:

> 'Information must be freely available. Unnecessary secrecy undermines public confidence that pollution has been properly controlled. The new system of public registers which the Act introduces will increases confidence in pollution control. Furthermore it will facilitate public participation in helping to protect the environment. It will mean that every individual can become an environmental watchdog in his or her own right.'

The following sections of this chapter will look in detail at the various statutory provisions which provide for both publicity and access to information. It will consider:

- provisions under the Environmental Protection Act 1990 relating to Integrated Pollution Control, Local Authority Air Pollution Control and Waste Management;

- provisions under the Water Resources Act 1991;

- Environmental Information Regulations 1992.

Both the EPA and the Water Resources Act provide for the creation of public registers, maintained by the regulatory authorities. The registers are required to be available for inspection at all reasonable times and copies of entries can be obtained for a reasonable charge. The specific statutory provisions are further supplemented by the Environmental Information Regulations which are described in detail. In relation to all of these provisions, information may be excluded from the registers on the grounds that its disclosure would be a threat to national security or breach commercial confidentiality.

Sections 20–22 EPA are concerned with the establishment of public registers of information and apply to both Part A processes controlled by HMIP and Part B processes controlled by local authorities. It should be noted that the registers held by the local authorities include information pertaining to the LAAPC processes and any Part A process controlled by HMIP which operate within their local authority boundary. In addition HMIP are required to provide the NRA with any details of discharges into controlled waters from prescribed processes, so that the NRA can include this information on their registers. The Environmental Protection (Applications, Appeals and Registers) Regulations 1991 supplement these provisions.

6.7.2   The Environmental Protection Act: IPC and LAAPC

These registers must be freely available to the public for inspection at all reasonable times. If members of the public wish to take copies of the documents, they will be permitted to do so for a reasonable charge. The Act does not define what constitutes a reasonable charge. The registers may be kept in any form.

The register contains details of:

- any application for an authorisation made to the authority;

- any representations made by any person required to be consulted by the authority;

- all authorisations granted;

- any application for the variation of the conditions of an authorisation under s 11(4)(b) of the Act;

- any variation notice, enforcement notice or prohibition notice issued by the authority;

- any revocation of an authorisation affected by the authority;

- any appeals made under s 15 EPA against a decision by the enforcing authority including details of the Secretary of State's determination of the appeal;

- any conviction of any person for any offence under s 23(1) of the Act including the name of the offender, the date of conviction, the penalty imposed and the name of the court;

- monitoring information obtained or provided which relates to the conditions of the authorisation;

- in a case where any such monitoring information is omitted from the register by virtue of its commercial confidentiality under s 22, a statement by the authority, based on the monitoring information obtained or provided to them, indicating whether or not there has been compliance with any relevant condition of the authorisation;

- directions given by the Secretary of State to the enforcing authority;

- any notice served on the applicant by the authority and of any information furnished in response to such a notice;

- any report published by an enforcing authority relating to an assessment of the environmental consequences of the carrying on of a prescribed process in the locality of premises where the prescribed process is carried on under an authorisation granted by the authority.

6.7.3	Environmental Protection Act: waste disposal

Similar provisions exist in relation to the information held by the Waste Regulatory Authorities which exercise powers under Part III EPA. Each Waste Regulatory Authority is under a duty, by virtue of s 64 to maintain a register containing details of:

- current or recently current licences granted by the authority;

- applications made to the authority for licences;

- applications for modification of licence;

- notices issued by the WRA effecting the modification, revocation or suspension of a licence or imposing requirements on a licence-holder;

- appeals against decisions of the WRA under s 43;

- certificates of completion issued by the WRA;

- of any offence on the part of the licence-holder;

- any action take by the WRA under ss 42 or 61 EPA;

- directions issued by the Secretary of State;

- such matters relating to the treatment, keeping or disposal of waste in the authority's area or any pollution of the Environment caused thereby;

- where any information is excluded by virtue of s 66 a statement indicating the existence of that information.

Provisions exist in relation to both the IPC/LAAPC registers and the Waste Licensing registers for information to be excluded either on the grounds of national security or commercial confidentiality.

- Exclusion on the grounds of national security: s 21 EPA (in relation to IPC/LAAPC) and s 65 EPA (waste) provide that information should be excluded if the Secretary of State determines that its disclosure would be contrary to national security. Alternatively, an applicant can make an application to exclude the information on the grounds that it is contrary to national security. In this instance, the Secretary of State must be notified. In both these circumstances there will be no reference to the excluded information in the register.

- In addition, ss 22 and 66 EPA allow information to be excluded if its disclosure would prejudice, to an unreasonable degree, the commercial interests of a person. An application can be made to HMIP, the local authority or the WRA for information to be excluded from the register and this is usually done at the same time as the application is made for the authorisation or Waste Management Licence. The enforcing authority has responsibility for determining what is commercially confidential (with a right of appeal to the Secretary of State) and it has 14 days to decide whether or not to exclude the information. If it fails to make a determination after 14 days, it is deemed to have decided that the information is commercially confidential and should be excluded. Where the authority decides that the information is not commercially confidential, it must give the applicant 21 days to appeal the Secretary of State. Where commercially confidential information is excluded, the register may still contain an outline description of the process. The Secretary of State also has the power to issue direct that certain information may be excluded.

Whether information will be regarded as commercially confidential depends upon whether it would prejudice, to an unreasonable degree, the commercial interests of the person concerned.

The Water Resources Act, like the EPA, makes specific provision for the maintenance of public registers relating to water pollution. The NRA is under a duty to keep public registers which must be available for inspection by the public at all reasonable times. Where an application for a discharge consent is made, the NRA must enter the details on the

6.7.4   EPA – exclusion of information from the public registers

6.7.5   Public registers relating to water pollution

register within 28 days. The register should provide the following information:

- details of any notices of water quality objectives or other notices served under s 83 WRA 1991;

- details of applications made for discharge consents;

- details of the consent, plus any conditions attached;

- the maximum levels of substances to be contained in the effluent;

- any notices served on the consent holder and any time limits;

- details of any samples of water or effluent taken by the NRA;

- the steps taken as a result of any sample taken;

- details of any discharges into controlled water which are controlled by HMIP under the system of Integrated Pollution Control;

- details of any directions issued by the Secretary of State.

Sampling information includes the content of effluent as taken, where the sample was taken from, date of sample, time of day and whether any action was required to be taken by NRA. Sampling information must be placed within two months of the sample if taken by NRA; or if taken by others, not more than 28 days from receipt of the information by the NRA. The register must also state whether the sample has been taken in compliance with the tripartite sampling requirements under s 219.

Any entry on the register has to be kept for five years; thereafter, only if it is necessary for the exercise of the NRA's pollution control function.

| 6.7.6 | Exclusions |

The Secretary of State can issue a certificate to exclude information where it would be contrary to the public interest to make it public, or where it is a trade secret.

| 6.7.7 | Other information in relation to water |

In addition to the pollution control registers, other public registers exist relating to trade effluent consents and are held by the sewerage undertakers (Water Industry Act 1991, s 196). Details of private water companies are held by the Director General of Water Services (Water Industry Act 1991 s 195). Information on abstraction and impounding licences is held which can provide further information about the water industry by the NRA under s 189 of Water Resources Act 1991.

In addition to the registers described above, pressure groups and individuals can obtain additional information from other sources, including environmental information held by local authorities. This should be available to the general public under the Local Government (Access to Information) Act 1985. In addition, the Clean Air Act 1993 provides that local authorities have powers to arrange for research and publicity with regard to air pollution. However, under s 34(2) it is a criminal offence to disclose any information obtained under the Clean Air Act provisions which is a trade secret. Details of hazardous substances consents can be found in registers maintained by the Hazardous Substances Authorities who are under a duty to maintain the registers by virtue of s 28 Hazardous Substances Act 1990.

6.7.8 Other sources of environmental information

In addition to these specific provisions for the establishment of public registers, the environmental Information Regulations 1992 make further provisions for the freedom of access to information on the environment held by public bodies. The requirements of the Directive go beyond the system of public registers; however, they are subject to a number of weaknesses. In particular, they include a long list of exceptions and provide no statutory right of appeal against a refusal to provide information.

6.8 Environmental Information Regulations 1992

The Regulations give effect to Directive 90/313 on Freedom of Access to Information on the Environment. They place a duty on 'every relevant person' who holds any information to which the Regulation applies to make the information available to every person who requests it, subject to the exceptions listed. The person supplying the information can make a charge for the supply of the information.

By reg 2(1) the Regulation applies to any information which relates to the environment. Information relates to the environment if, and only if, it relates to any of the following:

(a) the state of any water or air, the state of flora or fauna, the state of any soil or the state of any natural site or other land;

(b) any activities or measures giving rise to noise or any other nuisance which adversely affect anything mentioned in sub-para (a) above or are likely adversely to affect anything so mentioned;

(c) any activities or administrative or other measures (including any environmental management programmes) which are designed to protect anything so mentioned.

6.8.1	Information	Information includes anything contained in records; it therefore includes information held in registers, reports and returns, as well as computer records or other records kept otherwise than in a document.

| 6.8.2 | Relevant persons | The duty to furnish information is placed on 'relevant persons'. They are defined in the regulations as Ministers of the Crown, government departments, local authorities and other persons carrying out functions of public administration at a national, regional or local level and which have responsibilities in relation to the environment. The definition has a second limb and a person or organisation may be a relevant person if they have public responsibilities for the environment which do not fall within the above description but is under the control of a person falling within that description. This second limb is capable of including the privatised water companies and sewerage undertakers which have environmental responsibilities and are in the control of Ministers of the Crown and the NRA. In *Unison v South West Water* (1994), it was held that South West Water was an emanation of the State for the purposes of an EC Directive concerned with employment rights. It would therefore seem to follow that the water companies may also be subject to the regulations. However, this particular point has not yet been considered by the courts. |

It is clear that the definition includes information held by the Department of the Environment and the local authorities in their various capacities as well as the NRA and HMIP.

6.8.3	The duty to make information available	The duty to make information available is owed to the person requesting the information. Those persons or organisations that are subject to the duty to make information available must ensure that:

- every request made for information is responded to as soon as possible;

- no such request is responded to more than two months after it is made;

- where the response to such a request contains a refusal to make information available, the refusal is in writing and specifies the reasons for the refusal.

However the regulations make provision for the relevant person, subject to the duty, to:

- refuse a request for information in cases where a request is manifestly unreasonable or is formulated in too general a manner;

- impose a charge in respect of the costs reasonably attributable to the supply of the information;

- make the supply of any information conditional on the payment of such a charge;

- make the information available in such a form, and at such times and places, as may be reasonable.

The regulations allow for certain categories of information to be excluded from the requirements of disclosure. A distinction is drawn between information which must be excluded and other information which may be exluded depending upon the exercise of discretion by the relevant person holding the information.

6.8.4   Exceptions to
disclosure

Certain information must be regarded as confidential and therefore cannot be disclosed. It will be treated as such if:

- the information is treated as confidential and its disclosure in response to a request for information would contravene any statutory provision or a rule of law or would involve a breach of any agreement;

- the information is personal information contained in records held in relation to an individual who has not given his consent to disclosure;

- the information is held by the relevant person in consequence of having been supplied by a person who was not under, and could not have been put under, any legal obligation to supply it to the relevant person and has not consented to its disclosure;

- the disclosure of the information in response to that request would, in the circumstances, increase the likelihood of damage to the environment affecting anything to which the information relates.

In addition information may be treated as confidential in the following circumstances:

- information relating to matters affecting international relations, national defense or public security;

- information relating to, or to anything which is or has been the subject of, any legal or other proceedings (whether actual or prospective);

- information relating to the confidential deliberations of any relevant person or to the contents of any internal communications of a body corporate or other undertaking or organisation;

- information contained in a document or other record which is still in the course of completion;

- information affecting matters to which any commercial or industrial confidentiality attaches or any intellectual property.

6.8.5   Right of appeal

The regulations do not provide any specific right of appeal against a refusal to supply information. However, it is possible that a person could seek judicial review of a decision to refuse since the person from whom the information is requested is under a duty to provide it. Unfortunately, mounting a judicial review action is both difficult and expensive and it is unlikely that many individuals or pressure groups will seek this course of action. It was on this particular point that Friends of the Earth complained to the European Commission alleging inadequate implementation of the Directive.

Pressure Groups, Individuals and the Environment and Access to Information

The participation of citizens in the protection of the environment is recognised at international, European Community and national level. Inextricably linked with the desire to encourage and promote public participation is the recognition that access to information is vital.

Recognition of the need for public participation

Environmental pressure groups have been able to exert influence on the development of environmental law and policy particularly at the European level by lobbying.

Environmental pressure groups

Individuals and pressure groups can seek to ensure compliance with EC and domestic environmental law in the following ways:

- Complaining directly to the European Commission to persuade the Commission to take direct action against a Member State under the Art 169 procedure;

- Ensuring that the EC institutions themselves comply with the Treaty and EC Environmental law through an application for judicial review by the ECJ under Arts 173 and 175 EC Treaty;

- By means of judicial review in the national courts. This raises problems of legal standing and not all pressure groups will be able to satisfy the courts that they have the necessary sufficient interest. However the courts have shown a greater willingness to grant *locus standi* to the more well resourced and organised pressure groups such as Greenpeace;

- Individuals and pressure groups can bring private criminal prosecutions against persons committing environmental offences. However, in view of the burden of proof involved in criminal prosecutions and the legal costs involved, this again affords a limited opportunity;

- Consumers have been able to exert influence through their purchasing power. the demand for 'green products' and 'environmentally friendly' companies. This has shown itself to be a powerful tool in environmental protection and many companies are keen to promote their 'green credentials'.

Access to information

Access to information is vital. It is accepted that promoting better access to environmental information can improve environmental protection. Information on the state of the environment can be found in the public registers established under:

- Sections 20 and 63 EPA in relation to IPC/LAAPC and Waste Management licences;

- The Water Resources Act 1991.

Some information may be excluded on the basis of national security or commercial confidentiality.

Environmental Information Regulations 1992

The Environmental Information Regulations 1992 make further provision for environmental information to be made available to any person requesting it.

Chapter 7

Atmospheric Pollution

Atmospheric pollution is controlled by law in a number of ways and by means of various statutes, statutory instruments and EC Directives. The main controls are to be found in the Environmental Protection Act 1990 which has established a two-tier system of controlling emissions into the atmosphere from certain prescribed industrial processes; Integrated Pollution Control for the most seriously polluting processes and Local Authority Air Pollution Control for others (see Chapter 9). In addition, the provisions of the Clean Air Act 1993 deal with the emissions of dark smoke, grit and dust, and provide for the creation of Smoke Control Areas. The Environmental Protection Act also provides that certain emissions into the atmosphere (including odours and steam) may, if they are prejudicial to health or a nuisance, constitute a statutory nuisance and be controlled accordingly (see Chapter 14). The EC has also legislated to control air pollution, particularly in response to the transboundary nature of air pollution. It has enacted various EC Directives that establish minimum air quality standards and emission limits for certain products.

7.1 Introduction

Jonathan Porritt, in his book *Where on earth are we going?*, makes the claim that 'one day's breathing in Bombay is equivalent to smoking ten cigarettes'. Most people are aware of the health risks associated with smoking and have the choice as to whether or not they smoke. Unfortunately, we cannot exercise that choice about the air we breathe. The statistic quoted by Jonathan Porritt should not leave any room for complacency. The problems associated with air pollution are not confined to other parts of the world. Air pollution is a global problem. It affects all areas of the world, even rural and third world countries that are either affected by growing industrialisation or the consequences of pollution elsewhere. Because of the global nature of air pollution an international response is required. The international dimension is considered more fully below at para 7.10.

7.2 Problems of air pollution

Pollution of the atmosphere has long-term adverse environmental effects as well as damaging human health.

Air pollution is a global environmental issue. The depletion of the ozone layer, acid rain and climate change are issues high on the international agenda. Acid rain is created by the release

7.2.1 Environmental consequences, acid rain and global warming

of certain gases into the atmosphere: sulphur dioxide (SO_2), nitric oxide (NO) and nitrogen dioxide (NO_2). Together, NO and NO_2 are known as NO^x. In addition, ammonia, ozone and hydrocarbons also contribute to the formation of acid rain. Chris Rose, in his excellent book, *The Dirty Man of Europe*, makes the following statement:

'But Britain, too, has been quietly ravaged by acid rain. In the UK, lakes in Snowdonia National Park, most of mid-Wales, the Lake District, Cairngorms, Pennines and even on the Surrey heaths, are dead or dying from acidity. Peat lands, for which the UK is internationally important, and probably heaths, are being changed beyond recognition.'

Britain remains the Dirty Man of Europe so far as SO_2 and NO^x pollution is concerned, and will do so even when the EC Large Plant Directive is implemented by 2003.

The UK Government has published a strategy document on Climate Change in order to set out how it intends to fulfil its commitment to the 1992 Convention on Climate Change. The strategy includes a programme to control CO_2 emissions in order to reduce emissions to 1990 levels by the year 2000. However recent official projections suggest that, in fact, the UK's annual CO_2 emissions will rise from 158,000,000 to 168,000,000 tonnes between 1990 and 2000. Included in the range of measures designed to reach the targets is the introduction of VAT on domestic fuel and power and increased duty on petrol.

7.2.2	**Health problems associated with air pollution**

There has been considerable publicity about the links between air pollution and health. There appears to be a growing body of evidence which strengthens the link between exposure to particular pollutants and ill-health.

The air that we breath is a precious commodity. Pollution of it can result in breathing difficulties, increased incidence of asthma, cancer and even death. The relationship between various pollutants and different diseases is often disputed. However, considerable research has been carried out by a variety of organisations into various medical aspects of air pollution.

The Department of Health has its own expert Advisory Group on the Medical Aspects of Air Pollution Episodes (MAAPE). Since 1991, it has produced three reports on the relationship between health and the emissions of ozone; sulphur dioxide, acid aerosols and particulates; and oxides of nitrogen. The Committee on the Medical Effects of Air Pollutants (COMEAP) has also been asked by the Department of Health to advise on the possible links between asthma and air pollution because of concerns about a possible link between changing patterns of air pollution and increased General Practitioner consultations and hospital admissions for asthma. The Committee is due to report in 1995. As evidence of this growing concern the Department of Health and Department of the Environment have jointly supported the establishment of The Medical Research Council Institute for Environment and Health. Its function is to research the links between environmental quality and health and is collaborating with the World Health Organisation (WHO) on the possible effects of certain air pollutants.

The United States Environmental Protection Agency has carried out its own research which suggests that the emission of dioxins into the atmosphere can pose serious health risks. In particular, it suggests that dioxins can adversely affect development, reproduction and the immune system. However, the UK government appears to remain unconvinced about such findings. Major sources of dioxin emissions are from diesel combustion and steel-making.

Benzene, which is emitted into the atmosphere from vehicle exhausts and as a result of petrol evaporating (for example during vehicle refuelling) is a known human carcinogen.

The problems of air pollution are not new. Legislation aimed at controlling the acidic emissions from alkali works dates back to 1863, with the enactment of the Alkali Act 1863. The Act, like so many that followed it, was reactive; it was introduced following the recommendations of a Royal Commission to deal with the serious problems of pollution resulting from alkali works. Alkali works, in particular, were responsible for very damaging emissions of hydrochloric acid gas in large quantities. The 1863 Act was extended in scope in the Alkali Act of 1874, and both were consolidated in 1906 with the Alkali Works Regulation Act 1906. Among other things, this early legislation resulted in the appointment of an Alkali Inspector who was responsible for regulating alkali processes and the establishment of the concept of Best Practicable Means (see Chapter 1). The provisions of the 1906 Act are largely being phased oy by the programme of authorisations under the Environmental Protection Act (see Chapter 9). The 1906 Act still applies to those processes that have not yet been authorised under the IPC regime. HMIP has responsibility for enforcing the remaining Alkali Works Regulation Act provisions.

Legislation aimed at controlling smoke emissions was later introduced in the Public Health Acts of 1875 and 1936,

7.2.3   Historic controls

and also the Public Health (Smoke Abatement) Act 1926. These Acts were not successful in dealing with the problems of smoke pollution, and it was not until the Clean Air Act of 1956 that there was a comprehensive attempt to control all smoke emissions from domestic fires and commercial and industrial premises.

The Clean Air Act 1956, like the earlier legislation, was introduced to combat an existing air pollution problem. In 1952, some 4,000 people lost their lives as a result of the 'Great Smog'. Smogs, which occur more frequently now in countries like India, occur when fog combines with smoke particles. The result is that the fog is very dense (smog is a very apt description: it is really a smoke-filled fog) and visibility is reduced. A more serious consequence of smog, and the Great Smog in particular, is the impact on health. The Clean Air Act was introduced, and brought into effect some of the recommendations of the Beaver Committee which had produced a report, at the behest of the government, on the difficulties of controlling pollution from smoke. The Clean Air Act was extended in scope by the Clean Air Act 1968 and the provisions have now largely been consolidated in the Clean Air Act 1993, which is considered in more detail below.

| 7.3 | **Government policy and proposals for the future** | The government's policy in relation to air pollution is set out in *This Common Inheritance*. It is essentially concerned with the protection of public health. In the second-year report on the government's programme, there is a commitment to further action to reduce air pollution. In particular, it is suggested that, in addition to traditional legal controls, the government will also explore the use of different economic instruments. For example, measures to ensure that charges incurred by transport users reflect the full costs of the journeys. These costs include the costs to the environment. The proposed landfill tax in relation to waste is a further example of how economic and fiscal measures can be employed to reduce pollution or encourage recycling. |

7.3   **Government policy and proposals for the future**

The government's policy in relation to air pollution is set out in *This Common Inheritance*. It is essentially concerned with the protection of public health. In the second-year report on the government's programme, there is a commitment to further action to reduce air pollution. In particular, it is suggested that, in addition to traditional legal controls, the government will also explore the use of different economic instruments. For example, measures to ensure that charges incurred by transport users reflect the full costs of the journeys. These costs include the costs to the environment. The proposed landfill tax in relation to waste is a further example of how economic and fiscal measures can be employed to reduce pollution or encourage recycling.

7.3.1   *Air Quality: Meeting the Challenge*

More recently, the government has published its future proposals in the document, *Air Quality: Meeting the Challenge* which followed a discussion paper *Improving Air Quality*. The proposals include:

1   A new framework of national air quality standards and targets. Two main levels of air quality are proposed:
   - the first is a long-term target in which nine key pollutants will be rendered harmless to health and the environment. This target will be achieved through

measures such as the introduction of new plant and machinery;

- the second level is essentially a trigger or alert threshold which indicates when air quality is so poor that an immediate response would be justified to prevent serious damage to health. Such measures might include banning cars from city centres. Local authorities already have the legal powers to impose traffic restrictions, but as yet they have not used these powers to protect air quality.

The government is considering whether these targets should be placed on a statutory footing. The advantage of prescribing the targets in regulations is that they would then need to be secured through the system of control under Part I of the Environmental Protection Act. Section 7 of the EPA requires that conditions are attached to authorisations which enable statutory environmental qualities to be met. Pressure groups such as Friends of the Earth and the Clean Air Society maintain that the system will not work unless the targets are enshrined by law.

2   The second proposal is to establish a framework for local air quality management and, in particular, to concentrate action on those local areas where progress is slow in reaching the targets. It is proposed that local authorities will be responsible for reviewing air quality and that they will be under a duty to designate Air Quality Management Areas (AQMAs) if they are not attaining the air quality targets. The AQMAs would be controlled in a similar fashion to the Smoke Control Areas (see below at para 7.6.12). There are some doubts as to whether local authorities will have the resources to carry out these additional functions.

Local authorities will be required to draw up Air Quality Management Plans which set out their proposals for meeting air quality targets.

3   Vehicle emissions are seen as a major contributor to air pollution and the strategy suggests an action plan for transport to reduce the contribution of road transport to air pollution, particularly in urban areas. In AQMAs, local authorities will be required to appraise their development and transport policies against an air quality assessment. Planning Policy Guidance Note 23 on Planning and Pollution Control will be revised to reflect these changes. Planning Policy Guidance Note 13 on Planning and Transport already recognises the relationship between planning transport uses and air quality; however, it is not

clear to what extent its recommendations are currently being delivered through the system of development plans.

7.4   Current legislation

The local authorities (the district councils, London Borough Councils or the metropolitan districts), through their Environmental Health Departments and officers, play a key role in controlling air pollution. They are involved in three areas of air pollution control:

- providing authorisation for industrial processes governed by the Local Authority Air Pollution Controls contained in Part I EPA (see Chapter 9);

- enforcing the provisions of the Clean Air Act 1993;

- enforcing the provisions of Part 3 of the EPA in relation to those statutory nuisances which have an impact on the quality of air (see Chapter 14).

Emissions into the air are also controlled by Her Majesty's Inspectorate of Pollution thorough the system of Integrated Pollution Control described in Chapter 9. HMIP regulates the most seriously polluting industrial processes and, in doing so, controls not only emissions into air but also discharges into water or on land in order to secure the best practical environmental option.

Other controls exist under:

- The Health and Safety at Work Act 1974;

- European Community legislation;

- International Conventions and Protocols.

7.5   Local authority air pollution control

Local authorities are responsible for controlling the atmospheric emissions of certain prescribed industrial processes. Usually, it will be the district council or the London Borough Council that exercises these powers. Part I of the Environmental Protection Act establishes a two-tier system of control over certain prescribed industrial processes. Processes are prescribed for control under either system by the Secretary of State for the Environment by means of regulation. The Environmental Protection (Prescribed Processes and Substances) Regulations (as amended) identify those processes which fall under the central control of Her Majesty's Inspectorate of Pollution or the control of the relevant local authority. Part B processes in the regulations fall under the latter. In 1993/94, 903 applications for LAAPC authorisation were received by local authorities, bringing the total to date up to 13,778 applications. Unlike the IPC system, which is subject to a phased programme, the system of LAAPC has been fully implemented.

Where a process falls into Part B of the regulations, it must seek authorisation from the local authority in whose area the process is based. Local authorities are required to regulate the process so as to prevent or minimise the pollution of the environment due to the release of prescribed substances into the air. The system of LAAPC only permits the local authority to control atmospheric emissions, whereas the central system of Integrated Pollution Control enables the control of substances into all environmental media to secure the Best Practical Environmental Option (BPEO).

In regulating these prescribed processes, local authorities have the power to set down conditions in authorisations which secure the objectives laid down in s 7 of the EPA. In particular, processes should use the best available techniques not entailing excessive costs (BATNEEC) to prevent the release of substances into the air or, where that is not practicable by such means, to reduce the release to a minimum and to render harmless any substances that are released.

Local authorities enjoy the various powers of enforcement which HMIP exert in relation to the processes regulated under Part I EPA. Local authority inspectors also have the same powers as HMIP inspectors. These are described in Chapter 9.

It has already been stated that the first legislative controls over atmospheric emissions date back to the Alkali Act 1863. This early legislation did not however control the emissions of smoke from industrial processes. The use of coal and the consequent emissions of smoke and grit particles resulted in serious pollution problems and also health problems. The Public Health (Smoke Abatement) Act of 1926 testifies to the public health problems that smoke pollution can cause. However, it was not until the Clean Air Acts of 1956 and 1968 that there was any comprehensive attempt to control emissions of smoke, dust and grit from industrial premises The Clean Air Act 1956 was introduced to prohibit the emission of dark smoke from any domestic or industrial chimney. A chimney was defined as any structure or opening through which smoke is emitted. Its scope was extended by the Clean Air Act 1968 which prohibited emissions of dark smoke from any industrial or trade premises, even though the emission was not made from a chimney. The provisions of these Acts have now been consolidated into the Clean Air Act 1993. Enforcement of the Clean Air Act is by the local

7.6   The Clean Air Act 1993

authorities, who may act in respect of smoke arising within their areas or affecting their areas.

| 7.6.1 | Relationship between the Clean Air Act and Part I of the EPA |

Before considering the details of the Clean Air Act, it is important to note the relationship between these controls and the controls over atmospheric emissions under Part I of the EPA (Integrated Pollution Control and Local Authority Air Pollution Control). The provisions of Parts I–III of the Clean Air Act do not apply to any process regulated under Part 1 of the EPA. Section 41 of the 1993 Act excludes IPC and LAAPC processes from the date of authorisation.

| 7.6.2 | Offences under the Clean Air Act |

The Clean Air Act 1993 controls emissions of smoke, dust and grit by means of criminal offences. The following are the main offences:

- emission of dark smoke – from a chimney or from industrial premises other than from a chimney;

- emission of dust and grit from non-domestic furnaces;

- emission of smoke from a chimney in a Smoke Control Area;

- various offences relating to the installation of furnaces.

Prosecutions under most provisions of the Clean Air Act are dealt with in the magistrates' court.

| 7.6.3 | The 'Dark Smoke' Offences (ss 1 and 2) |

The Clean Air Act creates numerous criminal offences, including the so-called dark smoke offences. Sections 1 and 2 of the Act prohibit the emission of dark smoke from different categories of premises; s 1 requires the emission of dark smoke to be through a chimney whereas s 2 does not. The offences are strict liability offences, although various activities are exempted from the provisions.

Section 1 prohibits:

- the emission of 'dark smoke' from the chimney of any building (s 1(1)); or

- from a chimney which serves the furnace of any fixed boiler or industrial plant (s 1(2)).

The provisions cover dark smoke emissions from the chimneys of domestic premises as well as industrial or commercial. Where an offence has been committed under s 1(1), liability will rest with the occupier of the building from which the dark smoke is emitted. In the case of dark smoke emissions from a chimney serving a fixed boiler or industrial plant (s 1(2)), the person having possession of the boiler or plant will be liable if an offence is committed.

Section 2 prohibits:

- the emission of dark smoke from industrial trade premises.

However, unlike s 1, the s 2 emission need not be through a chimney. Trade or industrial premises are premises which are used for an industrial or trade purpose or premises on which matter is burnt in connection with any industrial or trade purpose. A s 2 offence may be committed either by the occupier of the premises or any other person causing or permitting the emission. In the case of *Sheffield City Council v ADH Demolition Ltd* (1984), it was held that premises could include a demolition site and that there was no requirement for the land to be covered by a building. The burning of rubbish on a demolition site may also amount to an industrial or trade process.

Smoke includes soot, ash, grit and gritty particles emitted in smoke. Dark smoke is defined by reference to a device known as the Ringlemann Chart. Smoke which is determined to be as dark or darker than shade 2 on the Ringlemann Chart is 'dark smoke' for the purposes of the Act. The Ringlemann Chart indicates differing shades of darkness. The chart consists of a piece of card with cross-hatching in black on a white background so that a known percentage of white is obscured. The chart needs to be placed at some distance from the observer who will then be able to see that the lines merge into different greyish/black shades. The different shades are numerically categorised; 0 equals white and 5 equals dense black. Shades 2–4 increase by degrees so that shade 1 indicates a 20% obscuration of the white, shade 2 equals 40%, and so on. In order to compare the shades with the smoke, it is necessary to place the card between the observer and the smoke (the chart is usually mounted on a wooden or metal frame). The observer usually stands about 50 feet from the chart in order to match the smoke colour with the chart. The matching should normally take place in good daylight conditions.

7.6.4   What is dark smoke?

By virtue of s 3 of the 1993 Act, a court must be satisfied in any legal proceedings for breach of s 1 that the smoke is as dark as defined. However, there is no requirement for an actual comparison of the smoke with the chart. It is sufficient that the court is certain that the method was properly applied and that the smoke was thereby determined to be dark.

There is no requirement in the Act for the defendant to have caused or knowingly permitted the discharge of dark smoke. The offence is a strict liability one. There are however a number of defences and exemptions which are considered below. Breach of s 1 is a criminal offence and a person may be liable on summary conviction to a fine of up to £3,000 (level 3) for emissions from private dwellings otherwise £5,000 (level 5).

| 7.6.5 | Notification that an offence has been committed |

The occupier of the premises must be notified of the offence by the local authority environmental officer 'as soon as may be'. This will usually mean that an environmental health officer or officer from the local authority advises the occupier verbally. However, the local authority is required to confirm this notification in writing within a period of four days. Failure to give notice will provide the defendant with a defence to any charges made under ss 1, 2 and 20. Unlike other pollution offences discussed in this book, the offence can only be tried by the magistrates' court.

| 7.6.6 | Strict liability and burden of proof |

The Clean Air Act presumes that there will have been an emission of dark smoke from industrial or trade premises in any case where material is burned on those premises and the circumstances are such that the burning would be likely to give rise to the emission of dark smoke. The burden of proof falls squarely with the occupier (or any other person causing or permitting the burning) to show that no dark smoke was actually emitted.

| 7.6.7 | Exemptions |

The Act provides certain exemptions from the above offences. These are contained in the Dark Smoke (Permitted Periods) Regulations 1958, which establishes the following exceptions whereby no offence is committed if the emissions of dark smoke are made within certain periods:

1   the emission of dark smoke is permitted for a defined number of minutes during an eight-hour period. The precise number of minutes depends on the number of furnaces which feed into the chimney and whether or not the emission involves the blowing of soot;

2   in any event, the continuous emission of dark smoke cannot at any time exceed four minutes and the continuous emission of black smoke must not at any time exceed two minutes in any half-hour period.

The Clean Air (Emissions of Dark Smoke) (Exemptions) Regulations 1969 also provide exceptions relating to the burning of certain materials in the open. The following are exempt from the s 2 offence:

1   burning timber and other waste material which results either from the demolition of a building or from the

clearance a site upon which there is building operation or engineering construction;

2   burning explosive which has become waste and any material which has become contaminated by such explosive;

3   burning tar, pitch or asphalt and other matter in connection with any resurfacing;

4   burning animal and poultry carcasses where the animals have died or have been slaughtered due to a disease;

5   burning containers which have been contaminated by any pesticide or toxic substance used for veterinary or agricultural purposes.

However, for these exceptions to apply, the person seeking to rely on the exceptions would need to satisfy certain conditions. Among other things, there is the requirement that there is no other reasonably safe and practicable method of disposing of the matter. Other conditions relate to the manner in which the burning takes place and that steps are taken to minimise the emission of dark smoke. The fire must be carried out under the supervision of the occupier of the premises concerned.

Section 1(4) provides that where a breach of the dark smoke provisions occur then a number of defences may be raised in any proceedings. These defences exist when a number of circumstances arise:

7.6.8   Defences

•   when lighting the furnace from cold; or

•   when there has been some unforeseeable and unavoidable failure of the furnace or apparatus connected with the furnace; or

•   when unsuitable fuel has been used when suitable fuel is unobtainable and that the least unsuitable fuel was used.

Garner's *Encyclopaedia of Environmental Law* suggests that the defence of lighting a furnace from cold might only be available in relation to the initial ignition of the furnace and not each time the furnace is restoked after a period (ie overnight) of being damped down.

These defences are all subject to the important *caveat* that all practicable steps were take to prevent or minimise the emissions of dark smoke.

As far as the s 2 offence is concerned, s 2(4) provides a defence if it can be proved that the emission was inadvertent and that all practicable steps had been taken to prevent or minimise it. It appears from the statute that both these elements will be required before a defendant can rely on the defence. 'Practicable' is defined here in a similar way to 'practicable' in the context of 'best practicable means'. Therefore, regard must be had to factors such as local conditions and circumstances; financial implications; and the current state of technical knowledge.

Finally, if the person charged with an offence under either of these sections has not been served with a written notification of the offence from the environmental health department of the local authority within the prescribed four-day period, this will provide him with an additional defence by virtue of s 51.

7.6.9 Grit, dust and fumes

Section 5 establishes similar offences to the dark smoke offences in relation to grit, dust and fumes. Grit is defined by the Clean Air (Emission of Grit and Dust from Furnaces) Regulations 1971, which also prescribes the limits of grit and dust emissions from certain specifications of furnaces. Dust does not include dust emitted from a chimney as an ingredient of smoke and fumes means any airborne matter smaller than dust.

It is an offence if, on any day, the grit or dust emitted from a chimney serving a specified furnace is over the prescribed emission limits laid down in the regulations. The occupier will be guilty of the offence unless he can successfully raise the defence that the best practicable means had been used to minimise or prevent the emission. It should be noted here that the defence requires the best practicable means to be employed rather than any practicable means. However, in circumstances where the regulations do not specify a prescribed limit (ie certain furnaces are not covered by the regulations) it will still be an offence for the occupier if he fails to use any practicable means to minimise the emission of grit or dust from the chimney.

7.6.10 Control over the installation of non-domestic furnaces

Section 4 of the 1993 Act provides that, before installing a furnace over a certain size (basically a non-domestic boiler), the person seeking to make the installation must obtain the approval of the local authority. The section also stipulates that all new non-domestic boilers should, so far as practicable, be smokeless. Any one who installs a furnace in contravention of this requirement is committing an offence, but if the local authority has approved the installation, it is deemed to comply with the requirements of the section.

Additionally all non-domestic furnaces over a certain energy value must comply with the provisions contained in ss

6–8. Furnaces falling under these sections must be fitted with local authority approved grit and dust arrestment equipment. The arrestors must be properly maintained and used, if used for the following purposes:

(i) to burn pulverised fuel; or

(ii) to burn, at a rate of 45.4 kg or more an hour, any other solid matter; or

(iii)to burn, at a rate equivalent to 366.4 kilowatts or more, any liquid or gaseous matter.

There are certain exemptions from these provisions and these are specified in s 7. In particular, the Secretary of State has used his powers under s 7 to prescribe by regulation that furnaces of a certain class may be exempted by introducing The Clean Air (Arrestment Plant) (Exemption) Regulations 1969. Alternatively, it is possible to apply to the local authority for an exemption under s 7. The local authority can only grant an exemption if it is satisfied that the emissions of grit or dust will not amount to a statutory nuisance (ie be a nuisance or prejudicial to health).

The local authority may also require the occupier of these furnaces to comply with certain monitoring requirements in relation to the measurement of grit, dust and fumes. In turn, the occupier has the right to request that the local authority make and record such measurements and the local authority will be required to do so from time to time. A right of appeal to the Secretary of Sate is available if the local authority refuses to approve the proposed equipment.

Section 14 empowers the local authorities to control the height of chimneys for the purposes of regulating air pollution. The thinking behind these controls is based on the principle of dilute and disperse. Tall chimney stacks are supposed to enable the more effective dispersion of pollution in order to dilute it to harmless levels. The control under s 14 exists in addition to the normal planning controls which the planning authority can exert.

If any one is seeking to:

• erect a new chimney to serve a furnace;

• enlarge an existing chimney to serve a furnace;

• replace a chimney with an increased combustion space

then they must make an application to the local authority for chimney height approval. The local authority will determine the application by reference to the Third Memorandum on

7.6.11   Control over chimney height

Chimney Heights which assists with the calculation on chimney heights. The local authority must take into account various factors and, in particular, must not grant approval for a chimney unless it is satisfied that its height will be sufficient to prevent, as far as practicable, the chimney emissions becoming prejudicial to health or a nuisance.

The local authority can either approve the chimney height with or without conditions. Once again, there is a right of appeal against the decision of the local authority to the Secretary of State.

7.6.12   Smoke Control Areas

The ability to establish Smoke Control Areas (SCA) is one of the principal features of the Act and provides a means by which local authorities can control, in particular, smoke from domestic properties. A local authority has the power to declare all or part of its area as a Smoke Control Area and does so by a Smoke Control Order. In addition the Secretary of State has the power, by virtue of s 19 to order, a local authority to designate a Smoke Control Area.

The Smoke Control Order may designate certain classes of building; it may exempt specific buildings or classes of buildings or fireplaces.

Once an area has been designated as a SCA, then an occupier of a building in the area is guilty of an offence if smoke (note, this includes any shade of smoke) is emitted from a chimney of that building. However defences are available if:

- the emission resulted from the use of an authorised fuel; or

- the emission resulted from the use of a fireplace exempted by regulations.

Authorised fuels are defined by the Smoke Control Areas (Authorised Fuel) Regulations 1991. Various regulations exempt certain classes of fireplace (the Smoke Control (Exempted Fireplaces) Orders).

It is also an offence to buy solid non-authorised fuel for use in a smoke control area (unless of course it is for an exempt fireplace) and it is also an offence to retail unauthorised fuel for unauthorised use in a SCA.

7.7   **Statutory nuisances relating to air quality**

The provisions relating to statutory nuisance are considered in Chapter 14. However, in the context of controls over air pollution, it should be noted that the following matters may constitute a statutory nuisance if they are either prejudicial to health or a nuisance:

(a) any premises in such a state so as to be prejudicial to health or a nuisance (this could cover odour emissions from such premises even though smell is specifically mentioned in (c) below);

(b) smoke, fumes or gas emitted from premises so as to be prejudicial to health or a nuisance;

(c) any dust, steam, smell or other effluvia arising on industrial, trade or business premises.

However, it should be noted that, in relation to (b) above, where the emission of smoke can be controlled under the Clean Air Act 1993 the statutory nuisance provisions do not apply. Therefore, this statutory nuisance is largely concerned with smoke which is less than 'dark' from non-domestic premise.

There is no doubt that the emissions from motor vehicles are a major source of atmospheric pollution. Ninety-eight per cent of the UK's benzene emissions arise from vehicle emissions. Eighty-seven per cent of the UK's carbon monoxide emissions come from petrol engined vehicles. Linked to these statistics is the further fact that vehicle emissions have increased by 50% since 1970, although there is some evidence of a downward trend since the introduction of cars fitted with catalytic converters. Vehicle emissions are also largely responsible for emissions of other pollutants such as 1,3 butadiene which has been shown to be linked to increased risks of lymphoma or leukaemia.

7.8   Pollution from motor vehicles

Pollution from motor vehicles is regulated in a variety of ways, in particular:

• The Road Traffic Act 1988;

• EC Directives on emissions from vehicles;

• There are many regulations (made either under various atatutes, or to implement EC Directives) which regulate both the construction of vehicles and vehicle parts in order to limit atmospheric pollution (and invariably noise pollution).

7.9   European Community legislation

The European Community had a relatively slow start in terms of its programme of legislation aimed at controlling air pollution. The first Directive establishing air quality standards was not adopted until 1980. Since then, the EC has adopted various measures aimed at combating atmospheric pollution, particularly in response to the growing awareness about acid rain. Generally speaking, EC air pollution measures can be categorised into the following broad types:

- Emissions from industrial plants

  Of particular importance is the Large Combustion Plant Directive. This is being implemented in the UK through the system of Integrated Pollution Control. In addition, Directive 84/360 established that new industrial plants must use the best available technologies not entailing excessive cost and Directive 89/369 deals with emissions from municipal waste incineration plants. More recently, the Commission has proposed a Directive setting up a system of Integrated Pollution Control which will control atmospheric emissions.

- Air pollution affecting the ozone layer and global warming

  Regulation 594/91 requires the reduction in the use of Chlorofluorocarbons (CFCs) of 85% from the 1986 levels by the year 1996 and a phasing out of their use entirely by 30 June 1997. This regulation has since been amended to include controls over HCFCs and methyl bromide. In 1990, the European Council of Ministers stated its intention to stabilise CO^2 emissions at 1990 levels by the year 2000. To this end, the Commission has proposed a new Community Strategy to limit carbon dioxide emissions. One of the proposals was to introduce a carbon tax. However, at the time of writing, the proposals have not reached any agreement and it appears that Member States will be free to adopt their own unilateral measures, but it is unlikely that a Community-wide tax will be adopted.

- Air quality standards

  A number of Directives lay down air quality objectives and limit values for sulphur dioxide, suspended particles, lead and nitrogen dioxide. The Commission has also proposed a Directive on ambient air quality assessment and management (Com (94) 109 Final). The aim of the proposed Directive is to define the principles of a common strategy to establish objectives for ambient air quality. Under the Directive, the Commission will be required to set ambient air quality objectives according to a fixed timetable. Member States will be required to take measures to ensure that the limit values set by the Commission are not exceeded. Unlike the UK government's proposals in *Meeting the Challenge* (see para 7.3.1 above) the European Commission wants to set legally-binding air quality standards.

- Vehicle emissions

  The Community has enacted various pieces of legislation which seek to harmonise the emissions from vehicles, particularly motor cars. Measures include Directive 76/716 on the sulphur content of gas oil, Directives 78/611 and 85/210 concerning the lead content of petrol the Commission has also proposed a variety of other measures, such as traffic management which are aimed at reducing vehicle emissions.

- Product quality standards

  It has already been noted that one way of controlling air pollution is to set emission limits for certain categories of products. The EC has used this particular approach to limit the lead content in petrol and to limit emissions from motor cars.

Air pollution is a global environmental issue and attracts international attention. The study of international environmental law falls outside the scope of this book, but the transboundary nature of atmospheric pollution in particular makes it necessary to include some commentary.

The United Kingdom has committed itself to a number of international conventions which require the government to take steps to reduce the emission of certain pollutants:

- 1979 Convention on Long Range Transboundary Air Pollution

  Agreed in Geneva in 1979, this Convention was not ratified by the UK until 1980. Signatories agreed to endeavour to limit and, as far as possible, reduce and prevent air pollution. The Convention resulted in three international protocols concerned with the reduction of sulphur dioxide (SO_2) emissions; emissions of oxides of nitrogen (NO^x); and emissions of volatile organic compounds (VOCs).

- The 1985 Vienna Convention for the Protection of the Ozone Layer

  Parties to the Vienna Convention, including the UK which ratified it in 1987, have agreed the Montreal Protocol on Substances that deplete the ozone layer. The protocol

7.10 Acid rain, global warming and the international dimension

requires the signatories to freeze and reduce the production of various CFCs and halons.

* 1992 Convention on Climate Change

This convention was agreed by over 150 parties at the United nations Earth Summit in Rio de Janeiro. The convention is aimed at reducing emissions of CO_2 and other greenhouse gases to 1990 levels by the year 2000. Signatories are required to prepare National Programmes to meet these targets.

Summary of Chapter 7

Atmospheric Pollution

Pollution of the atmosphere results in both long-term adverse Environmental consequences but also causes health problems and can cause death.

Problems of air pollution

The legal controls over air pollution are contained in:

Legal controls

- Part I EPA – Integrated Pollution Control and Local Authority Air Pollution Control – The system of LAAPC only permits the local authority to control atmospheric emissions, whereas the central system of Integrated Pollution Control enables the control of substances into all environmental media to secure the Best Practical Environmental Option (BPEO). For a detailed discussion of LAAPC and IPC see Chapter 9;

- The Clean Air Act 1993 – controls emissions of smoke, dust and grit by means of criminal offences.

The following are the main offences:

Offences and remedies

- emission of dark smoke

  - from a chimney; or

  - from industrial premises other than from a chimney;

- emission of dust and grit from non-domestic furnaces;

- emission of smoke from a chimney in a Smoke Control Area;

- various offences relating to the installation of furnaces.

  Section 1 prohibits:

- the emission of 'dark smoke' from the chimney of any building (s 1(1)); or

- from a chimney which serves the furnace of any fixed boiler or industrial plant (s 1(2)).

  Section 2 prohibits:

- the emission of dark smoke from industrial trade premises.

  Although the offences are strict liability certain exemptions and defences are available.

Section 5 establishes similar offences to the dark smoke offences in relation to grit and dust and fumes.

Section 4 of the 1993 Act provides that before installing a furnace over a certain size (basically a non-domestic boiler) the person seeking to make the installation must obtain the prior approval of the local authority.

Section 14 empowers the local authorities to control the height of chimneys for the purposes of regulating air pollution. The thinking behind these controls is based on the principle of dilute and Local authorities can take preventive action to reduce air pollution from smoke by designating an area as a Smoke Control Area.

In the context of air pollution the following provisions of s 79 EPA may provide a means by which the pollution can be abated by a local authority exercising its powers under the EPA in relation to statutory nuisances (For further detail see Chapter 16):

(a) any premises in such a state so as to be prejudicial to health or a nuisance (this could cover odour emissions from such premises even though smell is specifically mentioned in (c) below);

(b) smoke, fumes or gas emitted from premises so as to be prejudicial to health or a nuisance;

(c) any dust, steam, smell or other effluvia arising on industrial, trade or business premises.

Chapter 8

Water Pollution

This chapter is concerned with the legal control of water pollution and the measures which exist to prevent pollution and improve water quality. Water, like air, is vital for human existence, it is required to sustain human life. Pollution control is essential; without it, the waters from which we extract drinking water and water for the manufacture of food and drinks would become unfit for human consumption. Water is not only used for consumption, it is also necessary for a variety of domestic, industrial and agricultural purposes. However, once it has been used, it has to be returned to the environment, mostly as effluent discharge. It is not usually possible to return the water in the same state as it was when it removed, albeit treatment takes place to reduce its polluting effect. The water must be returned in some form or there would be a serious risk of the water courses drying up. Therefore, society is automatically faced, as a consequence of normal daily activity, with the problem of water pollution.

The chapter considers various issues relating to legal control over water pollution. For ease of reference, the main issues that will be considered are as follows:

- the problems of water pollution, how water pollution arises and the quality of the water environment;

- common law rights in relation to water;

- the development of legal controls;

- the water industry and the Water Industry Act 1991;

- controls in relation to drinking water;

- the National Rivers Authority;

- the main water pollution offences and the system of pollution prevention control exercised by the National Rivers Authority through the consent system under the Water Resources Act 1991;

- clean-up powers following a water pollution incident;

- preventive measures;

- the controls over discharges of effluents into sewers;

- the controls over water abstraction;

8.1   Introduction

- other statutory provisions which relate to water pollution, such as the Environmental Protection Act 1990;

- relevant EC legislation.

The statutory controls discussed in this chapter relate to what are known as 'controlled waters', which basically covers all inland waters, lakes, rivers, streams and also coastal waters. A full definition of controlled waters is provided at para 8.7.1 below. The chapter does not deal with the problems or controls in relation to marine pollution. Pollution of the seas is clearly a matter of great significance in environmental terms and generates considerable public concern, particularly following oils spills; however, since it is not generally covered in mainstream environmental law courses, it has not been considered here.

8.2 The problem of water pollution

8.2.1 Sources of water pollution

Water pollution takes many different forms. It may be categorised in terms of where the pollution takes place. Water pollution comes from three main sources:

- from a specified discharge outlet such as a pipe – this is the easiest source of water pollution to control;

- it can also arise from a more diffuse source, notably run-off from industrial plants and agricultural land. This type of diffuse pollution usually involves some kind of surface water run-off through contaminated land which finds its way into a water course. Or it can involve the percolation of agricultural pesticides to underground and surface water. Because it does not come from a clearly defined source, such as a pipe, it is particularly difficult to control;

- water pollution may occur as a consequence of an accidental spillage When this happens the 'polluter' may have committed an offence and may be responsible for the clean up.

Alternatively water pollution may be defined by reference to the pollutants themselves. The Royal Commission on Environmental Pollution has broadly divided pollutants into three groups:

- Sewage effluent – sewage effluent has the effect of reducing the oxygen content of water;

- Heavy metals – heavy metals and organochlorines can be particularly toxic and have the ability to persist for lengthy periods of time and also to accumulate in organisms;

- Other pollutants – this wide-ranging category covers a variety of industrial discharges, including organic and inorganic chemicals, oil, solid waste. These are generally less persistent than heavy metals but, nevertheless, can cause serious damage.

One measure of the state of the water environment or the level of water pollution is the classification of the quality of rivers produced by the National Rivers Authority. According to statistics published by the NRA in *The Quality of Rivers, Canals and Estuaries in England and Wales*, the 1990 survey of water quality showed that 89% of rivers and 90% of canals are classified as being of a 'good' or 'fair' quality and only 11 % of 'poor' or 'bad' quality. Although there was an overall improvement in water quality between 1958 and 1980, since 1980 there has been a slight net deterioration in water quality for rivers and canals. In the 1990 survey, 4% of rivers moved down in overall classification. It has been suggested, however, that the 1990 survey results were affected in part by changes in survey methods. The precise meanings of these classifications is provided in the section on water classification at para 8.8.

8.2.2   Water quality as an indicator of the level of water pollution

Another indication of the state of water quality is the number of pollution incidents over a given period. Again using statistics produced by the NRA, *Water Pollution Incidents in England and Wales 1993*, a total of 34,296 pollution incidents were reported in 1993, which represents an 8% increase over 1992. Of these, 25,299 (74%) were substantiated. Using the NRA's own classification system of incidents, 331 were classified as 'major' and, of these, agricultural pollution incidents constituted 19%, sewage pollution incidents 23%, industrial pollution 34% and transport 5%. Whilst, therefore, the majority of the incidents were classified as minor incidents, they still have a cost both in financial and environmental terms. During 1993, 277 incidents resulted in convictions (97% of prosecutions). The largest number of prosecutions were in respect of major or significant pollution incidents. One thing to remember in relation to these statistics is that they only cover the reported incidents. Although the NRA have actively promoted public awareness and set up a 24-hour 'hot-line' to encourage people to report pollution incidents, there will still be occasions when pollution or a pollution incident remains undetected.

8.2.3   Water pollution incidents

The National Rivers Authority categorises water pollution incidents under three headings:

1   Major incidents involve one or more of the following:

    a) potential or actual persistent effect on water quality and aquatic life;

b) closure of potable water, industrial or agricultural abstraction necessary;

c) extensive fish kill;

d) excessive breaches of consent conditions;

e) major effect on amenity value.

2 Significant pollution incidents involve one or more of the following:

a) notification to water abstracters is necessary;

b) significant fish kill;

c) measurable effect on invertebrate life;

d) water unfit for stock;

e) bed of watercourse contaminated;

f) amenity value to the public, owners or users reduced by odour or appearance.

3 Minor incidents involve suspected or probable pollution which, on investigation, proves unlikely to be capable of substantiation or to have no notable effect.

8.3   The common law and water pollution

Although the Water Resources Act provides the statutory mechanisms for controlling water pollution and prosecuting offenders, the common law still provides a means of redress for people who suffer damage from pollution. This is particularly the case in terms of water pollution. Chapter 4 has already considered the role of the common law in protecting the environment and some of the inherent difficulties in bringing common law actions. The case of *Cambridge Water Company v Eastern Counties Leather plc* (1994) was concerned specifically with liability for pollution of groundwater as a result of past pollution and is considered fully in Chapter 4. However, in relation to water pollution consideration needs also to be given to the position of riparian owners.

A riparian owner is a person whose property adjoins a watercourse such as a river or stream. According to the courts, the law relating to the rights of riparian owners is well settled. A riparian owner is entitled to:

'have the water of the stream, on the banks of which his property lies, flow down as it has been accustomed to flow down to his property, subject to the ordinary use of flowing water by upper proprietors, and to such further use, if any, on their part in connection with their property as may be reasonable under the circumstances. Every riparian proprietor is thus entitled to the water of his stream, in its natural flow, without sensible diminution or increase and without sensible alteration in its character or quality' *per* Lord McNaughton, *John Young & Co v Bankier Distillery Co* (1893).

The court went on to say, in this case, that any invasion of these riparian rights which caused actual damage to the natural characteristics of the water could constitute an actionable nuisance which the courts would address. A riparian owner can bring an action for damages or can seek an injunction.

In addition to a claim in nuisance, it may be possible for a riparian owner to make a claim in trespass (see *Scott-Whitehead v National Coal Board* (1987).

The attempts to prevent and control water pollution by legislation have been varied and date back to the 1860s. Since that time, various government administrations have introduced new controls and have established new criminal offences. The following section is intended to provide a very brief overview of the history of those controls. The first Act of Parliament to attempt to control water pollution was the Rivers Pollution Prevention Act of 1876. Although there had been previous Acts which had dealt with water pollution, they were primarily aimed at improving public health (the Public Health Act 1875), or the productivity of salmon fishing (the Salmon Fisheries Act 1861). The Rivers Pollution Prevention Act 1876 created several offences in relation to the discharge or dumping of certain specified solid matters into any stream; discharges of solid or liquid sewerage matter into any stream; or discharging poisonous, noxious or polluting liquid proceeding from any factory or manufacturing process. The 1876 Act also introduced a number of defences, including the defence that the 'best practicable means' were employed. Despite the creation of these offences the Act was regarded as unsuccessful.

The 1876 Act was repealed in 1951 with the enactment of the Rivers (Prevention of Pollution) Act. The 1951 Act created the offence of causing or knowingly permitting any poisonous, noxious or polluting matter to enter into a stream and it also introduced the first system of discharge consents. It also required all new discharge outlets to have a licence. However, any existing discharge outlets were not required to have a licence unless they were altered, or the discharge itself was altered or increased. The Rivers (Prevention of Pollution) Act 1961 extended the consent procedure to cover certain types of discharges that were operational before the 1951 Act, thus extending the coverage of the new licensing procedure. The 1961 Act also provided a much stricter regime insofar as it

8.4   Development of water legislation

removed certain defences that had been available under the 1951 Act. The Control of Pollution Act 1974 repealed both the 1951 and 1961 Acts.

8.4.1	The 1991 Water Acts	

The starting point in considering the current legislative controls is the Water Act 1989 which, although superseded by consolidating legislation in 1991, was the Act which established the National Rivers Authority. It also led to the privatisation of the water supply and sewerage services and the establishment of 10 private water service companies which had responsibility as water and sewerage undertakers. In 1991, Parliament passed five Acts which aimed to consolidate the various legislative provisions relating to all aspects of the water industry and control of water pollution. The main Acts were the Water Industry Act 1991 and the Water Resources Act 1991. The provisions of the Water Resources Act provide the main framework for control of water quality and quantity and are considered in detail throughout this chapter. The Water Industry Act contains provisions relating to water supply and sewerage services; however, some of its provisions are related to environmental protection, particularly in relation to the controls over the quality of drinking water. These are considered at para 8.5.

8.4.2   Other statutory controls

In addition to the controls within the main water legislation, various other statutes contain provisions which relate to the control and prevention of water pollution or the maintenance of water quality standards. These include:

- the Environmental Protection Act 1990;

- the Salmon and Freshwater Fisheries Act 1975;

- the Land Drainage Act 1994;

The provisions in these statutes are considered at para 8.18.

8.5   The water industry and the Water Industry Act 1991

The water industry covers a wide-range of diverse activities, all of which share a common involvement in the water cycle ranging from the collection and treatment of water and its supply to the provision of sewers and sewage works. It also covers those bodies involved in the control of pollution, the regulation and control of fishing, navigation, flood defence, land drainage, conservation and, of course, recreational activities. In addition, it includes those organisations concerned with the regulation of the above activities.

The water industry in its widest sense has undergone many changes since the 1940s, as a result of legislation particularly aimed at reorganisation and privatisation. Before

1948, the responsibility for water supply and also sewage disposal fell to the local authorities. In 1948, the River Boards Act established 32 River Boards which were organised on a catchment area basis. The River Boards had responsibility for most of the activities in the water industry including water supply and sewage disposal. In 1963 the River Boards were taken over by 27 River Authorities as a consequence of the 1963, Water Resources Act. The River Authorities had responsibility, among other things, for pollution control. However, it was not really until 1973 that there was any real attempt to achieve an integrated control of the industry. The Water Act 1973 established 10 Regional Water Authorities which took charge of managing the various water functions in the relevant river basin areas. The 1973 Act, however, did permit the continued existence of a number of statutory private water companies.

Although the Water Act 1973 was intended to provide a more coherent framework for control. it did not tackle one of the main problems that had thus far existed in the industry. The regional water authorities had responsibility for pollution control but were at the same time themselves major polluters in their capacity as operators of sewage disposal works. This 'game-keeper and poacher' scenario gave rise to a great deal of criticism of the water industry. Consequently, the industry went through further reorganisation in 1989 with the Water Act, which led to the privatisation of the water supply and sewerage services and the creation of the National Rivers Authority. In 1991, the government consolidated the legislation controlling the water industry and now the Water Industry Act 1991 provides for the regulation of water supply and sewerage.

The position today is that the supply of water and the provision of sewerage services rests with privatised water service companies (known as the water undertakers and the sewerage undertakers). In addition, there are also water companies which are only responsible for the supply of water and play no role in relation to sewerage services. The office of the Director General of Water Services was established to regulate the activities of the privatised water industry.

The Water Service Companies and Water Companies are responsible for the supply of drinking water. The legal controls which regulate their activities can be found in the Water Industry Act 1991. Although many of the provisions in this Act are outside the scope of this book, it is clear that the duty to provide wholesome drinking water is inextricably linked to the quality of water abstracted for such purposes.	**8.5.1 Controls relating to drinking water**

Section 67 of the Water Industry Act 1991 requires that water supplied for drinking purposes must be 'wholesome' at the time of supply. Section 70 makes it an offence to supply water unfit for human consumption which, if tried on indictment, can lead to an unlimited fine. Wholesome water is defined in the Water Quality Regulations 1989 which implements a number of EC Directives. The EC has played a key role in determining the standards of water used for drinking water. Member States are required to comply with the standards laid down in Directive 75/440 on Surface Water for Drinking which requires that surface waters that are used for drinking water are fit for the purpose. The Member States are also required to comply with the Drinking Water Directive (80/778).

8.6 The National Rivers Authority

The National Rivers Authority (NRA) is the main regulatory body with responsibility for controlling pollution of water, although it shares responsibilities with Her Majesty's Inspectorate of Pollution in relation to those industrial processes that are governed by the Integrated Pollution Control Regimes of the Environmental Protection Act (see Chapter 9). The NRA was set up in 1989 by the Water Act 1989 to provide integrated management of river basins and the water environment in England and Wales. It took over the functions previously exercised by the water authorities. The constitution, functions and powers of the NRA are now prescribed by the 1991 Water Resources Act, and all the following sections relate to that Act.

8.6.1 Composition and control of the NRA

Section 1 provides that the NRA is a body corporate (unlike HMIP which is part of the Department of the Environment) although, in fact, it is accountable to the Secretary of State for the Environment in a number of ways. The Secretary of State has the power to appoint members of the Authority; he can issue directions to the Authority; and, with the Minister of Agriculture, has the power to determine the Authority's financial duties. The Secretary of State also has jurisdiction to determine appeals made against decisions of the NRA and to intervene in certain applications to the NRA. Section 5 of the Water Resources Act provides significant powers for Ministerial directions to be issued to the NRA, but the NRA must always be consulted before such directions are issued, except in emergency situations. Since the NRA is a body corporate it does not enjoy any of the Crown's immunities or privileges.

The membership of the corporate body of the NRA may vary between eight and 15 members. Two are appointed by the Minister of Agriculture, Fisheries and Food whilst the remaining members are appointed by the Secretary of State for the Environment. In appointing members, the Secretary of State or the Minister must have regard to the desirability of appointing people who have, or have had, experience of, or shown some capacity in, some matter relevant to the functions of the Authority. The NRA is assisted by a number of regional advisory committees that act in a consultative role, providing advice on those areas within their spheres of influence. These committees were established under s 7 of the WRA 1991. There are three main advisory committees that operate on a regional basis. These are discussed more fully in Chapter 5.

When the National Rivers Authority was established in 1989, it inherited the functions of the water authorities relating to pollution control, water resource management, flood defence, fisheries, navigation and conservation and recreation. The responsibilities of the NRA are laid down in s 2 of the 1991 Act as follows:

8.6.2   Functions

(c) water resources (Part II of the Water Resources Act 1991);

(d) water pollution (Part III of the Water Resources Act 1991);

(e) flood defence and land drainage (by virtue of Part IV and other enactments);

(f) fisheries (by virtue of Part V and other enactments);

(g) navigation authority, harbour authority or conservancy authority which were transferred to the Authority by virtue of Chapter V of Part III of the Water Act 1989 (and other provisions);

(h) functions assigned to the Authority by any other enactment.

The NRA is required by s 16 of the Water Resources Act to generally promote the conservation and enhancement of the natural beauty and amenity of inland and coastal waters and of land associated with such waters; the conservation of flora and fauna which are dependent on the aquatic environment; and the use of such waters and land for recreational purposes. The way in which the NRA should carry out this duty is described in the Code of Practice on Conservation, Access and Recreation which was issued pursuant to s 18(1) and also in the Water and Sewerage (Conservation and Recreation) (Code of Practice) Order 1989. The NRA also has a duty to consider water supply issues and, by virtue of s 15, it must have regard, when exercising its powers, to the duties that are

8.6.3   NRA duties

imposed on any water undertakers or sewerage undertakers by Parts II–IV of the Water Industry Act 1991. For a further discussion of the National Rivers Authority and, in particular, details of its policy, see Chapter 5.

8.7	**Control over water pollution: an overview**

The Water Resources Act 1991 provides the main body of control relating to the prevention and control of water pollution in England and Wales. The National Rivers Authority is responsible for controlling pollution of 'controlled waters' and for achieving the improvements in water quality required in order to meet statutory water quality objectives.

The control of water pollution is exercised by the NRA through a system of authorised consents. Any discharges made into controlled waters must be authorised by the NRA (with the exception of discharges made from IPC-prescribed processes which are controlled by HMIP). The system of consents enables the NRA to control, by means of conditions, the nature and volume of contaminants discharged into water in order to achieve improvements in water quality. Discharges made without consent, or in breach of the conditions attached to a consent, constitute criminal offences. The NRA employs inspectors who have wide-ranging powers to secure compliance. In the event that there is a discharge into controlled waters without consent or in breach of consent conditions, the Authority has the power to prosecute. Various statutory defences exist. The NRA has established itself as a strong regulator and has shown itself willing to prosecute offenders. The fines for water pollution offences may be unlimited if a case is dealt with by the Crown Court and, indeed, some of the fines have been very high. In addition, under s 161 WRA, the NRA has the power to take action to avoid pollution of controlled water or to clean-up after an incident. It can then recover its reasonable costs from those responsible for the pollution. The costs of clean-up may well exceed any fine imposed by a court.

8.7.1   Controlled waters

The pollution controls which are provided for in the Water Resources Act apply only in respect of waters defined as 'controlled waters' and the NRA can only exercise its controls over pollution in relation to those waters. Section 104 of the Act provides a definition of controlled waters which includes:

1   inland fresh waters – including lakes, ponds, rivers or water courses above the fresh water limit;

2   ground waters – that is waters contained in the underground strata;

3   coastal waters – including all estuarine waters up to the fresh water limits of rivers and water courses.

These terms are defined much more fully in s 104 as follows:

1   Inland fresh waters means the waters of any relevant lake or pond or of so much of any relevant river or watercourse as is above the fresh water limit. 'Relevant lake or pond' means any lake or pond, including reservoirs, which, whether it is natural, artificial, above or below ground, discharges into a relevant river or watercourse or into another lake or pond which is itself a relevant lake or pond. The Secretary of State is empowered to provide by order that any lake or pond which does not discharge into a relevant river or watercourse or into a relevant lake or pond is to be treated as a relevant lake or pond, or to be treated as if it were not a relevant lake or pond as the case may be.

A 'watercourse' includes all rivers, streams, ditches, drains, cuts, culverts, dikes, sluices, sewers and passages through which water flows, except mains and other pipes which belong to the Authority or a water undertaker or are used by a water undertaker or any other person for the purpose only of providing a supply of water to any premises.

In *R v Dovermass Ltd* (1995), the Court of Appeal held that the words 'controlled waters' applied to watercourses such as streams, ditches, drains and so on, even where such watercourses had overflowed or dried up.

'Relevant river or watercourse' means any river or watercourse, including an underground river and an artificial river or watercourse, which is neither a public sewer nor a sewer or drain which drains into a public sewer. The Secretary of State has the power to provide by order that a watercourse of a specified description is to be treated for these purposes as if it were not a relevant river or watercourse.

The 'fresh water limit', in relation to any river or watercourse, means the place for the time being shown as the fresh-water limit of that river or watercourse in the latest map deposited by the Secretary of State with the Authority for that purpose.

'Ground waters' are defined as any waters which are contained in underground strata. An underground strata means strata subjacent to the surface of any land.

2   'Coastal waters' means waters which are within the area which extends landward from the baselines of the territorial sea as far as the limit of the highest tide or, in the case of the waters of any relevant river or watercourse, as far as the fresh water limit of the river or watercourse, together with the waters of any enclosed dock which adjoins waters within that area. The relevant territorial waters are those waters which extend seaward for three miles from the baselines from which the breadth of the territorial sea adjacent to England and Wales is measured. This definition is subject to the power of the Secretary of State to provide by order that any particular area of territorial sea adjacent to England and Wales is to be treated as if it were an area of relevant territorial waters.

8.8 Water classification

Water classification is an important tool in terms of defining the current state of controlled waters, and also in terms of monitoring improvements or deterioration in standards. Section 82 of the WRA (originally s 104 of the Water Act 1989) specifically provides the Secretary of State with the power to issue regulations which enable a classification of waters. However, before these provisions were enacted, a voluntary water classification had already been established. In the late 1970s, the National Water Council (NWC) established a system of water classification, which is gradually being superseded by the new statutory system. The NWC system has provided the principal means of monitoring water quality and has also been used as the basis for the Department of the Environment's five-yearly water quality survey.

8.8.1 The National Water Council water classification system

The NWC Water classification system is generally equated to potential uses of water and provides for the following broad classes:

- Good Quality – class 1a – water of high quality suitable for potable supply abstractions; game or other high class fisheries; high amenity value;

- Good Quality – class 1b – water of less high quality than class 1a but usable for substantially the same purposes;

- Fair Quality – class 2 – waters suitable for potable supply after advanced treatment; supporting reasonably good course fisheries; moderate amenity value;

- Poor Quality – class 3 – waters which are polluted to an extent that fish are absent or only sporadically present; may be used for low grade industrial abstraction purposes; considerable potential for further use if cleaned up;

- Bad Quality – class 4 – waters which are grossly polluted and are likely to cause nuisance.

It was in fact the Water Act 1989 which introduced a system for setting statutory water quality standards and objectives but the provisions are now to be found in ss 82–84 of the 1991 Water Resources Act.

8.8.2   Statutory water quality standards

Section 82 of the Water Resources Act 1991 enables the Secretary of State to make regulations which classify controlled waters according to certain criteria specified in those regulations. In accordance with this power, and also to implement EC Directives in this area, a number of regulations have already been made but the system is by no means complete. The classification of water is necessary before water quality objectives (under s 83) can be established. The criteria specified in regulations made under s 82 in relation to any classification of water must consist of one or more of the following requirements:

1   general requirements as to the purpose for which the waters to which the classification is applied are to be suitable (in other words water may be classified according to the use to which it will be put);

2   specific requirements as to the substances that are to be present in or absent from the water and as to the concentrations of substances which are or can be present in the water;

3   specific requirements as to the other characteristics of those waters.

The following regulations have been introduced under s 82:

1   Surface Water Classification Regulations 1989. These regulations give effect to the EC Abstraction Directive and prescribe a system for classifying waters according to their suitability for abstraction as drinking water;

2   Surface Water (Dangerous Substances) (Classification) Regulations 1989 and 1992, which give effect to the EC Dangerous Substances Directive by prescribing a system for classifying inland, estuarine and coastal waters according to the presence in them of concentrations of certain dangerous substances. The regulations list a number of dangerous substances and state the concentration of each which should not be exceeded in fresh or marine waters;

3   Bathing Waters (Classification) Regulations 1991, which give effect to the Bathing Waters Directive and which prescribe a system for classifying relevant territorial waters, coastal water and inland waters which are bathing waters.

| 8.8.3 | Statutory water quality objectives: s 83 |

Once a range of classifications has been established under s 82, the next step is to establish Water Quality Objectives (under s 83) so that the quality of a particular classification of water can be maintained and improved. Statutory Water Quality Objectives cannot be established until a relevant classification has been determined under s 82. The Secretary of State may, by serving a notice on the NRA specify:

(a) the classifications prescribed under s 82; and

(b) in relation to each specified classification, a date by which the water quality objectives are to be achieved.

A three-month period of consultation is required before objectives can be set. Water Quality Objectives may be reviewed by the NRA after five years.

| 8.8.4 | General duties to achieve and maintain objectives: s 84 |

Statutory Water Quality Objectives would be unachievable in the absence of some mechanism for enforcement. Therefore, ss 82 and 83 are backed up by s 84, which places a duty both on the Secretary of State and on the NRA to exercise their powers in such manner as ensures, so far as it is practicable, that the water quality objectives specified for any waters in a notice under s 83 are met. Therefore the NRA is required for the purpose of the carrying out this function to monitor the extent of pollution in controlled waters and to achieve the water quality objectives through the setting of consent conditions.

8.9   Discharge consents

The Water Resources Act creates a number of offences relating to the discharge of substances into controlled water. The details of the offences are considered at para 8.11. The most important practical exception to the principal offences relating to the pollution of controlled waters under the Act arises where the discharge concerned is the subject of a discharge consent granted by the National Rivers Authority or by means of authorisation from HMIP under the system of Integrated Pollution Control.

The National Rivers Authority can issue consents in relation to any discharge of trade or sewage effluent into controlled waters. The practical reality of these provisions is that an industrialist must obtain a consent for each discharge. Over one third of discharge consents are made in respect of the 10 water service companies who operate the sewage treatment works. A further third are from septic tanks. The Act provides that a person will not have committed an offence under s 85 if the discharge is carried out in accordance with a consent and the conditions included in the consent. The detailed provisions relating to the granting of the discharge consents are contained in Sched 10 to the Act.

Schedule 10 of the Act requires applications for discharge consents to be accompanied or supplemented by all such information as the NRA may reasonably require. The NRA has four months in which to determine the application. Failure to reach a decision within this time will result in a refusal of the application.

8.9.1   Applying for a discharge consent

The Water Resources Act provides for considerable publicity in relation to consent applications. Notice of applications must be published by the NRA in both the London Gazette and in a local newspaper. Copies of the application must be sent to every local authority or water undertaker within whose area the proposed discharge is to occur. There is an exception to this requirement where the discharge will have no appreciable effect on the waters into which the discharge is to be made. The Authority is then required to consider any written representations or objections to the application within the prescribed period. In addition, details of the consents granted are maintained on a public register (see Chapter 6).

8.9.2   Publicity requirements

Publicity requirements may be circumvented where the Secretary of State is satisfied that disclosure of information about the discharge would be contrary to the public interest or would prejudice, to an unreasonable degree, some private interest by disclosing information about a trade secret.

Consents may be granted subject to such conditions as the NRA may think fit. Conditions may include conditions matters relating to the nature, origin, composition, temperature, volume and rate of the discharges, and as to the periods during which the discharges may be made. Schedule 10 to the Act provides a list of conditions which may be attached but it should be noted that the list is non-exhaustive. In practice the NRA will also stipulate conditions relating to monitoring of discharges. The Authority will also often include a condition that the discharge of any new substance not specifically referred to in the consent is prohibited. Therefore, where an industrialist intends to discharge a new substance he is required to seek a variation of the consent.

8.9.3   Consent conditions

In determining whether to grant a discharge consent or deciding what conditions to attach, the NRA are obliged to take into account a variety of factors, most notably the water quality objectives for the receiving waters. The NRA has stated in its policy document on discharge consents and compliance that:

'Quality Objectives relating to environmental need and end uses of a receiving water are a fundamental cornerstone of discharge policy. Once the desired receiving water quality is identified, the necessary effluent quality to ensure achievement of the water quality objective can be achieved.'

The NRA will, therefore, take into account the water quality standards and objectives. Additionally it must also have regard to its environmental duties. A number of other factors will also be relevant in determining whether to grant a consent and the conditions to attach to it. These include:

- relevant EC standards in relation either to the substance discharged or the quality of the receiving water;

- the impact of the proposed discharge on downstream users and other uses of the waters, such as fishing and recreational uses;

- any representations made either by interested parties or as a result of consultation.

Once the NRA has determined the conditions that are to be included in a consent it is required to give those persons who made earlier representations 21 days in order to make further representations. The consent cannot be granted until this 21-day period expires.

8.9.4   Appeals

Provision is made for appeals against determinations of the Authority to be made to the Secretary of State. A person can appeal to the Secretary of State against the NRA's refusal to grant a consent; against the conditions in the consent; against a variation; or against revocation. The Secretary of State has four months within which to determine the appeal and failure to make a decision within that period will mean that the appeal has been refused. The Control of Pollution (Consents for Discharges) (Secretary of States Functions) Regulations 1989 set out the provisions in relation to appeals.

8.9.5   The charging scheme

The application of the 'polluter pays' principle requires that polluters should bear the cost of the regulatory regime that controls them. The National Rivers Authority levies a charging scheme for all new and revised consents. Details of the charging scheme are available in NRA publicity material

(*National Rivers Authority Scheme of Charges in respect of Discharges to Controlled Waters* (1991)). In addition, the NRA also charges consent holders an annual subsistence fee.

One of the problems faced by the NRA is that, when it was established, it inherited many consents which were granted before its establishment in 1989. Consents granted under COPA 1974 were automatically transferred to consents under the Water Resources Act. These pre-1989 consents reflect the requirements which were set at the time. However, the NRA has the power to vary the conditions of these consents or even to revoke them. This has been one of the major tasks faced by the NRA. In addition the NRA is also required to review consents that it has issued and will do so to ensure that conditions are altered to meet requirements specified by means of EC legislation or regulations.

8.9.6 Reviewing consents

The problem with the discharge consent scheme under the Water Resources Act is that it only applies to specific identifiable discharges from a known spot, ie through a pipe. Other more diffuse sources of pollution, such as agricultural run-off and accidental spillages, cannot be controlled by the discharge consent system. A further controversial limitation in relation to the water offences is the fact that discharges from abandoned mines are outside the NRA's control. This has generated much debate and criticism. According to estimates from British Coal there are over 10,000 abandoned mines. About 100 mines are, according to the NRA, causing 'significant pollution' and affect over 200 kilometres of rivers, streams and brooks. Following the discontinuation of mining, water levels in the mine rise when pumping ceases. The Environment Bill contains provisions relating to abandoned mines and provides that the exception will not apply to mines abandoned after 31 December 1999. This will do little at all to alleviate the present situation and may even result in mines bringing forward closure dates before 1999 to avoid these provisions.

8.9.7   Weaknesses in the consent system

The NRA has various powers at its disposal which enable it to ensure that authorised discharges comply with consent conditions, to investigate any breaches of consents and also to detect and investigate pollution incidents. The Authority can exercise control through the consent system, using its power to prohibit certain discharges or by varying or revoking a consent but these powers are limited.

8.10   NRA enforcement power

The NRA can serve notice on a person who discharges into controlled water prohibiting the discharge or prohibiting the

8.10.1   Section 86 prohibitions

continuation of the discharge. Alternatively, the notice may prohibit the discharge unless certain conditions are observed. It is an offence to discharge in contravention of the terms of a prohibition notice.

| 8.10.2 | Revocation and variation of consents | The original consent will state a period, which must not be less than two years, within which the NRA cannot vary or revoke the consent. Variation or revocation within that stated period can only occur with the agreement of the consent holder. However, after that period, the NRA can exercise its powers to vary or revoke a consent. The Secretary of State also has the power to direct the NRA to vary or revoke a consent. |

| 8.10.3 | NRA Inspectors | The Water Resources Act (ss 169–174) provides NRA Inspectors with significant investigative powers. Inspectors may: |

- enter any premises to ascertain whether an offence is or has been committed;

- carry out inspections, measurements, tests;

- remove samples of water, effluent, land or articles;

- carry out experimental borings;

- install and operate monitoring equipment.

8.11   Offences of polluting controlled waters

Section 85 of the Water Resources Act creates the following offences relating to the pollution of controlled waters. A person contravenes s 85 if he causes or knowingly permits:

1   any poisonous, noxious or polluting matter or any solid waste matter to enter any controlled waters or discharges trade or sewage effluent into controlled waters;

2   any matter, other than trade effluent or sewage effluent, to enter controlled waters by being discharged from a drain or sewer in contravention of a prohibition imposed under s 86;

3   any trade effluent or sewage effluent to be discharged into any controlled waters or from land (in England and Wales) through a pipe, into the sea outside the seaward limits of controlled waters;

4   any trade effluent or sewage effluent to be discharged in contravention of any prohibition imposed under s 86, from a building or from any fixed plant either onto or into any land or into any waters of a lake or a pond that are not inland fresh waters;

5   any matter whatever to enter any inland fresh waters so as
    to tend to impede the proper flow of the waters in a
    manner leading, or likely to lead to substantial
    aggravation of pollution due to other causes or the
    consequences of such pollution.

Definitions

• The terms 'poisonous, noxious or polluting matter' are not
  defined by the Act. In the case of *NRA v Egger (UK) Ltd*
  (1992), it was held that, in determining whether the
  offence of causing polluting matter to enter controlled
  waters has been committed, it is not necessary to
  determine whether harm has been done before the offence
  can be established.

• 'Effluent' means any liquid, including particles of matter
  and other substances in suspension in the liquid.

• 'Substance' includes micro-organisms and any natural or
  artificial substance or other matter, whether it is in solid or
  liquid form or in the form of a gas or vapour.

• 'Sewage effluent' includes any effluent from the sewage
  disposal or sewerage works of a sewerage undertaker but
  does not include surface water.

• 'Trade effluent' includes any effluent which is discharged
  from premises used for carrying on any trade or industry,
  other than surface water and domestic sewage. For the
  purposes of this definition, any premises wholly or mainly
  used (whether for profit or not) for agricultural purposes,
  fish farming, scientific research or experiment, are to be
  deemed to be premises used for carrying on a trade.

The offences under s 85 refer to the entry of substances or the
discharge of substances into controlled waters, but neither of
these terms are defined. The term 'entry' is much wider than
'discharge' and covers situations where matter is released into
controlled water as a result of an accidental spillage or leak.

The central feature of the offences contained in s 85 is that the
person must have caused or knowingly permitted the offences
to have happened. Since the Act fails to define the terms,
interpretation has been left to the courts, who have considered
what is required in a string of cases.

The leading case on the meaning of the term 'causing' is
Alphacell Ltd v Woodward (1972). In this case, the defendants
were charged, under s 2 of the River (Prevention of Pollution)

Act 1951, with causing polluting matter to enter a river. The case involved settling tanks which were located on the river banks. The tanks were used in the process of preparing manila fibres. As a result of an obstruction (caused by vegetation) the pumps, which should have prevented any overflow, became blocked. Consequently, the contents of the settling tanks overflowed from the tanks and entered into the river, causing pollution. The biochemical oxygen demand (BOD) of the discharge was above the level in the consent. The defendants argued that they had not 'caused' the polluting matter to enter into the river. However, the House of Lords held that the prosecution were not required to prove that the defendants had knowingly, intentionally or negligently caused the polluting matter to enter the river. To require otherwise would make it extremely difficult for the prosecution to satisfy the burden of proof and, as Viscount Dilhorne noted, a great deal of pollution would go unpunished. The Lords held that the act of the defendants in constructing and operating the settling tanks was a positive and deliberate act and one which led directly to the overflow and caused the pollution. Therefore the court determined that the offence was one of strict liability. It is worth restating part of the judgment put forward by Lord Wilberforce in this case, since it illustrates the common sense approach adopted by the court:

> 'In my opinion, "causing" here must be given a common sense meaning and I deprecate the introduction of refinements such as *causa*, effective cause or *novus actus*. There may be difficulties where acts of third persons or natural forces are concerned but I find the present case comparatively simple. The appellants abstract water, pass it through their works where it becomes polluted, conduct it to a settling tank communicating directly with the stream, into which the polluted water will inevitably flow if the level rises over the overflow point.'

Therefore, it is necessary to establish that there is a positive and deliberate act and that there is a causal link between that act and the discharge in question. This approach has been adopted in several cases, notably *Southern Water Authority v Pegrum* (1989) and *Wrothwell Ltd v Yorkshire Water Authority* (1984).

In *Wychavon District Council v National Rivers Authority* (1992), the Divisional Court had to consider whether a person had 'caused' pollution under s 107(1)(c) of the Water Act 1989, where he had failed to discover the source of the discharge of sewage effluent and undertake remedial measures causing sewage effluent to enter controlled water. The facts of the case illustrate the problem involved. The National Rivers

Authority alleged that the district council had caused raw sewage effluent to enter the River Avon on 11 and 12 March 1990. The sewage entered the river at a storm outflow. On 12 March the district council, acting as the agent for Severn Trent Water Authority, cleared a blockage in a sewer pipe and the pollution stopped. The question was whether the district council had 'caused' the pollution by failing promptly to discover the source of the discharge of sewage effluent in the river and then failing to clear the blockage as soon as possible.

Watkins LJ in his judgment cited the words of Lord Wilberforce in *Alphacell*:

'The subsection evidently contemplates two things – "causing", which must involve some active operation or chain of operations involving as the result the pollution of the stream; "knowingly permitting" – which involves a failure to prevent the pollution, which failure, however, must be accompanied by knowledge.'

Therefore 'causing' involves some active operation or some positive act. Applying this to the *Wychavon District Council* case, the court held that there had been no positive act on the part of the district council and they could not therefore be guilty of causing pollution. It seems, therefore, that the causing offence requires some positive act of participation on behalf of the accused and there is no need to prove that the defendant intended the offence or was guilty of negligence. In *R v CPC (UK) Ltd* (1994), the Court of Appeal reaffirmed this position and stated that the fact that some other person, as well as the defendant, might have 'caused' polluting matter to enter a river does not mean that the defendant should be acquitted. For a further discussion of the meaning of 'causing' see *National Rivers Authority v Yorkshire Water Services Ltd* (1993).

Price v Cromack (1975) provides a useful illustration of the differences between the 'causing' offence and the offence of 'knowingly permitting'. A farmer was charged with 'causing' pollution when a lagoon on his land failed and waste animal products were released into the river. The farmer had a contract with an animal products firm which allowed the firm to discharge animal waste products into the lagoons on the farmer's land. The farmer was acquitted of the causing charge on the basis that he had not caused the pollution, using the tests described above. Whilst he had permitted the build up of the waste on his land, he could not be said to have caused the pollution. Had he been charged with knowingly permitting pollution, then the verdict would probably have been different. This case also makes it clear that this is a separate and different offence to that of causing.

8.12.3 'Knowingly permitting'

8.12.4	Acts of vandalism and third parties

Although it has been stated that the causing offence is one of strict liability, the courts have been willing to take a more lenient position with regard to acts of third parties. In *Impress (Worcester) Ltd v Rees* (1971), the act of a trespasser provided a defence. Unfortunately, acts of vandalism can result in numerous environmental problems, ranging from graffiti to more serious pollution incidents. The Divisional Court was faced with the problem of vandalism in the case of *National Rivers Authority v Wright Engineering Co Ltd* (1993). The defendants, Wright Engineering, stored heating oil in a tank close to a surface water drain. The flow of oil was controlled by a tap, which was not fitted with any kind of lock. During the 1990 Christmas vacation, when the factory was closed, vandals interfered with the oil tanks, as a result of which oil from the tank was discharged down the surface drain and into controlled waters. Although there had been previous minor acts of vandalism at the factory, none of them had resulted in any serious consequence. The magistrates' court found that the discharged oil was the result of intervention by a third party and that their interference was not reasonably foreseeable by the defendants because the result was out of proportion to the other earlier and minor incidents. On appeal, the Divisional Court held that foreseeability was a relevant factor.

8.12.5	Proving water pollution: the problems of evidence

It has already been stated that NRA Inspectors have wide powers to enable them to investigate pollution offences. In carrying out their investigations, Inspectors have the power to take samples of water or effluent. The Act, however, provides strict controls in relation to the admissibility of the samples as evidence in legal proceedings. Section 209 states that the result of the analysis of any sample taken on behalf of the NRA in exercising any power under the Act will not be admissible in any legal proceedings in respect of any effluent passing from any land or vessel, unless the person who took the sample complies with certain requirements. It should be noted that these requirements apply whether the sample is taken of the effluent or the receiving water. The requirements are that the Inspector –

(a) on taking the sample, notified the occupier of the land or the owner or master of the vessel of his intention to have it analysed;

(b) there and then, divided the sample into three parts and caused each part to be placed in a container which was sealed and marked; and

(c) delivered one part to the occupier of the land or the owner or master of the vessel and retained one part, apart from the one he submitted to be analysed, for future comparison (s 209(1)).

If it is not reasonably practicable for a person taking a sample to comply with the requirements of s 209(1), those requirements are to be treated as having been complied with if they were complied with as soon as reasonably practicable after the sample was taken. These strict requirements were considered in *Attorney-General's Reference (No 2 of 1994) (1994)*. It was held that it is not necessary to inform a discharger that a sample is going to be taken, but it will suffice if the discharger is informed immediately after and that the requirement to divide the sample 'there and then' means that the division of the sample should be at or proximate to the site where the sample is taken.

The provisions of s 209 only apply to samples taken on behalf of the NRA and do not extend to other samples, for instance samples taken by pressure groups or anglers. In practice, samples taken by other organisations are likely to be challenged on scientific grounds as in the case of *Greenpeace v Albright and Wilson (1991)*.

Section 88 provides that a person will not be guilty of an offence under s 85, in respect of the entry or discharge of matter into controlled waters, if the entry or discharge is made under and in accordance with a consent provided by the NRA under the Water Resources Act. In addition to consents under the Water Resources Act 1991, it will also be a defence if the entry or discharge is made under and in accordance with:	**8.13 Authorised discharges and other defences** 8.13.1 Authorised discharges

- an authorisation for a prescribed process designated for central control under Part I of the Environmental Protection Act 1990 (see Chapter 9);

- a Waste Management Licence granted under Part II of the Environmental Protection Act (there is an exception where the offence is of discharging trade or sewage effluent or where a prohibition is in force);

- a licence granted under Part II of the Food and Environment Protection Act 1985 (authorising the deposit of waste at sea);

- s 163 of the Water Resources Act 1991 or s 165 of the Water Industry Act 1991 (concerned with discharges for works purposes);

- any local statutory provision or statutory order which expressly confers power to discharge effluent into water; or

- any prescribed enactment.

Therefore, any discharges made into controlled waters which are in compliance with conditions set down by either the NRA or HMIP will not be in breach of s 85.

8.13.2   Other general defences

In addition to the defence that a discharge is authorised under the provisions listed above, the Water Resources Act also provides a number of other defences in s 89.

A person will not be guilty of an offence under s 85 in respect of an entry of any matter into any waters or any discharge if:

(a) the entry is caused or permitted, or the discharge is made, in an emergency in order to avoid danger to life or health;

(b) that person takes all such steps as are reasonably practicable in the circumstances for minimising the extent of the entry or discharge and of its polluting effects; and

(c) particulars of the entry or discharge are furnished to the Authority as soon as reasonably practicable after it occurs (s 89(1)).

8.13.3   Specific exceptions

In addition to the above defences a number of discharges made in a number of specific situations are exempted from the provisions of the Act. A person will not be guilty of an offence under s 85 by reason of causing or permitting any discharge of trade or sewage effluent from a vessel (s 89(2)); and a person will not be guilty of an offence under s 85 by reason only of his permitting water from an abandoned mine to enter controlled waters (s 89(3)). This particular exception is one which has caused considerable controversy in view of the amount of environmental damage and water pollution that escapes from abandoned mines.

A further exception applies in relation to solid refuse from mines. A person will not (except in respect of the entry of any poisonous, noxious or polluting matter into any controlled waters) be guilty of an offence under s 85 by reason of his depositing the solid refuse of a mine or quarry on any land so that it falls or is carried into inland freshwater if the deposit is authorised by the NRA. Furthermore, a Highway Authority or other person entitled to keep open a drain by virtue of s 100 of the Highways Act 1980 will not be guilty of an offence under s 85 by reason of his causing or permitting any discharge to be made from a drain kept open by virtue of that section, unless the discharge is made in contravention of a prohibition imposed under s 86 (s 89(5)).

In deciding whether to prosecute pollution incidents, the NRA's Customer Charter states that the factors which the NRA will take into account include:

8.14   NRA prosecution policy and penalties

- whether any fish are killed;

- what (if any) remedial steps were taken by the polluter;

- whether the incident was avoidable.

The NRA differentiates between major and minor pollution incidents and it seems is much more likely to mount a prosecution if there is a major pollution incident. In practice, the NRA has demonstrated a willingness to bring criminal proceedings which is borne out by the statistics (see Chapter 5).

The Water Resources Act allows individuals as well as the NRA to commence legal proceedings for offences under the Act. One such private prosecution was brought by Greenpeace in *Greenpeace v Albright and Wilson* (1991). More recently Greenpeace brought an unsuccessful action against ICI in *Greenpeace v ICI* (1994). Greenpeace brought this latter private prosecution under s 85(1) WRA and the case illustrates one of the dangers faced by private prosecutors. Greenpeace was required to pay over £28,000 towards ICI's legal costs. Clearly, only large environmental pressure groups such as Friends of the Earth and Greenpeace can afford to run the financial risks of losing legal actions. However, in addition to traditional environmental pressure groups, the Anglers Associations have availed themselves of these rights as well as resorting to common law actions to secure injunctions or obtain damages.

8.14.1   Private prosecutions

A person who contravenes the provisions of Part III of the Water Resources Act 1991, or the conditions of any consent given under the Act, will be guilty of a criminal offence and liable:

8.14.2   Penalties for water pollution offences

(a) on summary conviction, to imprisonment for a term not exceeding three months, or to a fine not exceeding £20,000 or to both;

(b) on conviction on indictment, to imprisonment for a term not exceeding two years or to a fine (of unlimited amount) or to both (s 85(6)).

In *National Rivers Authority v Shell UK* (1990), Shell UK was fined £1,000,000 for polluting the River Mersey. Although this case is somewhat exceptional, it does illustrate the levels of fines that may be imposed for serious polluting offences.

| 8.14.3 | Criminal liabilities of directors and other third parties |

In the same way that s 157 of the Environmental Protection Act allows for personal liability, s 217 of the Water Resources Act also extends liability for water pollution offences to company officials. Section 217 states that, where a body corporate is guilty of an offence under the Act, then any director, manager, secretary or other similar officer may also be personally liable and be guilty of that offence. However, in order to secure a conviction under s 217, it is necessary to prove that the offence was committed with the consent or connivance of, or is attributable to any neglect on the part of, that person. In practice, this has been very hard to do and the regulatory authorities have rarely prosecuted company officials under either s 217 WRA or s 157 EPA. However, the fact that individuals cannot hide behind the company veil should provide a deterrence against negligent environmental management.

8.15 Disposal into sewers

The disposal of effluent into sewers is inextricably linked to water pollution. Industrial processes generate enormous quantities of waste which is either discharged on land as solid waste, emitted into the atmosphere or, in the case of liquid wastes, it may either be discharged into controlled waters or released into the sewers. The discharge of trade effluent into sewers is controlled directly by the sewerage undertakers, exercising their powers under the Water Resources Act, but also indirectly by the NRA. Sewerage undertakers grant consents for the disposal of trade effluent into the sewers but they are then required to obtain consent from the NRA to release the final treated effluent into controlled waters. The Water Industry Act regulates the discharge of trade effluents into sewers and s 87 WRA deals with the discharge of sewage effluent into controlled waters.

8.15.1 Discharges of sewage into controlled waters

Section 85 makes it an offence to discharge sewage effluent into controlled waters and, therefore, sewerage undertakers are required to obtain a consent from the NRA to legally discharge the treated sewage. Sewerage undertakers are subject to the same provisions as any other discharger. Although there has been some degree of flexibility in the setting of consent conditions, the NRA has been reviewing many of the undertakers discharge consents in order to impose stricter conditions, and the Authority has demonstrated that it is willing to prosecute for breach of conditions. Section 87 WRA deals specifically with discharges into and from public sewers. Under s 87, sewerage undertakers, however, do benefit from the availability of an additional defence which is not available to other dischargers. An undertaker will not be guilty of an offence under s 85 if the discharge is in breach of consent conditions where:

- the breach is attributable to a discharge which another person caused or permitted to be made into the sewer;

- the sewerage undertaker was not bound to receive the discharge into the sewer; and

- the undertaker could not reasonably have been expected to prevent the discharge into the sewer.

This defence recognises that sewerage undertakers deal with effluent from a variety of sources, which are treated and then discharged from the sewer or works under NRA consent. If the final discharge from the undertaker is in breach of consent conditions, the undertaker will not be guilty of an offence if the reason for the breach was due to the unauthorised discharge of effluent into the sewer, providing it can be shown that the undertaker could not reasonably have expected the unauthorised discharge into the sewer.

Given that sewerage undertakers are subject to the same controls as any other discharger (subject to the availability of the additional defence), they are required to maintain a tight control on the effluent they are prepared to accept into the sewers and, for this reason, the disposal of trade effluent into a sewer requires a separate consent from the sewerage undertaken under s 118 of the Water Industry Act.

8.15.2   Discharges of trade effluent into the sewers

The disposal of trade effluent into a sewer (through a drain or sewer) requires a consent under s 118, and it is an offence to discharge any trade effluent from trade premises otherwise than in accordance with the conditions of a consent from the sewerage undertaker. The application for consent is made by means of serving notice on the undertaker. At least two months' notice must be given of an intention to discharge and the notice has to provide details of the proposed discharge. Following the service of a notice, the sewerage undertaker has to decide whether or not to grant consent and the conditions to attach.

8.15.3   Trade effluent consents: s 118 WIA

Section 121 specifies the conditions that a sewerage undertaker may attach to a trade effluent consent. Ultimately, when

8.15.4   Discharges of sewage into controlled waters

framing conditions the sewerage undertaker must have regard for the conditions in its own consent under the Water Resources Act.

8.15.5   Special consents

Certain types of effluent, known as 'special category effluents', require a special consent because they are potentially harmful and are difficult to treat. The Trade Effluents (Prescribed Processes and Substances) Regulations 1989 as amended, prescribe the particular substances that fall into this category.

8.16   Preventive approaches to water pollution

In addition to the controls thus far discussed, the Water Resources Act contains provisions which enable a more preventive approach to water pollution, whereby harm is prevented by means of anticipatory action. Section 161, in particular, empowers the NRA to take action to avoid pollution of controlled waters. This section also equips the NRA with extensive clean-up powers and is considered more fully at para 8.17 below. In addition to s 161, ss 92–95 contain provisions relating to the prevention of pollution. These provisions are particularly useful in relation to more diffuse sources of pollution such as run-off arising from agricultural activities.

8.16.1   Section 92 WRA

Under s 92, the Secretary of State has the power to make provisions (by means of regulations) for:

- prohibiting a person from having custody or control of any poisonous, noxious or polluting matter unless prescribed works and prescribed precautions and other steps have been taken for the purpose of preventing or controlling the entry of the matter into any controlled waters;

- for requiring a person who already has custody or control of, or makes use of, poisonous, noxious or polluting matter to carry out such works for that purpose and to take precautions and other steps for the same purpose as may be prescribed.

Using these powers, the Control of Pollution (Silage, Slurry and Agricultural Fuel Oil) Regulations were introduced in 1991. These regulations require persons with custody of silage, livestock slurry or certain fuel oil to carry out works and take precautions and other steps for preventing pollution of controlled waters.

8.16.2   Water protection zones: s 93

A further mechanism for preventing water pollution is contained in s 93 WRA 1991 and allows for the designation of Water Protection Zones. Where the Secretary of State, after consultation with the Minister of Agriculture, Fisheries and Food considers that it is appropriate to prohibit or restrict the carrying on in a particular area of activities which he considers are likely to result in the pollution of any controlled waters, he may by order make provision:

- designating that area as a water protection zone; and

- prohibiting or restricting the carrying on in the designated area of such activities specified or described in the order.

The aim of designating an area as a Water Protection Zone is to prevent or control the discharge of poisonous, noxious or polluting matter into controlled water. The NRA is then responsible for determining which activities can take place within the Water Protection Zone and has the power to prosecute anyone contravening any restrictions in the zone.

In addition to the designation of Water Protection Zones, areas may also be designated as Nitrate Sensitive Areas under s 94. (Nitrate pollution cannot be controlled under the mechanisms of the Water Protection Zones). The Secretary of State for Environment and the Minister for Agriculture have the power to designate areas as Nitrate Sensitive Areas, where they consider that it is appropriate, in order to prevent or control the entry of nitrate into controlled waters as a result of anything done in connection with the use of any land for agricultural purposes. Designation of an area is made by Order and the Order may:

8.16.3   Nitrate sensitive areas: ss 94–95

- require, prohibit or restrict the carrying on, either on or in region to any agricultural land in the area, of specified activities; and

- provide for specified or determined amounts to be paid in compensation in respect of the obligations imposed as a result of the designation.

Where an area has been designated as a Nitrate Sensitive Area, and the relevant Minister considers it appropriate, he may enter into an agreement to allow for payments to be made to the owner of the freehold interest in any agricultural land in the area (or with the permission of the freehold owner, or with any other person having another interest in the land) where that person accepts obligations with respect to the management of the land or other obligations imposed under the agreement.

It has already been noted that, under s 161 of the Water Resources Act, the NRA has the power to take action to prevent pollution of controlled waters. Section 161 is

8.17   The clean-up of polluted water

particularly important because it gives the NRA the power to take action to either prevent pollution or to clean up watercourses where pollution has taken place. Subject to s 161(2), where it appears to the Authority that any poisonous, noxious or polluting matter or any solid waste matter is likely to enter, is entering or has entered any controlled water, the Authority will be entitled to carry out remedial works to clean up the pollution. The section provides that the following works and operations may be carried out:

- removing or disposing of the matter;

- remedying or mitigating any pollution caused by its presence in the waters; or

- so far as it is reasonably practicable to do so, of restoring the waters, including any flora and fauna dependent on the aquatic environment of the waters, to their state immediately before the matter became present in the waters.

Where the Authority carries out any such works or operations as are mentioned in s 161, it will be entitled to recover the expenses reasonably incurred in doing so. Expenses may be recovered from any person who caused or knowingly permitted the matter in question to be present at the place from which it was likely enter any controlled waters, or who caused or knowingly permitted the matter in question to be present in any controlled waters. The NRA can exercise these powers independently of any legal proceedings which they might instigate. In 1993, the NRA successfully used its powers under s 161 in respect of an incident in the Anglian Region where the NRA recovered £99,000 from a polluter for the costs of restocking fish. It appears that the NRA are intending to use these powers to clean up the contaminated aquifer at Eastern Counties Leather (see *Cambridge Water Company Limited v Eastern Counties Leather plc* (1994)). In practice, the clean-up costs may be very high and often greater than any fine imposed by the courts.

8.18   Control of water pollution under other legislation

8.18.1   Part I EPA 1990

Part I of the EPA introduces Integrated Pollution Control (IPC) as a system for controlling pollution from those more seriously polluting processes which are prescribed by the Act (see Chapter 9). In relation to those processes falling under the IPC regime, control of pollution into controlled water is transferred from the NRA to Her Majesty's Inspectorate of Pollution. Under the EPA, persons or companies wishing to operate a prescribed process must obtain an authorisation from HMIP which will control releases into all environmental media, including water. In determining whether to grant an authorisation, HMIP is required, where there is a release into controlled waters, to consult the NRA. Section 28 of the EPA also provides that HMIP shall not grant an authorisation if the NRA certifies that the release will result in, or contribute to, the failure of any quality objective in force under the Water Resources Act. Effectively NRA can specify the conditions to be set in the IPC authorisation in relation to the discharges, and it can also specify when a variation is required. HMIP is under a duty to include any conditions that NRA specify.

Additionally, Part II EPA, which is concerned with waste management, is also relevant. The Act requires consultation between the National Rivers Authority and the Waste Regulation Authority where the deposit of waste is likely to result in pollution of groundwater (see Chapter 12).

8.18.2   Part II EPA 1990

In addition to the offences established by the Water Resources Act, s 4(1) of the Salmon and Freshwater Fisheries Act 1975 provides that it is an offence where a person 'causes or knowingly permits to flow, or puts, or knowingly permits to be put, into waters containing fish or into any tributaries of waters containing fish, any liquid or solid matter to such an extent as to cause the waters to be poisonous or injurious to fish or the spawning grounds, spawn or food of fish'. Although the Water Resource Act provides the main provisions relating to water pollution, charges may be brought under s 4 where fish on their spawning grounds are actually injured.

8.18.3   Salmon and Freshwater Fisheries Act 1975

The Land Drainage Act 1994 came into effect in September 1994. Although it is largely concerned with flood defence and land drainage, it does require local authorities to have regard for the environment when carrying out land drainage and flood defence works.

8.18.4   The Land Drainage Act 1994

The quality of water is not simply determined by what is discharged into it. Water quality is inextricably linked to water quantity. If water levels are low, there is less water available to dilute waste and effluents and this may cause a reduction in water quality. Therefore, it is appropriate in a chapter on water pollution to consider the legal controls that exist in relation to the abstraction of water. The NRA is under a statutory duty to secure the proper use of water resources. Under s 19 WRA, the NRA is under a duty to conserve and increase the available water resources. The NRA therefore has to assess the need for new developments and ensure that the most appropriate schemes are licensed, taking into account

8.19   Water abstraction

the environmental impact of new developments on existing users.

Before legislation was enacted to control the use of water, the common law had developed various rules which determined rights of riparian owners to abstract water. These have largely been superseded by the legislation but need to be considered.

8.19.1 Riparian rights

Owners of property adjoining a river, known as riparian owners or occupiers, have the right to what the courts called the 'ordinary use of water flowing past their land'. In *Miner v Gilmore* (1859), Lord Kingsdown stated that:

> 'By the general law applicable to running streams, every riparian proprietor has a right to what may be called the ordinary use of water flowing past his land; for instance to the reasonable use of the water for his domestic purposes and for his cattle, and this without regard to the effect which such use may have, in case of a deficiency on a proprietor lower down the stream.'

Not only does this view have potentially detrimental consequences for riparian owners further down stream, it clearly takes no account of any environmental consequences of such actions. However, the position is qualified to the extent that uses which may be regarded as extraordinary can only be carried out if they do not cause harm to lower riparian occupiers. Therefore, if one riparian owner wished to use water for what would be described as an extraordinary use, they could only do so if would not harm the rights of others. This was the view taken in the case of *Rugby Joint Water Board v Walters* (1967), where the court stated that the water removed must either have no effect on the river or it must be returned to it substantially undiminished in quantity or quality. This more recent decision appears to reflect the changing attitude to the environment insofar as the decision is couched in terms of the quality of the river in its own right.

8.19.2 Legislative controls over water abstraction

As stated above, the common law rules have now been replaced by legislative controls over water abstraction. Growing concern about the problems of over-abstraction, water shortages, rivers drying out and the consequent loss of natural habitat led to legislative controls aimed at controlling the abstraction of water. The first attempts to provide a means of control were contained in the Water Act 1945, which provided some limited controls over water abstraction. However, it was the 1963 Water Resources Act which aimed to provide the first comprehensive control over water abstraction, as it prohibited the abstraction of water without an abstraction licence.

When the requirement for an abstraction licence was first introduced, many industrial companies had already been abstracting water for use in their industrial processes for many years. Section 33 of the 1963 Act provided a special entitlement for such users, automatically granting a Licence of Right to any person who was entitled to abstract water from a source or supply in a river authority area at the date that s 33 came into force, or to a person who had a record of five years continuous abstraction. These Licences of Right are presumed by the 1991 Water Resources Act; however, such licence-holders are now required to pay for their abstraction rights.

Abstraction licences are now granted by the National Rivers Authority. In order to apply for an abstraction licence, it is usually necessary to be either:

8.19.3   Abstraction licences under the Water Resources Act 1991

- an occupier of the land adjacent to the inland water; or

- an occupier of land above the underground strata from which the water is drawn.

The licence is issued to the occupier of land. Once his occupation ceases, the licence will lapse and the new occupier will need to notify the NRA if he wishes to take over the licence. Water undertakers are required to apply for a licence for the water that they abstract from water courses. Sections 27 and 29 provide various exceptions to the need to obtain an abstraction licence. Owners of the land through which water flows may use for domestic or agricultural purposes a maximum of 20 cubic metres each day without the need for a licence.

An application for an abstraction licence is made to the NRA in accordance with the Water Resources (Licences) Regulations 1965. The application must be accompanied by a fee. Notice of the application is publicised by the applicant in the London Gazette and a local newspaper. The NRA is required when considering an application for an abstraction licence to consider:

- representations made in response to publicity;

- representations made arising from consultation with bodies such as English Nature;

- the effect of the proposed abstraction on other existing licence holders;

- the effect on other users of the supply.

The NRA can attach conditions to licences which may require the abstractor to return the water to the watercourse after use.

8.19.4   Licence conditions

Monitoring of the amounts of water abstracted will usually be required as a condition of the licence. When considering whether to grant a licence or the conditions to be attached to it, the NRA must consider whether the grant of licence will prevent another current licence-holder, or someone extracting water for domestic or agricultural purposes, from abstracting their full entitlement. If the proposed abstraction will affect in this manner, then the NRA must refuse to grant a licence unless the person affected agrees to the grant of the new licence.

An abstraction licence may be varied either by the NRA acting on its own initiative or at the request of the licence-holder. If the NRA decides that it intends to vary a licence, then a licence-holder has a right of appeal to the Secretary of State. If the holder suffers damage as a result of the Secretary of State's decision, he may recover compensation from the NRA. Once a licence is granted, the NRA is not liable to derogate from the grant of the licence,

| 8.20 | **The European Community dimension** | In terms of its environmental policy, water pollution and its prevention was one of the first areas to be developed in the EC. The European Community has adopted over 25 specific pieces of legislation in the area of water protection, management and conservation. In general, the EC has adopted a variety of approaches to pollution control, such as establishing minimum quality standards, controlling the discharge of specific pollutants or defining product specifications. (See Chapter 3 for a further discussion of this point.) In terms of EC action in relation to water pollution, measures have concentrated on either establishing minimum water quality standards or preventing and controlling the discharge of dangerous substances into the aquatic environment. In the context of this book, it is not possible to provide a full description of all of the relevant EC water pollution measures; however, some are of considerable significance and merit individual attention. Council Directive 91/271 on Urban Waste Water Treatment is particularly important. This Directive requires the secondary treatment of sewage discharged to inland and coastal waters. Under the Directive, Member States are required to phase out the disposal of sewage sludge at sea by 31 December 1998. It is the cost of implementing these requirements that has made the Directive so controversial. |

In adopting an approach that aims to establish water quality standards, the EC has adopted a number of key Directives including Council Directives 75/440 and 80/778 on drinking water, 76/160 on bathing waters, 78/659 on waters for fresh water fish and 79/923 on shell fish waters.

The main Directive which aims to control dangerous substances released into the aquatic evironment is the framework Directive 76/464 on Dangerous Substances into Water. As a framework Directive it has subsequently been backed up by a number of so-called daughter Directives. The framework Directive provides two lists of deleterious substances which are to be eliminated (in the case of List 1 substances) or progressively reduced (in the case of List 2 substances). These are sometimes referred to as the 'black list' in relation to List 1 and the 'grey list' in relation to List 2. The progressive reduction of List 2 substances is to be achieved by the establishment of Community-wide threshold limits and quality objectives. The UK approach to the Directive has been different to that in other Member States. The Commission wanted to establish uniform fixed emission limit values for the substances identified in List 1. However, the UK approach has been to establish water quality objectives for the receiving waters and thereby allow varying emission standards to be set in different discharge consents. As a result of political compromise, the Directive allows each Member State to effectively decide itself whether they want to set the fixed emission limit values for various types of industry or to adopt the water quality approach put forward by the UK government and subsequently adopted in the UK. Therefore, the approach in the UK is as stated, to set water quality objectives which are met through the emission standards set through the consent system.

8.20.1   Control of dangerous substances

Summary of Chapter 8

Water Pollution

Offences

The main legislation governing water pollution is the Water Resources Act 1991 although other controls are exerted, particularly through the system of IPC under Part I of the Environmental Protection Act 1990.

The control of water pollution is exercised by the NRA through a system of discharge concents. The pollution controls provided for in the WRA apply only in respect of 'controlled waters'.

- Section 104 defines controlled waters.

- Sections 82–84 WRA 1991 allow for the establishment of quality standards (s 82) and Water Quality Objectives (s 83).

- Section 85 creates the various offences relating to the pollution of controlled waters.

- It is a requirement that a person 'causes or knowingly permits' the pollution.

  These are separate offences.

Defences are:

Defences

- Section 88 provides the main defence. If the discharge was in accordance with a discharge consent, an IPC authorities or waste management licence;

- Section 89 provides other general defences;

- Preventive action. The Water Resources Act also provides for preventive action to be taken, namely under s 92; s 93 (Water Protection Zones); ss 94–95 (Nitrate Sensitive Areas);

- Remedial action. Section 161 allows the NRA to take action to either:

  (a) prevent pollution of controlled waters; or

  (b) to clean-up water courses where pollution has taken place.

- Water abstraction. Abstraction licences are granted by the NRA exercising powers under the WRA 1991.

Chapter 9

Integrated Pollution and Air Pollution Control

The concept of Integrated Pollution Control developed out of the recognition that pollutants have effects on environmental media other than those into which they are directly released and that reducing opportunities for the disposing of wastes into one medium often increases the need to dispose of the wastes into another.

In its Fifth Report on Air Pollution Control in 1976, the Royal Commission on Environmental Pollution asserted the need for an integrated approach to pollution control to replace the single medium approach that had developed in the UK. The report stated that:

> 'The reduction of emissions to the atmosphere can lead to an increase in wastes to be disposed of on land or discharged to water. If the optimum environmental solutions are to be found, the controlling authority must be able to look comprehensively to all forms of pollution arising from industrial processes where different control problems exist.'

In practical terms, this means that where a manufacturer selects a manufacturing process which reduces or eliminates the need to discharge into water, this may have a knock-on effect in terms of the emissions he makes into the atmosphere or the amount of solid waste that needs to be disposed of. The single medium approach, which had developed in a largely piecemeal fashion in this country, could not take account of this inter-relationship between different environmental media.

The Royal Commission Report also referred to the 'transferability of pollution':

> 'The three principal forms of pollution – of air, water and land – are often very closely linked. In order to reduce atmospheric pollution, gases or dusts may be trapped in a spray of water or washed out of filters. This leaves polluted water, if not discharged to a sewer or direct to a river or the sea, can be piped into a lagoon to settle and dry out, leaving a solid waste disposal problem. The pollutant may even go full circle by blowing off the lagoon as dust.'

The report identified other examples of the transferability of pollution, such as water seeping through refuse tips and smoke from the incineration of rubbish or sludge. The absence

9.1 Background to the development of Integrated Pollution Control – the need for a multimedia approach

of a co-ordinated view, and the fragmented approach to pollution control that had developed in the UK, meant that this inter-relationship was largely ignored. Decisions on water discharges taken by the water authorities were largely taken in isolation of decisions made by the waste disposal authorities, the local authorities exercising their clean air functions or the Alkali Inspectorate. The Royal Commission could find little evidence of co-ordination between the various agencies. This lack of co-ordination meant that, in practice, industries that had been prevented from releasing hazardous substances into a particular medium could choose another means of disposal – for example burning or burying – and effectively divert the wastes into another medium where the regulatory regime and rules were different. The Royal Commission, therefore, recommended the need for a more co-ordinated approach or a cross-media approach so that pollutants were not simply transferred from one medium to another. There was clear evidence of the need for a new controlling authority which could control whole processes and achieve the best practicable environmental option. Such a body was not established for over 10 years until the creation of Her Majesty's Inspectorate of Pollution (HMIP) in 1987.

9.2   Integrated pollution control: achieving the best practical environmental option

In 1990, the Environmental Protection Act eventually established a new system of pollution control which aimed to fulfil the recommendations of the Royal Commission. The system is known as Integrated Pollution Control or IPC and is controlled by Her Majesty's Inspectorate of Pollution. Taking up the Royal Commissions recommendations, the system of IPC was established to prevent or minimise pollution of the environment due to the release of substances into any environmental medium and thus takes a cross-media approach. However, the system of IPC does not cover all industrial processes but concentrates only on the most seriously polluting processes. These seriously polluting processes will be regulated by a means of prior approval in which the process is required to obtain an authorisation from Her Majesty's Inspectorate of Pollution. In granting approval, HMIP must consider the impact of the process on all three environmental media and determine the means of operation that would give the 'best practicable environmental option'.

In its 12th Report in 1988, the Royal Commission dealt with the issue of best practical environmental option and defined it in the following way:

'The selection of BPEO requires a systematic approach to decision-taking in which the practicability of all reasonable options is examined and in which environmental impact is a major factor in the final choice.'

There is therefore a requirement that Her Majesty's Inspectorate considers the process as a whole and authorises the option that provides the most benefit or the least damage to the environment as a whole, at acceptable cost.

Part I of the Environmental Protection Act 1990, in fact, establishes two systems of pollution control:

- Integrated Pollution Control for the most seriously polluting processes which are regulated by Her Majesty's Inspectorate of Pollution; and

- Local Authority Air Pollution Control (LAAPC) for those processes which should not be allowed to operate without an authorisation, but are not so seriously polluting as to fall within the central control of HMIP. Local authorities regulate these less seriously polluting processes for the purposes of preventing or minimising pollution of the environment due to the release of substances into air (but not into any other environmental medium).

Section 6 EPA requires that certain prescribed processes must not be carried on, or certain prescribed substances must not be released into any environmental medium ,without prior authorisation from either HMIP or the relevant local authority. To carry on a prescribed process or discharge a prescribed substance without an authorisation is a criminal offence. Regulations prescribe two lists of processes, those in the 'A' List to be controlled by HMIP and those in the 'B' List to be controlled by the local authority in whose area the process takes place.

Where a process is prescribed for control by HMIP, then HMIP regulates, by means of the authorisation, releases into all environmental media. HMIP must take into account the process as a whole in terms of the releases into air, water and land. In reaching its conclusions about the levels of discharges and emissions, it is required to have regard to achieving the 'best practicable environmental option', known simply as BPEO. Where the process is designated for control by a local authority, the local authority can only regulate any emissions that such a process makes into air. That does not mean, of course, that processes designated for LAAPC only discharge into air. It means that such processes must seek an authorisation from the relevant local authority (which will be the district council or London Borough Council) for the air emissions and if they discharge into controlled waters they

9.3 Overview of IPC and LAAPC

will be required to seek a separate consent from the National Rivers Authority under the Water Resources Act 1991. Therefore, for these 'less seriously polluting' processes there is no 'integrated pollution control'.

For the purposes of Part I of the EPA, the definition of environment is 'all, or any, of the following media, namely the air, water and land; and the medium of air includes the air within buildings and the air within other natural or man-made structures above or below ground'.

The Secretary of State for the Environment has the power to issue regulations prescribing those processes and substances which should be subject to control under Part I of the Act and which should be subject to either Integrated Pollution Control or Local Authority Air Pollution Control. If a process falls into one of the categories listed in the regulations, then it must obtain an authorisation as specified in the regulations, ie from either HMIP or the local authority, depending on whether the process is an 'A' list process or a 'B' list process. The regulations do provide for a small category of exemptions. Authorisations from HMIP or the local authority may either be refused or granted subject to conditions and it is a criminal offence to operate a process in contravention of any specific condition or general conditions attached to such authorisations. Of particular importance, is the BATNEEC condition. The concept of BATNEEC has been discussed fully in Chapter 1.

One of the features of Part I of the EPA is the degree to which it is supplemented by further regulations which lay down the detailed provisions relating to applications, the operation of authorisations, public consultation, public registers, powers of inspectors, enforcement powers and appeals.

The provisions in Part I relate to both HMIP and local authorities, the Act refers to them as the 'enforcing authorities'. However, reference will usually be made in this chapter to HMIP only. Where there are differences between the IPC and LAAPC procedures then specific mention will be made.

9.4   Prescribed processes and substances

9.4.1   What is a process?

The definition provided in s 1 Part I EPA is that a process means any activities carried on in Great Britain, whether on premises or by means of mobile plant, which are capable of causing pollution of the environment. 'Activities' are further defined as industrial or commercial activities or activities of any other nature whatsoever (including, with or without other activities, the keeping of a substance). The term 'process', therefore, has been given a very wide meaning and it is clear from the definition that even storage (keeping a substance) may constitute a process if it is capable of causing pollution. Pollution of the environment becomes central to the definition of a process. It is defined in terms of the release into any environmental medium from any process of substances which are capable of causing harm to man or any other living organism.

Since it is an offence to 'carry on' a prescribed process without an authorisation, there may be a question as to what constitutes carrying on. Cases which have considered this question (albeit not within the context of the EPA), suggest that there must be an element of repetition or series of acts and that the person carrying on the process must have control and direction with regard to it.

The controls over emissions into the air and discharges into water contained in Part I of the EPA only relate to those processes which are prescribed for control. As stated earlier, the Secretary of State for the Environment has the power by virtue of s 2 EPA to prescribe, by means of regulation, those processes and substances which fall within Part I and thus require an authorisation under s 6. The Act states that any such regulations made may frame the description of the process by reference to any characteristic of the process or the area or other circumstances in which the process is carried on or the description of the person carrying it on. As far as the substances are concerned, the Act provides that the regulations may prescribe substances separately for each environmental medium and that they may also include details about the amounts over a period of time, or the concentrations of such substances, in order for them to be 'prescribed'.

Using his powers under s 2, the Secretary of State has enacted the following regulations which prescribe the processes and substances which should be controlled under Part I of the EPA. The following regulations have been enacted: the Environmental Protection (Prescribed Processes and Substances) Regulations 1991, which has been amended by the following Regulations – SI 1991 No 836, SI 1992 No 614, SI 1994 No 1271 and SI 1994 No 1329. The regulations provide for a number of exemptions and these are dealt with more fully below.

9.4.2 The Prescribed Processes and Substances Regulations

Schedule 1 of the Regulations contains the descriptions of processes prescribed for control, and Scheds 4–6 prescribe the substances subject to control. Schedule 1 of the regulations is broken down into chapters, each dealing with a broad industrial sector. Within each of these broad sector headings, there is a more detailed list of industrial processes. These are further sub-divided into Part A processes and Part B processes. Part A processes are subject to IPC and Part B processes are subject to LAAPC.

9.4.3   Industrial sectors

Schedule 1 breaks down into the following chapters which are based upon broad industrial sectors:

- Chapter 1 :   Fuel Production Processes, Combustion Processes and Associated Processes;

- Chapter 2 :   Metal Production and Processing;

- Chapter 3 :   Mineral Industries;

- Chapter 4 :   The Chemical Industry;

- Chapter 5 :   Waste disposal and Recycling;

- Chapter 6:   Other industries.

Within each of these chapters there is a further breakdown into more detailed industrial processes, so for example within Chapter 4 on the Chemical Industry the following processes are included:

- petrochemical processes;

- the manufacture and use of organic chemicals;

- acid processes;

- inorganic chemical processes;

- chemical fertiliser production;

- pesticide production;

- pharmaceutical production;

- the storage of chemicals in bulk.

For each of these processes there is more detailed description and also a breakdown between those activities which are classified as a Part A process (IPC) or a Part B process (LAAPC). The following example best demonstrates this:

Chemical fertiliser production:

- Part A:
  (a) the manufacture of chemical fertilisers;
  (b) the conversion of chemical fertilisers into granules;

- Part B:
  Nil.

In order to determine whether a process falls under Part A or Part B, it is necessary to find the description of the process in the regulations. So, for example, if you are trying to determine whether a factory that manufactures ink is subject to IPC or LAAPC, you would first of all need to determine which broad industrial sector it falls into. Since it is not obvious which broad industrial grouping it falls into, the best starting point is the chapter on Other Industries (Chapter 6). From there, one can find s 6.6 'the manufacture of dyestuffs, printing ink and coating materials'. Under this sub-section, the manufacture and formulation of printing ink is determined to be a Part B process. However, the process will only need an authorisation from the relevant local authority where the carrying on of the process is likely to involve the use of 100 tonnes or more of organic solvents in any 12-month period at the location in question.

9.4.4   How to find out whether a process is prescribed for IPC or LAAPC

Many companies operate large industrial plants where a number of different industrial processes are carried out at the same location. In the event that there is a dispute, or it is not clear which category (or indeed categories) a particular plant should fall into, Sched 2 of the Regulations assists with a number of rules of interpretation. The issue of which category a plant falls into is more than academic and has real practical implications for the plant concerned. An application for an authorisation from HMIP is considerably more expensive than one from the local authority. The rules of interpretation provide for, *inter alia*, those situations where a process appears to fall into two categories or where a plant undertakes a number of different processes falling into several categories. The rules are lengthy, but the most important one covers situations where a particular plant operates a process which overlaps Part A and Part B. In such circumstances, the whole process will be controlled centrally as an IPC process by HMIP.

9.4.5   What happens when a plant operates more than one process?

By virtue of s 2(5) EPA, the Secretary of State can also prescribe certain substances for control and, accordingly, the release of the prescribed substances requires authorisation under s 6. The list of prescribed substances can be found in Scheds 4, 5 and 6 of the Prescribed Processes and Prescribed Substances Regulations 1991. They are prescribed in relation to the environmental medium in which they are released:

9.4.6   Prescribed substances

• *Schedule 4: Substances released into the air*:
  Oxides of sulphur and other sulphur compounds;

Oxides of nitrogen and other nitrogen compounds;
Oxides of carbon;
Organic compounds and partial oxidation products;
Metals, metalloids and their compounds;
Asbestos (suspended particulate matter and fibres), glass fibres and mineral fibres;
Halogens and their compounds;
Phosphorous and its compounds;
Particulate matter.

- *Schedule 5: Substances released into water:*
  Mercury and its compounds;
  Cadmium and its compounds;
  All isomers of hexachlorocyclohexane;
  All isomers of DDT;
  Pentachlorophenol and its compounds;
  Hexachlorobenzene;
  Hexachlorobutadiene;
  Aldrin;
  Dieldrin;
  Endrin;
  Polychlorinated Biphenyls;
  Dichlorvos;
  1,2–Dichloroethane;
  All isomers of trichlorobenzene;
  Atrazine;
  Simazine;
  Tributyltin compounds;
  Triphenyltin compounds;
  Trifluralin;
  Fenitrothion;
  Azinphos-methyl;
  Malathion;
  Endosulfan.

- *Schedule 6: Substances released on to land:*
  Organic solvents;
  Azides;
  Halogens and their covalent compounds;
  Metal carbonyls;

Organo-metallic compounds;

Oxidising agents;

Polyclorinated dibenzofuran and any cogener thereof;

Polychlorinated dibenzo-p-dioxin and any congener thereof;

Polyhalogenated biphenyls, terphenyls and naphthalenes;

Phosphorous;

Pesticides;

Alkali metals and their oxides and alkaline earth and their oxides.

In total, HMIP is responsible for about 200 industrial processes and about 5,000 industrial plants.

The regulations provide for a number of situations where a process is exempt from the need to obtain an authorisation. In particular, a process cannot be taken to be a Part A process if the process cannot result in:

9.4.7   Exemptions

(a) the release to air of prescribed substances, or there is no likelihood that it will result in the release to air of any such substance except in a quantity which is so trivial that it is incapable of causing harm, or its capacity to cause harm is insignificant; and

(b) the release of prescribed substances into water except in a concentration which is no greater than the background concentration, or in a quantity which does not, in any twelve month period, exceed the background quantity by more than the amount specified in Sched 5 of the Regulations;

(c) the release on to land of any prescribed substances or there is no likelihood that it will result in the releases on to land of any such substance, except in a quantity which is so trivial that it is incapable of causing harm or its capacity to cause harm is insignificant.

A process cannot be a Part B process unless it will, or there is a likelihood that it will, result in the release into the air of one or more of the prescribed substances, unless the quantity which is released is so trivial that it is incapable of causing harm or its capacity to cause harm is so insignificant.

There are a number of additional specified exceptions. These include processes carried on in working museums which are intended to demonstrate matters of historical interest and processes carried on in schools for educational purposes. The running of aircraft, hovercraft, cars, trains and ships is also excluded. The list of exceptions are provided in s 4 of the Regulations.

| 9.5 | The need for an authorisation |

Section 6 of the EPA provides that:

> 'No person shall carry on a prescribed process after the date prescribed or determined for that description of process by or under regulations under s 2(1) ... except under an authorisation granted by the enforcing authority and in accordance to the conditions to which it is subject.'

Therefore, once it has been determined that a process is prescribed or discharges a prescribed substance, and also which regulatory regime it falls under, an application for an authorisation for that process must be made to the appropriate enforcement agency. It is only an offence for a person to carry on the prescribed process without an authorisation after the date prescribed or determined. Such dates have been prescribed by regulations issued under s 2(1) and these regulations prescribe a timetable for applications to be made to avoid an enormous influx of applications once the provisions came into force (see section below – Phasing in IPC: a rolling programme).

An IPC authorisation is required to operate:

- any process subject to IPC;

- any proposed new process in any IPC category;

- any existing process in any IPC category where a 'substantial change' in the process is proposed.

An application for IPC authorisation is made to the relevant regional office of HMIP. It should be noted here that, where the process is prescribed for LAAPC, the application for authorisation is made to the local authority in whose area the prescribed processes are (or are to be) carried on. LAAPC applications may also be made for prescribed processes carried on by means of mobile plant, in which case the application is made to the local authority in whose area the person carrying on the business has his principal place of business.

| 9.5.1 | Phasing in IPC – a rolling programme of applications |

Part I EPA was due to come into force in April 1990 but the implementation date was delayed by twelve months until April 1991. At the time of the EPA coming into force, many plants were operating under authorisations from previous legislation but they are still required to obtain an IPC authorisation from HMIP. However, given the large number of plants concerned, and the time it would take to process all of the applications, the government recognised that there would be a need to include provisions for a phased programme of applications. Consequently, a rolling programme of applications has been established, which requires applications to be made on a sectoral basis by a certain specified deadline.

Applications for authorisations must be made by the date prescribed in Sched 3 of The Environmental Protection (Prescribed Processes and Substances) Regulations 1991. As noted above, these regulations have since been amended by further regulations to take account of delays in the system. In practical terms, it is always advisable to contact HMIP to find out when the deadline is. They will specify a period within which applications should be submitted, for example, not earlier than 1 November 1995 and not later than 31 January 1996 for those processes covered in Chapter 6 'Other Industries'. HMIP actively take steps to ensure that all companies are aware of the deadlines well in advance. This is usually done in association with relevant trade associations and business organisations. Therefore, companies should normally be well prepared for the applications process and HMIP will have a good idea of how many applications to expect. In order to deal with the 546 applications from the chemical sector, HMIP was forced to second additional staff.

The first sector to be covered under this phased in programme were the combustion processes which satisfied the UK's community law obligations under the Large Combustion Plants Directive. Those existing processes that have not yet been required to seek authorisation will continue to operate under their existing regulatory regime.

As far as new plants are concerned, the phased-in programme is not applicable and an authorisation must be obtained before operation begins. This will usually happen at the same time as planning permission is sought for the development. The relationship between the IPC controls and the planning regime is considered more fully in the chapter on Planning and Pollution Control. HMIP may agree to a staged application for new developments, enabling HMIP and the operator to discuss the proposal at the design stage and moving on later to the detailed application.	9.5.2 New processes
There are also specific provisions for existing plants which undergo a substantial change. An existing plant is defined as one which has operated for the previous 12 months. Where modifications or alterations to the plant are proposed, which are deemed to amount to a substantial change, then the	9.5.3 Processes undergoing substantial change

operator is required to obtain an immediate authorisation, irrespective of the deadlines stated in the programme of applications.

9.5.4   What amounts to substantial change?

Substantial change is defined in s 10(7) as 'substantial change in the substances released from the process or in the amount or any other characteristic of any substance so released'. If a Process Guidance Note is available for the prescribed process, this will provide examples of changes which are either substantial or not. Changes which are not substantial may still require a variation of the conditions of the authorisation. Once again, it is advisable to seek the advice of HMIP.

9.6   IPC applications

Schedule 1 to the Act provides details about the form of the application and the information that it must contain. It also deals with the publicity requirements. In addition, the form and content of applications is specified in the Environmental Protection (Application, Appeals and Registers) Regulations 1991.

Applications to HMIP for authorisations to operate IPC processes require a substantial input from the applicants. A search through the IPC registers held at HMIP offices will reveal that some of the applications are supported by many hundreds of pages of documentation. It is estimated that most applications take between 100–500 man hours to prepare and, indeed, many are prepared on behalf of companies by specialist consultants. The cost of preparing an application varies but can be as much as £15,000 in some instances, although in most cases the figure will be well below that.

Applications must be made on the appropriate form, together with relevant supporting information. The following information is required:

- the name and address of the applicant ;
- if the applicant is a company, the registered number and office;
- the address of the premises where the prescribed process is being (or will be) carried on;
- a map or location plan;
- a description of the prescribed process;
- a list of prescribed substances used in connection with or resulting from the prescribed processes;
- a list of any other substances used in connection with or resulting from the prescribed processes and which might cause harm if released into any environmental medium;

- a description of the techniques to be used for preventing the releases into any environmental medium of such substances, for reducing the releases of such substances to a minimum and for rendering harmless any such substances which are released;

- details of any proposed releases of such a substance into any environmental medium and an assessment of the environmental consequences;

- proposals for monitoring the release of substances and the environmental consequences of such releases;

- details of how the process will comply with 'any specific conditions' and how the process will operate using the best available techniques not entailing excessive cost;

- any other additional information that the applicant wants the enforcing authority to take into account when considering the application.

The information provided in the application must be clear, comprehensive and, of course, accurate. In the first tranche of applications in 1991/92, the applications were reported to be of a very poor standard. Consequently, HMIP has taken steps to provide much more guidance to companies before making their applications. However, in the 1993/94 Annual Report the Chief Inspector still noted his disappointment at 'the lack of awareness demonstrated by some applicants about the releases from their premises'. HMIP can serve a notice on the applicant requiring further information to be supplied by a specified date.

One of the Government's intentions when HMIP was created in 1987 was that it should eventually become self-financing. One justification for this cost recovery scheme was that it would be an application of the 'polluter pays' principle, with those processes polluting the environment paying for the system of regulation that controls their very activities. However, the charging scheme has been controversial and, as yet, HMIP have not yet been able to generate sufficient income from fees and charges to become self-financing.

Section 8 EPA provides that fees and charges must be paid to the enforcing authority in accordance with a scheme laid down by the Secretary of State. Fees are payable in respect of:

- applications for authorisations;

- variations of authorisations;

- an annual subsistence charge.

9.6.1   Fees and charges

The annual subsistence charge is levied to cover the on-going costs of inspection, monitoring and enforcement by HMIP and as a contribution to the shortfall in the recovery of charges in previous years. An application to HMIP or a local authority must be accompanied by the requisite fee. HMIP produce guidance notes (*Fees and Charges for Integrated Pollution Control 1993–1993*) available to applicants advising on the fee structure. However, it would be difficult to describe the guidance notes or the system as basic and simple, which it evidently was intended to be.

The level of fees has increased since 1991. The current fees as laid down in *Fees and Charges for Integrated Pollution Control 1993–1994* is £2,750 per component for those processes which had previously been subject to air pollution control by HMIP under previous legislation, and £3,860 per component for those with processes coming under the control of HMIP for the first time. Bearing in mind that some processes can involve many components, the charges can be significant. In addition, authorisation holders are also required to pay an additional sum of £1,290 per component if they seek to make a variation to the authorisation. All authorisation holders are required to pay an annual subsistence charge of £1,730 per component. The fees for LAAPC processes are lower. The cost of an application is £965 and the annual subsistence charge is £60.

The penalties for not paying the annual subsistence charge are serious. If the applicant fails to pay the relevant annual subsistence charge, the enforcing authority can serve a written notice on the holder of the authorisation, revoking the authorisation (s 8(8)).

9.6.2	Processing the application

When the application is received, HMIP must either grant the authorisation, subject to any conditions required, or it must refuse the application. HMIP cannot grant an authorisation if they consider that the applicant will not be able to carry on the process in compliance with the conditions attached to the authorisation. They will, therefore, clearly have to establish that the applicant has the ability and means to ensure compliance. There is no requirement within Part I of the EPA that the applicant be a 'fit and proper person' in the same way that there is in relation to waste management licences contained within Part II of the Act. The Secretary of State has the right, if he thinks fit, to intervene in the processing of an application and issue directions to HMIP as to whether or not they should grant the authorisation.

Once an application is received, it should normally be decided upon within a period of four months. However, the period can be extended with the agreement of the applicant. In 1993/94, in 7% of cases the determination period was extended to more than 12 months. In an attempt to speed up the process, and also to ensure greater consistency between applications, HMIP have issued 'template' authorisations which are described as generic authorisations which can be applied to many industrial processes with the minimum of modification.

Consultation is an important part of the process of dealing with IPC applications. Before reaching a decision on an application, HMIP is required to carry out a consultation exercise and seek the views of a number of bodies. In all cases, the views of the Health and Safety Executive must be sought. In addition, the following organisations are consulted:

9.6.3 Consultation

- the Ministry of Agriculture Fisheries and Food (where the process is in Wales, then the Secretary of State for Wales will be consulted instead);

- the National Rivers Authority.

Where the IPC process involves the release of any substance into controlled water, then HMIP is required to consult with the NRA. HMIP cannot grant an authorisation where, in the opinion of the NRA, the discharge would result in, or contribute to, a failure to achieve any water quality objective. The NRA can also specify the conditions on which the authorisation is to be granted, by virtue of s 28 EPA:

- the Sewerage Undertaker, where the prescribed process involves or may involve the releases of any substance into a sewer;

- English Nature or the Countryside Council for Wales, where the process may involve releases of any substance which affects a site of special scientific interest;

- the harbour authority, where the process involves a release of any substance into a harbour;

- the district council in whose area the process will be carried on.

In addition to the consultation exercise, there are also provisions for the advertising of applications in order to ensure that other interested parties, such as local residents, have the opportunity to comment on the application. An advert must be placed in a local newspaper providing details about applications (for authorisation or variation).

9.6.4 Advertising

9.7   Conditions

Authorisations can either be granted subject to conditions or refused. The conditions imposed in an authorisation are the principal mechanism by which the enforcing authorities can control or prevent the releases of substances into the environment and by which the UK can not only abate pollution but fulfil its obligations under Community law and other international treaties.

In deciding upon conditions, HMIP and the local authorities are guided by s 7 EPA which deals specifically with conditions. As such, s 7 is of vital importance since it spells out what considerations HMIP and the local authorities must take into account and, importantly, what the objectives of the conditions are. It also introduces the concepts of BATNEEC and BPEO. Section 7 provides that both HMIP and the local authorities must include conditions which they consider appropriate for achieving certain stated objectives. In particular, conditions must be included which:

- the authority considers appropriate for achieving the objectives laid down in s 7(2) – BATNEEC;

- comply with any directions given by the Secretary of State for the implementation of obligations under EC or international law;

- comply with any limits or requirements, and achieve any quality standards or quality objectives, prescribed by the Secretary of State;

- comply with any requirements applicable to the grant of authorisations specified by or under a plan made by the Secretary of State under s 3(5) (see below);

- comply with any other directions given by the Secretary of State in relation to all authorisations, certain types of authorisation or an individual authorisation;

- appear to the enforcing authority to be appropriate.

Whatever conditions are laid down, it is important to note that they are all subject to certain administrative law principles – they must be necessary, they should be clear and of course they must be *intra vires*. In addition, no conditions can be imposed for the purposes only of securing the health of the people who work at the plant where the process is being carried on.

In setting conditions, not only must the enforcing authority take into account directions given by the Secretary of State, they must also set conditions which meet the objectives laid down in s 7(2) known as the BATNEEC conditions. Before considering the BATNEEC provisions in detail, it is important to consider the role that the Secretary of State plays in giving directions and making plans.

Section 7 refers to directions issued by the Secretary of State, to quality standards and objectives prescribed by him and also to plans. The Secretary of State is empowered to make such plans, directions and regulations by virtue of s 3.

9.7.1   The role of the
         Secretary of State

Section 3 empowers the Secretary of State for the Environment to make regulations which establish standards, objectives or particular requirements in relation to particular prescribed processes, or particular substances, and also to develop strategic plans aimed at reducing pollution. This power is significant in that it enables the Secretary of State to comply with obligations laid down in EC directives.

Using s 3, the Secretary of State can make regulations which lay down quality objectives or quality standards in relation to any substance which may be released in any medium. Regulations may also prescribe standard limits for the concentration of substances, the amount, or the amount in any period, which may be released, or even any other characteristic of that substance in any circumstance in which it may be released.

The Secretary of State can also, under s 3, make plans for:

9.7.2   Plans

- establishing limits for the total amount, or the total amount in any period, of any substance which may be released into the environment in the United Kingdom or any area within it;

- allocating quotas, as regards the release of substances, to persons carrying on processes in respect of which any such limit value is established;

- establishing limits so as progressively to reduce pollution of the environment;

- the progressive improvement in the quality objectives and quality standards established by the above-mentioned regulations issued under s 3.

The system of IPC enables HMIP to ensure that the UK complies with its obligations under Community law. In particular, HMIP is required to ensure that, in drawing up conditions of authorisations, the UK satisfies any quality standards or quality objectives laid down in EC Directives. Certain Directives are particularly relevant in this context, such as Directive 88/609 on the limitation of emissions of certain pollutants into the air from large combustion plants and Directive 84/360 on the combatting of air pollution from industrial plants.

9.7.3   Specific conditions

In the light of what has been said above, specific conditions may be imposed which state expressly the quantities and compositions of substances that can be released, when and where they can be released, the duration of the releases. In addition, the consultation with the NRA may result in the NRA specifying conditions which they think appropriate in relation to the discharge of any substance into controlled water. HMIP must include such conditions into the authorisation (s 28(3)(b)).

9.8   The BATNEEC condition

In setting conditions, both HMIP and the local authorities are required by virtue of s 7 to comply with the directions issued by the Secretary of State, discussed above, and also to meet the objectives laid down in s 7(2).

These objectives are:

- for ensuring that, in carrying on a prescribed process, the best available techniques not entailing excessive cost will be used;

- for preventing the release of substances prescribed for any environmental medium into that medium or, where that is not practicable, by such means for reducing the release of such substances to a minimum and for rendering harmless any such substances which are so released; and

- for rendering harmless any other substances which might cause harm if released into any other environmental medium.

This section is of the utmost importance. It introduces the concept of BATNEEC and requires that, in setting the specific conditions, the 'Best Available Techniques Not Entailing Excessive Cost' are employed to prevent releases or to render them harmless. The BATNEEC requirement applies to the specific conditions laid down by HMIP. However, in addition to those aspects which are specifically covered by a condition in the authorisation, s 7(4) states that there is also an implied general condition in every authorisation that, in carrying on the process, the person carrying it on must use BATNEEC to achieve the same purposes. The specific and implied general conditions relating to the 'Best Available Techniques Not Entailing Excessive Cost' are considered in detail below.

The concept of 'Best Available Techniques Not Entailing Excessive Cost', or BATNEEC as it is more simply known, is of vital importance. BATNEEC is to be used both in relation to expressly stated conditions and also as a general implied condition. It is, therefore, important to understand what is meant by the phrase. For a fuller discussion of the various elements of the BATNEEC concept see Chapter 1.

The purpose of using BATNEEC is to prevent the release of substances into the environment or, where that is not practicable, to reduce the release to a minimum and render any releases harmless. In the context of IPC and LAAPC, the types of conditions that fulfil the requirements of BATNEEC can relate to such things as:

- the actual technology and machinery used;
- the qualifications, training and supervision of the workforce;
- the design, layout and maintenance of the factory;
- the amounts, compositions, etc of the substances used in the process.

BATNEEC is not a fixed standard, it will alter over a period of time. For existing processes, BATNEEC is being introduced by means of conditions in authorisations which require a timetabled upgrading of the techniques involved. It should be noted that s 4(9) places both the Chief Inspector of HMIP and the local authorities in a position where they must follow developments in technology and techniques for preventing or reducing pollution of the environment in relation to the relevant processes.

Any aspect of the process which is not regulated by a specific condition is nevertheless subject to an implied BATNEEC condition, on the same lines as the BATNEEC objective described above. However, HMIP strive as far as possible to make the conditions in the authorisation specific, in order that there is less reliance upon the vagaries of depending on the implied general condition.

In order to achieve some degree of consistency between regions with regard to the interpretation of BATNEEC across a particular industry, sector or process, a number of guidance notes have been issued.

The local authorities and HMIP Inspectors are assisted in their IPC and LAAPC work by a number of published guidance notes issued by the Secretary of State. They are under a duty to have regard to the guidance provided. For IPC processes

9.8.1   What are the 'Best Available Techniques Not Entailing Excessive Cost' (BATNEEC)?

9.8.2   BATNEEC: The implied condition

9.8.3   Guidance notes

five industry guidance notes have been published covering the fuel and power sector, metal industry, mineral industry, chemical industry and the waste disposal industry. These provide general guidance for the industry sector. They contain information on the processes that fall within that sector, relevant EC Directives and information about available abatement technologies and techniques, sampling and monitoring. In practice, the content of the guidance notes indicates the approach that the authority is likely to take in the authorisation.

In addition to these general guidance notes, detailed process guidance notes are to be published covering over 200 individual processes.

Local Authority Air Pollution Guidance Notes have also been issued providing guidance on Part 'B' processes. General guidance notes are available, and provide very useful information on general matters such as the applications procedure, public registers, and the appeals procedure. These are supported by specific process guidance notes which give advice in particular on the techniques appropriate for the control of air pollution for individual processes. In addition, the Secretary of State has issued a further guidance note for local authorities on upgrading of existing processes and this adds to the information already given in the process guidance notes.

| 9.8.4 | **Failure to comply with conditions** |

Failure to comply with the conditions attached to an authorisation is an offence (s 6 EPA). This includes failure to comply with any of the specific conditions and also failure to comply with the implied BATNEEC condition. In the event that legal proceedings are brought concerning a failure to satisfy the BATNEEC condition, the burden of proof falls squarely on the operator. He must prove that there was no better available technique that could be used without entailing excessive cost.

| **9.9** | **Best Practical Environmental Option – BPEO** |

The important feature of Integrated Pollution Control is that it replaces the single medium approach to pollution control with an approach that takes into account the environment as a whole. Therefore, when HMIP are considering a process prescribed for central control, it must have regard, when drawing up the conditions of the authorisation, to all of the environmental media involved. Where the process involves the release of substances into more than one medium, the objective includes ensuring that the best available techniques not entailing excessive cost are used for minimising the pollution which will be caused to the environment as a whole by the releases, having regard to the 'Best Practicable Environmental Option', known as the BPEO. In other words, the aim is to minimise pollution by the application of BATNEEC having regard to the BPEO.

Unfortunately, the EPA does not provide a definition of what is meant by the Best Practicable Environmental Option. It is clear that it will involve a balancing exercise, taking into account ways in which, for example, a slight increase in air emissions might radically reduce discharges to water, and weighing up what is 'best' for the environment as a whole. Using this example, although emissions to air might be greater than if there were a single medium approach, the small increases in atmospheric emissions is more than offset by the reduction in water pollution. The Royal Commission definition (which is used by HMIP as a working definition) serves as useful guide into what is intended:

> 'A BPEO is the outcome of a systematic consultative and decision–making procedure which emphasises the protection and conservation of the environment across land, air and water. The BPEO procedure establishes, for a given set of objectives, the option that provides the most benefit or least damage to the environment as a whole, at acceptable cost, in the long term as well as the short term.'

9.10 Public registers

The provisions relating to access to information have already been covered in detail in Chapter 6. As in other parts of the EPA, and other environmental legislation, there is a requirement that information pertaining to IPC and LAAPC processes are maintained on public registers. Section 20 requires the HMIP and the local authorities to maintain public registers which contain information on:

- IPC applications;

- IPC authorisations;

- variation, enforcement and prohibition notices issued;

- revocations of authorisations;

- emission monitoring results provided to HMIP;

- details of any enforcement action taken by HMIP against operators;

- details of any appeals.

9.10.1 Exemptions from publicity requirements

There are only two exceptions to the requirement for information to be publicly available. By s 21, information may be excluded if it affects national security and, by s 22, a more widely-used provision, information may be excluded on the grounds of commercial confidentiality.

9.10.2   Exclusion on the grounds of national security

Under s 21, the Secretary of State for the Environment may issue directions requiring information to be left off the register:

'if, and so long as, in the opinion of the Secretary of State, the inclusion in the register of that information, or information of that description, would be contrary to the interests of national security.'

Where HMIP excludes information on this ground, then it must inform the Secretary of State that it has done so. It is possible that an applicant may wish information to be excluded on the grounds that they believe its inclusion would be contrary to the interests of national security. If this is the case, the person seeking to rely on s 21 should give notice to the Secretary of State specifying the information and indicating its apparent nature. The person must notify HMIP that he has done this and, as a consequence, the information cannot be included on the register until the Secretary of State has determined that it should be included.

9.10.3   Exclusion on the grounds of commercial confidentiality

It is much more likely, and indeed common, that a company will want to exclude information from the public registers because they do not want the public generally, or competitors specifically, to have access to such information. For example, a company may have pioneered a new process or product or may not want to reveal what raw materials are used. Provision is made for information to be excluded on the basis that the information is 'commercially confidential'. Section 22(11) defines commercially confidential information as information which, if it were contained in the register, would 'prejudice to an unreasonable degree the commercial interests of that individual or person'.

If a company wishes information to be excluded on this ground, then they must apply to HMIP for a determination. HMIP must reach a decision within a period of 14 days beginning with the date of the application for exclusion. Failure to make a determination within 14 days will result in the information being deemed to be commercially confidential.

By April 1993, some 666 applications had been submitted for IPC authorisation, of which 97 sought to exclude information from the public register on the grounds of commercial confidentiality. Twenty-one claims were rejected, 63 were accepted and the outcome of the remaining 13 was uncertain. Most of the applications for exclusion were based on arguments related to the technical details of the process.

Once an authorisation has been granted, it is possible to transfer the authorisation to another person. In the event that a company or business is sold, or is taken over, it will be necessary for the new owner to obtain an authorisation if they wish to carry on the process. Before entering into a contract for the sale of the business, the prospective owner would be well advised to establish that the business has the relevant authorisation, otherwise they might enter into a situation where they are themselves 'carrying on the process' and, consequently, acting in breach of s 6 by operating a prescribed process without authorisation.

Section 9 makes specific provision for the transfer of authorisations, and allows the holder of an authorisation to transfer the authorisation to another person who intends to carry on the process. The new holder must notify HMIP within 21 days of the transfer taking place. There is no requirement that HMIP is consulted before the transfer takes place. This contrasts with the situation in relation to Waste Management Licences, where the Waste Regulatory Authority would need to be satisfied that the new licensee was a fit and proper person. However, it would clearly be extremely prudent for the transferee to check the position with HMIP beforehand, since HMIP has the power to revoke a licence if it considers the holder cannot comply with the conditions.

9.11 Transfer of an authorisation

HMIP ensures compliance with the standards laid down by a number of means:

- regular site visits;
- analysis of monitoring data;
- investigation of problems and complaints;
- specifying on-line monitoring by the process operator.

9.12 Monitoring of IPC authorisation

HMIP is under a duty to review the conditions of the authorisations that it has granted. The Act requires that this happens 'from time to time' but in any event at least every four years. The Secretary of State has the right to alter this period by means of regulation.

9.12.1 Reviewing authorisations

The Environmental Protection Act arms HMIP and the local authorities with a wide range of powers to enable them to enforce the authorisations and the conditions of the authorisations that they have granted, and also to take action

9.13 Powers of enforcement

against processes that are operating without authorisation. The powers of enforcement include the following actions:

- variation and revocation of authorisations;

- enforcement and prohibition notices;

- powers to secure compliance with the above notices;

- power to enter property;

- power to carry out examinations and investigations;

- powers of seizure;

- power to take steps to remedy harm.

9.13.1 Variation of authorisations

It has already been noted that HMIP is under a statutory duty to review all authorisations at least every four years. As a consequence of that review, HMIP may decide that is necessary to alter or vary the conditions of the authorisation. A variation of an authorisation may be necessary to comply with new quality objectives or standards, or directions issued by the Secretary of State. An authorisation must be varied if the NRA gives notice in writing to HMIP that conditions relating to discharges into controlled waters should be varied (s 28(4) EPA).

Alternatively, the person carrying out the process may wish to make changes to the authorised process. For example, it might be the case that changes are made to the actual process or the substances handled or discharged, in which case it will be necessary for the authorisation holder to seek a variation of the authorisation. Sections 10–11 make provision for variation of authorisations by HMIP (s 10) or at the instigation of the authorisation holder (s 11).

9.13.2 Variation by HMIP

Section 10 enables HMIP (or the local authority) to vary an authorisation at any time in order to incorporate new conditions in line with the requirements of s 7. To vary the notice, HMIP must serve a written 'Variation Notice' on the holder of the authorisation, specifying the variations which it has decided to make and the date or dates from which the new conditions will have effect. Variation takes effect from the date specified in the notice. The authorisation holder will be required by the variation notice to inform HMIP, within a specified period, of what action it proposes to take to comply with the varied conditions. The authorisation holder will also be required to pay a variation fee. Sometimes, a variation will result in a substantial change to the process that is authorised. Where HMIP is of the opinion that, as a result of requiring variations there will be a substantial change, they must notify the authorisation holder of that opinion.

Section 11 deals with situations where the authorisation holder applies for a variation in the authorisation. An application may be made at any time by an authorisation holder requesting that the authorisation be varied. The application for the variation must be made on the prescribed form and must be supported by information prescribed in regulations and any other information that HMIP requires. When HMIP receives a request to alter or change a process it must consider the following:

9.13.3   Application for a variation

- whether the proposed change would involve a breach in any of the conditions of the existing authorisation;

- if it would not involve such a breach, whether they would be likely to vary the conditions of the authorisation as a result of the change;

- if the variation does involve a breach of the authorisation, whether or not it would consider varying the authorisation so that the change may be made; and

- whether the change would involve a substantial change in the manner in which the process is being carried on.

HMIP must, after taking these considerations into account, notify the applicant of its decision and the variations that it would consider making. The position then depends on whether the proposed changes amount to a substantial change or not. If they do not, then the applicant may apply for the relevant variations. If, on the other hand, HMIP determines that the proposed change would amount to a 'substantial change' and notifies the applicant accordingly, then the applicant must apply for a variation if he wishes to proceed with the changes. This differs from the former situation where the applicant has a choice of whether or not to apply for a variation. However, in practice, if HMIP has determined that a variation is required for a proposed change and the authorisation holder proceeds with the change without seeking the appropriate variation, they lay themselves open to the possibility of enforcement action from HMIP.

It has already been stated that HMIP can serve a written notice of revocation on the holder of an authorisation where the holder fails to pay the necessary charges associated with the authorisation (see Fees and Charges). In addition, HMIP is also empowered to revoke an authorisation at any time, by virtue of s 12, and can revoke an authorisation where it has reason to believe that the prescribed process has not been carried on at all or for a period of 12 months. The Secretary of State may also issue a direction to HMIP as to whether HMIP should revoke an authorisation.

9.13.4   Revocation of authorisations

Revocation of an authorisation is clearly an important enforcement tool, since it means that, once the revocation becomes effective, the prescribed process cannot continue to be carried on without an offence being committed under s 6. Therefore, it is important that the authorisation holder has adequate notice of revocation and the right of appeal. Section 12(1) provides that notice of revocation must be served in writing on the person holding the authorisation, and s 12(3) provides that it shall have effect from the date specified in the notice. The authorisation holder must have at least 28 days' notice from the date the notice is served and the date specified in the notice. HMIP can withdraw the revocation notice, or vary the date specified in it, at any time up until the date that the revocation takes effect.

An appeal against a decision of HMIP to revoke an authorisation must be made to the Secretary of State (see rights of appeal, para 9.15, below). Where an appeal is made, the revocation will not take effect until the final determination of the appeal or the withdrawal of the appeal (s 15(8)).

| 9.13.5 | Enforcement notices |

Section 13 provides HMIP with the power to serve an 'Enforcement Notice' on a process carrying out a prescribed process in two circumstances:

- if, in the opinion of HMIP, the person carrying out the prescribed process under an authorisation is contravening any condition of the authorisation; or

- is likely to contravene any such condition.

Therefore, HMIP is equipped to deal with situations where there has been a breach of the authorisation or it can take anticipatory action where it is of the opinion that a breach is likely to occur.

Procedurally, the notice must state that HMIP is of this opinion, it must specify the matters which constitute the contravention or which make a contravention likely, and it must also specify the steps that must be taken to remedy the situation and the date by which such steps must be taken. Once again, the Secretary of State has the power to issue a direction to HMIP as to whether HMIP should exercise its powers under s 13. Failure to comply with an enforcement notice is an offence (s 23).

| 9.13.6 | Prohibition notices |

Prohibition Notices are different to enforcement notices in that they are not aimed at dealing with situations where there has been, or is likely to be, a breach of an authorisation. The aim of the prohibition notice is to enable HMIP to take action in situations where the carrying on of the process involves an imminent risk of serious pollution.

Section 14 provides:

'If the enforcing authority is of the opinion, as respects the carrying on of a prescribed process under an authorisation, that the continuing to carry it on, or the continuing to carry it on in a particular manner, involves an imminent risk of serious pollution of the Environment the authority shall serve a notice (a "prohibition notice") on the person carrying on the process.'

There is no requirement for there to be a contravention of the authorisation. Section 14(2) specifically states that the prohibition notice may be served whether or not the manner of carrying on the process in question contravenes a condition of the authorisation. As with enforcement notices, the prohibition notice must state HMIPs opinion, specify the risks involved, specify what steps are to be taken to remove the risk and the period of time in which such steps should be taken. Where the notice applies only to a part of the prescribed process. then it may also apply conditions to that part of the process. The Secretary of State can issue direction to HMIP as to whether a notice should be served and what matters it should specify in it.

Failure to comply with an enforcement or prohibition notice is an offence triable either way. According to HMIP, it will always result in prosecution. However, HMIP can also seek an injunctive remedy from the High Court if it feels that a criminal prosecution will not provide a sufficient remedy. HMIP may wish to use this particular power to obtain an injunction in the event of a emergency situation.

9.13.7 Power to secure compliance with enforcement and prohibition notices

The powers of inspectors are wide and are provided for in a lengthy s 17. It is essential that inspectors have these powers in order to ensure compliance with the authorisations granted, and to identify instances where processes are being carried on without the appropriate authorisation. The powers that the Inspectors have are exercisable in relation to:

9.13.8 Powers of inspectors

a) premises on which a prescribed process is being carried on, or is believed (on reasonable grounds) to be carried on;

b) premises on which a prescribed process has been carried on and the condition of those premises is believed, once again on reasonable grounds, to be such as to give rise to a serious risk of pollution of the environment.

In order to fulfil the responsibilities of the inspectorate, inspectors are granted the following powers:

- to enter premises which the inspector believes it is necessary for him to enter – normally this should be at any reasonable time unless there is a situation in which the inspector is of the opinion that there is an immediate risk of serious pollution of the wnvironment, in which case the inspector can enter the premises at any time;

- to take with him any duly authorised person, equipment or materials – the inspector can be accompanied by a person authorised by the Chief Inspector (or in the case of LAAPC by a person authorised by the local authority), and a policeman. The latter may be needed in situations where the inspector has reasonable cause to apprehend any serious obstruction in carrying out his inspection. The inspector may also take any equipment or materials required for any purpose for which the power of entry is being exercised;

- to make such examination and investigation as may be necessary;

- to instruct that the premises or part of them be left undisturbed – the inspector may require that the premises or the part of the premises under investigation are not disturbed for as long as is reasonably necessary to enable him to carry out any examination or investigation;

- to take measurements and photographs and make recordings;

- to take samples of articles or substances – samples can be taken of any articles or substances found in, or on, the premises and also from the air, water or land in, on, or in the vicinity of the premises. Specific provisions relate to the possession, safekeeping and use in evidence of such samples;

- to require information from any person – the inspector can require any person whom he has reasonable cause to believe to be able to give any information relevant to any examination or investigation to answer such questions as the inspector thinks fit to ask. The person answering the questions will be required to sign a declaration of truth to the answers;

- to inspect any information and to take copies – the inspector can require the production of any information that he considers necessary, including information held on computer. He also has the right to inspect and take copies of such information or any entry in the records;

- to require facilities and assistance – here the inspector can require any person to afford him such facilities and assistance with respect to any matters or things within that person's control or in relation to which that person has responsibilities. So, for example, the inspector can require an engineer on the premises to show him how the monitoring and testing equipment is working (or not working, as the case may be);

- any other powers conferred by regulation by the Secretary of State – certain information can be withheld from the inspector if it is subject to legal professional privilege under s 17. This covers correspondence between clients and their solicitors or legal professional advisers.

Section 23 makes it an offence not to comply with the requirements of the inspector or to obstruct him in carrying out his duty.

Where a process has been operating without authorisation, in breach of conditions or in breach of an Enforcement or Prohibition Notice, then HMIP has the power (s 27) to remedy any harm that may have occurred. In this respect, remediation work can be carried out by HMIP and any costs incurred by the Inspectorate can be recovered from the offender. In addition, s 26 makes provision for the court to make an order for a person convicted of these particular offences to remedy the matter. The court can choose to do this in addition to, or instead of, imposing a fine.

9.13.9 Powers to take steps and remedy harm

Section 23 sets out the offences in relation to IPC and LAAPC processes. These include:

9.14 Offences

- operating a process without authorisation;

- failure to comply with a condition within an authorisation;

- failure to comply with an enforcement or prohibition notice;

- obstructing an inspector;

- failure to comply with the requirements of an inspector;

- providing false information on any records that are required to be maintained as a condition of the authorisation.

Through its monitoring and as a result of inspections. HMIP inspectors are usually able to detect breaches of authorisations, either as result of public complaints, or because there has been a pollution incident. Like the NRA,

HMIP relies on the information received from complainants and, to this extent, pressure groups and citizens can play a role in securing the enforcement of the environmental rules.

9.14.1   Public complaints

HMIP records the number of complaints that it receives about the processes under its control. These are published in the Inspectorate's quarterly reports. The increase in what are called 'justifiable' public complaints dates from 1992/3 and the trend for increasing numbers of complaints has continued, although HMIP has partly attributed this increase to a greater public awareness of the environment and of the role of HMIP.

9.14.2   Enforcement policy

In its guidance note to industry, HMIP states: 'Breaches of authorisation standards or other problems are normally dealt with quickly and effectively with the co-operation of the operator.' In practice, HMIP seeks to ensure compliance with authorisations informally and very often a letter from an Inspector will suffice to ensure that a breach is brought to an end or does not occur. Where an informal resolution proves to be unsatisfactory as a means of resolution, HMIP can issue either an enforcement notice or a prohibition notice (where relevant) or can bring a prosecution under s 23 of the Act. Prosecution is not automatic and depends upon the circumstances of each case, taking into account factors such as the potential harm and the attitude of the operator. HMIP will also consider what will be gained by a prosecution. HMIP has a policy of using the media as much as possible and publicises all notices and prosecutions. Adverse media attention may, in fact, be more compelling than the threat of prosecution for a company concerned abouts its environmental image. Failure to comply with an enforcement or prohibition notice does, however, result in automatic prosecution and HMIP is particularly single-minded about this.

In the first six months of 1994/95, HMIP served 45 enforcement notices and two prohibition notices. This represents an increase on the figures for the whole of 1993/4 when 43 enforcement notices and two prohibition notices were served.

9.14.3   Penalties

Section 23 lays down the various penalties for the offences created in the same section. The offence of carrying on a prescribed process without an authorisation, failing to comply with an enforcement or prohibition notice can result in a fine of up to £20,000 in the magistrates' court. On conviction on indictment, the penalty can increase to an unlimited fine or to up to two years' imprisonment.

Evidence suggests that the magistrates are willing to impose sizeable fines for offences committed under Integrated Pollution Control. For example, in a case brought by HMIP against Southern Refining Services (SRS) in 1994, Newbury magistrates imposed a fine of £12,000 for an air-pollution incident caused by SRSs procedures for dealing with residues from a distillation process. In addition the magistrates made an award of costs against SRS of over £6,000. The case concerned an air pollution incident which occurred as a result of an operator mistakenly adding quantities of the biocide sodium dichloroisocyanurate to a process instead of sodium carbonate. This resulted in the release of noxious fumes, including chlorine gas. The release lasted for 10–15 minutes. As a result of the incident, more than 20 of the company's workforce had to be treated for eye irritation. The company showed themselves willing to co-operate with HMIP during the subsequent investigation. The company was charged with, and pleaded guilty to, a breach of an IPC authorisation under s 23(1) of the EPA. Three breaches were identified by HMIP: failure to take all practicable means to prevent fugitive emissions; failure to provide staff with appropriate written operating instructions; and failure to label drums correctly. The case is interesting because the magistrates, unusually, took the turnover and the profitability of the company into account when determining the level of fine. The turnover of the company was reported to be £500,000 and its profit between £80,000 to £100,000.

Section 15 provides various rights of appeal in relation to all parts of Part I and, as such, it should be remembered is equally applicable to LAAPC. In addition to s 15, the Environmental Protection (Application, Appeals and Registers) Regulations 1991 provide detailed information about the appeals procedure. An appeal must be brought within two months.

9.15   Rights of appeal

A right of appeal lies with the person seeking the authorisation or the authorisation holder against the following:

- refusal to grant an authorisation;

- the conditions attached to an authorisation;

- refusal to grant a variation of an authorisation sought by the authorisation holder (under s 11);

- revocation of an authorisation;

- a variation notice, enforcement notice or prohibition notice.

In addition, s 22 allows a right of appeal concerning exclusion of commercially confidential information from the register.

The Secretary of State can take the following actions in appeal cases:

- affirm the decision taken by HMIP;

- where the decision was a refusal to grant an authorisation or a variation of an authorisation, the Secretary of State may direct HMIP to grant the authorisation or vary it accordingly;

- quash all or any of the conditions of an authorisation;

- quash a decision to revoke an authorisation;

- give directions as to the conditions to be attached to authorisations;

- quash, affirm or modify a variation, enforcement or prohibition notice.

9.15.1   The form of appeal

Although the appeal against the decision of the enforcing authority is to the Secretary of State for the Environment, in practice most appeals are dealt with under delegation by Inspectors. Section 15(3) enables the Secretary of State to refer any matter involved in the appeal to a person appointed by him, and that delegation also extends to the actual determination of appeal cases. The Inspectors have the same power as the Secretary of State in determining the outcome of appeals. The appeal itself may be in writing or, if requested by either of the parties or the Secretary of State, it may take the form of a hearing which may be held in private.

9.16   **IPC in practice**

Although HMIP produces a quarterly report on such matters as the number of applications, authorisations granted, complaints, and inspections, a more independent review of IPC in practice was carried out by Environmental Data Services Limited (ENDS). Their report *Integrated Pollution Control – The First Three Years* provides a comprehensive review of the workings of IPC since it was established.

A number of the survey's findings are noted below:

- The cost and effort required for the preparation of applications is significant;

- The report suggests that the quality of the applications is not satisfactory. It is claimed that many of the applicants are still failing to demonstrate a clear understanding of some of the basic requirements of IPC and that they do not comply with official guidance;

- According to its Director, HMIP is carrying out only 60% of the inspections it believes are necessary to achieve fully effective regulation (ENDS Report 239, December 1994). HMIP also accepts that the rising trend in complaints about processes under its control may reflect a deterioration in industry's environmental performance.

9.16.1   Proposals for change

In August 1994, the Department of the Environment issued a consultation paper on the proposed amendments to the Environmental Protection (Applications Appeals and Registers) Regulations 1991. The consultation paper suggests a number of proposals in relation to the information furnished in applications and the consultation with statutory consultees. In addition to these possible changes, the European Community has proposed an IPC initiative. In September 1993, the European Commission submitted a proposal for a Council Directive in Integrated Pollution Prevention and Control which is very similar to the IPC system in the UK. The stated purpose of the Directive is to provide procedures to prevent, wherever practicable, or to minimise, emissions from industrial installations within the Community. The directive requires Member States to designate a supreme competent authority to co-ordinate the licensing of each category of installation. Member States are required to ensure that there are no installations operating without a permit after the deadline of 30 June 2005.

9.17   The relationship between IPC and other areas of pollution control

Although the aim of IPC was to introduce a more integrated approach to pollution control, the system nevertheless still overlaps or duplicates other areas of control.

9.17.1   Waste

Processes that operate under an IPC authorisation are exempted from the Waste Management Licensing System. However, HMIP cannot attach any conditions to an IPC authorisation concerning the final disposal by deposit in or on land of controlled waste. Where a process involves the final disposal of controlled waste deposited in or on land, then HMIP must notify the relevant Waste Regulatory Authority. The person carrying on the process may then need to obtain a Waste Management Licence in addition to the IPC authorisation (see Chapter 10 on Waste Management).

9.17.2   Statutory nuisance

Section 79 EPA deals with the relationship between the controls under Part I of the Act and the statutory nuisance provisions under Part III. A local authority cannot institute summary proceedings without the consent of the Secretary of State in respect of a nuisance falling under s 79 if proceedings could be instituted under Part I. However, this provision does not prevent a citizen commencing their own action under s 82, or a local authority from serving an abatement notice under s 80.

| 9.17.3 | Water pollution | Where the IPC process involves the discharge of any substance into controlled water, then HMIP is responsible for controlling that discharge, not the National Rivers Authority. Consequently where the process is in compliance with an IPC authorisation, there will be no offence under s 85 of the Water Resources Act 1991. However, this division of jurisdiction is qualified to the extent that HMIP has a duty to consult the NRA where such discharges are being proposed. In particular, HMIP cannot grant an authorisation if the NRA decides that, in its opinion, the discharge will result in or contribute to a failure to achieve any Water Quality Objective which is in force (s 28). The NRA may also specify, in writing, conditions that they consider appropriate and HMIP must include any such conditions in the IPCs authorisation. In addition, the NRA has the right to give notice in writing to HMIP requiring further changes in conditions and these must be incorporated in authorisations by means of HMIP exercising its powers to vary the authorisation. |

| 9.17.4 | Discharge into sewers | Many IPC processes will involve the discharge of trade effluent into the sewers. Although the IPC authorisation will attach conditions concerning the discharge, the process operator will still require a discharge consent from the sewerage undertaker. |

| 9.17.5 | Planning control | The relationship between planning control and environmental control is covered in detail in Chapter 13. |

Summary of Chapter 9

Integrated Pollution Control and Air Pollution Control

Part I of the EPA introduces a new system of Integrated Pollution Control for the most seriously polluting processes. Less seriously polluting processes are regulated by a system of LAAPC.

IPC and LAAPC

- IPC processes are subject to central control by HMIP.

- To carry on a prescribed process a person must obtain an authorisation under s 6.

- This must be obtained within the deadline specified in the Prescribed Processes and Substances Regulation 1991, as amended.

Part I of the Environmental Protection Act 1990 establishes two systems of pollution control:

Pollution control

- Integrated Pollution Council for the most seriously polluting processes which are regulated by Her Majesty's Inspectorate of Pollution; and

- Local Authority and Pollution Control (LAAPC). Local authorities regulate only the atmosphere emissions of other prescribed processor.

- Section 6 EPA requires that certain *prescribed processes* must not be carried on or certain *prescribed substances* must not be released into any environmental medium without prior authorisation from either HMIP or the relevant local authority.

- Section 2 EPA enables the Secretary of State to issue regulations prescribing processes and substances for control. See The Environmental Protection (Prescribed Processes and Substances) Regulations 1991 S1 1991 No 472, as amended.

- Applications for all IPC processes are being phased in on a sectoral basis.

- Section 7 EPA – the conditions imposed in the authorisation are the principal mechanism for controlling the release of substances into the environment.

BATNEEC and BPEO

In particular, s 7 introduces the concept of BATNEEC.

Processes subject to IPC will be required to use the 'Best Available Techniques Not Entailing Excessive Cost' to minimise pollution to the environment as a whole; to achieve the Best Practicable Environmental Option (BPEO).

Information about all IPC and LAAPC authorisations is maintained on a public register, subject to exceptions under ss 21 and 22 EPA.

Enforcement

Enforcement is secured through the following:

- variation of revocation;
- enforcement and prohibition notices;
- power to enter property;
- pwer to examine, investigate and sieze;
- power to prosecute;
- power to take steps and remedy harm.

Rights of appeal

Appeal against HMIP decisions is made to the Secretary of State for the Environment.

Chapter 10

The Legal Regulation of Waste on Land

In May 1994, regulations came into force which resulted in a new system of waste licensing and also in a redefinition of the meaning of waste as previously defined in the Environmental Protection Act 1990. Combined with the relatively new changes introduced by the Environmental Protection Act, the regulation of waste has undergone considerable reorganisation in recent years. The EPA 1990 introduced substantial changes to the regulatory framework and the whole approach to be taken to waste management. Its provisions, particularly the introduction of a statutory duty of care and a much stricter licensing regime, have resulted in a legal framework which endeavours to regulate waste throughout its life cycle. In other words, the legislation aims to control waste from the point of production to the final deposit, from the 'cradle to the grave'. The EPA and the Waste Management License Regulations (which implement the EC Waste Framework Directive 75/442 as amended by Directives 91/156 and 91/692) resolve many of the defects that existed in the previous control of waste, namely the Control of Pollution Act 1974. Before considering the detailed legal controls of waste, it is valuable to have an understanding of some of the modern day problems associated with the management of waste.

10.1 Introduction

Since the industrial revolution, pollution of the landscape has been associated with the accumulation of unwanted waste materials. The UK is estimated to generate around 400 million tonnes of waste; the annual production of domestic rubbish alone exceeds 300 kg per person. Today the constant increase in wastes has become a major concern. The UK, Germany, France and Italy produce 85% of the total volume of wastes in the European Union and 78% of the dangerous substances. In addition to the increased volume of waste, there has been a significant change, since the 1950s, in the nature of waste generated. Although the volume of domestic waste has increased, the weight and density has decreased. Domestic waste is no longer largely cinders and ash, but contains more packaging materials, particularly plastics. This has resulted in the need for bigger dustbins and more frequent collections. Some evidence suggests that the use of larger dustbins results in the generation of more waste! About 90% of all household rubbish is tipped as landfill.

10.2 The problem of waste

About a third of the total waste generated in the UK is defined as 'controlled waste' (see para 10.6.1 below). Special wastes, which by definition are 'dangerous to life', are estimated to amount to about 2.5 million tonnes per year. The remaining waste is made up of waste from agricultural premises and radioactive waste. In addition, the UK currently also imports hazardous waste for specialist treatment.

10.2.1 Methods of disposal	In the UK, waste is largely disposed of by means of landfill (over 85% of controlled waste is disposed of in landfill). Other means of disposal include incineration, dumping at sea or chemical treatment. Only a small percentage of waste is incinerated. All means of disposing of waste raise objections, either from environmental protection groups or from residents who object to the disposal of waste in their locality. The NIMBY (not in my back yard) philosophy, if it can be called such a thing, is one which causes problems. We all generate ever-increasing amounts of waste but nobody wants to face the problems of disposing of it. Inevitably, the disposal of waste will become more and more problematic as the amount of waste increases and the land available for landfill decreases. Landfill sites will become a scarce resource.
10.2.2 Landfill and co-disposal	One of the particular problems faced in the UK arises out of the practice of co-disposal of waste. The UK now has a large number of abandoned landfill sites which have accepted a wide range of differing types of waste. Often the exact composition of landfill sites is unknown. Surface and ground water contamination by leachate discharges is a particular problem. Equally, the effect that these sites have on the environment is not known. In a study of 100 UK landfill sites, 54% performed no monitoring of ground water and 50% had no gas monitoring boreholes. Where monitoring had taken place, over 50% had found surface or ground water contamination and a further 50% had found gas migration. There has been considerable public concern about the problems surrounding landfill, not surprisingly since the build-up of methane can result in explosion. This happened in Loscoe in Derbyshire in 1986, where the garage of a house exploded due to a build-up of methane from a local landfill site.

It is clear from this that there is a need to manage more successfully the problems arising from the production of waste.

10.2.3 Incineration and other methods of disposal	Incineration as a means of waste disposal is not widely practised in the UK as compared to other European countries. According to the Royal Commission's 17th Report, UK

incinerators only accounted for 7% of waste arisings. In 1991 there were over 200 incineration plants in the UK licensed by Waste Regulatory Authorities. Thirty of these were municipal incinerators; most of the remaining incinerators were for clinical waste or were privately owned. Clinical Waste Incinerators had been exempt from pollution controls and waste licensing because they benefited from Crown Immunity. This was removed in 1991 following recommendations of the Royal Commission in its 11th Report.

There are considerable differences of opinion about the desirability of incineration as a means of waste disposal. There is concern about the polluting effects of incineration, particularly in relation to the emissions into air, as manifested in the case of *Gateshead Metropolitan Borough Council v Secretary of State for the Environment* (1993) (for a detailed discussion of this case see Chapter 13 – Planning and Pollution Control). On the other hand, incinerators can be beneficial in terms of the possibilities of energy recovery from wastes which can substitute for fossil fuels.

Although there are concerns about the polluting effects of incinerators, there are rigorous controls over their operation. Incinerators are controlled under the following regimes:

- Town and Country Planning Regime (see *Gateshead MBC v Secretary of State for the Environment*);

- Waste Management Licensing System;

- Integrated Pollution Control or Local Authority Air Pollution Control by the Health and Safety Executive.

Incinerators will need to meet the standards laid down in EC Directive 89/369 and there are existing uncertainties about whether they will manage to achieve these standards.

In response to the recommendations in the Royal Commission's Report on Incineration (17th Report), the government announced its intentions to draw up a waste strategy for England and Wales. At the time of writing, the government has issued its proposed strategy for consultation (*Waste Strategy for England and Wales*, Department of Environment, January 1995).

10.2.4   Waste strategy for England and Wales

The government's aims, as outlined in the draft strategy, is to apply the principle of sustainable development to waste management and to give priority to reducing waste. The key elements of the strategy are as follows:

- Various waste management options will be ranked into a hierarchy which will indicate their relative advantages and disadvantages *vis-à-vis* the environment;

- Improve the data available on waste production;
- Reduce the amount of waste produced by setting targets:
  (i) the target for household waste should be to keep its production at 1995 levels;
  (ii) reducing the amount of controlled waste going to landfill by 10% each year over the next ten years to achieve a target of 64% of waste going to landfill by 2005;
- Introducing the new landfill tax by 1996;
- Detailed targets are also set in relation to recycling;
- The establishment of a new DOE Task Force to provide more detailed information about waste, statistics, etc;
- To prohibit the export of waste and to allow export of hazardous waste for recovery to OECD countries in exceptional circumstances;
- To prohibit the import of waste, subject to a three year transitional period.

10.3	**The development of statutory waste controls**
10.3.1	Public health protection

The system of waste regulation in this country basically evolved out of public health functions. Before 1972, there was no legislation primarily concerned with the problems arising out of waste production and disposal. There were some basic provisions in the Public Health Acts of 1848 and 1936 which enabled local authorities to remove house and trade refuse and to require removal of any 'accumulation of noxious matter'. The 1936 Public Health Act placed the local authorities under a statutory duty to inspect their areas to detect 'statutory nuisances' including 'any accumulation or deposit which is prejudicial to health' (These provisions are now enacted by ss 79–82 of the Environmental Protection Act – see Chapter 14). However, the aim of this early legislation was to protect public health from the problems of disease and vermin associated with the industrial revolution rather than dealing with the environmental problems of waste.

10.3.2	Town and Country planning controls

The Town and Country Planning Act 1947 provided the first real preventive legislation requiring new developments, including waste disposal sites, to have planning permission. The deposit of waste on land is a development within the terms of the Town and Country Planning regime and therefore requires planning permission. Certain waste facilities may now require an environmental assessment to be carried out as part of the planning process. The relationship between the planning regime and pollution control legislation is also considered in Chapter 13.

Growing concern in the early 1970s about the detrimental environmental effects of waste led the government to set up two working groups on refuse disposal and toxic waste. The reports of these two groups provided the impetus for the Control of Pollution Act in 1974. However, before that legislation, the government introduced the Deposit of Poisonous Wastes Act 1972 in response to a series of incidents concerning indiscriminate dumping of toxic wastes. The 1972 Act is now repealed but it was the first attempt at statutory control of industrial waste disposal in the UK.

10.3.3   The Control of Pollution Act 1974

The Control of Pollution Act 1974 (COPA) was the first attempt at achieving a degree of comprehensive pollution control in the UK. It introduced the requirement for local authorities to make plans regarding the waste generated in their areas and also introduced a system of licensing to control sites where waste was deposited. The Act required all Waste Disposal Authorities (which were the county councils in England and the district councils in Wales and Scotland) to draw up a plan for the disposal of all household, commercial and industrial waste likely to be situated in its area. These plans were to be reviewed and modified by the waste disposal authority where appropriate. The authorities were placed under a statutory duty to publicise the draft plans, giving the public an opportunity to make any representations. In addition, there was a requirement that the Waste Disposal Authorities consult with the water authorities, other levels of local government and other relevant bodies. The plans had to include information on the types and quantities of waste which would arise in the area, or be brought into it during the period of the plan, the methods of disposal, the sites and equipment being provided and the overall cost. In addition, the authorities were also under a statutory duty to consider what arrangements could reasonably be made for reclaiming waste materials.

The 1974 Act introduced the requirement for a comprehensive licensing system for the disposal of waste on land, over and above the existing planning controls. It made it an offence to deposit household, commercial or industrial waste on land, unless the land in question was licensed by a Waste Disposal Authority. In May 1994, the site licence provisions of COPA were superseded by the Waste Management Licence system under the Environmental Protection Act 1990. Existing COPA Licences automatically transferred into EPA Waste

10.3.4   COPA – site licensing

Management Licences. Since many existing licence-holders will have obtained their licences under the COPA regime, it is necessary to compare the two systems in some detail.

10.3.5   Defects in the COPA legislation

The Control of Pollution Act was the first comprehensive piece of legislation to tackle environmental pollution in an integrated way, it covered, *inter alia*, controls over air pollution, noise nuisance and waste on land. In fact, the COPA legislation was used as a model for the EC Directive on Waste Management. However, the COPA legislation, despite its worthy attempts, was defective in a number of ways which reduced the effectiveness of the controls over waste in particular. The EPA which provides the current controls over waste on land was introduced to address some of these shortcomings. In particular, the COPA legislation was 'defective' in the following ways:

- the regulatory bodies were responsible for both waste regulation and waste disposal operations and this gave rise to a conflict of interest;

- the regulatory bodies had very limited powers to refuse a licence application or control the transfer of licences;

- only those licence conditions which related specifically to the licensed activity, ie the deposit of waste, could be enforced. Conditions relating to the management of sites and monitoring, for example, were unenforceable;

- licences could be surrendered at will. Disreputable licence-holders could surrender licences to avoid obligations and liabilities arising from the licensed site.

10.4   The Environmental Protection Act 1990 Part II – Waste on Land

As stated in the introduction to this chapter, the waste management regime in this country has undergone substantial reorganisation in recent years. Part II of the Environmental Protection Act was enacted to provide a more comprehensive regime for dealing with waste on land, and also to address some of the defects in the COPA system. The EPA, in true environmental law fashion, has largely been implemented by means of Statutory Instruments. In May 1994, the Waste Management Licence Regulations were finally introduced, bringing into force one of the final pieces of the jigsaw, namely the provisions relating to the licensing system. With a few notable exceptions (s 61 in particular), most of the provisions of the EPA relating to waste management are now in force and are operational.

The Environmental Protection Act did far more than re-enact the provisions of the Control of Pollution Act. It introduced a number of very significant changes in order to tighten up the control of the whole of the waste chain, not just the final deposit of waste. In particular, the EPA facilitated the shift from the concept of waste disposal under the provisions of COPA 1974 to the concept of waste management. The imperative behind the Act was that the legislative controls should relate to waste at all points on the waste chain. Essentially, control should be exercised from the point at which waste is produced and stored pending removal, to the point at which it is finally deposited. The main changes brought about by the EPA are discussed at length throughout this chapter but may be summarised as follows. The EPA:

- introduced a much stricter licensing system, particularly in relation to qualifications of licence-holders, licence conditions and surrender of licences;

- established a statutory duty of care over anyone who imports, produces, carries, keeps, treats or disposes of controlled waste;

- reorganised the functions of the regulatory authorities to avoid the poacher and gamekeeper scenario that existed under COPA.

In practical terms it is not easy to define what waste is. When does something become waste? Does it matter if the substance discarded by one person is used by another who regards it in a different light? For example, what is one person's waste may be a valuable raw material for another person or may have value for recycling purposes. Take waste paper for example: many toilet paper manufacturers promote their 'green' credentials by selling recycled paper products. For them, waste paper is a valuable raw material, but for people with waste paper to get rid of, it is just another waste produce that needs disposing of.

10.5   What is waste?

The legal definition of waste is equally complicated. The definition provided by s 75 of the EPA has now been amended by the Waste Management Licence Regulations 1994 in order to implement the provisions of the EC Waste Framework Directive 75/442, as amended in particular by Directive 91/156. DOE Circular 11/94 also provides guidance on the interpretation of the Directive and Regulations. Therefore, the definitions in s 75 should be read in conjunction with the Regulations. For the sake of completeness both definitions are provided.

10.6   Section 75 – waste and controlled waste

Section 75 EPA defines waste in very broad terms as:

(a) any substance which constitutes a scrap material or effluent or other unwanted surplus substance arising from the application of any process; and

(b) any substance and article which requires to be disposed of as being broken, worn out, contaminated, or otherwise spoiled.

In addition s 75(3) provides that anything which is discarded or otherwise dealt with as if it were waste shall be presumed to be waste unless the contrary is proved.

The starting point of the statutory definition is that something is waste if it is unwanted, surplus to requirements, needs to be disposed of, is discarded or otherwise dealt with as if it were waste. If what constitutes waste is interpreted by reference to the person disposing of the material, it will depend upon the facts of each case. Something can become waste either by being altered in some way, such as being damaged or contaminated, or by a decision on the part of the holder that he no longer needs or wants the material in question. In a consistent line of decisions, the courts have upheld the view that waste is defined from the point of view of the person producing or discarding it. This was the view taken by the Crown Court in *Long v Brooke* (1980), when it was held that, on its true construction, the statutory definition of waste (at the time s 30 COPA where the definition was identical to that given in the EPA) defines waste from the point of view of the person discarding it. Here, excavated material used for landscaping was held to be waste. In *Kent CC v Queensborough Rolling Mill* (1990), the matter in question concerned material that was used to shore up subsidence at a wharf-side site. It was held that the purpose to which the material was put was irrelevant. What was important was that the material had earlier been discarded and, when removed from the site, was waste within the statutory definition. The same approach to the term 'waste' has been adopted in relation to Town and Country Planning legislation. See *R v Rotherham Metropolitan Borough Council, ex p Rankin* (1990).

The question of what constitutes waste has also been considered by the European Court of Justice in *Vessoso and Zanetti* (1990). The Court of Justice had to consider whether the term waste in the Framework Directive on Waste included substances that could be recycled. The Court was clear in its judgment that waste under the Directive included materials intended for recycling, since it was waste as far as the disposer was concerned, irrespective of the intentions of the recipient. The case is important particularly in view of the fact that the Waste Management Licensing Regulations have incorporated the EC definition of waste into national law. National courts interpreting the UK Regulations are required to be consistent with the ECJ's decision in this case.

If the matter in question is not waste, or if the waste is not Directive waste, then the following provisions do not apply. Sections 75(4)–(7) define those types of waste that are 'controlled' by the Act. The definition of controlled waste is supplemented by the provisions of the Controlled Waste Regulations 1992, and includes household, commercial or industrial waste. The classification of the wastes into three broad heads is largely important in terms of the provisions relating to collection. For example, household waste is collected free of charge (with a few exceptions) whereas charges are made for the collection of commercial and industrial waste.

10.6.1   Controlled waste

- Household waste – includes waste from domestic properties, caravans, residential homes, educational establishments, hospitals, nursing homes (subject to regulations).

- Industrial waste – means waste from any of the following premises: factories (see Factories Act 1961); public transport premises; premises used to supply gas, water, electricity, sewerage, postal or telecom services; waste from construction or demolition operations is also termed industrial waste as is waste from contaminated land. Industrial waste is sometimes referred to as trade waste.

- Commercial waste – includes waste from premises used wholly or mainly for the purposes of a trade or business; or for the purposes of sport, recreation or entertainment, except household, industrial, mining, quarrying and agricultural waste, or any other waste specified in the Regulations.

Not all types of waste are 'controlled'. For example, waste from agricultural premises, waste from mines and quarries, explosive or most radioactive waste are not defined as controlled wastes. Litter is, however, classified as controlled waste – the subject of litter controls is dealt with in Chapter 11.

As stated earlier, the definitions of controlled waste in the EPA have now been amended by the Waste Management Licence Regulations 1994, in particular Regulation 24(8). The Regulations give effect to the definition of waste provided in EC Directive 91/156 which amends the Waste Framework

10.6.2   Directive waste

Directive 75/442. As a consequence, waste which is not 'Directive Waste' is not household, industrial or commercial waste.

Directive Waste is defined in the Directive and Regulations by reference to list of categories of waste. Directive Waste is any substance or object in the categories laid down in Sched 4 to the Regulations which the producer or the person in possession of it discards, or intends to discard, or is required to discard. These categories are as follows:

1   production or consumption residues;

2   off-specification products;

3   products whose date for appropriate use has expired;

4   materials spilled, lost or having undergone other mishap, including any materials, equipment, etc contaminated as a result of the mishap;

5   materials contaminated or soiled as a result of planned actions (eg residues from cleaning operations, packing materials, containers etc);

6   unusable parts (eg reject batteries, exhausted catalysts etc);

7   substances which no longer perform satisfactorily (eg, contaminated acids, contaminated solvents, exhausted tempering salts etc);

8   residues of industrial processes (eg slags, still bottoms etc);

9   residues from pollution abatement processes (eg scrubber sludges, baghouse dusts, spent filters, etc);

10 machining or finishing residues (eg lathe turnings, mill scales, etc);

11 residues from raw materials extraction and processing (eg mining residues, oil field slops, etc);

12 adulterated materials(eg oils contaminated with PCBs etc);

13 any materials, substances or products whose use has been banned by law;

14 products for which the holder has no further use (eg agricultural, household, office, commercial and shop discards, etc);

15 contaminated materials, substances or products resulting from remedial action with respect to land;

16 any materials, substances or products which are not contained in the above categories.

Inclusion in the list of categories, however, is not conclusive that the matter in question constitutes waste. The DOE circular which provides guidance on the Regulation states that 'the inclusion of a substance or object in one of the categories set out ... does not in itself mean that it is waste. The substance or object concerned must also be discarded'. Therefore, an object in one of the above categories will not be waste if, for instance, it is sent to a recovery operation or is sold to a specialist recovery operation. On the other hand, it should be regarded as waste, according to the DOE circular, if it is sent to a disposal operation, is discarded, abandoned, dumped or otherwise dealt with as if it were waste.

The Department of the Environment has overall control over the management of waste regulation through the auspices of Her Majesty's Inspectorate of Pollution. The Inspectorate supervises the Waste Regulatory Authorities and, as part of this supervisory function, employs Inspectors whose function is to check on the performance of the WRA. The Inspectors can take enforcement actions where a WRA is not carrying out its statutory functions.

The reasoning behind the administrative changes introduced in the EPA is that local authorities should no longer be able to act as both regulators and operators of waste disposal. Under the regulatory system established by the Control of Pollution Act, local authorities were in the position of regulating and operating their own waste disposal operations. The aim of the EPA was to remove what effectively amounted to the problem of local authorities acting in the capacity as both gamekeeper and poacher and the conflict of interest that naturally arose under such a system. Another principal reason for the changes was to ensure that waste disposal operations were no longer subsidised but run on a proper economic basis, with the charges reflecting the full economic cost of running the operation. In other words, the intention was to make waste disposal operations more competitive and subject to market forces.

The EPA therefore created three different levels of waste authority each with a different role in relation to waste management. These are defined in s 30 as:

10.7   The Waste Regulatory Authorities

- Waste Regulation Authorities (WRAs);

- Waste Disposal Authorities (WDAs);

- Waste Collection Authorities (WCAs).

10.7.1.   Waste Regulation
           Authorities (WRAs)

In England, the WRAs function in non-metropolitan counties is given to county councils. In the metropolitan areas, the WRAs are the district councils, with special authorities established for Greater London, Greater Manchester and Merseyside. Waste Regulation Authorities are intended to 'regulate' and, therefore, are free from any operational responsibilities. To this end, the WRAs also employs Inspectors who have considerable enforcement powers relating to entry on land, taking samples and so on. The role of the WRA Inspectors is to ensure that the waste licensing regime is being correctly complied with and that waste holders are complying with the statutory duty of care under s 34 of the Act (see para 10.15.1 below). The main functions of the WRA are as follows:

- preparation of waste disposal plans;

- control over the waste management licensing system;

- supervision of licensed activities;

- inspection of licensed land and landfill sites;

- maintaining the public registers;

- reporting to the Secretary of State.

The Secretary of State has the power to combining two or more Waste Regulation Authorities into regional authorities.

10.7.2   Waste Disposal
          Authorities (WDAs)

The WDA is normally also the county council in non-metropolitan areas and the district council in metropolitan areas. Special arrangements exist in London, Manchester and Merseyside. The functions of the WDA are:

- making arrangements for the disposal of controlled waste collected in the area by waste collection authorities;

- formation of waste disposal companies;

- provision of municipal waste sites for household waste to be deposited by residents;

- provision of transfer stations;

- waste recycling.

Section 51 places Waste Disposal Authorities under a duty to provide places where residents can deposit household waste and to arrange for the disposal of that waste and the waste collected by the waste collection authority.

Where a local authority is both a WRA and WDA then provisions in the EPA require the functions to be carried out 'at arms length'. Section 30(7) makes it the duty of each authority, which is both a Waste Regulation Authority and a Waste Disposal Authority, to make administrative arrangements to keep these functions separate. Details of the administrative arrangements in respect of this separation of functions must be submitted to the Secretary of State. This means that the actual operational functions of the WDA are not carried out by the authority itself but by a 'waste disposal contractor'. The waste disposal contractor can either be a private sector company or it can be a 'Local Authority Waste Disposal Company' (LAWDC). The LAWDC must be 'separate' from the main functions of the local authority, and it must compete on an equal footing with the private sector for the waste disposal contracts tendered by the WDA. The arrangements relating to LAWDCs are to be found in s 32 and Sched 2 of the Act.

10.7.3   Separation of functions

Section 30(5) defines a 'waste disposal contractor' as a person who in the course of business collects, keeps, treats or disposes of waste, being either:

(a) a company formed for all or any of these purposes by a waste disposal authority; or

(b) a company, partnership or individual (sole trader).

Waste Collection Authorities (WCAs) are the district councils or London Boroughs. Their functions are:

10.7.4   Waste Collection Authorities (WCAS)

- to arrange for the collection of household waste in their area;

- to arrange for the collection of commercial or industrial waste on request;

- to provide bins/receptacles;

- to collect waste and to deliver for disposal as directed by the waste disposal authority;

- to investigate and make arrangements for recycling.

Waste Collection Authorities are placed under a statutory duty to collect household waste free of charge (except where the waste is not reasonably accessible and other arrangements can be made). In certain prescribed cases, the WCA can make a charge for household waste collection. These cases are laid

10.7.5   Waste collection

down in the Controlled Waste Regulations 1992 Sched 2. They include large items, garden waste and other difficult wastes or waste produced from commercially-run residential premises.

The WCA also has a duty, if requested by the occupier of premises in its area, to collect any commercial waste from the premises or to arrange for the collection of the waste. In these cases, the WCA may charge a reasonable sum from the person making the request for the collection and disposal of the waste unless the authority considers it inappropriate to do so.

The Waste Collection Authority is required by s 48 to deliver the waste collected to such places as directed by the Waste Disposal Authority unless the WCA intends to recycle the waste. If the WCA is keeping the waste for recycling purposes it will still need to secure the consent of the WDA, since WDAs have the power to buy and sell waste for recycling purposes.

10.8   Waste planning and waste recyling

10.8.1   The Waste Disposal Plan

Section 50 of the EPA requires each Waste Regulation Authority to prepare a Waste Disposal Plan. In order to do this, the WRA must carry out an investigation to decide what arrangements are needed for treating or disposing of controlled waste within the area so as to prevent or minimise pollution to the environment or harm to human health. The Waste Disposal Plan should specify, *inter alia*, the kinds and quantities of controlled waste the WRA expects to find in its area, or to be transported in or out of the area; methods of disposal; licensing policy; the sites and disposal methods in use and expected to come into use; and the expected costs, for the period of the plan. The authority is also under a duty to have regard to the desirability, where reasonably practicable, of giving priority to recycling waste. In drawing up the plan, the WRA must consult the NRA, the Waste Collection Authorities in the area, other local authorities affected and representatives of the waste disposal and treatment industries in the area or likely to be in the area.

The WRAs should have regard to government policy on waste when preparing the Waste Disposal Plans. The draft plan is then submitted to the Secretary of State who can direct modifications. The final version is published and publicised and should also be kept under review. The Waste Disposal Plan does not have the same status as a Development Plan under the Town and Country Planning regime. As a consequence, a planning authority is not required to take the waste plan into account when taking planning decisions.

County planning authorities are required by the Planning and Compensation Act 1991 to prepare a Waste Local Plan or, at least, to combine a Waste Local Plan with a Minerals Local Plan. The Waste Local Plan addresses the land use implications of the authority's waste policies. Therefore, it deals with issues such as the need for sites and waste facilities and where these should be located, having regard to geological and hydrological considerations. The Waste Local Plan should not be confused with the Waste Disposal Plan which is prepared by the Waste Regulatory Authority.

10.8.2   The Waste Local Plan

In 1990, the UK government set targets for the recycling of household waste (25% of household waste). These targets are supposed to be met by the year 2000. However, according to government statistics, the current average recycling rate for household waste is just under 6%. Although s 49 of the EPA requires Waste Collection Authorities to prepare recycling plans to ensure that the targets are met, very few have made any real efforts to achieve the targets. In the 1994 budget, the government announced its intentions to introduce a tax on landfill in order to discourage disposal and encourage recycling.

10.8.3   Waste recycling policy and waste recycling plans

Waste recycling is largely the responsibility of the Waste Collection Authority, although both the WRAs and the WDAs have certain powers and duties in this regard. The main provisions relating to recycling are contained in the following sections of the EPA:

- Section 49 – Waste Collection Authorities are under a duty to investigate what arrangements can practicably be made for recycling household and commercial waste. They must prepare a waste recycling plan and keep it under review;

- Section 50(4) – Waste Regulation Authorities must consider the desirability of giving priority to waste recycling when drawing up the waste disposal plans. However they are only required to consider action which is reasonably practicable;

- Section 46(2) – the Waste Collection Authority can require household waste to be placed in separate receptacles if certain wastes are going to be recycled;

- Section 52 – has introduced a system of recycling credits to encourage recycling.

The Waste Collection Authority is required by s 49 to prepare a Waste Recycling Plan. The WCA in preparing the plan has to consider the effect that recycling proposals will have on the amenities in the locality and also the likely cost or saving to the authority. A copy of the plan should be made available for the public to inspect.

10.9   The waste offences

The principal means of controlling where and how waste is deposited is through the waste licensing system which is backed up by various sanctions. In particular, the EPA has tightened the controls over waste by establishing a number of waste offences.

10.9.1   Section 33 offences

Section 33 creates the main waste offences. By virtue of s 33(1) it is an offence to:

(a) deposit controlled waste, or knowingly cause or knowingly permit controlled waste to be deposited in or on any land, unless a Waste Management Licence authorising the deposit is in force and the deposit is in accordance with the licence;

(b) treat, keep or dispose of controlled waste, or knowingly cause or knowingly permit controlled waste to be treated, kept or disposed of:

- in or on any land; or
- by means of any mobile plant;
- except under and in accordance with a Waste Management Licence.

(c) treat, keep or dispose of controlled waste in a manner likely to cause pollution of the environment or harm to human health. (This offence operates independently of the licensing system.)

10.9.2   Section 33(1)(a): Unlawful deposit of waste on land

Section 33(1)(a) prohibits the deposit of waste on land without a Waste Management Licence (WML). The meaning of the term deposit was considered in the case of *Leigh Land Reclamation Ltd v Walsall Metropolitan Borough Council* (1991), where it was held that waste was deposited at landfill sites only when there was no realistic prospect of further examination or inspection and it had reached its final resting place. However, the Divisional Court in *R v Metropolitan Stipendiary Magistrate, ex p London Waste Regulation Authority* (1993) held that the decision in *Leigh* should no longer be followed on this particular point. The latter case involved a waste transfer station which the defendants were operating without a waste disposal licence (the case pre-dates the implementation of the Waste Management Licence system under EPA). The court held that the terms 'deposit' under s 3 COPA applied to temporary deposits as well as permanent deposits. The Department of the Environment also regards the term 'deposit' as including a temporary deposit on land pending disposal elsewhere. Consequently, it is the case that all storage of waste can be categorised as a deposit and therefore subject to s 33(1)(a).

Section 33(1)(b) covers a wide range of activities. It will be an offence to treat, keep or dispose of controlled waste, or to knowingly cause or knowingly permit it to be treated, kept or disposed of, in or on any land or by means of any mobile plant, except in accordance with a Waste Management Licence. The provision controls various activities which were not adequately controlled by the COPA legislation. The definition of what constitutes 'keeping' includes retention of any kind. Therefore, a person or company 'keeps' waste when it stores it on the premises pending removal by a waste collection contractor.

'Treatment' is defined in s 29(6), which provides that waste is treated when it is subjected to any process, including making it reusable or reclaiming substances from it.

The term 'disposal' is defined in the Waste Management Licence Regulations 1994 as any of the operations listed in Sched 4 to the Regulations. Schedule 4 lists a wide range of activities which constitute disposal, ranging from tipping of waste above or underground to the release of wastes into the seas.

Potentiall,y therefore, many thousands of business and industrial activities require a Waste Management Licence in order to avoid committing an offence under s 33(1)(b). It comes as no surprise, therefore, that certain activities are exempt from the WML system and, consequently, this provision. The exemptions are considered below at para 10.9.7 and para 10.10.2.

In both s 33(1)(a) and (b) it is an offence to 'knowingly cause' or 'knowingly permit' the deposit, treatment, keeping or disposal of controlled waste other than in accordance with a Waste Management Licence. The phrases 'causing and knowingly permitting' can be found in other pollution control legislation. However, in the context of the waste offences, the word 'cause' is prefixed with the requirement of 'knowingly'. The precise meanings of these terms have been considered in detail in Chapter 1, but are worth rehearsing again in relation specifically to cases involving waste. 'Causing' includes both acts or omissions which have a causal link with the pollution incident. There is no requirement for foreseeability (see *Alphacell v Woodward*). 'Knowingly permitting' requires that a

10.9.3   Section 33(1)(b): to treat, keep or dispose of controlled waste

10.9.4   Knowingly cause or knowingly permit

person has some knowledge of the matters that constituted the offence and allowed them to happen.

10.9.5   Section 33(1)(c) offence

The final offence in s 33 is different to the first two categories of offence in that it is not related to the Waste Management Licence system. Section 33(1)(c) makes it an offence to treat, keep or dispose of controlled waste in a manner likely to cause pollution of the environment or harm to human health. It makes no reference to knowingly causing or knowingly permitting, nor does it make it a defence to be operating in accordance with a Waste Management Licence. It is possible for a person to be operating in accordance with a Waste Management Licence and yet still be committing an offence under s 33(1)(c). All that is required is that treatment, keeping or disposal is likely to cause pollution to the environment or harm to human health. Because it is not linked to the licensing system, this particular offence came into force on 1 April 1992.

10.9.6   Other waste offences

In addition to the main offences created by s 33(1), the EPA also creates a number of other specific offences such as:

- s 33(5), which states that where controlled waste is carried in and deposited from a motor vehicle, the person who controls or is in a position to control the use of the vehicle shall be treated as knowingly causing the waste to be deposited, whether or not he gave any instructions for this to be done;

- making false statements when applying for a Waste Management Licence is an offence (s 44);

- s 60 creates the offence of interfering with a waste site and receptacle for waste unless that person has the consent of the relevant authority, contractor or other person;

- s 63(2) makes it an offence to deposit waste other than controlled waste in certain circumstances.

10.9.7   The household waste exemption

The main exemption from the waste offences is in relation to household waste. The offences do not apply in relation to household waste from a domestic property which is treated, kept or disposed of within the curtilage of the dwelling by or with the permission of the occupier of the dwelling (s 33(2)). In addition the Waste Management Licence Regulations exempt certain activities from the s 33(1)(a) and (b) offences (see para 10.10.2 below).

10.9.8   Defences

It is clear from the wording of s 33(1)(a) and (b) that an offence will not be committed if the deposit, treatment, keeping or disposal of controlled waste is in accordance with a Waste Management Licence and the conditions attached to the licence. Therefore, compliance with a WML and all its conditions will provide a defence to these two offences. Compliance with the terms of a WML, however, affords no defence in relation to a s 33(1)(c) offence, although in practice it may help to prove one of the other defences available.

Section 33 also provides a number of additional defences. To succeed, a person charged must prove:

(a) he took all reasonable precautions and exercised all due diligence to avoid the commission of the offence; or

(b) he acted under instructions from his employer and neither knew, nor had reason to suppose, that the acts done by him constituted a contravention of s 33(1); or

(c) the acts were done in an emergency to avoid danger to the public and that, as soon as reasonably practicable after they were done, particulars were given to the Waste Regulation Authority.

The courts will determine as a question of fact whether a person can rely on any of these defences.

The seriousness of the offences is reflected in the fact that a person committing an offence could be liable to an unlimited fine or even imprisonment for a period of up to two years. Section 33(9) details the penalties as follows:

10.9.9   Penalties

(a) on summary conviction, to imprisonment for a term not exceeding six months or a fine not exceeding £20,000 or both; and

(b) on conviction on indictment, to imprisonment for a term not exceeding two years or an unlimited fine or both.

The penalties are more serious if special waste is involved (see para 10.17 below). Prison sentences are rare for environmental crimes; however, the Crown Court has used its powers of prison sentencing on a number of occasions in relation to waste offences. In February 1995, the head of a waste disposal company was jailed for six months.

In most cases, the penalty for a waste offence will be a fine. Although the fine may not always be that great in relation to the company's resources, the poor publicity arising from a prosecution may be more damaging.

Section 157 of the EPA opens up the possibility of making company directors and managers personally liable. Where a waste offence has been committed by a company, the

10.9.10   Personal liability

directors and senior management may also be personally liable for the offence. However, it has to be proved that the offence was committed with their consent or connivance or be attributable to their neglect. In practice, this is often very difficult to prove.

10.10 The waste management licence system

It has already been stated that the licenaing system is the principal means of securing the control over waste. Therefore, the deposit, treatment, keeping or disposal of controlled waste which is permitted and in accordance with a Waste Management Licence will not amount to an offence under s 33(1)(a) and (b), although it should be remembered that even operations in accordance with a licence may constitute an offence under s 33(1)(c).

The system of Waste Management Licences is relatively new, only coming into force in May 1994 by means of the Waste Management Licence Regulations 1994. The Regulations were enacted some four years after the EPA, although this should be seen as an improvement to the COPA legislation, where some of the provisions took over ten years to come into effect (and others never came into effect!). Prior to the 1994 Regulations, the COPA licencing system remained in force. COPA-licensed sites automatically became EPA-licensed sites on 1 May 1994. The new system is complex and all waste producers need to determine, by reference to the Waste Management Licence Regulations, whether or not they need to obtain a Waste Management Licence or whether they are exempt. In the latter case they may still need to register with the Waste Regulatory Authority.

The licensing framework provided in Part II of the EPA has substantially extended the controls that can be exerted through the licensing system over waste handling. The Waste Disposal Licences issued under the provisions of the Control of Pollution Act centred upon the deposit of waste, and a number of defects in the legislation meant that certain activities were not adequately controlled. The new Waste Management Licences contrast with the COPA Waste Disposal Licences in more than just name. The EPA licences are Waste Management Licences and, as such, can encompass conditions relating to the overall management of the waste not just the final deposit. Combined with the statutory duty of care, it is intended that the system will provide much greater control over waste throughout its various stages of production and disposal.

The main changes in the licencing system are as follows:

- applicants for licences must satisfy the 'fit and proper person test';

- all aspects of the licence are enforceable at all times, ie not only when the disposal operations are in progress;

- the WRA must agree to the transfer of a licence because of the fit and proper person requirement;

- new arrangements in respect of surrender of licences.

Section 35 defines a Waste Management Licence as a:

> 'licence granted by a waste regulation authority authorising the treatment, keeping or disposal of any specified description of controlled waste in or on specified land or the treatment or disposal of any specified description of controlled waste by means of a specified mobile plant.'

10.10.1   Definition of a Waste Management Licence

Where a Waste Regulation Authority grants a licence, it will do so subject to any conditions that it thinks are appropriate. There are two different types of Waste Management Licence: the site licence and the mobile plant licence. The site licence is granted to the person in occupation of the land. Occupation is not defined but will be someone who has some degree of control associated with or arising from the presence on or use of land. The mobile plant licence is granted in respect of mobile plant which is defined under s 29(9) (subject to a power to further definition by Regulation) as: 'plant which is designed to move or to be moved, whether on roads or other land.'

The s 33(1)(a) and (b) offences can be committed by any one who deposits, keeps, treats or disposes of controlled waste on land or by means of mobile plant (with the noted exception of householders generating household waste on their premises). A wide range of people and activities are caught by this very wide definition. It extends well beyond the waste deposited on waste sites and transfer stations, but also includes, for example, waste which is produced by manufacturing firms, who either use waste as part of their production process (such as firms that receive waste paper for recycling). Equally, companies also produce quantities of waste which are kept on site pending removal by a waste disposal contractor. Most of these processes will be subject to controls either by the National Rivers Authority or by the IPC and LAAPC regimes. In most instances they will be exempt from the waste management licensing requirements and hence these two offences.

10.10.2   Exemptions

The power to exclude certain activities from the licensing regime is given to the Secretary of State by s 33(3). The Secretary of State can make regulations, excluding certain activities involving the deposit, keeping, treatment or disposal of waste, from the need to have a licence. When drawing up the list of exemptions, the Secretary of State is required to take into account the adequacy of other statutory controls and Council Directive 91/156, which also permits exemption where there are other adequate pollution controls. Consequently, the Waste Management Licence Regulations 1994 exempt certain activities that are controlled under other pollution legislation.

Regulation 16 provides that certain activities are exempt from the waste management licence system where they are controlled by other statutory controls. Therefore, IPC processes that do not include the final deposit of waste on land are exempt. The disposal of liquid wastes into water that are controlled under Parts II or III of the Water Resources Act are also exempt. The relationship between the waste licensing system and other areas of pollution control is dealt with more fully at para 10.18 below.

In addition over 40 specific activities listed in Sched 3 to the Regulations are also exempt.

The 1994 Regulations are complicated and, in practice, businesses will need to consult their relevant WRA to confirm whether a licence is required or not. In some instances, businesses may feel more confident taking legal advice, given the penalties for operating without a licence. Additional guidance is provided in Annex 5 of the DOE Circular accompanying the Regulations.

10.10.3   Registration for exempt activities

Regulation 18 of the 1994 Regulations requires that certain exempt activities must nevertheless be subject to a registration requirement. Failure to register an exempt activity with the relevant WRA is a criminal offence. The WRAs are under a duty to maintain a register which contains the names and addresses of all exempt activities. The registers are open to inspection by the public.

10.11   The applications procedure

Applications for a Waste Management Licence must be made to the appropriate WRA in writing accompanied by the fee payable under s 41. In the case of a mobile plant licence the relevant WRA will be the local authority in whose area the operator has his principal place of business. Section 36 deals with the applications procedure and determines the considerations that the WRA must take into account. No licence can be granted in relation to land unless there is planning permission or an established use certificate which authorises the particular use.

By virtue of s 36(3), a WRA may not reject an application that has been properly made unless:

- the applicant is not a fit and proper person;

- the rejection is necessary to prevent pollution to the environment, harm to human health or serious detriment to the amenities of the locality.

Therefore, there are only two grounds for refusal; these are considered more fully below. The WRA must either grant a licence or give notice of rejection within four months of receiving the application, unless an extension is agreed in writing with the applicant. Failure to deal with the application in the prescribed time is deemed a rejection.

As in other pollution control regimes discussed in this book, 'polluters' are required to pay for the system that controls them. The application of the 'polluter pays' principle in this instance means that charges are levied by the WRA for the following:

- applications for Waste Management Licences;

- applications for modification of the licences;

- transfers;

- surrender;

- subsistence, to cover the costs of the WRAs supervision of the licence.

10.11.1   Charges

Before reaching a decision on an application for a Waste Management Licence, the WRA must consult both the National Rivers Authority and the Health and Safety Executive (s 36(4)). In certain protected areas the application must be referred to English Nature or the Countryside Council for Wales. If there is any disagreement arising out of the consultation, then the matter must be referred to the Secretary of State for decision. The WRA is also required by the Waste Management Licence Regulations to have regard to the protection of groundwater when determining a licence application. The Regulations give effect to the Groundwater Directive.

10.11.2   Consultation

The WRA must be satisfied that the applicant is a 'fit and proper person' before it can issue a Waste Management Licence. This is an entirely new requirement introduced by

10.11.3   The fit and proper person test

the EPA and specifically addresses one of the principal defects in the COPA system, namely that almost any person could obtain a waste disposal licence irrespective of their 'track record' in waste management.

Section 74 provides that a person shall be treated as not being a fit and proper person if it appears to the authority:

(1) that he or another relevant person has been convicted of a relevant offence;

(2) that the management of the activities which are to be authorised by the licence are not or will not be in the hands of a technically competent person; or

(3) that the person to hold the licence has not made and has no intention of making or is no position to make financial provision adequate to discharge the obligations arising from the licence.

There are three elements to the test: the first relates to previous convictions for relevant offences; the second to the technical competence of the applicant; and the third to the applicant's financial position.

1   *The relevant offences* – These are set down in the 1994 Waste Management Licence Regulations, and include a range of pollution related offences. However, s 74(4) provides that, if the WRA considers it proper to do so in any particular case, it may treat a person as a fit and proper person notwithstanding that he has been convicted of a relevant offence. The WRA will clearly have to take into account matters such as the gravity of any previous offences and whether or not it was a one-off offence, possibly with mitigating circumstances. The fit and proper person test in this particular regard does not simply concern the applicant but also relates to other 'relevant persons' which includes (s 74(7)):

    •   any employee of the applicant who has been convicted of a relevant offence; or

    •   a company of which the applicant was a director, manager, secretary or similar officer and which has been convicted of a relevant offence; or

    •   where the applicant is a company, any current director, manager, secretary or similar officer of the company who has been convicted of a relevant offence, or was an officer of another company when that company was convicted of a relevant offence.

2   *Technical competence* – The management of the licensed facility must be in the hands of technically competent

persons. A person is technically competent if he holds one of the certificates awarded by the Waste Management Industry Training and Advisory Board (WAMITAB). The precise qualification is determined by reference to the type of waste facility and waste that it takes.

3   *Financial Resources* – The WRA will need to be certain that the licence-holder is in a position financially to be able to discharge the obligations arising from the licence. This means that the licence-holder will need to show that he has adequate financial resources to comply with the conditions of the licence and to meet any liabilities or remedial action if a pollution event occurs. In practice this is the hardest test for the local authority to apply.

Even if an applicant is deemed to be a fit and proper person, the WRA must not grant a licence if it is satisfied that rejection is necessary to prevent pollution of the environment or harm to human health. In most cases, this will not be an issue and the WRA should be able to impose sufficiently rigorous conditions to ensure that the activity does not harm the environment or human health.

10.11.4   Rejection necessary to prevent pollution

The WRA can refuse an application if the activity would cause serious detriment to amenities of the locality, but they cannot have regard to this particular aspect if the activity in question has planning permission. The justification for this is that questions of amenity will already have been taken into account by the planning authority.

It is a precondition to obtaining a site licence that the site has planning permission for such use. Section 36(2) provides that a licence shall not be issued 'for a use of land for which planning permission is required' unless a planning permission is in force. Section 191 of the Town and Country Planning Act 1990 provides that a certificate of lawfulness of existing use or development shall be treated as a grant of planning permission for the purposes of s 36(2)(a) of the EPA.

10.11.5   Planning and waste licensing

The objective of the licensing system is to regulate the day to day operation of waste facilities. This should be achieved by unambiguous conditions which leave the operator in no doubt as to what the required standards are and how they are to be met. Each condition should be necessary, comprehensive, unambiguous and enforceable otherwise it will be unreasonable. In addition, conditions need to comply with the guidance issued by the Secretary of State in Waste Management Papers.

10.12   Licence conditions

Section 35(3) provides that a Waste Management Licence will be granted on such terms and subject to such conditions as appear to the WRA to be appropriate, and these conditions may relate to the activities authorised, the precautions to be taken and the works to be carried out. In practice, conditions will be set which cover fundamental issues, such as the site infrastructure and site operation. They will also stipulate monitoring and record-keeping requirements, security and methods of avoiding nuisances. In practice, many of the conditions set in the licence will be the outcome of negotiation between the WRA and the applicant.

The conditions that can be included in a licence may relate to site preparation, site operation and, importantly, to matters affecting the site after the waste operation has ceased. One condition which may be attached is particularly important: s 35(4) enables a condition to be set requiring the holder to carry out works or do other things, even though he is not generally entitled to do them. It provides that any person whose consent would be required should grant or join in granting the holder of the licence such rights in relation to land as will enable the holder to comply with such a condition. This new power may cause considerable problems. The conditions may also extend to waste other than controlled waste (s 35(5)).

The Secretary of State has the power to make regulations specifying the conditions to be attached to the licences.

10.12.1 Variation of licences

Waste Management Licences can be varied either by the WRA or at the request of the licence-holder by virtue of s 37 EPA. The WRA is under a duty to vary the conditions of the licence where it is necessary to ensure activities 'do not cause pollution of the environment or harm to human health or become seriously detrimental to the amenities of the locality affected by the activities'. Where the WRA wishes to vary the licence because it considers a variation is desirable, then it may only vary the conditions if a variation is 'unlikely to require unreasonable expense on the part of the holder'. The Secretary of State also has the right to direct the WRA to modify conditions. Any variation of a licence must be effected by a notice served on the licence-holder. Alternatively, the licence-holder may want to seek a variation of the licence, for example to accommodate different types of wastes or to extend the operations. A licence-holder must apply to the WRA for a variation. Failure to determine an application to vary a licence within a period of two months, unless the period has been extended by agreement in writing, will result in the authority being deemed to have rejected the application. A licence-holder can appeal to the Secretary of State against the decision of the WRA regarding variation.

Waste operations are businesses run on commercial lines. Many are very profitable. Like all businesses, the ownership and control of the business can change hands. It is therefore necessary in such circumstances for there to be a transfer of the licence to the new owner/operator. Section 40 deals with the rights of transfer. A licence may be transferred on joint application of present holder and transferee. However, the WRA can only agree to the transfer if it is satisfied that the transferee is also a fit and proper person. As in the other provisions relating to licences, a right of appeal exists to the Secretary of State. If the WRA fails to determine an application for transfer within a period of two months (unless applicants agree in writing) the application will be deemed to have been rejected by the WRA.

10.12.2   Transfer of licence

The powers of revocation and suspension (provided in s 38) are available to the WRA dependent upon certain circumstances. A licence may be revoked in whole or in part, although it can only be partially revoked if the reason is due to the lack of technical competence of the management. The partial revocation of the licence allows for continuing obligations to be imposed on the licence-holder even if operation of the site is no longer permitted. Revocation can take place if:

10.12.3   Revocation and suspension of licences

- the licence-holder ceases to be a fit and proper person as a result of a relevant offence or the management is no longer in the hands of a technically competent person; or

- continuation of the licensed activities will cause pollution of the environment or harm to human health or serious detriment to amenities in the locality and these cannot be avoided by modifying conditions.

The WRA may suspend the licence in the following circumstances:

- the licence-holder is no longer a fit and proper person on the grounds of technical competence;

- the licensed activities have caused or are about to cause serious pollution of the environment or serious harm to human health;

- continuation of the licensed activities will continue to cause serious pollution of the environment or serious harm to human health.

Under s 38(6), the WRA has the power to suspend activities specified in the licence and s 38(9) provides that the authority may require the licence-holder to take measures to deal with the pollution or harm concerned. The licence-holder has a right of appeal. Suspension still takes affect pending the appeal but revocation does not.

10.13   Surrender of licences (s 39)

It is in relation to the surrender of licences that the EPA makes some very significant changes to the old COPA legislation. A fundamental flaw of the COPA waste regime was that licence-holders could surrender their licences at will. In point of fact, this is precisely what happened to many licensed sites in the months and weeks before the EPA provisions came into force in May 1994. Many COPA licence-holders surrendered their licences to avoid an automatic transfer to an EPA Waste Management Licence and the more stringent responsibilities that that entailed. In particular, operators taking this rather radical course of action were aware of the difficulties they would face in surrendering a Waste Management Licence. In short, the EPA provisions concerning the surrender of licences are much stricter and it is no longer possible for licence-holders to give up their licence at will. The provisions are to be found in s 39 EPA.

A Waste Management Licence may be surrendered by its holder, but in the case of a site licence it can only be surrendered with the agreement of the WRA. If the WRA accepts the application for surrender, it will issue the licence-holder with a 'certificate of completion'. However, the Waste Regulation Authority can only accept the surrender if it is satisfied that the condition of the relevant land is unlikely to cause pollution of the environment or harm to human health. In order to come to a decision about surrender, the WRA must first inspect the land and consider any information provided by the licence-holder about the state of the land. The WRA has three months to determine the application or a longer period if it is agreed in writing with the applicant. The WRA may, however, determine within that period that they cannot accept the surrender until certain information is supplied about the site or until it has undergone remedial works. For this reason, the Waste Manager should always keep accurate and detailed records about the wastes that have been deposited in order to facilitate and speed up the process of surrender.

Prior to agreeing to the surrender the WRA must refer the proposal to NRA and consider its views. If the NRA does not agree that the licence should be surrendered, the matter will be referred to the Secretary of State to resolve. Refusal to agree to surrender is subject to appeal to Secretary of State.

In all of the various provisions discussed above, it has been noted that the applicant or licence-holder has a right of appeal. The EPA provides a right of appeal to the Secretary of State against the WRA determination in the following instances:

10.14 Rights of appeal

(a) an application for a licence or a variation of the conditions of a licence is rejected;

(b) a licence is granted subject to conditions;

(c) the conditions of the licence are modified;

(d) a licence is suspended;

(e) a licence is revoked;

(f) an application to surrender a licence is rejected; or

(g) an application for the transfer of a licence is rejected.

An appeal must be made within six months of the relevant decision.

The WRAs have a general duty to monitor and supervise all licensed activities (s 42). They must take the necessary steps to ensure that the licensed activities in their area do not cause pollution of the environment, harm to human health or serious detriment to the amenities of the locality. They must also take steps to ensure that licence-holders comply with licence conditions.

10.15 Supervision and monitoring

In addition, the waste authorities will also carry out inspections of their areas to ensure that there are no unlicensed activities such as fly-tipping. Unlicensed waste disposal will constitute a breach of s 33 and it will be the WRAs that bring any prosecutions where they find such activities taking place.

Therefore, the WRAs employ inspectors whose function is to inspect and monitor sites. Section 69 enables WRAs, WDAs and also WCAs to appoint Inspectors. Waste Management Paper 4 (published by the DoE) provides the authorities with guidance on the powers provided under ss 69 and 70 EPA.

WRA Inspectors have wide powers to carry out the necessary monitoring and inspection required by the Act. In particular, they have powers to:

10.15.1 Powers of inspectors

• enter any premises which an inspector believes it is necessary for him to enter;

- make such investigations and examinations as are necessary in the circumstances;

- take photographs, measurements, recordings and samples of articles and substances on the premises including samples of land, air or water;

- require the dismantling of any article likely to cause pollution or harm to human health;

- take possession of that article to ensure that it is available in any proceedings under Pt II of the Act;

- question any person who he thinks can give him information;

- require the production of records, whether documentary or held on computer;

- seize or instruct that an article which he thinks is an imminent danger of serious pollution or harm to human health be rendered harmless even if this means destroying it.

However, the Act does not give inspectors entire discretion in exercising these powers. Section 69 provides certain safeguards. For instance, special procedures need to be adopted when taking samples. Of particular importance is s 69(7) which states that any answers given by a person questioned will not be admissible against him in criminal proceedings.

10.16   Clean-up powers

Section 59 EPA gives the WRAs and the Waste Collection Authorities powers to require the removal of controlled waste where the waste has been deposited in contravention of a Waste Management Licence. The authority may serve a notice on the occupier, requiring the waste to be removed, or steps to be taken to mitigate the consequences of the deposit. At least 21 days must be allowed, during which time the recipient has a right to appeal to the magistrates' court. Such an appeal must be allowed if the court is satisfied that the appellant neither deposited nor knowingly caused or knowingly permitted the deposit, or if there is a material defect in the notice.

If the occupier fails to take necessary action, then the authority can do so and charge the cost back to that occupier or, in appropriate cases, from the person who deposited or knowingly caused or knowingly permitted the deposit of waste.

Under s 61, the WRAs have a duty, where no site licence is in force, to inspect closed landfill sites and where it appears to the authority that the condition of the land is such that pollution of the environment or harm to human health is likely to be caused, the WRA is under a duty to do such works and take such steps (whether on the land affected or on adjacent land) as appear to be reasonable to avoid such pollution or harm. Unfortunately, the Environment Bill contains provision for the repeal of s 61. If the provisions had been implemented they would have imposed the strongest clean-up powers in environmental law.

10.16.1 Section 61: clean-up

One of the first pieces of legislation to deal with special wastes was the Deposit of Poisonous Wastes Act 1972, which made it an offence to deposit on land poisonous, noxious or polluting wastes in circumstances which may give rise to an environmental hazard. The Act also introduced new controls over the movement of dangerous wastes, and required those removing and depositing dangerous waste to notify the Waste Disposal Authority at least three days before doing so. This legislation was rushed through Parliament in response to the scares about dumping of toxic waste in the West Midlands. The definition of noticeable wastes in the 1972 Act were defined in a negative way as all toxic or dangerous waste not specifically excluded by regulations.

10.17 Special waste

The 1972 Act has since been repealed and replaced by provisions in the Control of Pollution Act 1974 and by further regulations. However, the subject of hazardous substances is also dealt with by a number of other statutes, which deal either wholly or in part with activities which give rise to hazardous substances and the controls that exist where escape or serious emergency might occur. It is not the intention of this book to deal with hazardous substances in the context of Health and Safety at Work and the regime that exists under that legislation for the handling of such substances, despite the fact that there is an indirect effect on the environment from these controls.

Control over special waste is still by means of the Control of Pollution Act 1974, although under s 62 EPA the Secretary of State is empowered to make provisions by means of regulations for the treatment, keeping or disposing of controlled waste that may be difficult or dangerous. As yet, this power has not been exercised, but may be used in the future to comply with EC Directive 91/689 which itself has been deferred due to difficulties in compiling a list of hazardous wastes. Although the special waste provisions are to be found in the COPA legislation, it is imperative to note that the duty of care provisions discussed above still apply to special waste.

10.17.1   Definition of special waste

Section 17 COPA provides that, if the Secretary of State considers that if controlled waste of any kind is or may be so dangerous or difficult to dispose of, he has the power to make special provision by means of regulation for waste of that kind. The Control of Pollution (Special Waste) Regulations were introduced in March 1981 to give effect to s 17 and are known as the s 17 Regulations. The Regulations define special waste by means of an inclusive list and set of criteria. The term special waste applies to the following:

(a) All medicinal products (as defined by the Medicines Act 1968, s 130) which are available only in accordance with a prescription (reg 2(1)(b));

(b) Any controlled waste which consists of or contains any of the substances listed in Sched 1 Part I (to the Regulations), if it is also dangerous to life, or has a flash point of 21 degrees Celsius or less.

10.17.2   Dangerous to life

One of the criticisms of the criteria laid down in the regulations is that they define special wastes not by reference to possible environmental damage but, instead, by reference to the possible effect on human health. The measure of whether something is dangerous to life is if the substance is likely to cause death or serious damage to tissue if a single dose of not more than 5 cm^3 were to be ingested by a child of 20 kg body weight; alternatively, if it is likely to cause serious damage to human tissue by inhalation, skin contact or eye contact on exposure to the substances for 15 minutes or less; or, finally, if it has a flash point of 21 degrees Celsius or less.

10.17.3   Consignment note system

Part II of the Special Waste Regulations establishes a mandatory system of consignment notes which must be prepared by the producer of special waste, before the waste is removed from the premises at which it is produced. The regulations require six copies of a standard form, known as the consignment note, to be prepared by the special waste producer. The system is complicated by the requirement that various parts of the form are completed at different times. However, the intention is that the system offers a record of all special waste movements. Producers of special waste have to keep records of all consignment notes for two years. Copies are sent to the WRA.

There is a separate EC Directive on Hazardous Waste as amended by 91/689. Council Directive 91/689 seeks to lay down a common definition of hazardous waste across the EC based on generic features and constituents of the waste. The deadline for the implementation of this Directive has been delayed as a consequence of the failure to draw up a list of hazardous wastes. When implemented these amendments will require some alteration of the definition of special waste under EPA s 62.

Additional controls are available under the Planning (Hazardous Substances) Act 1990. Prior to this, the control of developments under the Town and Country Planning regime could exert little control over the use of hazardous substances in developments. It was possible for factories and manufacturers to introduce new hazardous products and uses without requiring the need for further planning consent.

10.17.4 The Planning (Hazardous Substances) Act 1990

The Planning (Hazardous Substances) Act, which was brought into force on 1 June 1992, requires that the keeping of any hazardous substance on, over or under land, beyond small quantities, will require consent of the Hazardous Substances Authority (usually the London Boroughs, the district councils in metropolitan counties and the district planning authorities elsewhere). Before 'Hazardous Substances Consent' is given the Hazardous Substances Authorities consider whether the proposed storage or use of a hazardous substance is appropriate in a given location.

Part I of the EPA, which introduces Integrated Pollution Control, also contains some important controls over waste disposal; companies which are registered under IPC will be subject to controls by HMIP over their waste production, and some waste disposal facilities will themselves need to register under IPC, with the exception of landfill sites. Integrated Pollution Control authorisations issued by HMIP cannot include conditions which regulate the final deposit of waste on land. However, authorisations may regulate other forms of disposal, such as temporary disposal pending transfer. Such waste would, in line with the implied condition of IPC authorisations, need to be disposed of in a way that used the best available techniques not entailing excessive cost. Where an IPC process does involve the final deposit of waste on land, then HMIP must notify the Waste Regulation Authority of the area in which the process operates.

10.18 Relationship between the waste management regime and other pollution controls

10.18.1 Integrated pollution control

The consent of the National Rivers Authority must be obtained before a Waste Management Licence is granted. Before reaching a decision on an application for a waste management licence, the WRA must consult the National

10.18.2 Water pollution

Rivers Authority. If there is any disagreement arising out of the consultation, then the matter must be referred to the Secretary of State for decision. The WRA is also required by the Waste Management Licence Regulations to have regard to the protection of groundwater when determining a licence application. The Regulations give effect to the Groundwater Directive.

10.18.3   Town and country planning

Before a WRA can issue a Waste Management Licence, it must be satisfied that the waste management operation has planning permission by virtue of s 36(2) EPA. The applicant will need to demonstrate that he has planning permission or an established use certificate.

10.18.4   Statutory nuisance

Statutory nuisances may arise in relation to waste in two instances. The deposit of controlled waste, could amount to an accumulation, prejudicial to health or a nuisance under s 79(1)(e). Alternatively, the resultant smell from the waste could, if prejudicial to health or a nuisance constitute a statutory nuisance under s 79(1)(d).

Summary of Chapter 10

The Legal Regulation of Waste on Land

The terms waste and controlled waste are:

- defined in s 75 EPA, the Waste Management Licence Regulations 1994 and EC Directive 91/156.

Waste Regulation is in the hands of:
- Waste Regulation Authorities;
- Waste Collection Authorities;
- Waste Disposal Authorities.

Section 33 EPA establishes the main waste offences. An offence will not be committed under s 33(1)(a) and (b), if the deposit, treatment, keeping or disposal of controlled waste is in accordance with a Waste Management Licence.

Applications for a WML are made to the appropriate WRA accompanied by a fee. The WRA must consider whether:
- planning permission is in force;
- the applicant is a fit and proper person;
- rejection is necessary to prevent pollution.

Conditions will be attached which regulate the day-to-day operation of the waste site (s 35).

Waste Management Licences can be:
- varied;
- revoked;
- suspended.

- **Surrender** of licences is now subject to s 39 EPA. A licence cannot be surrendered until the WRA issue a certificate of completion.

- **Appeal**. The EPA provides a right of appeal to the Secretary of State against the determination of the Waste Regulation Authority.

- **Special Waste**. Special waste is still covered under the Control of Pollution (Special Waste) Regulations 1981 issued under s 17 COPA 1974.

EC Directive 91/689   EC Directive 91/689 as amended will, when implemented, result in the redefinition of special waste.

Chapter 11

Waste: The Duty of Care

One of the most significant features of the EPA was the introduction for the first time of a statutory duty of care which became effective from 1 April 1992. The Royal Commission for Environmental Pollution had recommended for some time the introduction of a statutory duty of care in relation to waste. In its Eleventh Report, *Managing Waste: The Duty of Care* (1985)), the Royal Commission recommended that a duty of care be placed on everybody involved in the waste chain, including waste holders who were not required to have a Waste Management Licence. They also argued strongly that such a duty of care be put on a statutory footing:

> 'The producer [of waste] incurs a duty of care which is owed to society, and we would like to see this duty reflected in public attitudes and enshrined in legislation and codes of practice.'

The duty of care is set out in s 34 of the Act and is supplemented by regulations made under s 34(5), the Environmental Protection (Duty of Care Regulations) 1991 and a Code of Practice. Any person who fails to comply with the duty imposed by s 34 or with the regulations commits a criminal offence. It is not necessary for any environmental damage to have been caused or for there to be a breach of s 33. All that is required is that there has been a breach of the duty of care. There is no statutory provision allowing for a civil action where damages have been caused as a result of a breach of s 34. On summary conviction, a breach of the duty of care can lead to a fine of £5,000 or on indictment an unlimited fine.

Section 34(1) provides that the duty of care applies to any person who imports, produces, carries, keeps, treats or disposes of controlled waste or, as a broker, has control of such waste. (DoE Circular 19/91 uses the short hand term 'waste holder' to refer to all persons who are subject to the duty.) Section 34(2) provides the only exception to the duty for occupiers of domestic premises who produce household waste on their property.

A broker is a person who may exercise control over waste, but may not necessarily hold it. For the purposes of the duty, they can be considered as sharing responsibility for any transfer of waste that they arrange with the actual parties who effect the transfer.

11.2 What does the duty of care involve?

Any person bound by the duty must:

'take all such measures applicable to him in that capacity as are reasonable in the circumstances:

a) to prevent any other person committing the offences in s 33;

b) to prevent the escape of the waste from his control or that of any other person;

c) to ensure that if the waste is transferred, it is transferred only to an "authorised person" or to a person "for authorised transport purposes"; and

d) when waste is transferred, to make sure that it is accompanied by a written description of the waste which will enable other persons to avoid a contravention of s 33 of the Act and to comply with the duty under s 34(1)(b) to prevent the escape of waste.'

11.3 Elements of the duty of care

11.3.1 To take all such measures applicable to him in that capacity as are reasonable in the circumstances

Section 34(1) requires anyone bound by the duty of care to take 'all such measures as are applicable to him in that capacity as are reasonable in the circumstances' to avoid a breach of the statutory duty.

This requirement needs to be considered in detail since it clearly limits the duty of care in two respects. First, duty holders are only required to take all measures that are applicable to them in their respective capacities. Second, such measures need to be reasonable in the circumstances. Therefore, the liability of the individual waste holder is limited and the duty is a subjective one. According to the Code of Practice which is intended to provide a guide for waste holders, a holder's capacity concerns his relationship with the waste in question, whether as a producer, carrier, keeper, treater, disposer or broker. Different measures are appropriate for different capacities. What is 'reasonable' is determined by reference to the circumstances. It is here that the Code of Practice is of importance since it provides guidance for waste holders on the measures that are reasonable in different circumstances. The circumstances which affect what is reasonable will include:

• what the waste is;

• the dangers it presents in handling and treatment;

• how it is dealt with;

• what the holder might reasonably be expected to know or foresee.

This element is central to the duty of care. A waste holder must not only take steps to ensure that he does not breach s 33. He must take reasonable steps to ensure that any other person who has control of his waste does not breach s 33. Therefore, for example, a waste producer can not relinquish responsibility for the waste produced on site once it is passed to a waste carrier. He must, as an absolute minimum, check that the waste is going to a licensed site which can take the particular type and quantity of waste and that the carrier is a registered carrier. Clearly, it is more prudent to draw up a contract with a carrier/waste manager which incorporates provisions that enable the waste producer to, *inter alia*, periodically check the site, check that records and transfer notes are being kept and to allow for termination of the contract in the event of the waste manager losing his licence. The contract should require the waste disposal contractor to comply with all of the relevant laws and licence requirements, and should ideally cover matters of liability, ownership of the waste, insurance and indemnities against liability. In practice, many arrangements are made without any written contract or are done by means of a standard contract which does not adequately cover all of the important issues.

The Code of Practice again provides good practical advice on complying with this element of the duty. However, it should be emphasised that compliance with the Code of Practice does not ensure that the duty of care is being adequately met.

In order to prevent the escape of waste, producers of waste should package it in such a way as to prevent escape and leakage whilst on site, in transit, or in storage. Consideration should be given to preventing its escape in subsequent transfer, with a view to the conditions which are likely, and the final method of treatment and disposal. Since escape can occur in a variety of circumstance, care will need to be taken to counteract all possibilities. For example, escape may occur where there is a spillage or where containers have been overfilled; it can occur even when adverse weather conditions result in waste being blown away or drain down storm drains. Vandals and animals may cause waste to escape, hence the need for security as well as containerisation. The waste producer, in particular, should take into account the time it will take for the waste to reach its final destination and the mode in which it will be carried or stored at a transfer station. Containerisation should be adequate for all of these different situations. For example, black bin bags will almost certainly be inadequate as they are almost guaranteed to

11.3.2 To prevent any other person committing offences under s 33

11.3.3 To prevent the escape of waste from his control or that of any other person

break open as soon as they are moved. This will be particularly important where the wastes include corrosive substances.

11.3.4 The transfer of waste to authorised persons and for authorised transport purposes

To comply with the duty of care, it is also essential to ensure that waste is only transferred to authorised persons or to a person for authorised transport purposes. These are defined respectively in s 34(3) and (4).

Section 34(3) states that the following are authorised persons:

- Waste Collection Authority;

- holder of a Waste Management Licence;

- persons exempted by regulations made by the Secretary of State under s 33(3);

- a registered carrier under s 2 of the Control of Pollution (Amendment) Act 1989;

- any person not required to be registered under the Control of Pollution (Amendment) Act 1989.

It is therefore necessary that transferors of waste should make sure that they are only transferring their waste on to an authorised person. If waste is being transferred to a carrier, then the carrier must be registered under the Control of Pollution (Amendment)Act 1989. Subject to limited exceptions (prescribed in the Controlled Waste (Registration of Carriers and Seizure of Vehicles) Regulations 1991), any person carrying waste in the course of their business, or in any other way for profit, must be registered with the Waste Regulation Authority. Anyone intending to transfer waste to a carrier should check that the person is registered (or exempt from the need to register) with the Waste Regulation Authority. The WRA maintains a register of waste carriers which is open to public inspection. It is necessary for the person handing over the waste to a carrier to check the actual certificate of registration since photocopies are not proof of registration. Moreover, the transferor should also carry out regular checks to ensure that the registration has not lapsed.

11.3.5 Authorised transport purposes

Section 34(4) lists the following as authorised transport purposes:

- the transport of controlled waste within the same premises between different places in those premises;

- the transport to a place in Great Britain of controlled waste which has been brought from a country or territory outside Great Britain not having been landed in Great Britain until it arrives at that place;

- the transport by air or sea of controlled waste from a place inside Great Britain to a place outside Great Britain.

Waste producers are responsible for ensuring that, when they transfer waste, the waste is accompanied by an adequate written description. The description must necessarily be sufficient to ensure that other waste holders in the waste chain can avoid committing offences under s 33.

The Environmental Protection (Duty of Care) Regulations 1991 (made under s 34(5)), which came into force on 1 April 1992, established a system of transfer notes and record keeping of waste transfers to help waste holders comply with this element of the duty of care. However, the transfer note does not necessarily provide the written description. The aim of this system is to enable the WRA to keep track of the movement of all wastes within their area, and a written description will still need to be provided when waste is transferred. The regulations place responsibilities on the transferor and transferee of waste to keep records of all waste transfers. On completion of the transfer of the controlled waste, both the giver and the receiver must complete and sign a transfer note. This includes:

- identification of the waste;

- quantity;

- whether it is loose or in container at time of transfer;

- place and time of transfer;

- name and address of both;

- whether the transferor is the producer or importer;

- if the transferee is authorised for transport purposes.

All parties involved in the transfer must keep a copy of the transfer note and the written description for at least two years. The WRA may serve a notice demanding copies of transfer notes and these must be supplied within seven days. While all transfers of waste must be documented, the regulations do not require each individual transfer to be separately documented. It is possible for a single transfer to cover multiple consignments transferred at the same time or over a period not exceeding a year. However, this can only apply where the description is provided before the first consignment and all the other consignments covered by the note are the same.

11.3.6   The written description

11.4   The Code of Practice

Section 34(7) empowers the Secretary of State to issue a Code of Practice for the purposes of providing practical guidance on how to discharge the duty of care (*Waste Management, The Duty of Care, A Code of Practice*). The Code recommends a series of steps which would normally be enough to satisfy the requirements of the duty. Its importance however is reflected in the fact that, by virtue of s 34(10), the Code of Practice shall be admissible in evidence and, if any provision of the Code appears to the court to be relevant to any question arising in the proceedings, it shall be taken into account in determining that question. It is therefore important that all those who are subject to the duty of care are familiar with the Code.

11.5   Breach of the duty of care

Any person who fails to comply with the duty of care, or the documentation requirements laid down in the Duty of Care Regulations, commits a criminal offence and will be liable, on summary conviction, to a fine not exceeding £5,000. On indictment, the Crown Court can impose an unlimited fine. Once again, directors and senior management may be personally liable for a breach of s 34. It is, therefore, in the interests of management to ensure that adequate training programmes and systems are in place to ensure that all relevant staff understand the requirements of the duty of care at all times.

Finally, breach of the duty of care could result in a person being deemed not to be a 'fit and proper person' for the purposes of obtaining or maintaining a Waste Management Licence.

11.6   Civil liability

It has already been noted that the Environmental Protection Act (under s 73(6)) provides a statutory civil remedy for any person who has suffered damages as a consequence of another person's breach of s 33. However, no such statutory remedy exists in relation to a breach of the duty of care. In addition, of course, damages may be available through common law actions such as nuisance.

11.6.1   EC Directive on civil liability for waste

Although the duty of care as currently defined does not apply strict liability to waste producers, it may be amended in the future, should the Directive on Civil Liability for Damage Caused by Waste be adopted. This Directive will radically alter the current liability of waste producers and waste controllers. The Directive, if adopted in its current form, will make a producer or controller of waste liable under civil law for damage or injury caused by the waste, irrespective of fault on their part. In addition, the draft Directive also contains proposals concerning liabilities arising out of co-disposal.

The problem of waste is perhaps more evident to the general public in the form of litter, which we see every day on the streets of our cities, towns and villages. Litter is a serious problem in the UK, a recent survey carried out by the Tidy Britain Group (formerly Keep Britain Tidy) shows that the public are likely to encounter litter in three-fifths of the environment, notably parks and play areas, carparks, high density residential areas and industrial sites. The most common items of litter are:

- cigarette ends;

- sweet wrappers;

- matchsticks;

- chewing gum;

- glass fragments.

The inclusion within the Environmental Protection Act 1990 of a chapter to deal specifically with litter is an indication of the extent of the problem, and shows a desire on the part of government to take stricter measures to 'keep Britain tidy'.

This section will examine the current regulatory framework controlling with litter.

Specific statutory control of litter began in 1958 with the enactment of the Litter Act. This was extended by the 1971 Act and was more recently consolidated in the Litter Act 1983.

The problem of litter was firmly placed on the government's environmental agenda with the publication, in 1989, of a DOE consultation paper *Action on Litter: The Government's Proposals for Legislation*. This consultation paper made clear the impetus behind such proposals:

'More and more people are concerned that in spite of increased efforts by many local authorities, private landowners, voluntary groups and individuals, the problem of litter shows no signs of abating. At the same time, public awareness, and the demand from both local authorities and individuals for tougher action, are growing. The government shares this concern, and is determined to take the measures needed to ensure that the problem can be, and is, tackled effectively.'

Although the EPA 1990 contains the bulk of the litter provisions, several of the provisions contained in the Litter Act 1983 are still in force and are central to the control of litter. Under s 3 of the Litter Act 1983 the Secretary of State for the Environment can make grants to assist any body working to change attitudes and prevent littering. Section 5 of the Litter

Act places local authorities under a duty to provide and maintain bins in streets and public places.

11.8.1 The Environmental Protection Act 1990

The result of this renewed awareness was that litter was included in the extensive environmental framework enacted by the Environmental Protection Act 1990, which replaces part of the 1983 Act. The new provisions contained in Part IV of the Environmental Protection Act 1990 largely consolidated the law on litter, repeating the offence, and it also creates further responsibilities for local authorities to address the problem of litter. Interestingly, under s 87(6) of the EPA 1990 local authorities are also encouraged to publicise the problems of litter, the aim of this being to bring about a change in attitude towards litter. It is widely acknowledged by the DOE and the Tidy Britain Group that only when the legislative sanctions are supported by such a change in attitude can the problems of litter be overcome. The provisions of the EPA may be having some success in countering the problems of litter as in 1993, the Tidy Britain Group reported that Britain was 13% cleaner than it was prior to the implementation of the EPA 1990.

11.8.2 The definition of litter

Litter has a wide interpretation; it can relate to anything except natural matter, such as overgrown vegetation or fallen leaves; nor does it include dog faeces, which, although it is classed as litter, is subject to a different regulatory regime.

The definition of litter is not restrictive as the offence relates to what is *done* with the litter, rather than what it *is*. In short, the definition of litter refers to waste materials on the ground rather than in a litter bin or other receptacle.

11.8.3 Responsibility for litter control

Control of litter rests with the principal litter authorities defined under s 86(1) of the EPA (namely the county councils, district councils and London borough councils) which have a duty to ensure that land is kept clear of litter and refuse. In order to determine the standards of cleanliness, the Secretary of State for the Environment has issued a Statutory Code, which sets standards of cleanliness and the areas to which they apply.

The Code of Practice is based on four standards of cleanliness:

- Grade A – no litter or refuse;

- Grade B – predominantly free of litter and refuse, apart from small items;

- Grade C – widespread distribution of litter and refuse with minor accumulations; and

- Grade D – heavily littered with significant accumulations.

These standards relate to 11 categories of zones which are defined in the code, ranging from residential areas, parks, recreational grounds and shopping areas to local roads and highways. The zone in which the land is classed determines the standards expected and the time in which the standard must be rectified should it fall.

Under s 95 of the EPA, the principal litter authorities are under a duty to maintain public registers containing information relating to orders of litter control areas under s 90(3) and street litter control notices issued under s 93.

Each litter authority has a duty in respect of highways and roads in its area. Roads and highways are to be kept as clean as is practicable, the standard which will be required is set out in the DOE Code of Practice on Litter and Refuse.

The SSE, under s 90, has issued the Litter Control Areas Order 1991 (SI 1991/1325) which designates land which may be the subject of a litter control order. Types of land to be controlled include:

11.8.4   Litter control areas

- public car parks;

- industrial estates;

- inland beaches or seashores; and

- shopping centres.

Land may also be designated by reference to its ownership or the activities carried out upon it.

The litter authorities can designate any such land as a litter control area if the presence of litter is detrimental to the amenities of the locality. Designation of an area will require full council agreement and public consultation must also take place.

Under ss 93 and 94 the litter authority may issue a street litter control notice with the aim of preventing accumulations of litter or refuse in any street or open land. A notice will be served on the occupier of the premises associated with the street litter problems where:

11.8.5   Street litter control notices

- there is recurrent defacement by litter or refuse of any land, being part of the street or open land adjacent to the street, which is in the vicinity of the premises; or

- the condition of any part of the premises which is open land in the vicinity of the frontage and is detrimental to the amenities of the locality because of the litter or refuse; or

- the premises produces types and quantities of litter or refuse which is likely to cause the defacement of any part of the street.

The Street Litter Control Notices Order 1991 (SI 1991/1324) specifies prescribed premises and land for the purposes of s 94. The notice will specify requirements relating to the clearance of the litter or refuse from a specified area. Failure to comply with a notice is an offence and is punishable by a fine not exceeding level 4 on the standard scale.

This provision is particularly useful in relation to fast-food outlets whose premises are often surrounded by the debris of empty cartons and wrappings.

| 11.8.6 | Litter abatement notices | Under s 92 of the EPA, the principal litter authority is permitted to serve a litter abatement notice upon a site which is defaced by litter or refuse, or that there is a possibility of such defacement recurring. The notice may contain time limits for the improvement of the site. |

Under s 92 of the EPA, the principal litter authority is permitted to serve a litter abatement notice upon a site which is defaced by litter or refuse, or that there is a possibility of such defacement recurring. The notice may contain time limits for the improvement of the site.

The litter abatement notice must be served on the occupier of the land, or, when the land is unoccupied, on the owner. The person upon whom the notice is served may appeal to a magistrates court.

Failure to comply with a litter abatement notice is an offence and any person may be liable to a fine not exceeding level 4 on the standard scale, and for one-twentieth of this amount for every day the offence continues.

Under s 92(9), if the owner or occupier upon whom the notice is served fails to comply with the requirements of the notice, the litter authority has the power to enter the land and clear the litter or refuse, and may then recover the costs from the responsible party, but not where the site in question is crown land or if it belongs to a statutory undertaker.

11.8.7   Abandoned shopping and luggage trolleys

Although not commonly thought of as litter, abandoned trolleys contribute to the detrimental appearance of an area. Under s 99 of the EPA, litter authorities are given power to seize trolleys found on any land in the open air. Section 99 emphasises that litter authorities should consult those responsible for the trolleys, such as train stations, airports and supermarkets, as to the operation of the legislation. A result of such consultation may be the creation of schemes for the collection of trolleys, which would reduce or eliminate the problems and would be less demanding on local authority resources. This reinforces the government's commitment to changing attitudes to the control of litter.

It is a criminal offence to throw, drop or deposit litter under s 87 of the EPA:

> '(1) If any person throws down, drops or otherwise deposits in, into or from any place to which this section applies, he shall, subject to subsection (2) below, be guilty of an offence.
>
> (2) No offence is committed under this section where the depositing and leaving of the thing was –
>
> (a) authorised by law, or
>
> (b) done with the consent of the owner or occupier or other person or authority having control of the place in or into which that thing was deposited.'

It is also an offence to throw litter from a vehicle, although a prosecution will normally only take place where the litter is thrown by the driver of the vehicle who can be identified by DVLC records.

Prosecution under s 87 is usually left to the police through the Crown Prosecution Service. The principal litter authorities can also prosecute an offender.

It is rare for a prosecution to be brought following a member of the public reporting the littering offence. A prosecution will succeed where there is strong evidence identifying the person responsible, the location of the littering and a description of the litter.

If a person is found guilty of this offence, under s 87(6), the maximum penalty is level 4 on the standard scale, which is currently £2,500. As an alternative to prosecution it may be more appropriate informally to caution the litterer about his behaviour.

In many cases, the litter authority may feel it is more appropriate to issue a fixed penalty notice to the litterer. This is currently £10 although under s 88(7) the SSE may substitute a different amount. The litterer will have 14 days to pay, failure to do so can result in a prosecution under s 87.

The litter authorities also have the power to appoint litter wardens to issue the fixed penalty notices.

In addition to the powers and duties of the litter authorities, the EPA makes provision for individuals to take action in respect of litter. The may also be the possibility of an action under the common law.

The EPA 1990 also confers a right on private individuals to take action on litter. Under s 91 of the EPA any member of the public affected by the presence of litter or refuse on land may, after giving five days' written notice, apply to the magistrates' court for a litter abatement notice.

Proceedings under s 91 are brought against the person who has the duty to keep the land or the highway clear under ss 89(1) and 89(2) of the EPA 1990.

The fees for this have recently been reduced from £30 to £3.50 for making a complaint, £3.50 for the issue of a summons and £16.50 for an Abatement Order, which are payable at the various stages of the process. Non-compliance with a litter abatement notice can result in fines of up to £2,500 with additional fines accruing every day the terms of the notice are not met.

| 11.8.13 | Common law liability for litter |

In the case of *Gregory v Piper* an action was brought in respect of rubbish rolling against a wall was held to constitute trespass. This was possible because trespass is actionable *per se*, it does not require proof of damage.

However, it will generally be difficult to bring a common law action in respect of litter because of the problems of finding the responsible party. The common law may be an inappropriate means of resolving the problem because of the time delay and costs that are involved. See further Chapter 5, Civil Liability and the Common Law.

Waste: The Duty of Care

One of the most significant features of the EPA was the introduction for the first time of a statutory duty of care which became effective from 1 April 1992.

The duty of care is set out in s 34 of the Act and is supplemented by Regulations made under s 34(5), The Environmental Protection (Duty of Care Regulations) 1991 and a Code of Practice.

The duty of care

Any person who fails to comply with the duty imposed by s 34 or with the Regulations commits a criminal offence. 1t is not necessary for any environmental damage to have been caused or for there to be a breach of s 33. All that is required is that there has been a breach of the duty of care.

Breach of the duty of care

Section 34(1) provides that the duty of care applies to any person who imports, produces, carries, keeps, treats or disposes of controlled waste or, as a broker, has control of such waste.

Section 34(2) provides the only exception to the duty for occupiers of domestic premises who produce household waste on their property.

Any person bound by the duty must: 'take all such measures applicable to him in that capacity as are reasonable in the circumstances –

(a) to prevent any other person committing the offences in s 33;

(b) to prevent the escape of the waste from his control or that of any other person;

(c) to ensure that if the waste is transferred, it is transferred only to an "authorised person" or to a person "for authorised transport purposes"; and

(d) when waste is transferred, to make sure that it is accompanied by a written description of the waste which will enable other persons to avoid a contravention of s 33 of the Act and to comply with the duty under s 34(1)(b) to prevent the escape of waste.'

Litter

Litter is a serious problem in the UK. The main legislative provisions controlling litter are contained in Part IV EPA 1990 and the Litter Act 1983, parts of which still remain in force.

Legislative control of litter

Section 87 EPA creates the criminal offence of throwing, dropping or depositing litter.

Under s 86(1) EPA litter is under the control of the principal Litter Authorities.

A statutory Code of Practice sets standards for cleanliness.

Section 90 allows land to be designated as a Litter Control Area.

Section 95 requires maintenance of public registers relating to Litter Control Areas.

Any member of the public can take proceedings against litter offenders under s 91 EPA.

Chapter 12

Contaminated Land

The problems of contaminated land are not new. There is evidence to suggest that land uses dating back to Roman times have been responsible for causing some of the contamination we know today. More recently, many industrial uses of land are responsible for the widespread problems of contamination across the country, in both urban and rural areas. The control of contaminated land is a newer phenomenon which has attracted significant interest in recent years. This is largely as a result of major incidents of contaminated land, such as those at Love Canal, USA, in the late 1970s, and a similar incident at Lekkerkerk in The Netherlands, in which residents of housing estates suffered illness and death from the effects of buried toxic waste. Following considerable attention from central government, control was proposed through public registers of land which may be contaminated, under s 143 of the Environmental Protection Act 1990.

The attempted introduction of 'public registers of land which may be contaminated', under s 143 of the Environmental Protection Act 1990, attracted a great deal of attention to the issue of contaminated land, and although s 143 is to be repealed, it began a lengthy debate as to the possible forms of regulation of contaminated land, which has resulted in the provisions now contained in the Environment Bill.

This chapter will examine the nature of contamination, the problems it poses, and how the legal regulation is framed. It will also consider more practical implications associated with the relationship between legal regulation, or the lack of it, and the ownership of contaminated land.

12.1   Introduction

Contamination can refer to a variety of contaminants put into the environment by various sources which can be man-made or naturally occurring. This chapter will only refer to contamination which occurs in land as a direct or indirect result of industrial processes, not to naturally-occurring contamination such as radon or naturally-existing heavy metals.

The definitions of contamination and contaminated land can vary significantly. Problems have arisen because the different professions associated with contaminated land

12.2   Definition

interpret it according to varying factors, for example: the particular contaminants involved and the period of time for which the land has been contaminated.

There is no universally accepted definition of contamination, although several organisations have prepared their own working definitions:

- Department of the Environment – '... land which represents an actual or potential hazard to health or the environment as a result of current or previous use.'

- Royal Commission on Environmental Pollution – 'Contamination refers to the introduction or presence in the environment of alien substances or energy ... Contamination is a necessary but not sufficient condition for pollution.'

- NATO/Committee on Challenges to Modern Society (CCMS) – 'Land that contains substances which, when present in sufficient quantities or concentrations, are likely to cause harm, directly or indirectly, to man, to the environment or, on occasion, to other targets.'

- British Standard Code of Practice for the Identification and Investigation of Contaminated Land – 'Land that contains any substance that, when present in sufficient concentration or amount, may present a hazard. The hazard may:
  a) be associated with the present status of the land;
  b) limit the future use of the land; and/or
  c) require the land to be specially treated before particular use.'

For the purposes of this chapter, contaminated land can be understood as a general concept – meaning land which has been contaminated as a result of a previous or current use – irrespective of the hazards it may pose. This general definition follows the spirit of those proposed by the DoE, NATO/CCMS, and the Royal Commission on Environmental Pollution. Although it is recognised that such definitions bring with them limitations, it is necessary to have a general understanding of what is meant by contamination.

Contamination of land can occur in a number of ways, most commonly by the use to which the land is put as this will often involve hazardous or contaminating substance being released into the ground.

Some of the most commonly found examples of contaminated land are:

- old gas works sites;
- land previously used for industrial purposes;
- waste disposal operations;
- old sewage works and sewage farms.

All of these land uses can present a hazard to the health of workers on the site, and occupiers of the site, as well as to those on adjacent land.

Details of other contaminating land uses were published in the first Consultation Paper on Contaminated Land published in May 1991, which contained many obvious examples of industries which are potentially contaminating: for example, the chemical industry, the petrochemical industry and the rubber industry. However, also included were some land uses which may be thought to be more mundane, such as dry cleaning outlets on the high street.

No comprehensive survey of contaminated land has been undertaken across the UK and, as a result, there is no accurate figure of exactly how much land is affected. Department of the Environment estimates suggest that between 50,000 to 100,000 sites are affected with some degree of contamination, covering some 27,000 hectares of land. However, experience of contaminated land in the US and in some Member States of the EC has shown that, until a full survey is undertaken, the number of sites affected by contamination is always underestimated.

12.3   The extent of the problem in the UK

The major hazards presented by contaminated land are those to human health and to the environment. Advice issued in DOE Circular 21/87 and Health and Safety Executive publications stresses the possible hazards for workers involved with the redevelopment of contaminated sites, and occupiers and users of buildings situated on contaminated land. There is also the possibility that contamination might affect the fabric of any building on the site, as recognised in Sched C of the Building Regulations.

12.3.1   Risks associated with contaminated land

Contamination is a particular problem in residential areas; for example, houses with gardens, schools and playing fields which, if they are contaminated, can present a direct path for the contamination to pass to humans and harm health, eg through children eating soil and from eating home-grown produce.

The problems caused by contaminated land were highlighted by several occurrences of contamination, both nationally and internationally.

12.3.2   Incidents of contamination

The first major incident was discovered in Spring 1979, at Love Canal, USA, where toxic waste which had been buried in a 'hole in the ground' resurfaced. Unfortunately, the site upon which it had been dumped had been developed as a residential area, comprising houses, schools, parks and shops. The toxic waste appeared as an 'oily black gook' in the back gardens and basements of the houses. The ill-effects of this contamination were widespread, with residents alleging miscarriages, birth defects, cancer, and many mysterious illnesses, although these were never affirmed by federal government research. The incident at Love Canal attracted international attention and prompted the US government to enact stringent regulation of toxic waste and contaminated land in the form of the Comprehensive Environmental Response Compensation and Liability Act 1980.

This was followed by a similar incident at Lekkerkerk in the Netherlands, which provided the impetus for the Dutch Government to take action and legislate on the problem of contaminated land.

The UK has not been immune from problems of contamination. Several incidents have been caused by escaping methane; for example a bungalow at Loscoe in Derbyshire exploded due to a build up of methane, and a similar incident at the Abbeystead Pumping Station, in which a man tragically died in the explosion.

The existence of contamination in land can also pose a threat to groundwater. This is a particularly important consideration in the south of England where up to 80% of drinking water is abstracted from underground aquifers. The link between contaminated land and polluted groundwater was recently identified in the case of *Cambridge Water Company v Easter Counties Leather plc* (1994), which will be discussed later in the chapter.

12.4   Government recognition of the problem of contaminated land

It is only relatively recently that there has been any recognition of the problems, let alone any attempt to regulate them. Since the late 1970s, the government has been well aware of the issues associated with contaminated land because of the scrutiny the whole area has received in various reports and examinations. The DOE itself has established a Contaminated Land Branch, which looks at the problems of contamination, and can commission minor surveys of contaminated land in England and Wales.

This marked the first official recognition of the problems of contaminated land in the UK. The ICRCL's original objectives were to offer practical advice and guidance to local authorities and developers on the redevelopment of such land, and to sponsor research into issues associated with contamination. In reality, the ICRCL has little strength, it merely operates as a co-ordinating body with only two full-time members of staff. Its membership includes representatives from the DoE, Ministry of Agriculture, Fisheries and Food, Scottish Office, Welsh Office, Department of Health and the Health and Safety Executive, thus indicating the wide range of interests involved with contamination.

12.4.1 The establishment of the Interdepartmental Committee on the Redevelopment of Contaminated Land

In its 10th Report, *Tackling Pollution: Experience and Prospects*, the RCEP considered the issue of public access to wnvironmental information held by pollution control authorities.

With reference to contaminated land, the RCEP recommended that records of such land should be kept and that a DOE planning circular should be issued to local planning authorities in order to clarify the position of a contaminated site in the planning process.

12.4.2 Royal Commission on Environmental Pollution

The House of Commons Select Committee on the Environment has twice examined the issue of contaminated land. It was originally anticipated that the Report on Toxic Waste (1989) would also include contaminated land. However, as the Committee looked deeper into the issue of contamination, they felt it would merit an examination as a separate issue.

As a result of this recommendation, in the following year the House of Commons Select Committee on the Environment undertook an Inquiry into Contaminated Land (1990). The Committee examined the issue of contamination in detail. Its main recommendations were that records of contamination should be created and open to the public and that a comprehensive framework of regulations should be established.

12.4.3 House of Commons Select Committee on the Environment

Until the enactment of the Environmental Protection Act 1990, there was no specific regulation of contaminated land. This was due to a number of factors:

12.5 Legislative control of contaminated land

- it was only discovered that contamination was an environmental hazard relatively recently, and even now further research needs to be done into the problems of contamination and its remediation;

- although there is a significant contamination problem across the European Union, surveys undertaken in the member States have revealed large amounts of contamination:
  - The Netherlands   110,000 contaminated sites;
  - Denmark   20,000 contaminated sites;
  - Germany   100,000 contaminated sites.

Despite this large problem of contamination, the EC has not formulated any regulatory regime for dealing with contaminated land. As a result of this, the UK government has not been forced to take action to implement EC legislation in this area.

Some sort of indirect control is, however, exerted through a number of EC Directives: for example Directive 80/68, the Groundwater Directive, which aims to prevent the pollution of groundwater by certain substances, and to reduce or eliminate any damage caused by pollution.

The EC is also working on a draft Directive on Civil Liability for Damage Caused by Waste, which is designed to attach liability for pollution and contamination to those involved in the waste disposal process. For further discussion see Chapter 11 on Waste.

12.5.1   Controls existing before the Environmental Protection Act 1990

Prior to the enactment of the Environmental Protection Act 1990, control of contaminated land fell within public health legislation, the town and country planning system, and several miscellaneous legislative provisions, many of which are still in force today.

12.5.2   Public health

The first legislative provision to deal with the problems of contamination were ss 54 and 92 of the Public Health Act 1936. Section 54 prevented the erection or extension of a building on land which has been filled up with 'any material impregnated with faecal or offensive animal or offensive vegetable matter, or is ground upon which any such material has been deposited'. In such circumstances, the local authority could not permit development because of the perceived risk to public health.

Although the fundamental objective of the provision was to safeguard public health, it also had the indirect effect of preventing development on contaminated sites. The extent to which this provision has been relied upon in the area of contaminated land is unknown.

Section 92 has now been re-enacted by s 80 of the EPA 1990, which is discussed below and in greater detail in Chapter 14, Statutory Nuisance.

The Occupiers' Liability Acts place an occupier of land under a general duty to ensure that visitors, and in some cases trespassers, are kept reasonably safe from injury. This is of limited application because it is very rare that contamination will lead to injury of the kind covered by the Act.

12.5.3   Occupiers' Liability Acts 1957 and 1984

Under the Health and Safety at Work Act, an employer is under a duty to ensure that his workplace is as safe as is reasonably practical for employees and visitors. This is of particular importance where the workplace is classed as a contaminated site, for example when it is undergoing redevelopment or remediation. This is supported by a Health and Safety Executive Guidance Note, 'Protection of workers and the general public during the development of contaminated land'.

12.5.4   Health and Safety at Work Act 1974

There is currently much discussion as to the relationship between planning control and environmental protection. It is currently addressed by the Planning Policy Guidance Note *Planning and Pollution Control*, issued in July 1994.

12.6   Town and Country Planning legislation

The PPG emphasises the importance of consultation between planning and pollution control authorities and highlights the interrelationships between them. The recent case of *Gateshead Metropolitan Borough Council v Secretary of State for the Environment* (1994) has established judicial guidance in this area. For further discussion on this area see Chapter 13.

The regulation of contaminated land can fall quite properly within either of the planning law or environmental law regimes, as can be seen with the attempts to register contaminated sites under s 143 of the EPA 1990, and controls drawn from other areas of this Act and the Water Resources Act 1991 which both seek to achieve protection of the wnvironment. Guidance originally issued by the DoE, and more recently updated by Planning Policy Guidance Note 23, asserts that contamination is material planning consideration which must be taken into account at every stage of the planning process.

Whilst it is clearly recognised that contamination is essentially an environmental problem, there are many planning policy issues which support the redevelopment of contaminated land:

12.6.1   Planning policy issues and contaminated land

- the government's emphasis on the redevelopment of such sites, in programmes such as Action for Cities;

- it relieves pressure on the green-belt;

- the regeneration of unsightly areas can improve the look of an area and may often attract new investment;

- beneficial to the residents of an area to improve the visual amenity of the site.

There are also several factors which support the control of contaminated land within the planning system:

1   the town and country planning system provides a comprehensive framework for controlling land use and regulating development; and

2   it is often at the redevelopment stage that the potential for contamination becomes apparent.

12.6.2	Circular 21/87

The Department of the Environment Circular 21/87 affirmed the position of contaminated land within the planning regime. In Circular 21/87, advice was given to local planning authorities as to the priorities which should be attached to contaminated land in the development plan system. It also established that contamination should be regarded as a material planning consideration, which should be taken into account at every stage of the planning process.

12.6.3	Planning Policy Guidance Note 23

Planning Policy Guidance Note 23 has now replaced Circular 21/87. It restates the aims of the government in relation to contaminated land:

'... where practicable, brownfield sites, including those affected by contamination, should be recycled into new uses and the pressures thereby reduced for greenfield sites to be converted to urban, industrial or commercial uses. Such recycling can also provide an opportunity to deal with the threats posed by contamination to health or the environment.'

The PPG explicitly defines the local planning authorities' functions in relation to contaminated land. They have an overall duty to examine any unacceptable risks to health or the environment which are presented by any planning project; therefore, they must exercise caution in discharging their planning functions in the following stages:

1   In the preparation of development plans and policies, the local planning authority must take account of contamination and its effects on health and the environment. At this stage, it may be appropriate for the local planning authority to formulate more specific policies relating to contaminated land;

2   Before an application for planning permission is submitted, it may be appropriate for the local planning authority to discuss issues arising from a proposed development with the developer in order to bring to his attention the possibility of contamination. It may also be possible to discuss the issue with a wider range of consultees, such as the Waste Regulatory Authority, the National Rivers Authority, HMIP and the Health and Safety Executive;

3   In considering the application for planning permission for the development of a contaminated site, the local planning authority must determine whether the developer's proposals take account of any contamination. If the authority feels that there is insufficient knowledge of the contamination then they may grant outline planning permission, pending an investigation of the site and the formulation of a cost-effective solution;

4   If the local planning authority is satisfied with the proposals for development, then it may grant planning permission to which may be attached conditions. Such conditions may require, for example, that a full investigation of the site is undertaken, or that the developer informs the local planning authority of the presence of significant unsuspected contamination encountered during the redevelopment;

5   Once planning permission has been granted, the local planning authority should issue a separate notice stating that the responsibility for safe development and secure occupancy rests with the developer.

The local planning authority has the option of attaching planning conditions to a planning permission to ensure that the condition of the land corresponds with its end use; this is a recognised method of controlling problems of contamination. To be valid, the condition must comply with the principles established in *Newbury District Council v Secretary of Sate for the Environment* (1980), namely:

(i)   it must serve some useful planning purpose;

(ii) it must fairly and reasonably relate to the permitted development; and

(iii) a condition must not be manifestly unreasonable.

Under s 215 of the Town and Country Planning Act 1990, the local planning authority has the power to secure the tidying up of any land in their area which is in such a condition to

12.6.4   Planning conditions

12.6.5   Section 215, Town and Country Planning Act

'adversely affect' the amenity of the area. The local planning authority can serve a notice on the owner and occupier of the land requiring that such steps be taken to remedy the condition of the land within a certain period. Failure to comply with the provisions of the notice is a criminal offence under s 219, and the local planning authority may also enter the land and undertake the work required by the notice. In such circumstances, the authority can recover the expenses from the owner of the land. It is not known to what extent these powers have been used to remediate contamated land.

| 12.6.6 | Limitations of the town and country planning system |

Although the town and country planning system clearly does play an important role in the regulation of contaminated land, it does have several fundamental drawbacks. The first is that contamination has only recently been recognised as an issue which merits regulation, and has therefore been slotted into an existing framework which does not provide any specific control.

Also, the town and country planning system exists to control development, rather than to prevent it – for example, an average 94% of planning applications are granted each year.

Another major reason for the ineffective control of contaminated land within the planning system is that planning applications are dealt with by local planning authorities which often have neither the expertise nor the resources to deal with contaminated land.

It is also essential to look at the fundamental objectives of the planning system,

'Essentially the [town and country planning] system is designed to regulate the development and use of land in the public interest ... Properly used, it can help to secure economy, efficiency and amenity in the development and use of land' (Planning Policy Guidance Note 1).

This basic objective can only be met where the local planning authority balances the needs of stimulating the local economy, possibly providing employment or local housing with environmental issues. Often the former will be deemed more important because it is not the function of a local planning authority to 'prevent, inhibit or delay development which can be reasonably permitted' (PPG1).

For these reasons, the control of contamination cannot fall solely within the planning system, but must also be controlled under environmental legislation which is specifically aimed at some of the environmental problems associated with contaminated land.

No specific statutory control of contamination was attempted until the enactment of s 143 of the Environmental Protection Act 1990. Under this section, local authorities were to be placed under a duty to compile and maintain public registers of land which may be contaminated. The section was a late amendment to the EPA, appearing at the third reading in the House of Lords, and therefore received little debate and scrutiny by Parliament, which gives the overwhelming impression that the section was not properly thought through. A long consultation period followed the inclusion of s 143 of the EPA, the primary purpose of which was to ascertain the format of the proposed registers, although it soon became clear that the consultation was initially necessary to discuss the issue of registration, and subsequently regulation in general. In total, to date, four consultation papers have been issued by the Department of the Environment.

The earlier consultation papers issued in May 1991 and June 1992 were both very prescriptive, detailing the proposed form of the registers and the contaminating uses which would be deemed to contaminate the land. Both of these Consultation Papers attracted a considerable amount of criticism, the most vociferous condemnation coming from the property industry, concerned that blight would be attached to any property included on the register. It was thought that this would be particularly damaging at a time of recession.

The proposals contained in the Consultation Papers also created a split in the environmental lobby: on the one hand, there were those who approved of the registers as part of a wider campaign for better information on the environment, and, on the other, there were those who feared that such a register would increase pressure on greenbelt and countryside sites.

The proposals mooted by the DOE were clearly unsatisfactory and the opposition to them prompted the need to reconsider the possible forms of regulation of contaminated land.

On 24 March 1993 it was announced by the Secretary of State for the Environment that the proposals for s 143 registers were to be withdrawn and that the problems of contaminated land were to be the subject of a 'wide-ranging review'.

The results of the review were announced in a Consultation Paper published in March 1994, entitled *Paying for our Past*. It considered the regulation of contaminated land in detail, establishing the basic principles of the government's contaminated land policy:

12.7   The Environmental Protection Act 1990: proposals for control under s 143

12.7.1   Paying for our past

- the prevention of a further generation of contaminated land;

- to act on existing contamination where it poses a threat to human health or the environment;

- the remediation of sites to a standard at which they are suitable for their intended use;

- the minimisation of financial and regulatory burdens; and

- to encourage the redevelopment of contaminated sites.

The general tone of *Paying for our Past* seemed to be one of uncertainty, with questions being posed as to how the regulation of contaminated land might be framed. It was intended that these questions should be answered by responses from 'anyone who wishes to let the DOE know their views'.

12.7.2	Framework for contaminated land

The issues raised in the third consultation paper and the responses submitted to the DOE in response to it have recently been addressed in *Framework for Contaminated Land*, the fourth consultation paper issued in November 1994. This most recent offering from the DOE contains firm proposals for the regulation of contaminated land.

The proposed regulation is to come through the Environment Bill which will contain new provisions to extend statutory nuisance law to cover contaminated land and which will be regulated by the local authorities. Registers of the contaminated sites will be compiled, but at a much less comprehensive level than was proposed by s 143, which is now being repealed by the Environment Bill.

Proposals contained in the Environment Bill are based on the established statutory nuisance legislation contained in the Environmental Protection Act 1990. The changes are intended to provide 'greater clarity and certainty' in the application of the law relating to contaminated land. Under these new proposals, the local authorities will be under a duty to inspect their areas from time to time to identify contaminated land, and closed landfill sites. Once these sites are identified, remediation must be considered, which must include an assessment of the state of the land or its impact on water or adjacent sites, and the undertaking of works to remedy the effects of the contamination. The proposals differentiate between contaminated sites, landfill sites and 'special sites'. Local authorities will be empowered to issue remediation notices to secure the assessment and clean-up of contaminated sites (see para 1.11.2).

Despite these proposals, no comprehensive legal basis for the regulation of contaminated land has yet been established. Instead we must look to a variety of provisions drawn from numerous other statutory sources which may be applied to problems of contamination.

The enactment of the EPA was of great importance to the control of environmental pollution and the minimisation of environmental damage, as has been discussed elsewhere in this book. Although there is only one section in the Act relating specifically to contaminated land, there are several other sections which potentially have an impact on its regulation. The relevant sections of the Act are discussed below.

12.8   The Environmental Protection Act 1990: its general application to the control of contaminated land

Part I of the Act contains provisions relating to Integrated Pollution Control. These provisions are of some significance to contaminated land as the application of IPC and local authority Air Pollution Control can contribute to the reduction of contaminated sites. The authorisations issued by HMIP contain references to the effects of the process on the land and also on the implications to the food chain.

12.8.1   Part I of the EPA

Part II of the EPA relates to the waste on land provisions. It is of particular importance with regard to contaminated land. In the UK, closed landfill sites account for approximately 20% of sites which are deemed to be contaminated. The incidents at Loscoe in Derbyshire and at Abbeystead highlight the dangers of escaping methane from landfill sites.

12.8.2   Part II of the EPA

The tightening up of regulation of the waste disposal process can only have a beneficial effect on the reduction of contaminated land, increasing accountability of those involved with waste management. This is particularly true with regard to surrender of Waste Management Licences, which may no longer be surrendered at will. Surrender can only take place when the Waste Regulation Authority is convinced the site is unlikely to cause pollution or harm.

Section 59 gives waste regulation and collection authorities the power to deal with waste that has been fly tipped in their area. The powers conferred on these authorities are to act immediately where it is necessary to prevent pollution of land, water or air, or harm to human health. or where there is no occupier of the land, or where the occupier is innocent in relation to the deposit.

12.8.3   Section 59 EPA

Section 61 of the EPA had the potential to make a significant contribution to a contaminated land policy. Unfortunately,

12.8.4   Section 61 EPA

this provision has not been implemented, and it will be repealed by the Environment Bill when the latter comes into force.

Section 61 would have placed the Waste Regulation Authorities under a duty to inspect closed landfill sites in their area, to determine whether any site is in such a condition that it may cause pollution of the environment or harm to human health because of the concentration and accumulation in, and emission or discharge from, the land of noxious gases or liquids caused by deposits of controlled waste on land. In these circumstances, the WRA would have been empowered to undertake remedial works and recover the expenses from the owner of the land.

Although s 61, on face value, appeared to have the potential to combat problems of contaminated land arising from former waste disposal sites, it was limited, for a number of reasons:

(i) the financial burden on the local authority meant that the necessary funding may not always have been available;

(ii) the provisions only related to registered landfill sites and therefore the effects of illegal dumping were not tackled.

12.8.5   Sections 79–83 EPA

The statutory nuisance provisions of the EPA may offer some form of relief for members of the public who are affected by a contaminated site. Categories of statutory nuisances are laid out in s 79(1).

Those relating to contaminated land are:

(a) any premises in such a state as to be prejudicial to health or a nuisance;

(b) any accumulation which is prejudicial to health or a nuisance.

The key features are 'prejudicial to health' and 'nuisance', which are discussed in detail in Chapter 14.

Local residents can report the nuisance which must then be investigated by the local authority, who must also undertake regular investigations of the area. If a nuisance is found, the local authority is required to serve an abatement notice:

• requiring the abatement of the nuisance or prohibiting or restricting its occurrence or recurrence;

• to require the execution of works and the taking of steps to prevent the nuisance.the nuisance will be served on either:

   • the person responsible;

   • the owner or occupier of the premises.

In the event of non-compliance with this notice, the local authority may carry out the work and recover the expenses from the responsible party. Failure to comply with an abatement notice is a criminal offence punishable by fines of up to £20,000, although there are some limited defences.

Statutory nuisance provisions are particularly important in the field of contaminated land as they can force the clean-up of the site in question at the expense of the owner or the responsible party.

A recent example has shown the importance of the statutory nuisance provisions in relation to contaminated land. Land owned by the Ministry of Defence in Hampshire was found to be seriously contaminated with asbestos and heavy metals, which had arisen following the dumping of industrial and military waste. The 192 dwellings situated on the land had to be evacuated because of the threat to health. The local authority issued an abatement notice under s 80 of the EPA 1990, which prohibited reoccupation of the land until remedial work had been carried out.

Current proposals contained in the Environment Bill for the regulation of contaminated land reflect the importance attached to the statutory nuisance provisions. These are discussed later in the chapter.

Land contamination and water pollution are closely linked because there is potential for the contamination to leach into the water or groundwater, thereby causing pollution which is often very difficult to clean-up. This is particularly the case with groundwater. This link between contaminated land and water pollution was illustrated in the recent case of *Cambridge Water Company v Eastern Counties Leather plc*, which will be discussed below.

12.9   Controls under water legislation

The protection of controlled water courses is an essential function for the NRA, in order that the water quality standards and objectives are met and maintained. The protection of groundwater is also an important consideration for the NRA, particularly in the south-east of England where groundwater is an essential resource.

12.9.1   The role of the National Rivers Authority

The NRA has a proven track record for prosecuting those who cause or knowingly permit controlled water courses to be polluted. In the first two years of the NRA (1989–1991), there were 496 prosecutions in the industrial sector; 404 prosecutions in the agricultural sector; and 54 prosecutions against water companies.

In some of the most notable cases, the NRA secured substantial achievements, large fines were imposed on the polluter, who also had to pay for clean-up and often financed a sweetener. For example in *NRA v Shell UK* (1990), Shell were fined £1,000,000 and paid a massive £1,400,000 in clean-up costs.

12.9.2	Section 161 Water Resources Act

Section 161 of the Water Resources Act 1991 contains provisions to allow the NRA to carry out certain works or operations if it appears likely that any poisonous, noxious or polluting matter or any solid waste is likely to enter controlled water. The costs may then be recovered from the responsible party.

It is probably s 161 which will be of great significance in countering problems of contamination, because of the NRA's strong enforcement record and their willingness to prosecute. The link between land use and water pollution should mean that the NRA will make full use of this provision, particularly where sensitive water quality objectives are threatened.

12.10 Common law remedies

A detailed explanation of the principles and the application of the torts of nuisance, negligence, trespass and the rule in *Rylands v Fletcher* is given in Chapter 4. This section will examine the application of these torts to problems of contaminated land.

12.10.1	The implications of *Cambridge Water Company v Eastern Counties Leather plc*

The *Cambridge Water Company* case is of great significance in the application of the common law to problems of contaminated land. It was first thought that the case should be brought under s 161 of the Water Resources Act 1991. However, the Act was not in force at the time the pollution occurred therefore it could not be used. The full facts of the case are stated in chapter e and are briefly summarised below.

Cambridge Water Company purchased a site in 1975, which included a licence to abstract water, which the water company intended to do. The Cambridge Water Company was unaware that the land was contaminated by spillages of the solvents used by the two defendants at Eastern Counties Leather, which happened prior to 1975. The contaminants rendered the water coming out of the borehole owned by Cambridge Water to be unfit for human consumption under an EC Directive of 1980, which was to be integrated into domestic law by July 1985.

The plaintiffs, Cambridge Water Company, claimed damages from the defendants in nuisance, negligence and under the rule in *Rylands v Fletcher*. The case attracted considerable attention in its passage through the High Court, the Court of Appeal and, finally, the House of Lords, as all those with an interest in historic liability for pollution awaited a conclusive statement of where the liability would lie.

The House of Lords found that Eastern Counties Leather could not be liable for the contamination of the borehole because there was no foreseeability of damage. The Law Lords stated, *inter alia*, that the imposition of liability for historic pollution should be dealt with by Parliament rather than by the common law, in order to promote a greater degree of certainty:

> 'It is more appropriate for strict liability in respect of operations of high risk to be imposed by Parliament, rather than by the courts. If such liability were to be imposed by statute, the relevant activities can be identified and those concerned can know where they stand. Furthermore, statute can, where appropriate, lay down precise criteria establishing the incidents and scope of such liability.'

However in *Framework for Contaminated Land*, it is stated that the House of Lords' decision in *Cambridge Water Company v Eastern Counties Leather plc* provided for a better understanding of the common law in the area of contaminated land, and as such it 'provides a sensible balance between the interests of all potential parties'. Because of the clarification of civil liability for contamination arising from the case, there are no proposed legislative amendments to the common law.

The most likely potential liability for contaminated land is in nuisance. Both public and private nuisance must be considered along with statutory nuisance.

12.10.2   Section 161 Water Resources Act

Private nuisance consists of unlawful interference by a person with another's use or enjoyment of his land. There are a wide variety of 'actions in pollution' cases that may be used in an action relating to contaminated land, although aside from the well-publicised case of *Cambridge Water Company v Eastern Counties Leather plc*, there is little evidence of other cases being used. The limitation associated with the tort of nuisance is that the plaintiff must show that he has some proprietary interest in the land.

Public nuisance is an unlawful act which materially affects the life, health or property, or the reasonable comfort and convenience, of a class of Her Majesty's subjects who are affected by it. It is classed as a crime and prosecutions are brought by the Attorney-General. Any person who suffers damage over and above that suffered by the general public may bring an action for compensation.

| 12.10.3 | Negligence | In order to succeed under the head of negligence, the plaintiff must establish that the defendant owed a duty of care, that this was breached and resulted in foreseeable physical damage. Because of the high standard of care which is associated with hazardous contaminants, it may be possible that negligence might offer more scope than the tort of nuisance; however, this potential is limited by two factors: |

- it is particularly difficult for an action in negligence to succeed because of the essential requirement to establish the duty of care and the subsequent breach of this duty. This will be particularly difficult if the landowner can prove adherence to technical standards, or that he took professional advice; and

- it is necessary for the plaintiff to establish that some physical damage was caused by the breach of the duty of care, as pure economic loss is not sufficient grounds for an action in negligence.

However, the main drawback associated with an action in negligence is with establishing causation and evidence of breach of the duty of care, a problem common to many of the 'environmental' torts.

| 12.10.4 | The rule in *Rylands v Fletcher* | The rule in *Rylands v Fletcher* imposes strict liability if a substance is brought onto the land or if it collects upon the land and then escapes. This is limited by the fact that, where the substance is kept on the land, it must be by a non-natural user, ie that the use has to be special, bringing with it an increased danger to others, not just an ordinary use which offers benefit to the community. An example of the application of this principle came in *Read v Lyons* (1947), in which it was held that a munitions factory in wartime could not amount to a non-natural use of land. |

In the *Cambridge Water Company* case, it was established that foreseeability of damage is a prerequisite for the recovery of damages under the rule in *Rylands v Fletcher*.

| 12.10.5 | Trespass | The application of the common law principle of trespass is rarely used in cases regarding pollution, as the trespass must be intentional or negligent. Trespass is actionable *per se*, therefore there is no need to prove damage. Injunctions are readily available if an action under this head succeeds. |

| **12.11** | **Practical problems posed by contaminated land** | The problems posed by land contamination must also be discussed alongside the legislative framework which controls contaminated land. The legal control of contaminated land – whether it be by statute or by the common law – often dictates |

the action which must be taken at a more practical level, particularly with regard to the purchase of a contaminated site.

The lack of current statutory guidance creates many difficulties for those involved with contaminated land because the legal limits of liability are far from certain. This uncertainty has been exacerbated by the threat of legislation, first under s 143 of the EPA 1990, and currently with the proposals contained in the Environment Bill. Also, the stringent regulatory regime which is in place in the USA, and several EC Member States, is of considerable concern for those who fear that such a framework may inevitably be established in the UK.

Problems associated with contaminated land frequently become apparent only when the land becomes available for redevelopment, usually at the time of purchase, and it is often at this stage that action is taken.

12.11.1 The purchase of contaminated land

The existence of contamination can have very serious implications in the purchase of a site, as it can blight a site, it may preclude the development of the site for certain end-uses, and it may require extensive, costly remediation to be undertaken. If undetected, it could potentially lead to liability under statute and under the common law, as outlined earlier in the chapter.

The appearance of the s 143 registers, which would have assisted prospective purchasers and developers, made the property industry very nervous about the prospect of contamination. They feared that the creation of such registers would lead to widespread blight of contaminated sites, thus damaging the property market, a particularly worrying prospect at a time of recession. It was probably a result of their responses to the government's proposals that the registers of 'land which may be contaminated' were abandoned. The fact that the provisions of s 143 will be repealed provides them with little comfort because of the uncertainty of what form any regulation may take in the future. The uncertainty means that the issue cannot be ignored and any purchase of land must be carried out under the knowledge that the land may be contaminated.

The principle of *caveat emptor* – let the buyer beware – still applies to land transactions, although reform of this principle has been considered by the Conveyancing Standing Committee of the Law Commission in its 1989 Report, *Let the Buyer be Well Informed*. This report examined the possibility of abolishing the doctrine of *caveat emptor*, a move which would

12.11.2 *Caveat emptor*

bring England in line with other European jurisdictions. The proposal of placing a duty on the seller to disclose all material facts about the property was not accepted, on the basis of two major concerns:

- it would probably require the seller to conduct a survey of the land, which would in turn increase conveyancing costs, be time-consuming, and would not necessarily be conclusive in regard to any contamination on the site; and

- extending the seller's duty from actual to constructive knowledge has fundamental weaknesses because of the difficulty in defining what would be material facts from the point of view of both the seller and the buyer.

The Committee also expressed concern at the prospect of a radical alteration of a well-established and well-understood legal principle.

Despite the Committee's recommendation that the principle of *caveat emptor* should be retained, it also took the view that 'there is room for more forthcoming candour on the part of property sellers'. This observation has yet to be backed by the force of law.

The retention of the principle of *caveat emptor*, therefore, places the onus on the buyer to do all he can to ensure that he knows the condition of the land. There are several reasons for ensuring that a full environmental survey of the property is undertaken prior to purchase:

- for the simple reason that the buyer should know what he is getting for the money; he may be able to renegotiate the price, taking account of the presence of any contamination on the site;

- to avoid the imposition of liability, either by statute or under the common law;

- so that any contamination can be accounted for in the plans for the development of land;

- the buyer may be concerned about the environmental threats posed by the land or worried about its effects on human health.

The principle of *caveat emptor* means that there is no obligation on the seller voluntarily to disclose any information about the state of the land. However, if the vendor is asked specific questions then he must answer them honestly. In the case of *Nocton v Ashburton* (1914), the Court of Appeal stated:

'When a purchaser, with a possible view of making an offer for the property, seeks information from the vendor, the vendor, of course, is bound to the best of his ability to supply him with accurate information.'

In addition, the vendor must also be aware of the provisions of the Property Misdescriptions Act 1991, particularly when making statements as to the fitness for purpose of the site and its past uses. Defences available in the Act include due diligence, and that the seller has taken all reasonable steps to ensure that his statement is true.

It is also possible that a seller's statement relating to the quality of the land may amount to a misrepresentation, a statement of fact which has induced the representee to enter into a contract which does not form part of that contract. In *Gordon v Selico* (1986), the deliberate concealment of dry rot was held to be a fraudulent misrepresentation.

The s 143 registers were to have made the conveyancing process for contaminated land considerably easier, as there is provision on the Local Search and Enquiry Form to acknowledge an entry on the public register of 'land which may be contaminated'. Since there are no registers, this provision on the form no longer has to be acknowledged. However, there are other means of determining information about contamination, for example through local planning authority registers, registers kept by the old waste disposal authorities, trade directories and local knowledge. There is a three-stage survey which should be undertaken by the purchaser to assess correctly the state of the land.

12.11.3   Site investigations

The first stage is known as a 'desk study' of the land. This will establish a general picture of current and previous land use. Information for this survey can be drawn from a variety of sources, such as the aforementioned registers and trade directories, newspaper archives which might contain information about any polluting activities on the site, local history society records, aerial photographs and Ordnance Survey maps.

Stage two involves an actual survey of the land and analysis of samples taken, and is usually most effective when following a thorough desk study, because knowledge of the previous activities and their location is essential for understanding the potential for contamination and helps to focus the search. Samples of the land will be taken on a systematic basis using established techniques, and these samples will then be tested to give detailed information as to the extent of the contamination. This is an essential part of the process as it should give an accurate picture of the condition of the site.

Stage three is contingent upon the earlier stages. If contamination is revealed, then some sort of remediation will be required depending upon the end use of the site. Options for the reclamation of a site will obviously depend on such factors as the severity of the contamination and the financial resources available. Options include excavation and disposal of the contamination and encapsulation. Remediation can be very expensive, costing anything from £700,000 to £3,000,000 per hectare.

| 12.11.4 | Table of costs for site investigation and remediation of contaminated land |

It appears to be accepted that the costs of carrying out these three stages can be as follows:

Desk Study	£200–£1,000
Site Investigation	£2,000–£20,000 plus
Treatment	
Removal	£10–£50m^3
Cover	£10–£40m^3
Biotreatment	£40–£50m^3

It should be noted that other methods of remediation are available, such as thermal and chemical treatment of the contamination, although precise costs are unknown.

These costs are mere estimates, although it should be remembered that the nature of the contamination will have a great impact on the costs of remediation. Indeed it is not unknown for costs to amount to £3,000,000 per hectare.

| 12.11.5 | Contractual terms |

Parties to the purchase of land may also account for problems and costs associated with contamination within the contract for the sale of the land. This is common practice in the USA and is becoming increasingly common in the UK and other EU Member States. The success of the proposed terms will obviously depend on the bargaining strength of the parties involved.

Although the costs involved in a survey of the site, as detailed above, may seem very high, it is prudent that the remediation costs are known at an early stage in order that negotiations can take place with regard to the purchase of the land rather than bearing the costs of clean-up liability at a later date. Property transactions in the USA and in Europe often include warranties and indemnities in respect of contamination, often included at the insistence of the buyer or the lessee, although as yet this is a little known practice in the UK. It is possible for a contract to be made conditional upon satisfactory site investigations or remediation completed by the seller before the sale. The buyer may seek a reduction in the sale price to cover the costs of remediation.

Of course, parties to the sale of contaminated land also have the option to withdraw completely due to the risky nature of the sale. However, this should be done when it is evident that the contamination problem is very large and very serious. In the main, contamination can be dealt with by environmental engineers, although, as already illustrated, this can be a very costly process. The drafting of the contract will obviously depend upon the enquiries carried out during the purchase of the land, and will rely upon the expertise of several professions, including solicitors, probably an environmental consultant and possibly an environmental engineer.

12.12 The financial implications of contaminated land

12.12.1 Financial responsibility for contaminated land

The clean-up of a contaminated site is a very costly operation, even in its most simple form. Because of the expense involved, and the emphasis on the reuse of 'brownfield' sites, financial backing for the redevelopment of such sites must be available. It is not always possible in these cases to ensure that the 'polluter pays' principle applies, where the original polluter can be identified. It is often the case that the site will be 'orphaned', with no party claiming responsibility. It would be unrealistic to expect a developer to pay for the land and for the costly clean-up, which may mean that the redevelopment of the site is not economically viable. This proposition would be contrary to the current governmental policy on contaminated land and urban renewal, and to the wishes of the property industry.

This view is echoed in *Framework for Contaminated Land*, in which it is stated that, where possible, costs should follow responsibility, in other words that the 'polluter pays' principle should apply. However, it is recognised that this is particularly difficult when dealing with historical pollution, although there is no intention to impose financial burdens, which it is feared would 'discourage enterprise' – enterprise which, in turn, contributes to the redevelopment of contaminated land.

12.12.2 Banks and lending institutions

Banks and other lending institutions are becoming increasingly aware of the problems posed by land contamination, largely because of the precedents set in the USA where, at both federal and state level, there are very stringent environmental laws in place. The most well-known regulation is under the US Comprehensive Environmental Response and Compensation Liability Act 1980, which imposes a strict duty on a wide range of parties and also established a 'superfund', drawn from taxes on polluting industries, which should be used to clean-up land.

Unfortunately, about 80% of this money is used in administration and legal costs. Judicial interpretation of the 'superfund' legislation has produced some worrying results for the lending institutions, notably the *US v Fleet Factors* case which imposed financial liability for clean-up on a lending institution which had no influence on the day-to-day running of the operation causing the contamination.

The discovery that land is contaminated may have a big influence on the lender's security for several reasons:

- the land can become worthless because it is unusable without remediation and the remediation may be more costly than the value of the land;

- financial liabilities for clean-up as imposed by a pollution control agency may render the owner unable to meet repayments. Liability is most likely to fall on a lender when the land is repossessed and the lending institution assumes ownership status and then becomes liable for clean-up costs themselves.

For these reasons, many financial institutions are now requiring that environmental audits are undertaken before any major loans are agreed.

The concept of environmental due diligence, already of great importance in the US and many Member States of the EU, is being increasingly recognised in the UK. It forms an essential part of a comprehensive environmental management regime and requires that a full environmental survey is carried out, prior to the purchase of a site, and that any processes carried out meet established environmental standards. It really means that care is taken throughout the whole operation to ensure that little or no environmental damage is caused and that no liability can be attributed to that operator.

12.12.3   Grant aid

In the absence of any statutory financial liability being imposed on either a responsible party, a developer or a local authority, it is maintained that bodies such as English Partnerships (the name of the Urban Regeneration Agency for England) and the Welsh Development Agency will tackle dereliction and contamination, in their functions established by the Leasehold Reform, Housing and Urban Development Act 1993.

It is also possible to seek grant aid from central government for the remediation of contamination. The main grants available at present are the Derelict Land Grant and the City Grant. However, the grants system is currently under review and the functions of the Urban Regeneration Agency are yet to be established in relation to contaminated land.

Derelict Land Grant is one of the major sources of finance available to encourage the return of derelict sites to beneficial use. Resources available for 1991/1992 amounted to £88,000,000.

12.12.4   Derelict land grant

Under s 3 of the Derelict Land Act 1982, power is conferred on local authorities to carry out works to bring into use, reclaim or improve any derelict, neglected or unsightly land. Provision is also made for other public bodies, voluntary organisations, private firms and individuals to receive grant aid under this scheme.

In order to be eligible for a DLG, it is not enough for the land to be merely derelict. Priority is given to hard end use development, and forecasts of the intended use of the sites would have to show that, after reclamation, the site would attract development which would provide employment, investment or housing. If a grant were permitted, the rate at which it would be provided would vary according to location because of the regional distribution of the grant.

A fundamental flaw in the use of derelict land grant for the redevelopment of contaminated land is that not all contaminated land is derelict, nor is all derelict land contaminated. However, a high proportion of derelict land is thought to be contaminated, and most of this fits the category of 'orphaned sites'.

The DLG scheme is currently being revised by English Partnerships with a view to creating a more systematic approach.

City Grant has been available since May 1988, its purpose being to provide support for private sector redevelopment. In 1991/1992 approximately £96,700,000 was available under the City Grant scheme.

12.12.5   City grant

City Grant is available for capital projects which benefit urban sites, by bringing derelict land and buildings back into use, that could not be undertaken without grant-aid. In order to be eligible for City Grant aid, a project must demonstrate that:

• it has a completed capital value in excess of £500,000;

• it will provide new jobs or housing;

• it will provide significant environmental improvements;

• it will generate further development in the area.

Priorities for the allocation of City Grant are to City Challenge areas and the 57 other assisted areas, with applications outside these areas rarely successful.

Of the two major forms of grant-aid available, City Grant appears to be the most popular because it can allow for some profit margin in the redevelopment, thereby stimulating the property industry. Derelict Land Grant cannot provide for any profit margin because it is calculated on the basis of the net losses incurred by the project.

12.12.6	Urban renewal programmes

There are a variety of other urban renewal projects which can provide some financial assistance in the remediation of contaminated land, although that is not their exclusive purpose. These include the Urban Programme, which is intended to deal with a range of inter-related economic, environmental, social and housing problems resulting from long-term changes in the local economies of special areas. The Urban Development Corporations have as their objective the regeneration of around 15,800 hectares of run-down inner-city areas, they can reclaim sites and offer financial assistance to private sector development.

12.12.7	Insurance

In certain situations, it may be possible to make an insurance claim which may assist with the redevelopment of a contaminated site. The ability to claim insurance is, however, limited as the attitude of the insurance industry is changing with regard to environmental issues, largely because it is becoming aware of the large claims being made on insurance in the USA and in Europe. The availability of insurance is an important issue for would-be owners of contaminated land to consider, as it may contribute towards clean-up or meeting claims for damages.

The two types of policies covering the environment are public liability policies and environmental impairment liability policies.

12.12.8	Public liability policies

Public liability policies are the more traditional type of policy and it is important to note that they were not specifically drafted with environmental problems in mind. Most manufacturing industries will have these in place to cover their potential liabilities to third parties. These policies can only be used for sudden and accidental events; cover for the clean-up of a neighbour's site contaminated by gradual migration would not be available therefore. There would be no cover for contamination of the owner's site because cover can only be third party.

Environmental impairment liability policies were first introduced in the 1970s. EIL policies cover gradual pollution, as well as sudden and accidental events. These policies are generally very expensive and are generally restrictive in terms of the scope of the cover offered.

Once the insurance industry became aware of the extent of the financial liability associated with incidents of environmental pollution, they began to limit the application of insurance policies. As a consequence of this, environmental insurance is not always offered and, if it is, it will depend on such factors as the probability of the incident and the extent of the losses from such an incident. If insurance cover is granted, it is very likely that the policy will contain some or all of the following exclusions:

- the event must be accidental, not deliberate;
- cover is third party only;
- there is no cover for criminal penalties.

The future availability of environmental insurance is in doubt, particularly in respect of pollution that has yet to occur, and this is an issue which is under considerable discussion.

Alternative solutions may be necessary in order to provide cover for operations affecting the environment, particularly as the government seems to be stressing a system of voluntary responsibility for contamination. The future may lie with a scheme involving members of industry banding together to provide their own insurance cover, in the absence of any commercially available policy. The EC is also becoming involved with this type of cover in attempting to institute an insurance pool, available across the European Union.

There can be no doubt that more stringent regulation of contaminated land will be enacted in the future, as it is an area of growing concern. With over 50% of new residential development being on 'brownfield' sites, there has to be a comprehensive regulatory framework to prevent a disaster on the scale of that at the Love Canal in the USA. Such a framework would have to provide for the identification of contaminated land, and more comprehensive guide-lines as to the applicable clean-up standards, both of which are lacking in the existing system of control.

The overwhelming view from all those involved with contaminated land is that regulation of some form will be implemented at some time in the near future. The proposals contained in the Environment Bill have considerably

12.12.9 Environmental impairment liability policies

12.12.10 Limitations

12.12.11 The development of insurance

12.13 The future development of contaminated land regulation

strengthened this view. However, it is of some concern that the proposals contained in the Environment Bill are not as stringent as they might be, particularly in comparison with the American experience of superfund. Many parties involved with contaminated land will still feel that there may be much tougher legislation to come, which will create more onerous liability, and are wary of the future regulatory framework for contaminated land.

A further issue which requires clarification is that of liability for historic pollution, in order to determine who should pay for the remediation of the contamination. This may be clarified by the introduction of the ECs Directive on Civil Liability for Damage Caused by Waste, which is currently in draft form (see Chapter 11).

Summary of Chapter 12

Contaminated Land

There is no universally accepted definition of contaminated land although it is generally taken to mean land which contains potentially hazardous substances which do not naturally exist in the land. Hazards are presented to man and the environment generally.

It is proposed that a definition of contaminated land should be contained in the Environment Bill. It is also estimated that there are between 50,000–100,000 contaminated sites in the UK.

There is currently no specific legislative control of contaminated land, although it was proposed that, under s 143 of the EPA 1990, there should be public registers of land which may be contaminated. This section is to be repealed under the Environment Bill. Indirect control of contaminated land is, however, exerted through various statutes:

- Town and Country Planning Act 1990;
- Water Resources Act 1991;
- Environmental Protection Act 1990:
- Part I – Integrated Pollution Control;
- Part II – Waste on Land;
- Sections 79–83 – Statutory Nuisance Provisions.

The common law torts of nuisance, negligence, trespass and the rule in *Rylands v Fletcher* can also be used to provide redress for damage caused by contaminated land, as was illustrated in *Cambridge Water Company v Eastern Counties Leather plc*.

Contaminated land poses many practical problems. The absence of legislative guidance and control creates particular difficulties, particularly in the purchase of a contaminated site. This is recognised by banks and financial institutions who are aware of the potential liability of a contaminated site. It is recommended that the following steps be taken by a purchaser:

Definition

Legislative control

Common law actions

Practical problems

- desk study;

- site investigation;

- remediation.

Grant aid

Grant aid may be available in limited situations. Insurance cover for contaminated land, as with other environmental problems, is limited.

Environmental Bill and the Environment Agency

It should be noted that the Environmental Bill will make considerable changes to the regulation of contaminated land, bringing it within the control of local authorities and the newly created Environment Agency. The proposed regulatory regime is to be based on the existing statutory nuisance provisions contained in the EPA 1990.

Chapter 13

Planning and Pollution Control

Although environmental law has evolved to the extent that it is a new branch of law in its own right, it is nevertheless closely inter-related with other areas of law, particularly planning law. Environmental law, by its very nature should not be seen as a 'specialist' subject in isolation. The environmental lawyer needs to be aware of other areas of law that operate alongside the main environmental controls discussed in this book. For instance, many environmental problems affect land and property interests, notably contaminated land, which in turn has a real effect on the acquisition of land, the conveyancing procedure and the availability or otherwise of insurance against potential liabilities arising from the contaminated land. However, it is the area of planning law with which environmental law coincides to the greatest extent. This is reflected in the fact that the two 'disciplines' are now often taught together as 'planning and environmental law' courses.

This close relationship manifests itself in a number of ways. On the one hand, planning authorities can take environmental considerations into account when drawing up development plans and granting planning permissions, and the question is really to what extent they can do this bearing in mind that there are specific regulatory authorities exercising statutory pollution prevention controls. This is particularly apt when the planning authority is being asked to grant planning permission for industrial processes which are clearly going to pollute the environment. Bearing in mind that industrial processes will require both planning permission and authorisation from either HMIP, the NRA, the Waste Regulatory Authority or, indeed, the local authority itself exercising its pollution control powers, where do the boundaries lie between such controls? An associated issue arises once planning permission has been granted. Does the grant of planning permission provide a defence in nuisance claims?

In addition there are specific pieces of legislation which are aimed at protecting the environment but which are implemented and enforced through the planning and development control system. The Environmental Assessment Directive is the main legislation which falls into this category. It is clearly an 'environmental' control mechanism aimed at

13.1 Environmental law and planning law

preventing environmental harm; however, it finds its place within the framework of the town and country planning law and the development control system. Equally, the more recent Habitats Directives, which is an EC environmental protection measure, impacts once again upon the town and country planning regime.

13.1.1 The nature of the problem	The whole relationship, therefore, between planning and environmental law is particularly topical and one which warrants detailed consideration. As local planning authorities have become increasingly aware of environmental issues they have sought to control potentially polluting developments through the planning control system. The issue of how far they can go in taking environmental considerations into account when determining planning applications has recently been considered by the Court of Appeal in *Gateshead Metropolitan Borough Council v Secretary of State for the Environment* (1993), and has also been addressed specifically by the Department of the Environment in two recent Planning Policy Guidance Notes on *Planning and Pollution Control* and *Planning and Noise*.
13.1.2 Overview of the chapter	This chapter is not intended to provide a detailed coverage of the planning regime that exists in the UK. However, it is worth considering in brief how the planning system works. Following this brief section, the chapter will concentrate on the following issues:

- the way in which local planning authorities can take environmental considerations into account when preparing development plans;

- the ruling in *Gateshead Metropolitan Borough Council v Secretary of State for the Environment*;

- the guidance given in the Planning Policy Guidance Note on *Planning and Pollution Control* (PPG 23);

- the effect of planning permission on subsequent nuisance claims;

- environmental assessments;

- the impact of the EC Habitats Directive on planning.

13.2 Overview of planning law in the UK	The planning system in this country provides the principal means for controlling development in bothurban and rural areas. Planning authorities are responsible for determining whether development can take place, and where it can take place, and in this way they have exercised significant control over both the landscape and the general environment.

Planning authorities are required to take into account various considerations when reaching planning decision. Their sole concern is not the environment, although it is a material consideration which they may take into account. Inevitably, other considerations come to the fore – such as the need to have sufficient housing and economic development. However, it is clear that wherever development is allowed – for example, out-of-town shopping centres and major road schemes – there will be environmental consequences. Out-of-town shopping centres are particularly notable: by their very nature, they tend to be located away from residential areas and people must use cars or public transport to reach them. As a consequence, there are more vehicle emissions than there would be if people were 'just nipping to the local store' and the demand for new roads increases. In addition, it is often the case that smaller local shops find it difficult to compete with the new breed of superstores and shopping malls and often eventually close down, once again forcing shoppers to travel further to shops and also resulting in the decline of town and city centres. This is just one of many examples of how planning decisions affect the environment.

The government's planning policy is largely set out in Planning Policy Guidance Notes (PPGs) which are issued by the Department of the Environment. These notes are supplemented by Circulars produced by the DOE and, for Wales, the Welsh Office. The aim of the PPGs is to provide a policy framework against which local planning authorities can exercise their powers under the town and country planning legislation. A number of PPGs define the government's policy in relation to the environment and provide specific advice on how planning decisions should be taken in relation to various factors. The following list is not exhaustive but indicative:

13.2.1   National planning policy in relation to the environment

- PPG7 – *The Countryside and the Rural Economy*. This states that the guiding principle in the countryside is that development should benefit the rural economy and 'maintain and enhance the environment';

- PPG21 – *Tourism*. This recognises the positive benefits that tourism developments can have in terms of the environment, because tourism often depends upon a high quality environment;

- PPG12 – *Transport*;

- PPG24 – *Planning and Noise*. This is considered more fully in Chapter 15;

- PPG23 – *Planning and Pollution Control*. This PPG was introduced to clarify some of the problems relating to the overlap of functions between planning authorities and pollution control authorities and is considered more fully below.

13.2.2   Planning permissions

Most proposed developments are required to obtain planning permission before the development can go ahead and the developer must seek such permission, therefore, from the appropriate planning authority. In England, this is usually the district council, London Borough Council, Metropolitan District Council or the county council. The applicant has to supply the local planning authority with the necessary information in order for the authority to take a decision as to whether permission should be granted or not, and the conditions, if any, that should be attached to such permission. The local planning authority can refuse to make a decision on the application until the applicant has supplied sufficient information.

There is a presumption in favour of development and, in fact, the applicant does not have to demonstrate the need for the development but the planning authority has to provide reasons why an application should be refused. Planning Policy Guidance Note 1 (1988) on *General Policy and Principles* states clearly that there is a presumption in favour of development. The presumption in favour of development was general unless the proposed development would cause harm to 'interests of acknowledged importance'.

The situation has altered, however, with the introduction in 1991 of s 54A of the Planning and Compensation Act 1991. This required 'greater consideration to be given to the role of development plans in determining planning applications'.

In dealing with applications for planning permission 'regard is to be had to the development plan' and 'the determination shall be made in accordance with the plan unless material considerations indicate otherwise'.

On a final note it is interesting to note that, when the Planning and Compensation Act 1991 was going before Parliament, it contained a provision that would have placed a duty on both the Secretary of State and local planning authorities to have regard to the desirability of securing sustainable development when discharging any of the planning functions. Unfortunately, the provision was defeated.

This Common Inheritance envisaged a major role for planning authorities in ensuring that development plans are drawn up so as to take environmental considerations comprehensively and consistently into account. Development plans provide the main framework against which applications for planning permission are determined. The *raison d'être* behind development plans is that they provide a rational and consistent basis for making planning decisions. The development plan therefore acts as a guide but it is not prescriptive. The development plan is not a single document but comprises a number of plans. In the county council areas it consists of the structure plan, the local plan, the minerals local plan and the waste local plan. In metropolitan areas the development plan is called the Unitary Development Plan (UDP). In PPG23 it is stated that 'development plans are an important vehicle for promoting environmental protection through integrated land-use planning policies'.

In drawing up development plans, planning authorities are required to have regard to national and regional planning policy and they are legally required to include policies in respect of the improvement of the physical environment. Planning authorities must have regard to the environmental policies as stated in the Planning Policy Guidance Notes. For example, PPG12 states that the planning system, and the preparation of development plans in particular, can contribute to the objectives of ensuring that development and growth are sustainable. As a result of PPG12, some planning authorities have begun to think about strategic Environmental Assessment in developing their planning policies. Some particular authorities have led the way in this field; however, in general, the majority of authorities have shown little evidence of this strategic thinking. In November 1993, the government provided further guidance to authorities in *Environmental Appraisal of Development Plans: A Good Practice Guide*.

Development plans must also comply with any EC requirements. This includes, notably, the Waste Framework Directive; therefore, for example, development plans must take account of government guidance on waste disposal policy. In this way, development plans are necessarily required to take on board environmental considerations.

As yet, however, there is no legal requirement to carry out any kind of strategic environmental assessment in relation to the development planning process. Although environmental assessments are required in relation to specific project types (see below), there is no similar procedure in relation to the strategic planning stage.

13.3 Environmental appraisal and development plans

13.4   *Gateshead Metropolitan Borough Council v The Secretary of State for the Environment*

The relationship between planning and environmental controls is one that has received considerable recent attention. The case law on how far planning authorities could concern themselves with environmental matters has resulted in uncertainty and confusion (see *Stringer v Minister for Housing and Local Government* (1971)). The case of *Gateshead Metropolitan Borough Council v The Secretary of State for the Environment and Northumbrian Water Group plc* (1993), in particular, highlighted the uncertainties in this area.

Gateshead Metropolitan Borough Council, the local planning authority, refused outline planning permission for a clinical waste incinerator to be built in Gateshead. The refusal was based on the grounds that the applicant, Northumbrian Water Group plc, had failed to supply sufficient information to demonstrate that the plant would operate without causing a nuisance to the surrounding locality, including the possible release of noxious substances. The developers appealed against the authority's decision and a public local inquiry was held. In his report to the Secretary of State, the inspector recommended that the Secretary of State dismiss the appeal on the grounds that 'the impact on air quality and agriculture in this semi-rural location is insufficiently defined' and that 'public disquiet regarding fears as to environmental pollution and, in particular, dioxin emissions cannot be sufficiently allayed to make the proposed development of a clinical waste incinerator on this site acceptable'.

However, the Secretary of State chose to act against the inspector's recommendation and granted planning permission. The Secretary of State accepted that the pollution arising from the incinerator and its impact on neighbouring land uses could constitute a material consideration. However, he also stated that:

> 'While the planning system must determine the location of facilities of this kind, taking account of the provisions of the development plan and other material considerations, the Secretary of State considers that it is not the role of the planning system to duplicate controls under the Environmental Protection Act 1990.'

He went on to assert that the controls under the EPA were adequate, but recognised that it is necessary to take account of the impact of potential emissions on neighbouring land uses when considering whether or not to grant planning permissions; control of these emissions, however, should be regulated by Her Majesty's Inspectorate of Pollution.

Gateshead Council appealed against the Secretary of State's decision, but their appeal was rejected by both the

High Court and the Court of Appeal. The High Court held that the existence of a stringent pollution control regime under the Environmental Protection Act 1990 was a material consideration in a planning decision. Lord Justice Glidewell, in the Court of Appeal, accepted that the two systems of control overlapped. However, the Court of Appeal upheld the decision of the High Court and stated that the potential for environmental pollution would be a material consideration when determining planning applications but so would the existence of a system of environmental control administered by pollution control authorities.

Following the Court of Appeal's judgment in this case, the Department of the Environment issued specific guidance to the local authorities exercising planning and pollution control functions, on the nature of the relationship between the two. Unfortunately, the guidance still leaves room for some doubt, and it is suggested that this is one issue which will continue to receive attention in the future.

In July 1994 (two years after it was issued in draft), the government issued the long-awaited Planning Policy Guidance Note (PPG) 23 on the relationship between planning and pollution control. The guidance was particularly welcome in view of the conflicting case law and was intended to provide comprehensive guidance on the relevance of pollution to the exercise of planning functions. In fact, the DOE had circulated a consultation draft but the final draft was delayed until the outcome of the *Gateshead* case. The guidance given in the final version largely reflects the decision of the Court of Appeal in that case.

13.5 The government's response: Planning Policy Guidance Note 23

The aim of the Guidance Note was to clarify the relationship between the functions of local planning authorities and the various but separate statutory responsibilities exercised by both local authorities and other pollution control authorities principally under the Environmental Protection Act 1990 and the Water Resources Act 1991.

The main theme in the PPG is that the planning system should not seek to duplicate controls which are the statutory responsibility of other bodies. In other words planning authorities should not seek to duplicate the controls exercised by HMIP, the NRA or the WRA or local authorities exercising their pollution control functions. They should, however, ensure that there is close co-ordination among those involved in regulating a particular plant or process. Both the planning and pollution control systems are designed to protect the environment from potential harm but 'with different objectives'.

The PPG makes the following specific comments:

- The planning system should not be operated so as to duplicate controls which are the statutory responsibility of other bodies (including local authorities in their non-planning functions);

- Planning controls and pollution controls are separate but complementary;

- Decisions on planning applications for developments which may give rise to pollution must be made in accordance with the development plan, unless material considerations indicate otherwise, and they must also be made in accordance with relevant EC Directives;

- Planning authorities need to consult the relevant pollution control authorities in order that they can take account of the scope of the requirements of the relevant pollution controls. However, it is clearly stated that planning authorities should work on the assumption that the pollution control regimes will be properly applied and enforced. Lack of confidence in the effectiveness of controls imposed under pollution control legislation is not a legitimate ground for the refusal of planning permission;

- The planning system focuses on whether the development itself is an acceptable use of the land rather than the control of the processes or substances themselves.

13.5.1   What matters will be material considerations where the development may have adverse environmental impact

The guidance does go on to reassert that planning decisions must still be decided by reference to the development plan unless material considerations indicate otherwise. It identifies the matters which will be material considerations where there is a planning application for a development which may have an adverse environmental impact. These include:

- the availability of land for a potentially polluting development, taking into account its proximity to other development or land use which may be affected;

- the sensitivity of the area;

- the impact on amenity;

- any particular environmental benefits accruing from the project;

- the state of the site, whether it is contaminated or not;

- the proposed after-use of the site and feasibility of achieving restoration;

- prevention of nuisance from smoke, fumes, gas, smell or noise, vermin, birds or overblown litter;

- impact on road and other transport networks;

- feasibility of restoring land to standards sufficient for appropriate after-use.

Whilst the PPG does settle some issues, there are still some areas that remain less clear. This is reflected in the PPG itself, which recognises that in some areas there will still be an overlap.

13.5.2   Problems with the PPG

In particular, it states that there may be other (material) considerations which a planning authority may take into account to the extent that they have land use implications. It goes on to say, however, that these are likely to be the responsibility of the relevant pollution authority who will be able to advise on the extent to which they will be able to address those considerations through the pollution control mechanisms. Consequently, the weight to which the planning authority can attach to such considerations will be reduced to 'the extent that they are able to be addressed by the pollution control authority in carrying out its statutory responsibilities'. These 'other' considerations which are subject to this rather blurred line of responsibility are those areas which cause most environmental concern, namely:

- the possibility of land contamination arising from the proposed development, and protection and remediation measures as appropriate;

- the impact of any discharge of effluent or leachates, which may pose a threat to current and future surface or underground water resources or adjacent areas;

- the risk of toxic releases, whether on site or on access roads;

- the waste generated by the development, including that arising from the preparation and construction phases, and proposed arrangements for storage, treatment and disposal.

It should be remembered that these considerations can only be taken into account to the extent that they have land use implications.

There is also still concern about the nature of the relationship as defined in the PPG. A number of planning authorities will still be concerned about leaving the matters specified to the pollution control authorities. Once planning permission has been granted for a project by the planning authority, it is unlikely that HMIP will in practice refuse to authorise the project and will rely instead on ensuring that emissions and discharges are controlled by the developer using the best available techniques not entailing excessive cost, even though these emissions/discharges could still result in damage. This argument was put forward by Gateshead Council, but was not accepted by the Court of Appeal. Glidewell J asserted that HMIP should not consider that the grant of planning permission inhibits them from refusing to authorise a process if they (HMIP) decide that a refusal is necessary. Although this may theoretically be the case, it is not borne out by statistics, which suggest that HMIP are unlikely to refuse to grant authorisation for a process that has planning permission.

The PPG states that planning authorities must be confident that the pollution control authorities are performing their functions, and it is also the case that, having once granted planning permission, the authority cannot then refuse it if it is not satisfied with the pollution controls exercised by the other statutory bodies. The problem, however, remains that there is no requirement that a developer submits his IPC application before or simultaneously with the planning applications. Planning authorities are therefore required to take planning decisions in the absence of conclusive evidence that the emissions would be unacceptable. Planning authorities can ask HMIP whether a process is likely to be authorised and HMIP are required to help.

13.6   Planning permission and nuisance

The issue of the relationship between planning and environmental law has also raised its head in the context of claims for nuisance. Once planning permission is granted for a development, there is inevitably some change in the character of an area. The Court of Appeal in the case of *Gillingham Council v Medway Dock Co* (1993) had to consider whether the grant of planning permission could effect a change in the character of a neighbourhood and thus prevent a claim in nuisance.

It is a well-established principle in the law of nuisance that the locality in which the nuisance is alleged will have a bearing on whether a nuisance action will succeed. The question then is: to what extent will the grant of planning permission alter the characteristics of a neighbourhood and provide a defence against a nuisance action? In the *Gillingham*

Council case, planning permission had been granted to the Medway Port Authority for the construction of a port on the site of the former Chatham Royal Navy Dockyard. The Royal Navy Dockyard, when it was operational, had not generated much traffic, unlike the new port facility. Local residents complained to the local authority about the noise and other pollution from the 'round the clock' heavy goods vehicle traffic to and from the port. In proceedings against the Port Authority, the Council sought to restrain the passage of the heavy goods vehicles through the neighbourhood at night because it constituted a public nuisance. (For a discussion of nuisance see Chapter 4). The court held that the grant of planning permission could alter the character of the area and may have the effect of rendering 'innocent activities which prior to the change would have been an actionable nuisance'. It was held accordingly that the noise from the traffic was not an actionable nuisance.

However, this ruling has since been considered by the Court of Appeal in *Wheeler v JJ Saunders Ltd* (1995). Planning permission was granted for two pig-weaning houses. An action in private nuisance was brought because of the smells generated by the pigs. The defendants in the action sought to rely on the *Gillingham* case by arguing that the grant of planning permission for the pig houses meant there could not be an actionable nuisance. This argument was rejected by the Court of Appeal which held effectively that the grant of planning permission was no defence in nuisance. Staughton LJ was clear that:

> 'the court should be slow to acquiesce in the extinction of private rights without compensation as a result of administrative decisions which could not be appealed and were difficult to challenge.'

At the beginning of this chapter it was stated that the relationship between planning and environmental law is also evidenced by the fact that there is legislation which is aimed at protecting the environment but which is part of the town and country planning system. The remaining sections of this chapter deal with these instances. The most important legislation to be considered is in relation to environmental assessment.

The subject of environmental assessments is one which has generated considerable academic and legal attention. It has also been subject to a considerable degree of controversy and almost resulted in a legal action by the European Commission against the United Kingdom for failure to comply with its

13.7   Environmental assessment and planning

Community law obligations. One of the problems with environmental assessments is the jargon used. Sometimes they are referred to as Environmental Impact Assessments (EIAs), which is the American term or, alternatively, Environmental Assessments (EAs). The latter description will be used in this chapter although the meanings of the two are the same.

Environmental impact assessments were first introduced in the United States of America by the National Environmental Policy Act 1970. The experience of environmental assessments in the United States resulted in over 200 voluntary environmental assessments being carried out in the UK prior to 1988. However, there was no legal requirement to conduct an environmental assessment in this country until 1988 when the UK implemented the EC Directive on the Assessment of the Effects of Certain Private and Public Projects on the Environment.

13.7.1	Council Directive 85/337

Council Directive 85/337 was adopted by the EC Council in July 1985 and was required to be implemented into the domestic legal systems of the Member States by 3 July 1988. The Directive required all Member States to adopt all measures necessary to ensure that, before consent is given, projects likely to have significant effects on the environment by virtue, *inter alia*, of their nature, size or location are made subject to an assessment with regard to their effects. In other words, it made it a requirement that, for certain types of project, there must be an assessment of the effects of that project on the environment before planning permission is granted.

13.7.2	Background to the Directive

The Directive is arguably one of the most significant (and possibly controversial) pieces of EC legislation to be enacted. Despite its brevity, it took almost 16 years to be agreed. The difficulties in getting the agreement of the Member States to the Directive were largely because it was the first piece of EC legislation to be concerned with broad-based land issues and because it went to the very heart of the decision-making processes in the Member States. Both the UK and Denmark, in particular, were strong objectors to various parts of the Directive and, in fact, the UK had voted against agreement until it secured various amendments to the proposal. The UK government held the view that the system of development control existing under the town and country planning legislation provided a more effective method of assessing the environmental impacts of proposed projects.

As stated in the introduction, the implementation and application of the Environmental Assessment Directive has not been entirely straightforward. The Directive itself has been likened to a Framework Directive, laying down basic principles and procedural requirements. The Member States have then had considerable discretion in terms of the detailed implementation. It is in the implementation of the Directive that most problems have arisen.

13.7.3 Implementation in the United Kingdom

The Directive itself only runs to 14 Articles and three Annexes and yet it has given rise to a remarkable quantity of secondary legislation in the UK involving 19 Statutory Instruments. The principal means of implementation has been through the land use planning system by virtue of the Town and Country Planning (Assessment of Environmental Effects) Regulations 1988. These regulations came into effect on 15 July 1988 (some 12 days later than the date for compliance). The regulations were accompanied by an explanatory Department of the Environment Circular. The purpose of the Circular was to give guidance on the new procedures. The 1988 Regulations have since been amended by the Town and Country Planning (Assessment of Environmental Effects) (Amendment) 1994 which made a number of modifications to the categories of projects which may come up for assessment. These also are accompanied by a Circular issued by the Department of the Environment. Since most environmental assessments are made under the town and country planning system rather than the other specific regulations, this chapter will refer only to those procedures.

The UK government initially took the decision to implement the Directive by means of Statutory Instrument, using powers under s 2 of the European Communities Act 1972, rather than by primary legislation. However, since 1988, the Planning and Compensation Act 1991 (s 15) has provided the Secretary of State with the power to make regulations extending the categories of projects which are to be the subject of environmental assessment beyond those listed in the Directive. This power was exercised when the Secretary of State introduced the amending regulations mentioned above. As a consequence, privately financed toll roads were added into Sched 1 and the following into Sched 2:

- wind generators;

- motorway service areas;

- coast protection works.

Although the government had promised to add further categories of projects, namely: water treatment plants; golf courses; and trout farms, these were not included in the 1994 Regulations.

13.7.4   The aims

The Directive was based on a belief that, by improving the procedure by which planning decisions are taken, the quality of the subsequent decisions will improve from an environmental perspective. In other words, the Directive focuses on procedural rather than substantive obligations. It does not ensure or require that Member States refuse planning permission for projects that are damaging to the environment, only that they are informed of the environmental consequences before a decision is taken. The final decision on whether a project goes ahead or not, in the light of the environmental assessment, rests with the competent national authority. Thus the principle of subsidiarity is preserved.

The aim of an environmental assessment is to improve the planning process so that the effects on the environment are taken at the earliest possible stage in all the technical planning and decision-making processes. In short, EAs fulfil the policy that preventive action should be taken, that it is better to prevent the creation of pollution or nuisances at source rather than subsequently trying to counteract their effects.

A more specific statement about the aims of environmental assessments is provided in the DOE Circular which explains the main aims as follows:

'Formal environmental assessment is essentially a technique for drawing together, in a systematic way, expert qualitative assessment of a project's environmental effects, and presenting the results in a way which enables the importance of the predicted effects, and the scope for modifying or mitigating them, to be properly evaluated by the relevant decision-making body before a decision is given. Environmental assessment techniques can help both developers and public authorities with environmental responsibilities to identify likely effects at an early stage, and thus to improve the quality of both project planning and decision-making.'

**13.7.5   What is an
environmental
assessment?**

'Environmental assessment' refers to the process of deciding whether or not a project should get permission or approval. It involves the collection and assessment of information on the environmental effects of a project and the presentation and consideration of that information in the decision-making process. An integral part of the environmental assessment process is the submission of an environmental statement:

- Environmental statement – this refers to the information that is submitted by the applicant alongside his application for planning permission. The details of what should be included in the environmental statement are covered below. It should be noted that the phrase 'environmental statement' is not used in the Directive but is used in the implementing regulations;

- Environmental information – this is broader than the information supplied in the environmental statement. It encompasses any representations made by the statutory consultees and public following consultation and publicity.

It is the responsibility of the person seeking the planning permission for a project or development to carry out the assessment and prepare the statement. He must therefore seek advice at an early stage as to whether or not an impact assessment is required. Equally, the developer must bear the cost of preparing the statement which, if consultants are employed, can amount to a considerable amount of money – some consultants charge between £20,000 and £50,000 for carrying out the assessment and preparing the statement.

The Directive makes a distinction between two categories of projects listed in Annex 1 and Annex 2. Those projects listed in Annex 1 will always be subject to an environmental assessment (other than in certain individually determined and exceptional cases), whereas for those falling in Annex 2 the requirement is discretionary. According to the Directive, Annex 2 projects are subject to an assessment only where Member States consider their characteristics so require it. However, the Directive requires Member States, in interpreting these provisions, to have regard to the general obligation in the Directive that projects 'likely to have significant impact' should be subject to assessment.

13.7.6   **Projects which require an environmental assessment**

Annex 1 and Annex 2 are referred in the Town and Country Planning (Assessment of Environmental Effects) Regulations as Scheds 1 and 2 projects. The schedules have been amended by the 1994 Regulations which were introduced by means of s 15 of the Planning and Compensation Act 1991. These new regulations extend the range of projects to include ones which currently are not required by the Directive. According to the regulations:

- Schedule 1 Projects – must be the subject of an environmental assessment;

- Schedule 2 Projects – only require environmental assessment where there are 'likely to be significant environmental effects by virtue of factors such as the nature, size or location of the project'.

13.7.7   Schedule 1 projects

The following types of project are listed in Sched 1:

(a) The carrying out of building operations, or the change of use of buildings or other land (where it is a material change) to provide any of the following:

- crude oil refineries;
- thermal power stations;
- nuclear power stations or other nuclear reactors;
- installations for the disposal of radioactive waste;
- integrated works for the initial melting of cast-iron and steel;
- installations involving asbestos extraction, processing or transformation;
- chemical installations;
- motor ways and major roads;
- trading ports;
- special waste incineration, treatment or landfill.

The list of types of projects in Sched 1 is exhaustive.

13.7.8   Schedule 2 projects

Schedule 2 lists numerous types of development which are broken down into broad industrial sectors. For projects which fall into Sched 2 an environmental assessment is only required if the project is likely to have significant effects on the environment by virtue of factors such as their nature, size or location. The broad headings under Sched 2 include, for example, agriculture, the extractive industry and energy.

An example of the breakdown under each of these headings is shown below in relation to the extractive industries:

'2 Extractive industry:

(a) extracting peat;

(b) deep drilling, including in particular:

– geothermal drilling;

– drilling for the storage of nuclear waste material;

– drilling for water supplies;

but excluding drilling to investigate the stability of soil.

(c) exacting minerals (other than metalliferous and energy producing minerals) such as marble, sand, gravel, shale, salt, phosphates and potash;

(d) extracting coal or lignite by underground or open-cast mining;

(e) extracting petroleum;

(f) extracting natural gas;

(g) extracting ores;

(h) extracting bituminous shale;

(i) extracting minerals (other than metalliferous and energy-producing minerals) by open-cast mining;

(j) a surface industrial installation for the extraction of coal, petroleum, natural gas or ores or bituminous shale;

(k) a coke oven (dry distillation of coal);

(l) an installation for the manufacture of cement.

Projects serving national defence purposes are not covered by the Directive.

13.7.9   Exemptions

An environmental assessment is only required for projects listed in Sched 2 where the relevant planning authority decides that circumstances and characteristics of the project require it. The regulations state that the decision whether or not an assessment should be carried out depends upon whether such projects :

13.7.10   Projects likely to have significant effects on the environment

'are likely to have significant effects on the environment by virtue of factors such as their nature, size and location.'

Unfortunately the regulations do not define what is meant by 'significant' but DOE Circular 15/88 provides additional guidance. In deciding which Sched 2 projects should be subject to an environmental assessment, the matter to be considered is the likelihood of significant environmental effects. The Circular lays down three general criteria as to whether the environmental effects are likely to be significant:

(a) whether the project is of more than local significance in terms of its size and physical scale;

(b) the sensitivity of the location of the development;

(c) the polluting effect of the development and whether or not it is likely to give rise to complex or adverse effects.

Where projects are on a small scale but are in particularly sensitive or vulnerable locations then consideration should be given to the need for an environmental assessment where the project is likely to have significant effect on the special character of the protected site. This will be of relevance, for

13.7.11   Projects located in vulnerable locations

example, in national parks or sites of special scientific interest. However, it is worthy of note that there is no automatic presumption that an environmental assessment is needed for developments in such areas.

13.7.12   Indicative thresholds

The Directive specifically included provisions which enabled Member States to establish the criteria or thresholds necessary to determine which of the projects of the type listed in Annex 2 are to be subject to an assessment. It is in this area that implementation has particularly varied between Member States. A number of Member States, including the UK, chose to set thresholds which determine whether an EA is necessary or not. However, even in the setting of thresholds, the approach has differed. The approach taken by the Dutch Government, for instance, was to set very rigid thresholds below which an EA is not required and above which it will be. The problem with this approach is that it ignores the fact that there may well be small developments which fall below the rigid threshold but which are nevertheless seriously damaging to the environment. The method used in the UK has been much more flexible but lacks the certainty of the Dutch approach.

The approach taken by the UK has been to establish (by means of the Circulars) certain criteria (see above) and also to lay down indicative thresholds. DOE Circular (15/88) lists the thresholds for identifying Sched 2 projects. In doing this, however, it recognises the difficulty of prescribing such hard and fast quantitative thresholds and, as such, they do not provide a simple test as to the determination of whether an environmental assessment is required. The Circular states that the purpose of the thresholds are to assist authorities further in identifying whether a proposed development would be likely to have significant effects. The Circular emphasises that the decision whether a project is likely to have significant effects must be made on 'the basis of the particular circumstances of the individual project'. This case by case method certainly enables a flexible approach to be taken, so that projects within the criteria or above the thresholds may not necessarily require an environmental assessment and, equally, projects outside the criteria or below the thresholds could still be likely to have significant environmental effects and thus require an environmental assessment.

These indicative thresholds are found in Appendix A to Circular 15/88. Circular 7/94 contains the indicative thresholds for the new types of projects added to Sched 2 by the 1994 Regulations. Some of the thresholds are listed below as an indication of the types of thresholds that are included.

Whilst the approach adopted is intrinsically flexible, allowing for the exercise of discretion by the planning authority, it does of course mean that an applicant will not always be able to refer to the regulations and categorically determine whether an environmental assessment is required (unless the project is clearly a Sched 1 project). Therefore, unless the developer wishes to conduct an assessment on a voluntary basis, he or she will need to take advice from the relevant planning authority. The determination of whether an environmental assessment is required is made by the planning authority, subject to appeal by the Secretary of State. One of the problems inherent in this flexible, case by case system is, in fact, that the thresholds will not always provide satisfactory guidance for a local authorities themselves.

An applicant may, at any time prior to making a planning application, seek an opinion from the local planning authority as to whether or not a proposed development falls within Scheds 1 or 2. For Sched 1 projects, this should be relatively simple even for the applicant to determine, but it will not always be straightforward in relation to Sched 2 projects because of the requirement of 'significant environmental effects'. Where a developer thinks that an EA may be required he should be encouraged to seek advice from the planning authority at the earliest possible stage, he can either do this informally or he may seek a formal determination. Where the applicant seeks a formal determination, then the authority must notify the applicant of its decision within three weeks of receiving the request, unless a longer period is agreed with the applicant. The planning authority may request further information if considered necessary.

13.7.13 Advice from the planning authority whether an environmental assessment is required (reg 55)

If the authority decides that an environmental assessment will be required, it must state the reasons why it has come to that decision. The determination is also recorded in the public register. The applicant then has the choice of complying with the authority's determination or appealing to the Secretary of State (see below). Either a project requires an environmental assessment or it does not, there is no possibility of a simplified environmental assessment. The aim of this pre-planning determination is to minimise delay and uncertainty for the developer.

If the developer submits an application for planning permission without seeking advice or a determination from the authority, he may find that this delays the procedure. Where an application for planning permission is made, and the authority considers that an EA is required, then it must notify the applicant within three weeks, stating its reasons. If this happens, then the developer can either accept the planning authority's requirements or appeal to the Secretary of State. If he does not indicate that he will submit to the EA process or lodge an appeal within a further three weeks, the planning applications is deemed to have been refused, with no right of appeal to the Secretary of State.

13.7.14   A right of appeal

A right of appeal against the planning authority's determination lies with the Secretary of State. As the EA system is part of the town and country planning system, the normal appeals against non-determination of planning decisions applies. The Secretary of State will normally give his determination within three weeks and he too must also provide a written statement outlining the reasons for his decision. This decision is judicially reviewable.

The Secretary of State also has the additional power to issue his own direction that an EA is required, even if this preliminary procedure has not been initiated by the developer. He may also overrule a decision by a planning authority that an EA is not required.

13.7.15   Voluntary environmental assessments

In some instances, the applicant will decide to conduct an environmental assessment and submit an environmental statement on an entirely voluntary basis. It has already been noted that, prior to the introduction of the legislation in 1988, there were over 100 voluntary EAs submitted. Some developers will carry out an environmental assessment as a matter of good practice or to develop good public relations.

13.7.16   Carrying out the environmental assessment: what does it involve?

The environmental assessment involves a number of stages. It requires the collection of environmental information and the carrying out of a consultation exercise both of which will enable the developer to prepare the environmental statement The developer or applicant is encouraged to seek the advice from the relevant planning authority about the extent of the environmental assessment process and the detailed content of the environmental statement before its preparation has begun. This is known as scoping.

13.7.17   Scoping

The term 'scoping' refers to a stage when the developer, along with the relevant authorities and the consultees, decides upon the key issues which the environmental assessment needs to address. The DOE guide contains a checklist which is intended to serve as a basis for discussion between the developer and the authority about the scope of the assessment and statement. Whilst the checklist is long, it is made clear that it is not intended that all of the issues raised need to be considered, or at least considered with the same degree of detail. The environmental statement should focus on the most significant impacts. Once again, this is a good practical reason why the applicant should discuss the matter with the planning authority before starting what can be a considerably expensive exercise. This is reinforced by the fact that the planning authority can require the applicant to supply further information after the submission of the environmental statement.

Within the context of the regulations, the environment is defined as including the physical environment: human beings, flora, fauna, soil, waste, climate, the landscape, the interaction between any of these, material assets and the cultural heritage. Not only is the definition wide, it also includes long- and short-term effects as well as direct and indirect effects. Where there are any adverse effects, the developer should describe what mitigating measures can be used and how effective they will be.

13.7.18 Effects on the environment

A key element of the environmental assessment is the emphasis placed upon public participation and consultation. The DOE Guidance Note states that the preparation of the environmental statement should be a collaborative exercise involving discussions with the following:

13.7.19 Publicity requirements

- the local planning authority;

- the statutory consultees; and

- the public.

There are, therefore, extensive publicity requirements. Once the planning authority has determined that an EA is required to support a planning application, it must make this determination known on the public register. This gives the public the first opportunity to find out about the project. However, where the developer has not sought a determination from the planning authority, then there will be no such record on the public register. The public then has the opportunity to comment when the environmental statement is published. Enough copies of the statement must be provided so that the planning authority can consult with the statutory consultees and, in addition, a reasonable number of copies must be provided for sale to the public.

The publicity requirements also extend to the applicant. He is required to publish a notice in a local newspaper and also to post notices on the site, with information about where and when the environmental statement (ES) can be inspected or purchased. Unfortunately, some environmental statements have been prohibitively priced, despite the fact that developers are only supposed to make a reasonable charge.

| 13.7.20 | Opportunity for public consultation |

Following publication of the ES, the public has 21 days to inspect it before it is formally submitted with the application for planning permission. The planning authority then has up to 16 weeks to determine the planning application. During the 21 days following receipt of the planning application and ES, the public has the opportunity to make representations. The planning authority must then consider any representations made when it considers the application and the ES.

| 13.7.21 | Statutory consultees |

The planning authority must notify the statutory consultees of the EA and must allow them at least 14 days within which to comment on the ES. Then the planning authority is under a duty to take their comments into account before reaching the planning decision. The statutory consultees are the:

- National Rivers Authority;

- Health and Safety Executive;

- Countryside Commission;

- English Nature;

- HMIP

and any body which would have been consulted pursuant to a General Development Order (such as the National Rivers Authority, Health and Safety Executive). In addition, the authority must also send a copy of the planning application and the environmental statement to the Secretary of State.

| 13.7.22 | The environmental statement |

The aim of the environmental statement is to provide an objective account of the significant environmental effects which the project is likely to give rise to. The environmental statement is a document or a series of documents submitted by the developer in support of the planning application. There is no prescribed form. However, Sched 3 of the regulations lays down the minimum requirements for the coverage of an environmental statement. It must contain information on the following:

(a) a description of the proposed development comprising information about the site and the design and scale of the development;

(b) the data necessary to identify and assess the main effects which that development is likely to have on the environment;

(c) a description and assessment of the likely significant effects, direct or indirect, which the development is likely to have upon its environment explained by reference to its possible impact upon the following:

- human beings;
- flora and fauna;
- soil;
- water;
- air;
- climate;
- landscape;
- interaction between any of the above;
- material assets;
- cultural heritage;

(d) where significant adverse effects are identified, a description of the measures envisaged to avoid, reduce or remedy those effects; and

(e) a non-technical summary of the information provided above.

In addition to these minimum requirements, the Department of the Environment's *Guide to Environmental Assess-ment* also provides some advice on what other information might be included in the environmental statement. One of the perceived shortcomings in the statement is that there is no requirement to discuss alternative plans or specifications, although the statement may include in outline the main alternative structures (if there are any) and a main reason for choosing the development proposed. However, there is clearly no obligation to do this and in fact ESs rarely do.

The developer is responsible for preparing the statement; however, he is able to obtain any relevant existing information from the statutory consultees. The planning authority will normally have notified the statutory consultees that an ES is being prepared. The consultees can make a reasonable charge for supplying such information. In 1994, the Department also published, for consultation, a draft guidance specifically on the preparation of environmental statements. This guidance is aimed at developers and their advisers and covers matters such as the methods of prediction and the evaluation of impacts. In particular, the appendices provide much more specific and detailed information regarding, *inter alia*, the effects on humans, land, ecology, water, air and climate. It also emphasises the importance of a systematic approach to gathering information and the carrying out of a 'scoping' exercise.

13.7.23   **Impact on the planning process**

Planning permission cannot be granted for a project which falls within the regulations (see below) unless the developer carries out an environmental assessment (EA) and submits an environmental statement (ES). The planning authority must then consider the information contained within the ES before granting planning permission. Therefore, the ES and responses made by the consultees and public (the environmental information) become material considerations which the authority must take into account. The planning authority may request further information from the applicant – for instance, on how they intend to overcome or mitigate against any of the problems raised by the statutory consultees or the public, although this is relatively unusual.

It was stated at the outset that the Directive was based on an act of faith that, by introducing the EA into decision-making procedures, the subsequent decisions would improve in relation to the environment. However, neither the Directive nor the Statutory Instrument requires a planning authority to refuse consent for a project assessed to be damaging to the environment. Planning authorities are, however, now required to provide a written statement that they have taken the ES into account in reaching their decision. There is no duty to indicate what weight has been given to it. The ES and the various submissions made by the statutory consulates and the public becomes a 'material consideration', to which the planning authority must have regard.

One further implication is that the normal eight-week period for consideration of planning applications is extended to 16 weeks. This period will not start until the ES is submitted.

13.8   **Enforcing the regulations**

The Council of Ministers took over 16 years to agree the Environmental Assessment Directive, which is indicative of the controversial nature of the subject. It has already been stated that the UK was reluctant to accept the proposal, believing that the town and country planning system provided adequate controls to protect the environment. In addition to this, the Directive has been problematic because of the amount of discretion that is given to Member States in relation to Annex 2 projects. This discretion in relation to implementation has resulted in a variety of means of transposal into domestic law. Finally, the exercise of discretion by planning authorities themselves in relation to Annex 2/Sched 2 projects has generated concern. It is not surprising, therefore, that issues relating to the implementation of the Directive and enforcement of the UK Regulations have come to the fore. In 1991, the European Commission investigated seven separate complaints arising from alleged non-compliance in the UK.

Because it is largely local planning authorities which determine whether an EA is required, the scope for third parties to challenge their decisions is by means of judicial review. The applicant has a right of appeal to the Secretary of State but under town and country planning law. Interested third parties have no such right and, therefore, the only available course of action is to seek judicial review of the authority's decision. It is clearly not within the scope of this book to discuss the procedural or substantive issues of judicial review (although for additional comment (see Chapter 6). However, there have been a number of applications for judicial review regarding the Environmental Assessment Regulations.

In *R v Swale Borough Council and Medway Ports Authority, ex p The Royal Society for the Protection of Birds* (1991), the RSPB applied for judicial review against a grant of planning permission made in favour of the Medway Ports Authority for the reclamation of a 250-acre area of mudflat near Sheerness in order to construct a storage area for import and export cargoes. The site was of significant importance to migrating birds. The planning permission was granted by the Borough Council without any environmental assessment being required or carried out. The RSPB challenged the planning permission, by means of judicial review, on the grounds that the project was a Sched 1 project or a Sched 2 project with significant effects, and therefore the planning permission was unlawful without consideration of an environmental assessment. The case is interesting because it raised a number of important issues:

13.8.1   Judicial review

- Whether environmental pressure groups have the 'sufficient interest' required to bring judicial review proceedings. In the circumstances of the case, the RSPB were granted *locus standi* because they had a legitimate expectation of being consulted since the planning authority had supplied written assurances that it would, in fact, be consulted. (For a further discussion of the position of pressure groups in judicial review proceedings, see Chapter 6);

- The court held that the decision as to whether or not a project falls within one of the schedules or has significant effects was a matter exclusively for the planning authority, subject to challenge only on the grounds of *Wednesbury* unreasonableness (*Associated Provincial Picture Houses v Wednesbury Corporation* (1948)). The court considered that the question of classification was a matter of fact and degree and not law;

- The court also dealt with one of the issues that has caused some considerable problems. In some instances, planning permission is sought for a project which is part of a much wider future development for which permission is not yet sought. In other words, there is an incremental approach to the development. The court recognised that such an approach could present a possible means of defeating the aims of the Directive. However, it held that the question of whether or not a development was of a prescribed category had to be answered strictly in relation to the development applied for, not for any developments beyond it. On the other hand, the court did say that, in considering the possible environmental effects of a Sched 2 project, it was proper to regard the smaller project as 'promoting the larger development and thereby likely to carry in its wake the environmental effect of the latter'.

This action was followed by a case brought by the RSPB against the Secretary of State on the grounds that the Secretary of State acted unlawfully in excluding the 22 hectares of the Medway Estuary mudflats from the protection afforded under the EC Birds Directive. The Court of Appeal, however, upheld the Secretary of State's action by deciding that it was not unlawful for the area to be excluded. In the case, the court had to consider whether or not economic factors should be taken into account as part of the designation process or only after the designation of the area. The RSPB has appealed against this decision and the case is currently before the House of Lords. At the time of writing, the House of Lords had requested a preliminary ruling on the provisions of the Directive. It remains to be seen whether the RSPB will succeed in this litigation.

In *R v Secretary of State for Transport, ex p Surrey County Council* (1993), Surrey County Council has sought judicial review against the Department of Transport's decision to build link-roads alongside the M25. The grounds put forward are that the Secretary of State for Transport has refused to publish comprehensive details of his plans, and is treating the link-roads as separate schemes. Surrey County Council argue that it is impossible to assess accurately the consequences of widening the M25 without knowing the consequences of further widening in the future. At the time of writing this case had yet to be considered.

Judicial review has not been confined to the national courts. In 1994, Greenpeace initiated an action under Art 173 of the EC Treaty, against the European Commission. The action concerned the Commission's failure to require an environmental assessment for a project in the Canary Islands to which ecu 40M had been awarded from the EC Structural Funds. The Structural Funds provide financial assistance from the Community for those projects in the regions which are 'lagging behind'. The project was an oil-fired power plant. The difficulties of individual's challenging acts of the Community institutions under the provisions of Art 173 have already been discussed in Chapter 2. Natural or legal persons may only seek review by the Court of Justice of a decision addressed to themselves, or failing that against:

> 'a decision, which although in the form of a regulation, or a decision addressed to another person, is of direct and individual concern to the person seeking review.'

The European Court has placed a very restrictive interpretation on what constitutes direct and individual concern and has effectively barred many applicants from having the requisite standing to pursue such an action.

Implementation throughout the Member States has been varied, often taking place after the formal date of compliance, 3 July 1988. As noted above, the date of transposition of the Directive into UK law was 15 July, some 12 days after the deadline. The late implementation of the Directive has given rise to problems in relation to so-called 'pipeline' projects where planning permission was agreed prior to the implementation of domestic legislation but after 3 July 1988, when implementation should have taken place. In such circumstances, where permission has been given, the question has been whether the project should nevertheless have been subject to an EA on the basis of the Directive being directly effective. (For a discussion of the principle of direct effect, see Chapter 2.)

The question was considered in *Twyford Parish Council v Secretary of State for the Environment and the Secretary of State for Transport* (1992). The case involved the proposed section of the M3 motorway through Twyford Down, a project which has generated a great deal of environmental protest. The implementing regulations governing such road schemes are the Highways (Assessment of Environmental Effects)

13.8.2   Action before the Court of Justice

13.8.3   Delayed implementation, 'pipeline projects' and the direct effect of the Directive

Regulations 1988. Under those regulations, projects that had been approved prior to 21 July when the regulations came into force were specifically exempted from the scope of the regulations. The question was, therefore, was this exemption a correct implementation of the Directive? If it was not, then was the Directive capable of direct effect?

In *Wychavon District Council v Secretary of State and Others* (1994), Wychavon District Council had refused planning permission to a company who wished to erect a number of poultry houses for broiler production. The company appealed and the appeal was upheld by the planning inspector. However, during the appeal the Council argued that the company had intentionally underestimated the number of birds that they intended to rear, that the appeal was in reality a new application and that, if that was the case, an environmental assessment was required. The original application for planning permission pre-dated the introduction, on 15 July 1988, of the Environmental Assessment Regulations. The inspector nevertheless upheld the appeal and, consequently, Wychavon District Council applied to the High Court to have the inspector's decision quashed.

The court held that the Directive was not directly effective, on the basis that some of the Articles in the Directive could not satisfy the requisite test of clearness and precision. This would seem to contradict previous case law, where it has been held that it is possible for certain parts of a Directive to be directly effective even if others are not. The court also had to consider whether the EA regulations should be interpreted, so far as possible, to meet the requirements of the Directive (following the ruling of the Court of Justice in *Marleasing SA v La Commercial Internacional de Alimentacion SA, Case 106/89*). The Divisional Court was unwilling to do this, stating that there was no scope for the introduction, in the circumstances, of the doctrine of 'indirect effect', because no amount of interpretation could actually get around the fact that the commencement date of the regulations was 15 July. Since the original application for planning permission was before 15 July, the requirements of the regulations did not apply.

The question of the direct effect of the Directive was finally considered by the European Court of Justice in *Bund Naturschutz in Bayern EV and Others v Freistaat Bayern and others* (1992). The Court of Justice, in its first ruling on the Environmental Assessment Directive, was asked to consider the issue in a reference from a Bavarian court. The Environmental Assessment Directive was not transposed into

German law until 12 February 1990 and did not come into effect until April 1990. Under the German law (known as the UVPG) an exemption from the Directive was provided for pending consent procedures notified when the UVPG came into force. On 7 and 9 July 1988, the Bavarian Highways Department lodged consent applications for the plans of two sections of the new B15 federal highway in Bavaria. Under the UVPG, they were exempt from the Directive and no environmental assessment was carried out. On 16 December 1991, the government of Lower Bavaria approved the projects. An action was brought against the Federal State of Bavaria by an ecological organisation. In the proceedings before the Bavarian court, three questions were referred to the Court of Justice under the preliminary rulings procedure. Essentially, the questions were concerned with whether or not the Directive could be interpreted as allowing a Member State which had transposed the Directive after the deadline, to waive the obligations under the Directive by enacting transitional provisions for the project where the consent procedure was initiated after the deadline for compliance with the Directive, but before the coming into force of the national law implementing it.

The European Court held that there was nothing in the Directive which could authorise Member States to exempt transitional projects initiated after the Directive had come into force. They asserted that the Directive should have been implemented in full by the date for compliance.

The aim of the EC Directive was to improve the planning decision-making process by ensuring that the environmental effects of projects are taken into account at the earliest possible stage. One of the requirements of the Directive was that the European Commission review the implementation of the Directive five years after its adoption. The question is how successful has the Directive been? In order to answer this question the following points must be examined.

13.9 How successful has the Directive been?

When the Environmental Assessment Regulations were introduced into the UK, it was originally thought that they would generate only a dozen or so qualifying projects each year. This was an enormous underestimation. In fact, to date, there have been over 200 EAs a year with an estimated increase in the figure to about 300 a year. However, this quantitative measure does not reflect on the qualitative nature of EAs, nor does it reveal anything about the nature of planning decisions taken where EAs have been carried out. However, EAs have generated considerable research by the

13.9.1 The number of environmental assessments

European Commission itself and also by Universities such as the University of Manchester EIA Centre.

13.9.2   Evaluation by the   In 1993, the European Commission reviewed the implementa-
           European Commission   tion of the Directive, comparing its implementation in all of the Member States. In fact, as stated earlier, the Directive required the Commission to undertake this review after five years of operation and to publish its findings, but the review was delayed until 1993. By July 1991, all Member States had taken steps to approve some new legal measures relating to the Directive. Implementation varied considerably from State to State. The Commission published a report with its findings which can be briefly summarised as follows:

(a) there has not been a uniform application throughout the Member States;

(b) problems and doubts over which Annex 2 projects required an environmental assessment;

(c) concern about the poor quality of environmental statements;

(d) weak consultative practices;

(e) the failure of the authorities to adequately take account of the assessment findings in the decision making process.

This latter point reflects one of the inherent weaknesses of the Directive, insofar as it was based on the view that the introduction of environmental assessments in the planning decision-making process would inevitably lead to better decisions respecting the environment. Described by some as 'an act of faith', the Commissions report indicated that, in part, that faith was misplaced.

In addition to the Commission's evaluation, the Environmental Impact Assessment Centre at the University of Manchester also carries out its own research and surveys of EIAs in the UK and throughout the world. They have echoed the Commission's view about the quality of EAs and, in their research, have found that a high proportion of environmental statements have been unsatisfactory in terms of completeness and objectivity. More alarming was the finding that a number of projects were not being required to carry out EAs because the planning authority had not even considered the issue of whether one was needed or not.

As a consequence, the European Commission has come forward with a proposal to amend the 1985 Directive in order to remove some of the uncertainties that surround it. If the Directive is adopted in its current form, it will require implementation by 30 June 1996. The main proposals for change in the draft Directive are as follows:

(1) Extending the list of Annex 1 and 2 projects and tightening the definitions of certain Annex 2 projects. The 'revised' Annex 2 list would include:

- all intensive fish or shellfish farming;
- urban development projects, including shopping centres and car parks;
- road upgrading;
- coastal and maritime works;
- golf courses;
- camping and caravan sites;
- leisure centres;

(2) For Annex 2 projects, the relevant authorities would be under a duty to 'screen' projects to assess whether an environmental assessment is required. A new Annex 2(a) is proposed, which would introduce criteria that the relevant authorities must have regard to in determining whether the environmental impact of the project is significant. These relate to the characteristics of the project (its size, resource consumption, and the amount of waste it will generate) and to the sensitivity of the surrounding area. The authorities would then be required to publish their decisions on this screening exercise;

(3) In response to poor quality of environmental statements, it is proposed that an extra stage is introduced in order to ensure that environmental statements contain the information that is set out in Annex 3 of the Directive. This is known as 'scoping' and involves the identification of the key issues to be addressed by the environmental assessment. The authorities will be placed under a duty to inform the developer in advance what information he should provide. This would be done in consultation with the developer and also the statutory consultees;

(4) The Commission proposes a tightening up of the consultation procedures by allowing for earlier consultation with the statutory consultees and the public;

(5) The final proposal concerns the actual decision-making by the relevant planning authority. The planning authorities will be placed under a duty to 'take into consideration' the information obtained from the developer and the consultees when reaching its decisions. The authority will be under a duty to publish its decision and, significantly, it

will be required to state its reasons and considerations in reaching that decision. Therefore, planning authorities will have to state their reasons, for example, in deciding to grant planning permission despite receiving unfavourable responses from the statutory consultees or the public. This could lead to the possibility of more judicial review challenges against planning decisions by third parties.

13.10 The EC Habitats Directive

The EC has made further inroads into the planning regime by means of two Directives which are aimed at protecting birds and natural habitats. The EC Directive on the Conservation of Natural Habitats and of Wild Fauna and Flora (known as the Habitats Directive) and the Wild Birds Directive are both environmental protection measures, but have been implemented principally through the town and country planning system. They have resulted in a reduction in the discretionary power of planning authorities in relation to projects affecting certain designated areas.

Under the Habitats Directive, Member States are required to designate sites on land and at sea to form part of a European network called 'Nature 2000'. The network is made up of Special Areas of Conservation (SACs) under the Habitats Directive and Special Protection Areas (SPAs) under the Birds Directive.

In October 1994, the government brought into force the Conservation (Natural Habitats etc) Regulations 1994 which gave effect to the Directives.

The Regulations provide for the following:

1   The conservation of natural habitats and, in particular, for the selection, registration and notification of sites to be protected under the Directive. These sites are known as European Sites;

2   The management of such sites, including the control of damaging operations on them, special conservation orders in relation to them and for by-laws and compulsory purchase orders in relation to them;

3   The protection of designated species of wild animals and plants. Criminal offences are created in relation to the taking, killing or disturbance of such designated animals and plants;

4   The adaptation of planning and related controls to ensure the protection of the European Sites. This point is considered more fully below.

Part 4 of the Regulations deal specifically with the planning controls in relation to the designated sites and, in doing so, amends the Town and Country Planning Act 1990.

The Regulations make the following amendments to the planning controls in relation to areas designated under the Directive:

- restriction on the grant of planning permission where European Sites are likely to be affected.

The regulations result in a restriction on the granting of planning permission for developments likely to significantly affect a Special Protection Area designated under the Birds Directive, or a Special Area of Conservation under the Habitats Directive. It should be noted that SPAs and Special Areas of Conservation (SACs) are known collectively as European Sites.

Where planning permission is sought for a development which is likely to have a significant effect on a European Site, then the planning authority must make an appropriate assessment of the implications for the site in view of the sites conservation objectives. This does not apply where the proposed development is directly concerned with or necessary to the management of the site.

The assessment will involve the planning authority in a process of consultation with the relevant conservation body (English Nature) and also, if the authority considers it necessary, the public.

The authority can only grant planning permission once they have ascertained that the development will not adversely affect the integrity of the European Site. The only exception to this arises where the planning authority is satisfied that there is no alternative solution and that the development must go ahead for 'imperative reasons' of overriding public interest which may be of a social or an economic nature. In these circumstances, the authority may approve the planning permission even if the integrity of the site is adversely affected. However, if the site in question hosts a priority natural habitat type or a priority species, the only overriding interests can be reasons relating to human health, public safety or because there are beneficial consequences of primary importance to the environment.

If the planning authority decides that the proposed development will adversely effect the integrity of a European Site, then it has a duty to consider whether any adverse effects might be overcome by a planning obligation. Failing this, the planning authority must revoke or modify the planning permission. The authority can also remove the building or works in order to overcome the adverse effects.

Review of existing planning permissions which are likely to affect a European Site

The Regulations also require the review of existing planning permissions which have not been fully implemented and which are likely to affect a European Site. It does not apply to planning permissions where the development has been completed.

In addition to the Regulations, a new Planning Policy Guidance Note on Nature Conservation was issued (PPG9: *Nature Conservation*).

Planning and Pollution Control

Planning law and environmental law are closely linked and the relationship between them has generated considerable controversy in recent years.

Environmental law and planning law

The town and country planning legislation enables local planning authorities to control development in urban and rural areas and this allows environmental concerns to be taken into account as 'material consideration' in the planning decision process.

Various Planning Policy Guidance Notes recognise the relationship between the environment and other policy areas such as transport, tourism and the protection of the countryside.

Planning policy guidance notes

Planning Policy Guidance Note 23 deals specifically with the relationship between planning and pollution control, in particular:

* the planning system should not duplicate statutory environmental controls;

* the respective systems are complementary.

The PPG reflects the judicial decision in the case of *Gateshead Metropolitan Borough Council v Secretary of State for the Environment* (1993).

EC Directive 85/337 requires an environmental assessment of certain projects seeking planning permission. The Directive which is a preventive environmental measure has been implemented through the town and country planning regime.

Environmental assessment and planning

The Directive has largely been implemented by the Town and Country Planning (Assessment of Environmental Effects) Regulations 1992.

The aim of the environmental assessment is to improve the planning process so that the effects on the environment of a proposed project are considered within the planning decision process.

Schedule I projects must be the subject of an EA whereas Sched 2 projects only require an EA where there are likely to be 'significant environmental effects'.

'Significant environmental effects' is not defined in the Regulations. DoE Circular 15/88 provides guidance and indicative thresholds.

The Conservation (Natural Habitats etc) Regulations 1994 give effect to the EC Habitats Directive and the Wild Birds Directive. The impact of these EC environmental measures is again felt through the development control system.

Chapter 14

Statutory Nuisance

Chapter 4 considered the ways in which the common law can provide a means of protecting the environment and some of the inherent difficulties faced when bringing common law actions. Common law actions are now supplemented by the provisions of ss 79-82 of the Environmental Protection Act 1990, which provides that certain matters may constitute 'statutory nuisances' and as such may, if not abated, result in criminal offences. The control of statutory nuisances rests largely with the local authorities through their environmental health departments. However, it is also possible for a 'person aggrieved' by a statutory nuisance to commence proceedings in the magistrates' court in order to secure the abatement of the nuisance. The purpose of putting certain nuisances on a statutory footing was to provide a quicker and cheaper means of dealing with nuisances than by means of a common law action.

The current provisions for statutory nuisances can be found in ss 79–82 EPA 1990. However, the provisions are not new and, in fact, the EPA consolidates provisions from legislation dating back to the Public Health Act (PHA) 1936, which first placed certain nuisances on a statutory footing in recognition of the growing health problems associated with industrial development and some of the limitations of the common law in addressing these problems. The Public Health Act 1936 has now been repealed and re-enacted by the EPA where the definitions of the statutory nuisances are largely identical. One of the problems with this straight forward re-enactment is that there has been no redefinition of the statutory nuisances which were introduced by the PHA 1936 to protect public health, but are now intended to protect the environment. Although the statutory nuisances were intended to control pollution, it was within the context of protecting public health but not protecting the environment *per se*. In addition to the original list of statutory nuisances, the noise nuisances are drawn from the Control of Pollution Act 1974 and also the more recent Noise and Statutory Nuisances Act 1993. Many of the cases cited in this chapter concern the PHA provisions but are still relevant in the context of the EPA.

14.1   Introduction

14.2   What are the statutory nuisances?

The matters or activities that constitute statutory nuisances are listed in s 79 as follows:

(a) any premises in such a state as to be prejudicial to health or a nuisance;

(b) smoke emitted from premises so as to be prejudicial to health or a nuisance;

(c) fumes or gases emitted from premises so as to be prejudicial to health or a nuisance;

(d) any, dust, steam, smell or other effluvia arising on industrial, trade or business premises and being prejudicial to health or a nuisance;

(e) any accumulation or deposit which is prejudicial to health or a nuisance;

(f) any animal kept in such a place or manner as to be prejudicial to health or a nuisance;

(g) noise emitted from premises so as to be prejudicial to health or a nuisance;

(ga) noise that is prejudicial to health or a nuisance and is emitted from or caused by a vehicle, machinery or equipment in a street;

(i) any other matter declared by any enactment to be a statutory nuisance.

It should be noted that point (ga) was added by the Noise and Statutory Nuisances Act 1993. These particular nuisances will be considered in greater detail in Chapter 15.

14.3   Prejudicial to health or a nuisance

The list of matters that may potentially constitute statutory nuisances is wide and covers many different situations, ranging from noise as a result of a domestic argument or party to the accumulations of waste materials on a site. In practice, many of the matters that are statutory nuisances are very localised incidents which may not generally be regarded as major or serious environmental problems. However, it is at the local level that most people are concerned about and aware of environmental problems. A vacant site used for dumping rubbish may not have serious or global environmental consequences but can cause considerable problems for people living and working near the site. It may attract vermin, it may give rise to noxious or offensive smells and it may result in a loss of local amenity. In that sense, the vacant site affects the environment of those affected by it and as such is no less of an environmental problem to the people concerned.

However, the matters listed in s 79 are not automatically statutory nuisances. They become so if they are either prejudicial to health or a nuisance. The definition includes two separate and alternative limbs and it is not necessary to show that a matter is both a nuisance and prejudicial to health. This was affirmed in *Betts v Penge Urban District Council* (1942), where it was held that it is not necessary to show that a matter complained of is prejudicial to health in order for it to constitute a statutory nuisance. The Divisional Court held that it was sufficient to show that the matter (in the case in point, the matter concerned the state of premises) was such as to interfere with personal comfort for there to be a statutory nuisance.

Section 79(7) defines 'prejudicial to health' as meaning 'injurious, or likely to cause injury'. This definition includes two limbs: 'injurious to health' ie actual harm, and 'likely to cause injury' ie anticipated harm. The definition is the same as that given in the 1936 Public Health Act. Its meaning was considered by the Divisional Court in the case of *Coventry City Council v Cartwright* (1975). The case concerned a vacant site owned by the City Council. The Council took no steps to prevent people from depositing household refuse and building materials, such as brick, tarmacadam, earth, scrap iron and broken glass, on the site. A complaint was made by a local resident that the deposits constituted a statutory nuisance in that there was an accumulation or deposit which was prejudicial to health and a nuisance. The argument that it was a nuisance was based on the loss of amenity, an argument rejected by the court. However, the case is important because of its consideration of the meaning of the phrase 'prejudicial to health'. Initially, the magistrates found that the building materials on the site were prejudicial to health on the basis that anyone entering the site might injure themselves on the rubble, and they consequently made an abatement order. However, on appeal, their decision was overturned by the Divisional Court. The Divisional Court concerned itself with the question of whether or not the inert materials on the site could be prejudicial to health and in doing so came to the conclusion that it could only be prejudicial to health if it was likely to cause a threat of disease or attract vermin. It was held that the definition of prejudicial to health did not encompass inert materials which could cause physical injury to people who walk on it. In reaching this decision, the court considered that the statute (in the instant, the PHA 1936) defined prejudicial to health as meaning 'injurious or likely to cause injury to health' and concluded that this did not extend to

14.3.1 Prejudicial to health

physical injury from cuts and the like. In his judgment, Widgery CJ stated that, in relation to the words prejudicial to health: 'the underlying conception of the section [s 92(1(c) PHA 1936] is that that which is struck at is an accumulation of something which produces a threat to health in the sense of a threat of disease, vermin or the like.'

14.3.2   What is meant by nuisance?

The courts have equated nuisance in this context with common law nuisance, private or public, with the focus primarily on private nuisance, therefore involving interference with enjoyment of property. In *National Coal Board v Neath Borough Council* (1976), it was held that the word 'nuisance' meant either a public or a private nuisance at common law. It therefore involved an act or omission materially affecting the comfort and quality of life of a class of the public or an interference for a substantial period with the use and enjoyment of neighbouring property. It should be noted that, like the common law nuisance, the interference must be with neighbouring property (*National Coal Board v Thorne* (1976)).

The problem with using the common law notion of private nuisance is that there is no clearly applicable standard. As was shown in Chapter 4, of the features of the common law of nuisance is the achievement of a balance between competing rights, with each case turning on its facts. Where there is no actual physical damage to person or property, but only a reduction in the enjoyment of a property (for instance as a consequence of loud noise or offensive smells), then the courts have also indicated that much will depend upon the location where the nuisance is complained of. In the often quoted case of *Sturges v Bridgman* (1879). Thesiger LJ stated that 'what would be a nuisance in Belgrave Square would not necessarily be so in Bermondsey'. This narrow approach is problematic in the context of environmental protection. Environmental problems often transcend spatially-defined areas and should not be seen in such narrow terms. Moreover, it is precisely in the industrial and run-down areas where there are more likely to be statutory nuisances occurring, and there is no justifiable reason why in these more vulnerable areas the protection of the law should be less than in those areas where the chances of statutory nuisances occurring are more remote.

14.3.3   Interference with personal comfort

The courts have also tended to require demonstration that the nuisance interferes with a person's personal comfort as opposed to land or physical possessions, largely because the concept of statutory nuisance was based on the need to protect public health. This was aptly demonstrated in *Wivenhoe Port v Colchester Borough Council* (1985), where the court held that, in fact, nuisance in the context of statutory nuisance did not have its wide common law meaning but should be confined to personal discomfort. In the judgment, Butler J made the following statement:

'To be within the spirit of the Act [Public Health Act 1936] a nuisance to be a statutory nuisance had to be one interfering materially with the personal comfort of the residents, in the sense that it materially affected their well-being although it might not be prejudicial to their health. Thus, dust falling on motor cars might cause inconvenience to their owners; it might even diminish the value of their motor car; but this would not be a statutory nuisance. In the same way, dust falling on gardens or trees, or on stock held in a shop would not be a statutory nuisance. But dust in eyes or hair, even if not shown to be prejudicial to health, would be so as an interference with personal comfort.'

Here Butler J refers to the 'spirit of the Act', which was intended to protect public health. However, the statutory nuisances are now contained in the Environmental Protection Act which has as its *raison d'être* the protection of the environment and thus quite different aims to the Public Health legislation. The restrictive approach adopted by the courts would not serve such aims, indeed dust falling on grass and trees is precisely the type of activity which stimulates or causes environmental problems.

The restrictive approach adopted by the courts has been criticised by the House of Commons Environment Committee who, in their report on *Contaminated Land* (1990), recommended that the concept of nuisance should not be given such a restrictive interpretation but should be capable of being used to protect the natural environment as well as public health. Unfortunately, the government rejected this particular recommendation, claiming that it would result in local authorities being 'inundated with requests to take action from well-intentioned, but over-enthusiastic residents who had read a report in the *New Scientist* or had been influenced by a *Panorama* programme'. It therefore seems that the statutory nuisance provisions offer a means of protecting public health and interests in land but only a limited means of protecting the environment in its own right.	14.3.4 Criticisms of the present approach
In practice, the local authority environmental health officer will make an initial determination whether the matter complained of constitutes a statutory nuisance on the basis of it being prejudicial to health or a nuisance. The officer will therefore be required to take into account the nature of the	14.3.5 Identifying a statutory nuisance

neighbourhood and also whether the matter complained of amounts to a nuisance in common law or is just (as sometimes happens) a vexatious complaint.

14.3.6 Burden of proof

Within the context of proceedings involving statutory nuisances, the burden of proof which applies is the criminal one. In other words, it must be established beyond reasonable doubt that the matter complained of exists and that the defendant is responsible for it.

14.4 Exemptions

Section 79(2)–(6) provide a number of specific exemptions from the list of statutory nuisances. These are dealt with below under each category of nuisance:

- Section 79(1)(a) – Any premises in such a state as to be prejudicial to health or a nuisance. Premises does not simply mean buildings but is defined in s 79(7) as including land and any vessel other than one powered by steam-reciprocating machinery. the definition clearly encompasses the garden of a dwelling house. This particular head of statutory nuisance has been used on occasions by council house tenants to force the council to deal with council house problems;

- Section 79(1)(b) – Smoke emitted from premises so as to be prejudicial to health or a nuisance. This particular statutory nuisance was not included in the Public Health Acts but replaces provisions from the Clean Air Act 1956. Premises occupied by the armed forces are exempt from this section, as are certain activities listed in s 79(3) such as smoke emitted from a chimney of a private dwelling within a smoke control area and dark smoke emitted from a chimney of a building serving a boiler or furnace. These latter exempt activities will not constitute a statutory nuisance under Part III EPA but are controlled under the provisions of the Clean Air Act 1993;

- Section 79(1)(c) – Fumes or gas emitted from premises so as to be prejudicial to health or a nuisance. Section 79(1)(c) only applies to domestic premises;

- Section 79(1)(d) – Any dust, steam, smell or other effluvia arising on industrial, trade or business premises so as to be prejudicial to health or a nuisance. Steam emitted from a railway locomotive engine is exempted. This is the only statutory nuisance which is limited to industrial, trade or business premises. The terms 'industrial, trade or business' have been given a wide interpretation and include activities such as manufacturing and service activities such as banking;

- Section 79(1)(e) – Any accumulation or deposit which is prejudicial to health or a nuisance. This has been held to mean 'an accumulation of something which produces a threat to health in the sense of a threat of disease, vermin or the like' (*Coventry City Council v Cartwright* (1975)). In this particular case, the accumulation of building materials, scrap iron and broken glass was not an accumulation that was prejudicial to health, insofar as it would not cause a threat to health within the meaning given. The fact that the materials could cause injury when walked on was not relevant;

- Section 79(1)(f) – Any animal kept in such a place or such a manner as to be prejudicial to health or a nuisance. Both smells and noise from animals may constitute statutory nuisances;

- Section 79(1)(g) – Noise emitted from premises so as to be prejudicial to health or a nuisance. Noise nuisance was previously contained in the Control of Pollution Act 1974 (ss 58 and 59). Noise is defined as including vibration. Aircraft noise (other than noise from a model aircraft) is exempt from this provision but controlled under other specific legislation. As in the smoke nuisance, premises occupied by the armed forces are exempt from this particular section;

- Section 79(1)(ga) – Noise that is prejudicial to health or a nuisance and is emitted from or caused by a vehicle machinery or equipment in a street. This new statutory nuisance will be considered in full in Chapter 15 on noise;

- Section 79(1)(h) – Any other matter declared by any enactment to be a statutory nuisance. This catch-all provision enables other statutory nuisances created by any other act to be dealt with under the statutory nuisance procedures of the EPA.

Section 79(1) places all district councils and London Borough Councils under a duty to inspect their area from time to time to detect any statutory nuisance which ought to be dealt with under ss 80 and 80A of the Act. They are also under a duty to take such steps as are reasonably practicable to investigate complaints made by people living in the area about statutory nuisances. The duty is therefore two-fold. The local authority has to carry out its own checks and has to respond to complaints made. In practice, it is the environmental health departments and officers that are responsible for enforcing this legislation and they will carry out the inspections and	**14.5 Responsibility of the local authorities**

deal with the complaints. In some areas, particularly the large cities, some local authorities have night patrols who are concerned primarily with noise control.

| 14.5.1 | Duty to inspect |

The duty to inspect and detect statutory nuisances is tempered by the requirement that these inspections only have to be carried out from time to time. One of the problems here is that the expression 'time to time' is not defined by the Act, thus making the obligation very imprecise.

| 14.5.2 | Duty to respond to complaints |

The duty to respond to complaints was established by the EPA. Prior to its introduction, local authorities were not actually required to respond to complaints made although in practice complainants provided useful information about the occurrences of statutory nuisances within the local authority area. The duty to respond to complaints made by people living in the area is qualified by the fact that the authority only has to take such steps as are reasonably practicable to investigate the complaint. Again, this expression is not defined and could potentially cause problems. Local authorities are increasingly finding that they are facing severe financial problems. Whether the authority can take into account its own financial situation in determining what is reasonably practicable is not clear. However, if the Secretary of State finds that a local authority is in default of these duties, he can, by virtue of Sched 3, transfer the function to himself.

| 14.5.3 | Local authorities' investigative powers |

In order to carry out their functions of inspection and investigation, local authority environmental officers can enter any land with the people and equipment that they consider necessary. The officers can also carry out any inspections, measurements and tests and can also take away samples and articles. These powers are provided by Sched 3 to the EPA. The purpose of the inspection and investigation is to establish whether or not there is a statutory nuisance (or whether one is likely to occur) and to gather any evidence which may be needed in subsequent court proceedings. Once a local authority environmental officer is satisfied that a statutory nuisance is occurring, or is likely to occur, then an abatement notice must be served.

14.6   Abatement notices

Section 80 provides that an authority must serve an abatement notice when it is satisfied that a statutory nuisance:

- exists;

- is likely to occur; or

- is likely to recur in its area.

Therefore, the authority can take preventive action in order to stop a statutory nuisance happening. The requirement to serve the abatement notice is mandatory. The authority has no discretion once it is aware of the statutory nuisance. However, the section does not say anything about the need for the likely occurrence to be imminent. It is enough that it is likely to occur. Also, when one considers that the concept of prejudicial to health also extends to 'likely to cause injury', the local authority must serve an abatement notice if it believes that circumstances exist which make injury likely.

Although there is no prescribed form for an abatement notice, it must nevertheless state the following in a manner which is clear and understandable to the recipient:

14.6.1   The form of the notice

- the nature of the statutory nuisance;

- the action or works required to abate it;

- time limits for compliance;

- the rights of appeal to the magistrates' court.

The abatement notice can impose the following conditions:

(i) requiring the abatement of the nuisance or prohibiting or restricting its occurrence or recurrence;

(ii) requiring the execution of such works, and the taking of such other steps, as may be necessary for any of these purposes.

The provisions regarding the serving of abatement notices are contained in s 80. Normally, the local authority is required to serve the notice on the person responsible for the nuisance. Where the nuisance arises from any defect in the structural character of a building then the notice should be served on the owner of the premises. In circumstances where the person responsible for the nuisance cannot be found, or the nuisance has not yet occurred, then the notice must be served on the owner or occupier of the premises. In relation to vehicles, machinery or equipment, the person responsible will be the driver or operator.

14.6.2   Who must the notice be served on?

The person responsible for the nuisance is defined in s 79(7) as the person to whose:

- act;

- default; or

- sufferance

the nuisance is attributable.

This is a wide definition and could include not only the person who created the nuisance, but also a third person/party who failed to take any appropriate preventive or corrective action where they had some legal requirement to do so. It can also include third persons who, on becoming aware of the problem, took no steps to remedy the situation. This was confirmed in the 1925 case of *Clayton v Sale UDC* (1926), where an owner was held liable for a statutory nuisance on his land consequent upon the activities or defaults of another. It would also appear that a local authority could serve a notice on a previous owner of land, rather than the current owner, if it decides that the previous owner was the person who caused the nuisance rather than the present owner. The terms 'owner' and 'occupier' are not defined.

14.6.3   What if more than one person is involved ?

Section 81(1) deals with the situation where more than one person is responsible for the statutory nuisance. In these circumstances, s 80 still applies to each of the persons, irrespective of whether or not what any one of them is responsible for would, by itself, amount to a statutory nuisance. Therefore, if two persons are involved in an action which jointly amounts to a statutory nuisance, they will both be responsible for the statutory nuisance even if their individual actions do not by themselves amount to such a nuisance. Although the abatement notice should be served in the first instance on the person responsible for the nuisance, this should be read as meaning that the authority is obliged to serve separate notices on all the parties that may have contributed to the statutory nuisance.

14.7   Appeals against an abatement notice

A person upon whom an abatement notice is served is entitled to appeal against it by making a complaint to the magistrates' court. He must be informed of this right in the abatement notice. Where a person decides to lodge an appeal, they must do say within 21 days from the day when the abatement notice was served. The grounds for appeal are not laid down in the EPA but are provided in the Statutory Nuisance (Appeals) Regulations 1990. The grounds are:

1   The abatement notice is not justified by s 80 EPA – the appellant would be arguing that the matter did not constitute a statutory nuisance;

2   The abatement notice is defective or contains an error;

3   The authority has unreasonably refused to accept compliance with alternative requirements, or that the requirements laid down in the abatement notice are unreasonable or unnecessary;

4   The period for compliance in the notice is not reasonably sufficient for the purpose;

5   There has been an error in the service of the notice – for example, the notice has been served on the wrong person. An appeal may also be made if the appellant argues that it is 'equitable' for the notice to be served on some other person, either *instead of* the appellant or *as well as* him. Whether the wrong person has been served will be determined by reference to s 80(2);

6   The best practicable means were used to counteract the effect of a nuisance from trade or business premises;

7   In relation to a nuisance under s 79(1)(g), the requirements imposed by the abatement notice are more onerous than the requirements which may have been determined by means of other noise controls under the Control of Pollution Act 1974.

The magistrates' court has wide powers when dealing with appeals against abatement notices. It can:

•   correct any procedural defect in the notice, quash the notice or vary the notice;

•   dismiss the appeal;

•   make such order as it thinks fit regarding:
    (a) any works which need to be carried out and the contribution to be made by any person to the cost of the work; or
    (b) the proportion of expenses that a local authority may recover from the appellant and from any other person.

In general, the lodging of an appeal will not suspend the abatement notice and the person served with the notice will still therefore be required to comply with the conditions of the notice. However, this general provision does not apply in circumstances where:

14.7.1   Effect of an appeal upon an abatement notice

•   the abatement notice requires expenditure on works and that the expenditure required would be out of proportion to the expected public benefit; or

•   the abatement notice states that the nuisance is injurious to health; or

•   the nuisance is likely to be of limited duration so that the suspension of the notice would render it of no use or practical effect.

These provisions are to be found in the Statutory Nuisance (Appeals) Regulations.

14.8 Non-compliance with an abatement notice

Section 80(4) establishes that it is an offence for a person served with an abatement notice either to contravene or fail to comply with any requirement or prohibition imposed by the notice, without reasonable excuse. If an abatement notice is not complied with, the authority that has issued the notice has three options:

- abate the nuisance;

- institute summary proceedings; or

- take proceedings in the High Court.

14.8.1 The authority can abate the nuisance

The authority can abate the nuisance and do whatever may be necessary in execution of the notice (s 81(3)). A typical example of this is where audio equipment is removed to abate a noise nuisance. The authority can take this course of action irrespective of whether they take proceedings for non-compliance. In the event that the authority does take action either to abate the nuisance or prevent it happening, then it can, by virtue of s 81(4), recover any expenses reasonably incurred. This would normally be from the person whose acts or omissions caused the nuisance. If that person is the owner of the premises, the expenses can be recovered from any person who is for the time being the owner of them. This would cover situations where, for instance, a previous owner caused a nuisance, but the present owner could be made responsible for the reasonable expenses incurred by the authority. Should the matter of cost recovery go before the court, the court has the power to apportion the expenses between persons whose acts (or omissions) caused the nuisance, in a manner that the court considers fair and reasonable.

The Noise and Statutory Nuisance Act 1993 provides additional assistance to the local authorities in the form of a newly inserted s 81(a), which enables the local authority serving a notice to recover costs, to make a charge on the premises owned by the person in default. This provision was in fact included in the 1936 Public Health Act but was not incorporated into the 1990 EPA.

14.8.2 The authority can institute summary proceedings

If a person commits an offence under s 80(4), the authority can institute proceedings in the magistrates' court. The penalty for nuisance offences depends on whether the nuisance has occurred on industrial, trade or business premises or not. For nuisances arising on non-industrial, trade or business premises, the maximum penalty is £5,000 plus a further £500 for each day that the offence continues after the conviction. However, where the nuisance occurs on industrial, trade or business premises the maximum fine is £20,000 (but no additional daily fines can be made).

The third option available to the authority against a person who fails to comply or contravenes with an abatement notice is to take proceedings in the High Court (s 81(5)). This option is available if the authority is of the view that proceedings in the magistrates' court (under s 80(4)) would afford an inadequate remedy. The aim would be to secure an injunction to secure the abatement, prohibition or restriction. The authority can take this course of action even if summary proceedings have not been exhausted and, equally, there is no requirement that the authority has suffered damage from the nuisance. Failure to comply with an injunction may result in a prison sentence. In *Bristol City Council v Huggins* (1995), Mr Huggins was jailed for three months for breaching an injunction which was obtained by Bristol City Council after two prosecutions under the Environmental Protection Act failed.

14.8.3   The authority can take proceedings in the High Court

Any person who contravenes or fails to comply with the terms of an abatement notice, without reasonable excuse, is guilty of an offence (s 80(4)). However, s 80(7) provides a defence of best practicable means. Subject to certain exceptions, it will be a defence to prove that the best practicable means were used to prevent or counteract the effects of the nuisance. Before considering the specific defence of best practicable means, it needs to be noted that s 80(4) provides that it will only be an offence to contravene or to fail to comply with the requirements or prohibitions of an abatement notice without reasonable excuse.

14.9   Defences against non-compliance with an abatement notice

In the case of *Saddleworth Urban Development Corporation v Aggregate and Sand* (1970), it was held that lack of finance could not constitute a reasonable excuse. However, reasonable excuses can include special difficulties in complying with the notice, such as ill health (*A Lambert Flat Management Ltd v Lomas* (1981)).

14.9.1   What is meant by 'reasonable excuse'?

Section 80(7) provides the defence that the best practicable means were used to prevent or counteract the nuisance. The definition provided in s 79(9) EPA states that 'best practicable means' is to be interpreted by reference to the following provisions:

14.9.2   The 'best practicable means' defence

(a) 'practicable' means reasonably practicable having regard among other things to:

- local conditions and circumstances;
- the current state of technical knowledge; and
- the financial implications;

(b) the means to be employed include;

- the design, installation, maintenance and manner and periods of operation of plant and machinery; and
- the design, construction and maintenance of buildings and structures;

(c) and

(d) the test is to apply only so far as compatible with any;

- duty imposed by law;
- with safety and safe working conditions; and
- with the exigencies of any emergency or unforeseeable circumstances.

In circumstances where a code of practice under s 71 of Control of Pollution Act 1974 (noise minimisation) is applicable, regard must be given to the guidance given in the code (see Chapter 15).

| 14.9.3 | Limitations to the BPM defence |

The 'best practicable means' defence is, however, only available where the nuisance arises on industrial trade or business premises. Section 80(8) lists its availability as follows:

- in the case of nuisances (a), (d), (e), (f) or (g) the defence is only available if the nuisances occurs on industrial, trade or business premises;

- if the nuisance falls under category (ga) then the defence is generally not available unless the noise is emitted from or caused by a vehicle, machinery or equipment being used for industrial, trade or business purposes;

- in the case of smoke emitted from premises (79(1)(b)) the defence of best practicable means is not available except where the smoke is emitted from a chimney;

- the defence of best practicable means is not available at all in relation to the nuisances under s 79(1)(c) and (h).

| 14.9.4 | What is BPM in practice? |

The onus is on the company or business seeking to rely on the defence to prove that the best practicable means were employed. The issue of whether the costs of employing BPM and the effect on profitability was considered in *Wivenhoe Port v Colchester Borough Council* (1985). The Port Authority argued that it had used the best practicable means but was not able to use certain dust arrestment equipment because of the cost and impact on profitability. The court accepted that the profitability of the defendant was a relevant factor to be taken into account, but went on to say that the company needed to show, on the balance of probabilities, that the operation would go from profit to loss, or become so uneconomical that the company could not profitably continue if the dust machinery was used.

Section 82 EPA provides that any person aggrieved by a statutory nuisance has the right to complain to the magistrates' court in order to obtain a court order to bring the nuisance to an end. Failure to comply with a court order under the section is an offence.

14.10   Action by citizens

The provision enables any person who is aggrieved by the nuisance to commence proceedings. There is no requirement that the complainant is an occupier of premises or a neighbour of adjoining premises. The phrase 'person aggrieved' has appeared in various other statutes and has been widely interpreted by the courts. In *Attorney-General (Gambia) v N'Jie* (1961), Lord Denning asserted that the words 'person aggrieved' should not be subjected to a restricted interpretation. However, he went on to say that they:

> 'do not include, of course, a mere busybody who is interfering in things which do not concern him; but they do include a person who has a genuine grievance because an order has been made which prejudicially affects his interests.'

It seems, therefore, that a person must at least be in some way prejudicially affected by the alleged nuisance. More recently in *Sandwell Metropolitan Borough Council v Bujok* (1990), a council tenant alleged that the defective state of her council house gave rise to a statutory nuisance under the 1936 PHA. Mrs Bujok was entitled to bring proceedings against the council as a person whose health, and that of her family, was prejudicially affected by the premises. Section 82 is of particular value when the person concerned is complaining about a statutory nuisance created by a local authority and has been useful in enabling people to bring actions against the local authority in respect of council houses and premises which are prejudicial to health or a nuisance. The fact that the local authorities act as the statutory bodies responsible for controlling statutory nuisances does not provide them with any immunity against actions against them, as can be seen in the *Sandwell* case.

Aggrieved persons can only commence proceedings to secure the abatement of an existing nuisance or its recurrence. They cannot, under these provisions, bring an action to prevent a statutory nuisance, since the magistrates' court, unlike the local authority, does not have anticipatory powers.

14.10.1   Section 82 Proceedings

When a person complains to the magistrates' court, then there is a requirement that the defendant is informed, in writing, of the matter complained of and that such action is going to be taken. For noise nuisances, the complainant must give three days' notice but the period of notice is 21 days in respect of the other nuisances. Before taking action in proceedings brought under s 82, the magistrates must be satisfied that one of the following conditions exists:

- the alleged nuisance exists; or

- an abated nuisance is likely to recur on the same premises, or in the same street.

The court can make the following orders:

(a) requiring the defendant to abate the nuisance within a specified time and to carry out any works necessary for that purpose;

(b) prohibiting a recurrence of the nuisance and requiring the defendant to carry out any necessary works to prevent the recurrence. A time period for carrying out such works will be specified in the order;

(c) the magistrates can also impose a fine of up to £5,000;

(d) the court can order the relevant local authority to do anything which the convicted person was required to do by the court order, after it has given the authority the opportunity to be heard.

Where the nuisance is such as to render premises unfit for human habitation, the court can prohibit the use of the premises for human habitation until the court is satisfied that the premises have been made fit for such a purpose.

Failure to comply with a nuisance order from the magistrates is an offence and can result in a fine of up to £5,000 (plus £500 for each day that the offence continues).

Statutory Nuisance

Certain matters contained in s 79 EPA may constitute statutory nuisances if they are prejudicial to health or a nuisance. Prejudicial to health is defined as 'injurious or likely to cause injury'. The nuisance limb is equated with common law nuisance but the courts have tended to require demonstration that the nuisance materially affects personal comfort.

Prejudicial to health or a nuisance

Local authorities are under a duty to inspect their areas and also to respond to complaints concerning statutory nuisances. If a local authority is satisfied that a statutory nuisance exists or is likely to occur or recur, it must serve an abatement notice.

The abatement notice must clearly state requirements for abating the nuisance, works required and time for compliance.

Responsibilities of the local authorities

A right of appeal against the abatement notice exists to the magistrates' court. the appeal must be brought within 21 days of service of the notice (s 80(3)) on the grounds stated in Statutory Nuisance (Appeals) Regulations 1990.

Right of appeal

Non-compliance with an abatement notice is an offence (s 80(4)).

A local authority can:

1   abate the nuisance themselves and recover costs;

2   commence summary proceedings in the magistrates' court for failure to comply with the notice;

3   take proceedings in the High Court if on the belief that (1) and (2) will not provide a sufficient remedy.

Non-compliance

Section 82 provides that a person aggrieved by a statutory nuisance may complain directly to the magistrates' court.

Action by citizens

Chapter 15

Noise Pollution

Noise is a natural consequence of everything that we do. It forms part of our everyday background and, for the most part, we just accept it or at least tolerate it. Nevertheless, noise has the capacity to cause conflict between those who are making it and those who hear and do not want to hear it! In most instances, noises will not cause people to complain, but there are clearly circumstances where either the volume, duration or repetition (or all three) will cause sufficient aggravation to cause the recipient of the unwanted noise intrusion to take legal action, or in some instances resort to more dramatic measures. Most people are familiar with complaints between neighbours about excessive noise from loud music or lawnmowers, but these complaints rarely lead to legal proceedings. However, people are increasingly concerned about neighbour noise, noise from busy roads, construction sites, factories or airports, to name but a few examples. They are also more aware of the effects that noise can have upon them and are, consequently, more likely to complain.

Modern industrial society generates an enormous quantity of noise and it will increase as more and more aeroplanes arrive and depart at airports and as more and more cars take to the roads. There are also more opportunities for creating noise in a society which relies heavily on domestic appliances (the noisy washing machine and lawnmower). Stereo and audio equipment has become more sophisticated and commonplace and people are able to play music at high volumes. The dawn of the ghettoblaster and the personal stereo means that loud music is something which frequently occurs in the street as well as in the home. Although there is a general assumption that rural areas are quieter they are not without their own noise problems. Heavy machinery used in farming can also be a source of aggravation to local residents – see *Chapman v Gosberton Farm Produce* (1993) (below at para 15.5.3). Many people who move out of the inner cities and urban areas to the country are surprised at the lack of the peace and quiet that they had envisaged.

Neighbourhood noise, that is the noise outside people's homes, is a particular area of growing concern. In a 1990 survey carried out by the Building Research Establishment

15.1 The problem of noise pollution

15.1.1 Neighbour noise

(BRE) of 1,000 dwellings, it was found that 56% of them were exposed to daytime noise levels exceeding the World Health Organisation recommended level above which noise levels cause annoyance.

Neighbour noise complaints are the greatest source of noise complaints in England and Wales. Research from the University of Salford's Department of Housing and Environmental Health indicates that some 25% of complaints to local authorities relate to general household noise. The number of complaints about neighbourhood noise has increased in recent years. In 1992/93 there was an increase of almost 30% in neighbourhood noise complaints in England and Wales compared to 1991/92. The growing concern has prompted new proposals for more effective and speedy controls. The proposals are discussed in detail at para 15.12 below.

Although unwanted noise or excessively loud noise may be aggravating to those who do not wish to hear it, does it have any harmful effect? Unlike other types of pollution discussed in this book, noise is transient, it exists at the time that it is generated and cannot be said to have a permanent harmful effect on the environment in the same way that toxic wastes can contaminate land. Nevertheless, it can have long-term or even permanent detrimental affects on people's hearing, health or mental well-being.

15.1.2   Damage to health

Noise can be damaging to health in a variety of ways, very much depending upon the susceptibility of the recipient. Some of the health problems can be quite serious. For example, it is not unknown for sudden or violent noises to cause cardiac arrest in people and animals. It is certainly the case that low flying military aircraft can cause sheep to abort. Sudden noise can result in the tightening of the blood vessels resulting in the reduction of blood to the body. Excessive levels of noise continued over a sustained period can cause serious damage to hearing and may even cause hearing loss (noise-induced hearing loss). There are many types of employment or jobs that expose workers to enough loud noise to cause this type of hearing loss. Equally, deafness may occur as a result of a very sudden and loud noise.

Loss of sleep – and the associated health problems arising from loss of sleep – is a more common complaint. Aeroplane noise, in particular, has a much more significant impact on sleep loss than do other noises. Residents living close to major airports, notably Heathrow, will testify to this particular problem. Loss of sleep can result in a person becoming irritable, they may find it difficult to concentrate and it may in turn result in a diminution of physical well-being and health.

CS Kerse, in his book *The Law relating to Noise*, notes that exposure to excessive noise can result in a range of physiological effects. Quoting Dr Samuel Rosin, he states that:

> 'At an unexpected or unwanted noise, the pupils dilate, skin pales, mucous membranes dry; there are intestinal spasms and the adrenals explode secretions. the biological organism, in a word, is disturbed.'

Noise may also cause serious mental problems. In one particular case, *Middlesborough County Council v Stephens* (1993), the continuous playing of the song 'I will always love you' recorded by Whitney Housten was enough to cause the neighbour to suffer what was described as 'psychological torture'. Even if noise does not cause a particular physical problem, it can, if it continues over a long period of time or at anti-social hours, cause the listener to become aggravated, weary and aggressive. In short, it can affect the quality of life. It has even been reported in an article in *The Times* that in the last three years at least twenty people have lost their lives in noise disputes. Some, it is claimed, have committed suicide; others were killed during confrontations with neighbours. Such is the nature of noise pollution, that it can drive people to these lengths.

Whilst excessive or continued levels of noise may be unacceptable, certain levels of noise must be accepted in order that modern society can function. Construction sites, for instance, generate a significant amount of noise from mobile plant, pneumatic drills, etc and cause many local residents to complain. Yet we nevertheless expect and, in most instances, welcome new developments which can create jobs and which can enhance towns and cities. All activities and processes generate noise and we all expect to be able to continue those activities without interference from others. This raises certain problems regarding the legal regulation of noise, in that there will necessarily be a balancing act between the rights of individuals, groups or companies to make noise and the rights of others not to suffer at their expense. This weighing of considerations is familiar in the common law of nuisance where the courts have to consider whether what is complained of is unreasonable.

The other problematic feature of controlling noise is that it is a particularly subjective problem. What amounts to intolerable noise for one person may be disregarded or even considered desirable by others. Pop concerts and parties are a typical example. Some people will be able to accept certain levels of noise, whereas others may suffer in terms of their mental or

15.2 The problems of legal control over noise

15.2.1 The subjectivity of noise problems

physical health as a consequence of that same noise. The sensitivity of human hearing varies and other factors, such as age, can play a large part in determining responses.

15.2.2   Measuring noise

Despite the fact that responses to different noise vary widely, it is possible to measure sound objectively. Sound can be measured either in Hertz (Hz) which measures the frequency of sound (the number of pressure variations per second) or in decibels. The decibel (dB(A)) measure is more widely used because it provides a better measure of the response of the human ear to loudness as the ear responds to changes in the noise level. The Control of Noise (Measurements and Registers) Regulations 1976 prescribes the decibel as the method for measuring noise in relation to the legal controls discussed in this chapter. In addition, they also provide some guidance on how noise levels can be calculated when it is not possible to make a precise measurement. The courts are familiar with the use of decibels as measurements of noise, although they will often seek a further description of the noise from the complainant. In *Halsey v Esso Petroleum Co Ltd* (1961), the use of decibels was affirmed by the court and an indication was given as to the effect of different levels of noise: 'between 40 and 60 decibels the noise is moderate, and between 60 and 80 it is loud. Between 80 and 100 it is very loud and from 100 to 120 it is deafening.'

15.3   **Nature of legal controls**

Traditionally, noise problems have been addressed through the common law, principally by means of private nuisance actions. However, in more recent times, legislation has been introduced which attempts to control noise levels in different ways. In general, measures seek to control the level of emissions either through product specifications or preventive action by means of prior consents. Alternatively, adverse levels of noise can be controlled through mechanisms which enable regulatory authorities to take measures to abate noise nuisances. In the first instance, legislation exists to set precise noise emission levels for particular classes of machinery and vehicles and, in addition, there are a number of Codes of Practice which set out recommended noise levels for the likes of intruder alarms and icecream van chimes. Predicted noise from construction works can be regulated in advance by means of a noise consent issued by a local authority.

The other mechanism for dealing with noise pollution is through a system of sanctions. In some instances, noise can be controlled where it constitutes a statutory nuisance. Local authorities have various powers which enable them to abate noise nuisances and bring criminal proceedings if the person responsible for the noise nuisance ignores the abatement notice.

In addition to these legal measures, the levels of noise can to some extent be controlled in the first instance through good planning which takes account of the potential noise generation of developments at the planning stage. Planning authorities are in fact required to consider the problems of noise when taking planning decisions in order to avoid noise nuisances occurring. Planning Policy Guidance Note 24 gives guidance to local authorities on the use of their planning powers to minimise the adverse impact of noise.

Each of these mechanisms is considered more fully below. In addition, consideration is given to the government's recent proposals to tighten up the 'noise laws' in view of some of the shortcomings of the present regimes.

The main statutory provisions which relate to noise are as follows:

15.3.1   The main statutory provisions

- Control of Pollution Act 1974;

- Environmental Protection Act 1990;

- Noise and Statutory Nuisance Act 1993;

- Town and Country Planning Act 1990;

- Health and Safety at Work Act 1974;

- Land Compensation Act 1973;

- Civil Aviation Act 1982.

The latter three statutes deal, respectively, with the problems of noise in the workplace; public authorities' duty to insulate buildings against noise created by public works such as road building; and noise generated from civil aircraft. These are matters which fall outside the main environmental controls and will not be considered in this chapter. However, it should be noted that in relation to the Civil Aviation Act 1982 it is not possible to bring an action in either trespass or nuisance in relation to noise generated from the flight of civil aircraft. Noise from civil aircraft is covered by a separate regime under regulations. The main areas of control which are dealt with in this chapter are:

- Common law actions;

- Noise constituting a statutory nuisance;

- Noise on construction sites;

- Noise Abatement Zones;

- Controls over noise in the street (loudspeakers, burglar alarms);

- Noise emission regulations;

- Planning and noise;

- EC controls over noise.

15.4   Common law

It is well-established that adverse noise can constitute an actionable nuisance at common law. Noise may give rise to either a public nuisance or a private nuisance – see Chapter 4 for a detailed discussion of common law actions. In some circumstances it may be both. In *Halsey v Esso Petroleum Co Ltd* (1961), it was held that a noise nuisance from tanker lorries at night on the public highway was both a public and a private nuisance. Private nuisance actions are the most common.

A private nuisance is one which interferes with a person's use or enjoyment of land or some right connected with it. In order to bring an action, damage must be suffered. In terms of noise nuisances, the damages may be physical since vibrations may result in property damage or may damage hearing. However, it is more likely that a noise nuisance will interfere with a person's enjoyment of property through, for example, loss of sleep. There is no need to establish that the noise complained of is injurious to health to establish that it constitutes a nuisance (*Vanderpant v Mayfair Hotel Co Ltd* (1930)).

As shown in Chapter 4, the courts are required to balance the rights of the owner of land to do what he wants against the rights of the owners of neighbouring land to be free from interference. For an interference to be actionable in private nuisance, it must be unreasonable. This necessarily involves the court dealing with each case on its merits, taking into account all the relevant circumstances. The courts have developed a number of general principles and will take into account a number of factors, which have already been considered but are restated here in relation specifically to noise.

15.4.1   A temporary interference is less likely to a nuisance

As a general rule, the courts have found that a temporary interference is less likely to constitute a nuisance than one which is permanent or occurs regularly. This is a particular problem in relation to noise nuisances. A classic example of this reasoning can be found in the case of *Leeman v Montagu* (1936). Here, it was held that the noise from cockerels sounding their dawn chorus (note, *one* dawn chorus) was not an actionable nuisance, whereas if the noise from the cockerels had taken place in a residential area for weeks, that damages and an injunction may have been granted.

It is well-known that the courts will take into account the character of an area when determining whether an action is unreasonable and constitutes a nuisance (*Sturges v Bridgman*). The logical conclusion of this in relation to noise is that in peaceful suburban areas the courts are more likely to regard noise as a nuisance than in built-up industrial areas. The nature of the area is clearly a factor to be taken into account. However, this does not exclude the possibility of bringing an action in private nuisance in industrial areas nor does the fact that an area is already noisy remove the possibility of success. In *Roskell v Whitworth* (1871), a congregation at a Roman Catholic Church succeeded in obtaining an injunction to restrain the use of a steam hammer in an iron and steel works because it interfered with their prayers and the comfortable enjoyment of the rectory house. See also *Rushmer v Polsue and Alfieri Ltd* (1906). The recent case of *Gillingham Borough Council v Medway (Chatham) Dock Co Ltd* (1992) considered the extent to which the grant of planning permission for a development could change the character of a neighbourhood. For a discussion of this case see Chapter 13.	**15.4.2 Locality**

The courts have also demonstrated some reluctance to interfere with noise arising from construction sites. This reflects the principle that the courts have regard to the nature and desirability of the operation that is causing the alleged nuisance. In *Andreae v Selfridge* (1938), the defendant company was developing a site close to the plaintiff's hotel. It was held that, if operations of this particular nature were reasonably carried on, and all proper steps are taken to ensure that no undue inconvenience is caused to neighbours, then the neighbours must put up with the noise. The courts have effectively recognised that building operations cannot happen without noise and that they are usually only short-lived operations where the benefits outweigh the temporary discomforts. Legislation now exists to control the noise from construction sites (ss 60 and 61 COPA 1974) although it may still be possible to bring a private action in nuisance.

15.4.3   Nature of the activity causing the noise

It is well-established that, for an interference to be actionable, it must be one which affects an ordinary person and not one who is abnormally sensitive, see *Heath v Brighton Corporation* (1908).

15.4.4   Sensitivity of the plaintiff

Finally, in relation to noise nuisances the courts have been willing to take into account the malicious intent of the parties. In *Hollywood Silver Fox Farm Ltd v Emmet* (1936), the court

15.4.5   Intent of the parties

granted an injunction to the plaintiff which restrained his neighbour from firing his guns during the breeding season of the mink. The guns were being fired by the defendant from spite, following an argument between the two of them.

15.4.6	Remedies	The main remedies available in private nuisance are an injunction or damages. The advantage of common law actions, despite the problems noted, is that they enable plaintiffs to seek damages. If the intention of the plaintiff is to bring an end to the noise problem, a swifter and cheaper remedy is to ask a local authority to commence proceedings under the statutory nuisance provisions of the Environmental Protection Act.

15.5   Noise as a statutory nuisance

Chapter 14 dealt with the main framework of control over statutory nuisances contained in ss 79–82 of the Environmental Protection Act 1990. This section deals specifically with noise as a statutory nuisance. The provisions in the EPA relating to noise nuisances were amended by the Noise and Statutory Nuisance Act 1993, which received Royal Assent in November 1993. The majority of the new provisions came into force in January 1994. In particular, the 1993 Act incorporated a new statutory nuisance into the EPA at s 79(1)(ga).

15.5.1   Section 79(1)(g) and (ga) EPA 1990

Section 79(1)(g) and (ga) of the EPA provide that noise can be a statutory nuisance in the following circumstances:

- Section 79(1)(g) 'noise emitted from premises so as to be prejudicial to health or a nuisance'; and

- Section 79(1)(ga) 'noise that is prejudicial to health or a nuisance and is emitted from or caused by a vehicle, machinery or equipment in a street'.

The EPA does not provide any particular definition of noise other than to say, in s 79, that it includes 'vibration'.

15.5.2   Noise from premises

Like all of the statutory nuisances in s 79 of the EPA noise from premises may only constitute a statutory nuisance if it is either:

a) noise emitted from premises so as to be prejudicial to health; or

b) noise emitted from premises so as to be a nuisance.

This particular statutory nuisance was not included in the Public Health Act 1936 but was drawn from ss 57–59 of the Control of Pollution Act 1974. Under the COPA legislation, the term 'premises' was not defined. In *Tower Hamlets LBC v Manzoni and Walder* (1984), the court held that the term 'premises' did not include a street and therefore noise from a street could not be controlled under the statutory nuisance provisions of COPA. The Environmental Protection Act, however, provided a definition of 'premises' as including land. It remains unclear whether this definition encompasses a street.

For a discussion of what is meant by the terms 'prejudicial to health' and 'a nuisance' in the context of statutory nuisance (see Chapter 14). However, in the context of this particular head of statutory nuisance, the meaning of 'prejudicial to health' was considered in *Southwark London Borough Council v Ince* (1989). It was held that a house which was inadequately insulated against noise, so that noise from a nearby railway adversely affected the occupants, was a statutory nuisance because it was prejudicial to health.

Since noise is much more likely to interfere with enjoyment, rather than cause injury or be injurious to health, the nuisance limb needs some further definition. In general, the nuisance limb of statutory nuisance is based on the common law concept. This means that when the court is required to consider whether noise constitutes a nuisance it will take into account various matters, including:

- the duration and time of the noise;

- the nature of the activity giving rise to the noise;

- the harm suffered by the person affected;

- the neighbourhood in which the noise took place.

It also means that, in practice, the environmental health officer, who is usually responsible for exercising the local authority's statutory nuisance functions, will need to make a similar determination.

This particular statutory nuisance was incorporated into s 79 of the EPA by the Noise and Statutory Nuisance Act 1993. The amendment was made largely because the Environmental Protection Act did not provide sufficient protection from noise in streets. A street is defined as a 'highway and any other road, footway, square or court that is for the time being open to the public'. It is clear that a great deal of noise is generated in streets not only from vehicles but from icecream vans, people playing loud music and, of course, the interminable sounds of car alarms going off. Not all street noises are covered. Certain exceptions are provided: it does not apply to noise created by traffic, the armed forces or by political demonstrations (or demonstrations supporting or

15.5.3 Noise in a street which is emitted from a vehicle, machinery or equipment

opposing a campaign or cause). Traffic is understood to mean vehicles in motion.

Section 79(1)(ga) only refers to street noises emitted from vehicles, machinery or equipment. The question remains about the position of noise which emanates from the street but is not emitted from any of these particular sources.

| 15.5.4 | Noise abatement notices |

As with the other statutory nuisances, it is, in practice, the local authority environmental health officer who has to assess a situation to determine whether the noise is either prejudicial to health or a nuisance. This may involve the officer in taking noise measurements, where this is possible. Once an environmental health officer or local authority is satisfied that a statutory nuisance exists, or is likely to occur, then an abatement notice must be served on the person responsible. This will be the person whose act, default or at whose sufferance the noise is attributable. Where the noise is made from a vehicle, the abatement notice should be served on the owner and driver. Where the noise comes from machinery or equipment, then it should be served on the person who is for the time being the operator.

In circumstances where the noise nuisance has not occurred, or arises from an unattended vehicle, machinery or equipment, the abatement notice should be served on the person responsible for the vehicle. If that person cannot be found, the abatement notice can be affixed to the vehicle following a determination of the authority to that effect. This particular provision was introduced by the 1993 Act and is now contained in s 80(a) of the EPA. The abatement notice must specify the time for compliance; with noise nuisances that may be immediately. Non-compliance with an abatement notice without reasonable excuse is a criminal offence.

| 15.5.5 | Defences |

There are a number of defences available in relation to noise nuisances, some of which are not available in relation to the other non-noise statutory nuisances. The defences available are as follows:

- Reasonable excuse. It will be a defence if the defendant can prove that there was a reasonable excuse for non-compliance. A birthday celebration or party will not constitute a reasonable excuse;

- The Best Practicable Means defence. Where a noise nuisance has been alleged in relation to noise from a vehicle, machinery or equipment, then it is a defence to show that the best practicable means (BPM) were used to prevent or counteract the nuisance. The defence is only available where the vehicle, machinery or equipment is used for industrial, trade or business premises (s 80(8)(aa) EPA). The defence was considered in *Chapman v Gosberton Farm Produce Co Ltd* (1993). A company in Boston, Lincolnshire, received prepacked horticultural produce from heavy goods vehicles during the night time. Complaints were made to the district council about the noise from the lorries and also about the noise from the refrigeration equipment. In proceedings before the magistrates, the company argued that the best practicable means had been used to counteract the effect of the noise. The company maintained that they had sought planning permission to erect a soil bank and screening as part of a wider application to extend their business and this fulfilled the best practicable means. The magistrates accepted this defence, but their decision was overruled by the Divisional Court. The upper court held that the burden of proof in establishing the BPM lies on the defendant and it could not be said that a simple planning application was enough to discharge the burden of proof since the application for planning permission had not been determined.

In considering what constitutes best practicable means in this context, s 79 adds an additional factor not relevant in other statutory nuisances. In circumstances where a Code of Practice (issued under s 71 COPA) is applicable, then regard must had for the guidance given in the code.

• Codes of Practice. Section 71 of the Control of Pollution Act 1974 enables the Secretary of State to prepare and approve codes of practice for the purpose of giving guidance on the appropriate methods of minimising noise in relation to specified types of plant and machinery. Codes of practice issued under s 71 include Construction and Open Sites; Audible intruder alarms; Ice-cream Van Chimes; Model Aircraft.

• Additional defences. In addition, s 80(9) contains a defence specific to a failure to abate a noise nuisance or act in accordance with a prohibition or restriction in a noise abatement notice. The basis of this defence is essentially that the local authority has given its consent to a particular level of noise under the provisions of ss 60–67 of COPA and that the abatement notice attempts to impose a higher standard. The provisions of ss 60–67 are described more fully below.

| 15.5.6 | Failure to comply with an abatement notice | Local authorities have three options available to them in the event that a person fails to comply with an abatement notice (see Chapter 14). As far as noise nuisances are concerned, the environmental health officer has the powers to take steps to abate the noise. This may mean that the officer removes stereo/audio equipment. If the noise is from a car alarm the officer has the power to open the vehicle, if necessary by force, and immobilise the offending alarm. The expenses incurred by a local authority in abating a nuisance can be recovered with interest (s 81A EPA). The local authority can also place a charge on the premises. This new provision was inserted into the EPA by s 10 of the Noise and Statutory Nuisance Act 1993. |

15.5.6 Failure to comply with an abatement notice

Local authorities have three options available to them in the event that a person fails to comply with an abatement notice (see Chapter 14). As far as noise nuisances are concerned, the environmental health officer has the powers to take steps to abate the noise. This may mean that the officer removes stereo/audio equipment. If the noise is from a car alarm the officer has the power to open the vehicle, if necessary by force, and immobilise the offending alarm. The expenses incurred by a local authority in abating a nuisance can be recovered with interest (s 81A EPA). The local authority can also place a charge on the premises. This new provision was inserted into the EPA by s 10 of the Noise and Statutory Nuisance Act 1993.

15.5.7 Section 82: a person aggrieved

The right exists in relation to all of the statutory nuisances for a person aggrieved to make a complaint in the magistrates' court. Before a person can do this, they must give notice – in relation to noise nuisances, three days' notice is required rather than the standard 21-days notice.

15.6   Noise control measures under the Control of Pollution Act 1974

The main statutory provisions controlling noise can be found in Part III of the Control of Pollution Act 1974 which replaced the Noise Abatement Act 1960. The Control of Pollution Act includes a number of measures which enable local authorities to control various aspects of noise. In particular, ss 60 and 61 introduced the first legislative controls over noise from construction sites.

15.6.1 Noise on construction sites (ss 60 and 61)

The Control of Pollution Act provides the means by which local authorities can control the level of noise in their areas arising from construction works. The definition of construction extends to the erection, construction, alteration, repair or maintenance of buildings, structures or roads. It also includes demolition and dredging works. Where it appears to a local authority that any of these activities are being, or are going to be, carried out on premises then the authority can serve a notice imposing requirements as to the way in which the work is to be carried out (s 60(2)). It is not necessary that a nuisance exists, or could occur, for the authority to resort to these powers. Sometimes local authorities will publish details of the notice in the local press.

The Notice can specify the following:

- plant and machinery which must or must not be used;

- permitted hours of operation;

- noise levels by reference to the time of the day or to a part of the site;

- the time within which the notice is to be complied;

- the execution of works necessary for the purpose of the notice.

When the local authority issues its powers under s 60 it must take into account the matters specified in s 60(4) which are:

- relevant Codes of Practice issued under s 71 COPA;

- the need to ensure that the best practicable means are employed to minimise noise;

- the need to protect people in the locality from the effects of noise.

It should be noted that the definition of best practicable means under s 72 COPA is very similar to the definition provided under the EPA (s79(9)). The local authority is required to serve the s 60 notice on the person who appears (to the local authority) to be either carrying out or going to carry out the works. In addition, a notice can also be served on the person(s) who are responsible for or controlling the carrying out of the works. In *City of London Corporation v Bovis Construction Ltd* (1989), it was held that it was sufficient that the notice was served upon the person having control of the site even if the contractor actually doing the work is not served.

It is an offence not to comply with a s 60 notice without reasonable excuse. The magistrates can fine up to £5,000, with a daily fine of £50 for continuing offences. However, it is possible to raise the defence of reasonable excuse. The phrase 'reasonable excuse' is not defined in the Act but was considered in the case of *City of London Corporation v Bovis* where Lord Bingham stated that 'Nothing much short of an emergency, unless an event beyond a party's control, could in my view provide a reasonable excuse for contravention in a case such as this.' Where a party fails to comply with the s 60 notice, the local authority also has the option to apply for an injunction. The court may grant an injunction where it appears that the criminal proceedings will not provide an adequate remedy to ensure compliance with the notice and to protect the inhabitants from noise.

A right of appeal exists against a s 60 notice providing the appeal is made within 21 days of service. The grounds for appeal are set out in the Control of Noise (Appeals) Regulations 1986. An appeal can suspend the notice unless the notice expressly states otherwise.

15.6.2   Prior consents for construction site noise (s 61)

Given that local authorities have powers to restrict construction noise under s 60, contractors have the right to reach some agreement with the local authority, in advance of the works taking place, about the levels and timing of noise that will take place. Section 61(3) of the Act provides that contractors can apply for consent prior to the construction work taking place. To do so, the applicant must provide details of the work that is to be carried out and also the method by which it is to be carried out. In addition, details must be given regarding the measures that will be taken to minimise the noise resulting from the works. If the authority considers that the application contains sufficient information and that no s 60 notice would be served if the steps proposed are observed, then it must grant a consent. The authority has the right to attach conditions to the consent. In setting conditions, it must take into account the relevant codes of practice, the best practicable means and the need to protect persons in the locality from noise.

The authority must respond to the application for prior consent within 28 days of receipt of the application. The authority can either refuse or approve the application or, alternatively, it may agree subject to conditions. An applicant can appeal if the authority refuses to give its consent, fails to deal with the application within the 28 days, or attaches conditions to which the applicant objects. An appeal is made to the magistrates' court and must be lodged within 21 days after the expiry of the 28 days.

It is an offence to carry on the works other than in compliance with the terms of the consent. Obtaining the prior consent from the local authority can prove to be valuable since the existence of a consent can protect the contractor from any statutory nuisance proceedings brought by a local authority. However, the consent does not provide the same protection in relation to actions brought by private individuals (under s 82 EPA). The existence and compliance with a prior consent will not provide a defence in such actions. A citizen can also seek an injunction in respect of a noise nuisance irrespective of whether there is a s 60 prior consent. Although prior consent would appear to be a sensible step for any contractor, in practice relatively few have applied under these provisions. One of the suggested reasons for this is the view that contractors have thought that the local authorities would be too restrictive in setting conditions. Contractors have preferred to run the risk of proceedings under s 60.

15.7   Noise abatement zones

In addition to the specific powers in ss 60–61 COPA, local authorities can also take preventive action to control noise by designating noise abatement zones. The provisions relating to noise abatement zones are found in ss 63–67 of COPA. Section 63 of the Act makes provision for local authorities to designate all or any part of their area as a noise abatement zone. If they wish to do so, local authorities will make a Noise Abatement Order specifying the types or classes of premises to which the order applies. Originally, such an order had to be confirmed by the Secretary of State; however, this requirement was removed by the Local Government and Planning Act 1980.

Where a local authority designates an area as a noise abatement zone, it must measure the level of noise emanating from those classes of premises specified by the order. It is also under a duty to maintain a noise level register of all measurements taken. In a noise abatement zone it is an offence to exceed the level of noise recorded in the noise level register without the written consent of the local authority. The local authority can consent to a noise level being exceeded by virtue of s 65 and any consent may be subject to conditions Where such consent is denied by a local authority, an applicant can appeal to the Secretary of State. Where the local authority consents to the registered level being exceeded, then this is also recorded in the register.

If the local authority records a measurement in the register, then it is obliged to serve a copy of that record on the owner or occupier of the premises from which the measurement was taken. Any person who is served with a copy of a record has the right to appeal against the record to the Secretary of State within 28 days by virtue of s 64. The Control of Noise (Appeals) Regulations 1975 provides for the appeals procedure. The precise methods of measurement are determined by the Control of Noise (Measurement and Registers) Regulations 1976.

In addition, the local authority can require the reduction of noise emanating from premises covered by the noise abatement order. The local authority will issue a noise reduction notice which will state:

- that the level of noise must be reduced to the stated levels;

- the noise level allowable at different times of the day and on different days;

- what steps are to be taken to achieve the noise reduction; and

- the deadline for achieving the noise reduction.

The noise reduction stated in the notice must be practicable and achievable at a reasonable cost. It must also generate some public benefit. Parties served with a noise reduction notice have the right to appeal to the magistrates' court against the notice (the appeal must be made within three months).

15.8   Noise from loudspeakers (s 62)

The noise from loudspeakers is controlled by s 62 of the Control of Pollution Act 1974 which provides that loudspeakers are not to be operated in streets at all for advertising any entertainment, trade or business. There is a blanket ban as far as advertising is concerned. Loudspeakers may be used for other non-advertising purposes but they may not to be operated in any event between 21.00 and 08.00 the following morning. The Secretary of State can reduce these times but he has no power to extend the period. Section 62(2) provides exceptions for the use of loudspeakers:

- at any time in the street for, *inter alia*, various public service reasons, such as the police, the ambulance or fire service or the National Rivers Authority;

- used in an emergency;

- used inside vehicles for the entertainment of passengers;

- used by ice-cream vans (or vans selling perishable foods) can play music between 12.00 and 19.00;

- loudspeakers used at pleasure fairs.

In relation to the last three of these exceptions, there is a *caveat* that the noise must not give cause for reasonable annoyance.

The Noise and Statutory Nuisance Act 1993 amended s 62 COPA in order to allow local authorities to permit the use of loudspeakers in certain circumstances where it would otherwise be a breach of s 62.

15.9   Noise from burglar alarms

There cannot be many people who have not been annoyed by the sound of burglar alarms going off for what sometimes seems like forever in the middle of the night. Burglar alarms are designed to be noisy and to arouse attention, that is their very purpose. But all too often they go off for no other reason than the operator has misused the system or a 'door has blown open'.

Section 9 of the Noise and Statutory Nuisance Act 1993 enables local authorities to adopt a regime to deal with the problem of burglar alarms. Local authorities may impose obligations on installers of audible intruder alarms, and occupiers (or any person entitled to occupy if the premises are unoccupied) to ensure that where alarms are fitted they comply with requirements to be set out in regulations by the Secretary of State. When a burglar alarm is installed, the police must be notified of details of current key holders and the local authority must be informed of the police station where that information has been recorded. Where an alarm sounds for more than one hour and is giving persons living or working in the vicinity reasonable cause for annoyance, the local authority officer has the power to enter the premises and turn it off. The officer cannot use force to do this. However, the environmental health officer, accompanied by a police officer, can enter forcibly if a warrant has been obtained.

The alarm must comply with the prescribed requirements and, in particular, there must be a 20-minute cut-out device. Powers of entry are provided.

One way of reducing noise generated by certain types of transport, machines or activities is to set source emission standards. This is the approach that has been taken in a number of EC Directives.

15.10   Emission standards

EC legislation controls noise for a variety of types of machinery including:

- lawn mowers;
- motorcycles;
- cars, buses and goods vehicles;
- tractors;
- construction plant and machinery.

The Secretary of State has the power under s 68 COPA to make regulations which reduce or limit the noise caused by plant or machinery both inside and outside factories and construction sites.

The town and country planning regime can play a large part in either causing or reducing noise problems. Bad planning can result in noisy developments being built alongside more noise sensitive developments. For this reason, planning authorities are required to consider the potential for noise problems in the exercise of their planning functions. In 1994 a new Planning Policy Guidance Note (PPG24) was introduced on planning and noise. The PPG replaces advice previously given in DOE Circular 10/73. The PPG provides advice to local authorities on how to use their planning powers to minimise the adverse impact of noise. In particular, it outlines

15.11   Planning and noise

the considerations that should be taken into account when the authority is considering planning applications for activities which will generate noise and also for proposals in noise-sensitive areas. The PPG highlights the measures that may be taken to control noise. Theses include:

- ensuring that there is adequate distance between the source of noise and noise-sensitive areas;

- engineering solutions to reduce noise at the point of generation;

- controlling the times when noise-generating activities can take place.

15.11.1 Noise exposure categories

In addition, the PPG introduces the concept of 'noise exposure' categories for residential developments. When determining an application for a residential development near a source of noise, such as a motorway, planning authorities must firstly determine into which of the four Noise Exposure Categories (NECs) the proposed site falls, taking account of noise levels during the day and night. The for NECs are rated A–D. An 'A' category means that noise need not be considered as a determining factor in granting planning permission, whereas a 'D' category means that planning permission should normally be refused. Annex 2 of the PPG sets out detailed 'noise exposure' categories.

15.11.2 Planning conditions

Local planning authorities can grant planning permission for a development subject to conditions which are aimed at minimising noise levels. PPG24 is useful once again in that it describes the sorts of conditions that might be used to achieve this objective. For example, the planning authority can lay down conditions which determine that construction work cannot begin until a scheme for protecting a noise-sensitive development has been approved by the authority.

15.11.3 Building regulations

There can be no doubt that poor sound insulation, particularly in flats, is a contributing factor to neighbour noise problems. However, new buildings must comply with building regulations which can, to some extent, prevent noise problems occurring. The Building Regulations 1991, enacted under the Building Act 1984, are designed to secure the health, safety, welfare and convenience of people in or about buildings. Schedule 1 to the 1991 Regulations contains the various technical requirement relating to building structures and covers various aspects relating to noise insulation. It is an offence to carry out building works in contravention of the building regulations.

In October 1994, the Department of Environment established a Noise Working Party to review the effectiveness of neighbour noise controls contained in Part III of the EPA (the statutory nuisance controls discussed above at para 15.5). The Working Party made the following recommendations which have, at the time of writing, been issued for consultation:

15.12   Proposals for change

- Good practice guidance should be made available to local authorities on the management of noise services;

- Local authorities should be encouraged to provide information to residents about their authority's noise complaints service. They should promote public awareness of neighbour noise issues;

- There should be general guidance on the sorts of noise problems that might constitute a statutory nuisance;

- Local authorities should be able to respond to public complaints outside working hours;

- There should be more streamlined arrangements in relation to obtaining warrants to enter premises to temporarily confiscate noise making equipment or to silence intruder alarms;

- A code of practice should be issued to the police and to local authorities to encourage effective local arrangements for dealing with noise complaints;

- There should be a specific power of temporary confiscation of noise-making equipment and local authorities should be able to levy an administrative charge for its return. Additionally, local authorities should be able to seek permanent confiscation of noise-making equipment following prosecution;

- There should be a separate criminal offence in relation to night time noise disturbances.

Summary of Chapter 15

Noise Pollution

Noise 'pollution' is of growing concern both in terms of the increasing amount of noise that is generated by modern society and also because of the growing awareness of the problems it can bring. Noise, and in particular neighbourhood noise, account for a large share of complaints to local authorities.

The problem of noise pollution

Noise has traditionally been controlled at common law, principally in private nuisance actions. The courts will take into account a number of factors in determining whether noise constitutes an actionable nuisance including:

The problems of legal control

- the duration and time of the noise;

- the nature of the activity giving rise to the noise;

- the harm suffered by the person affected;

- the neighbourhood where the noise took place.

Noise may also constitute a statutory nuisance under the provisions of s 79(1)(g) and (ga) of the EPA as amended by the Noise and Statutory Nuisance Act 1993:

Noise as a statutory nuisance

- Section 79(1)(g) – 'noise emitted from premises so as to be prejudicial to health or a nuisance'; and

- Section 79(1)(ga) – 'noise that is prejudicial to health or a nuisance and is emitted from or caused by a vehicle, machinery or equipment in a street'.

Local authorities are under a duty to serve an abatement notice in order to bring the noise nuisance to an end or to prevent it occurring. The provisions relating to the service of abatement notices and local authority powers are detailed in Chapter 14.

Duty of local authorities

Noise is controlled under the provisions of ss 60–67 of the Control of Pollution Act. In particular:

Control of Pollution Act 1974

- Noise on construction sites is covered in ss 60 and 61. Local authorities can serve a s 60 notice to control the noise from construction (or demolition works). Alternatively, a contractor may obtain prior consent from the local authority under s 61;

- Local authorities can take preventative action by designating noise abatement zones (s 63). It is an offence to exceed the noise levels recorded in the noise level register without the prior consent of the local authority;

- Loudspeaker noise is controlled under s 62 COPA;

- Noise from burglar alarms is controlled by s 9 of the Noise and Statutory Nuisance Act 1993.

Emission standards

In addition to these various controls, certain products, particularly motor vehicles, are governed by regulations which specify noise emission limits. The EC has also legislated extensively in this area.

Planning and noise

The adverse effects of noise can be minimised through good planning. The town and country planning regime enables local planning authorities to attach conditions to planning permissions which are aimed at reducing the impact of noise. Planning authorities are also guided by Planning Policy Guidance Note 24.

Appendix

The following is a reproduction of Art 130r–t of the Treaty. The words in italics are those introduced by the Treaty on European Union 1992.

Article 130r–t

Article 130r

1   Community policy on the environment shall contribute to the pursuit of the following objectives:

- preserving, protecting and improving the quality of the environment;
- protecting human health;
- prudent and rational utilisation of natural resources;
- promoting measures at international level to deal with regional or worldwide environmental problems.

2   Community policy on the environment shall aim at a high level of protection taking into account the diversity of the situations in the various regions of the Community. It shall be based on the *precautionary principle and* on the principles that preventive action should be taken, that environmental damage should as a priority be rectified at source and that the polluter should pay. Environmental protection requirements must be integrated into the definition and implementation of other Community policies.

In this context, harmonisation measures answering these requirements shall include, where appropriate, a safeguard clause allowing Member States to take provisional measures, for non-economic environmental reasons, subject to a Community inspection procedure.

3   In preparing its policy on the environment, the Community shall take account of:

- available and scientific data;
- environmental conditions in the various regions of the Community;
- the potential benefits and costs of action or lack of action;
- the economic and social development of the Community as a whole and the balanced development of its regions.

4   Within their respective spheres of competence, the Community and the Member States shall co-operate with third countries and with the competent international organisations. The arrangements for Community co-operation may be the subject of agreements between the Community and the world parties concerned, which shall be negotiated and concluded in accordance with Art 228.

The previous sub-paragraph shall be without prejudice to Member States' competence to negotiate with international bodies and conclude international agreements.

Article 130s

1   The Council, acting in accordance with the procedure referred to in Art 189c and after consulting the Economic and Social Committee, shall decide what action is to be taken by the Community in order to achieve the objectives referred to in Art 130r;

2   By way of derogation from the decision-making procedure provided for in para 1 and without prejudice to Art 100a, the Council, acting unanimously on a proposal from the Commission and after consulting the European Parliament and the Economic and Social Committee, shall adopt:

- provisions primarily of a fiscal nature;
- measures concerning Town and Country Planning, land use with the exception of waste management and measures of a general nature, and management of water resources;
- measures significantly affecting a Member State's choice between different energy sources and the general structure of its energy supply.

The Council may, under the conditions laid down in the preceding sub-paragraph, define those matters referred to in this paragraph on which decisions are to be taken by a qualified majority.

3   In other areas, general action programmes setting out priority objectives to be attained shall be adopted by the Council acting in accordance with the procedure referred to in Art 189b and after consulting the Economic and Social Committee.

The Council, acting under the terms of para 1 or para 2 according to the case, shall adopt the measures necessary for the implementation of these programmes.

4   Without prejudice to certain measures of a Community nature, the Member States shall finance and implement the environmental policy.

5   Without prejudice to the principle that the polluter should pay, if a measure based on the provisions of para 1 involves costs deemed disproportionate for the public authorities of a Member State, the Council shall, in the act adopting the measure, lay down appropriate provisions in the form of:

- temporary derogations; and/or
- financial support from the Cohesion Fund to be set up no later than 31 December 1993 pursuant to Art 130d.

The protective measures adopted pursuant to Art 130t shall not prevent any Member State from maintaining or introducing more stringent protective measures. Such measures must be compatible with this Treaty. They shall be notified to the Commission.

Article 130t

Recommended Reading

Adams and McManus, *Noise and Noise Law: A Practical Approach*, Wiley Chancery (1994).

Ball and Bell, *Environmental Law*, Blackstone Press (1994).

Birnie and Boyle, *International Law and the Environment*, Oxford University Press (1992).

Blumm, *Environmental Law*, Dartmouth (1992).

Brazier, *Street on Torts*, Butterworth (1993, 9th edn).

Cairney (edn), *Contaminated Land*, Blackie Academic and Professional (1993).

Croner, *Environmental Management* (loose-leaf).

Department of the Environment, *River Quality, Classification of Quality of Waters* (1992).

Freshfields Environment Group, *Tolley's Environmental Handbook: A Management Guide*, Tolley (1994).

Garner, *Environmental Law*, Butterworth (loose-leaf).

Great Britain – House of Commons Select Committee on the Environment, *Toxic Waste*, HMSO (1989).

Great Britain – House of Commons Select Committee on the Environment, *Contaminated Land*, HMSO (1990).

Harpwood, *Lecture Notes on the Law of Tort*, Cavendish (1993).

Harrison, 'What shall we do with the contaminated site?' *JPL* (September 1992) pp 809–16.

Environmental Law and Management.

Environmental Policy and Practice.

Journal of Planning and Environment Law.

The ENDS Report.

Water Law.

Kiss and Shelton, *Manual of European Environmental Law*, Cambridge University Press (1994).

Kramer, *European Environmental Law Casebook*, Sweet & Maxwell (1993).

Kramer, *Focus on European Environmental Law*, Sweet & Maxwell (1992).

Langham, 'Contaminated land: the legal aspect', *JPL* (September 1993) pp 807–15.

Malcolm, *A Guidebook to Environmental Law*, Sweet & Maxwell (1994).

McManus, *Environmental Health Law*, Blackstone Press (1994).

Moore, *A Practical Approach to Planning Law*, Blackstone Press (1994).

National Rivers Authority, *Recommendations for a Scheme of Water Quality Classification for Setting Statutory Water Quality Objectives* (1992).

National Water Council, *River Water Quality, the Next Stage. Review of Consent Conditions* (1978).

Polden and Jackson, *The Environment and the Law: A Practical Guide*, Longman (1994).

Porritt, *Where on Earth are we Going?*, BBC Books (1990).

Rose, *The Dirty Man of Europe: The Great British Pollution Scandal*, Simon & Schuster (1990).

Telling and Duxbury, *Planning Law and Procedure*, Butterworths (1993, 9th edn).

Tromans, *The Environmental Protection Act 1990*, Sweet & Maxwell (1994, 2nd edn).

Index